Reformations Old and New

Essays on the
Socio-Economic Impact of Religious Change
c. 1470–1630

Edited by

BEAT A. KÜMIN

SCOLAR
PRESS

Published by
SCOLAR PRESS
Gower House
Croft Road
Aldershot
Hants GU11 3HR
England

Ashgate Publishing Company
Old Post Road
Brookfield
Vermont 05036–9704
USA

British Library Cataloguing in Publication Data

Reformations Old and New: Essays on the Socio-Economic
    Impact of Religious Change, c. 1470–1630.
    (St Andrews Studies in Reformation History)
    1. Reformation.   2. Church history—Modern period, 1500–
    3. Church history—Middle Ages, 600–1500.   4. Church and
    social problems—Europe—History.
    I. Kümin, Beat A.
    270.5

ISBN 1–85928–220–2

Library of Congress Cataloging-in-Publication Data

Reformations old and new: essays on the socio-economic impact of
    religious change, c. 1470–1630/edited by Beat A. Kümin. 1st ed.
        p.   cm. (St Andrews Studies in Reformation History)
    Includes bibliographical references and index.
    ISBN 1–85928–220–2 (cloth)
    1. Reformation—Europe.   2. Europe—Social conditions—16th
century.   3. Europe—Social conditions—17th century.   I. Kümin,
Beat A.   II. Series.
    BR309.R396   1996
    274'.06—dc20   96–14677
                                                                                      CIP

ISBN 1 85928 220 2

Typeset in Sabon by Manton Typesetters, 5–7 Eastfield Road, Louth,
Lincolnshire, LN11 7AJ

Printed in Great Britain by the Ipswich Book Company, Suffolk

Contents

List of tables, figures, and maps

Preface

The genesis of this book can be reconstructed with great precision. It was first conceived, so to speak, on 7 August 1993 in a dormitory of the majestic Stonyhurst College in Lancashire, venue of the Third Annual Meeting of the 'European Reformation Research Group'. The papers read on that occasion clearly clustered around two main themes: Reformation historiography on the one hand, and the socio-economic impact of religious change on the other. There was a general feeling at the time that the quality and variety of this research deserved a wider audience, and the *spiritus rector* of the group, Andrew Pettegree, suggested that Bruce Gordon and myself be entrusted with the preparation of two complementary collections of essays. The appearance of this volume, following shortly after *Protestant History and Identity in Sixteenth-Century Europe*, completes this twin project, and I am grateful to the editors of the 'St Andrews Studies in Reformation History' for accepting the finished manuscript into their series.

Stonyhurst, of course, was just the beginning, and subsequent meetings of the group at St Andrews and Warwick Universities, supplemented by some outside input and many informal discussions, have helped to give the collection its final shape. Given my limited editorial experience, I set about the task with some apprehension, and yet encouraged by the general consensus that it was one of the objectives of the exercise to provide 'new people' with a platform to present their work. Throughout, the contributors have proved extremely cooperative, and I am grateful for their readiness to revise and refocus their original work in line with the emerging themes of the volume. It has been a great pleasure to be at the centre of such an international effort and to see the essays develop. My thanks must go to William G. Naphy for his valuable general advice, Ken Farnhill for his help with some of the translations, and to Bruce Gordon for providing me with an advance copy of his introduction to the 'sister' collection.

Each of the authors, no doubt, would want to make his or her own acknowledgements, but collectively we should express our thanks to the organizers of the various conferences, in particular Andrew Spicer, Penny Roberts, Peter Marshall, and the members of the St Andrews Reformation Studies Institute, to the staff of the Pepys Library, as well as to Alec McAulay and Caroline Cornish at Scolar Press for their advice and professional help. The editor personally is grateful to his college and to the Swiss National Science Foundation for their generous support.

BK
Magdalene College, Cambridge
1996

Notes on contributors

Arnoud-Jan A. Bijsterveld is a postdoctoral research fellow with the Netherlands Organization for Scientific Research (NWO) at the Vrije Universiteit in Amsterdam and author of *Laverend tussen Kerk en wereld: De pastoors in Noord-Brabant 1400–1570* (Amsterdam, 1993), as well as of several articles on the North Brabant clergy.

Richard Cahill is Director of the Middle East Studies Centre in Cairo and completed a dissertation on Philipp of Hesse and the early Reformation. He is the author of 'The Damned Anabaptists in the textual history of the Augsburg Confession', *Nederlands Archief voor Kerkgeschiedenis* (1995).

Patrick Carter is a research fellow at the Department of History, McMaster University, Hamilton, Canada, and author of a number of essays on clerical taxation and financial administration in early modern England. He is currently engaged in a study of the economic impact of the Reformation upon the English parish clergy.

Peter Dykema is a Ph.D. candidate and a member of the Division for Late Medieval and Reformation Studies, University of Arizona, Tucson; he has co-edited a collection of essays on *Anticlericalism in Late Medieval and Early Modern Europe* (Leiden, New York, Cologne, 1993).

Timothy Fehler is Assistant Professor of History at Furman University, Greenville, South Carolina, where he teaches early modern European history. He has completed a dissertation on social welfare in early modern Emden (University of Wisconsin–Madison, 1995).

Per Ingesman is a senior research fellow of the Department of Church History, University of Aarhus, Denmark, and author of *Ærkesædets godsadministration i senmiddelalderen* (Lund, 1990). He has co-edited a number of books on Danish history, most recently *Danmark i Senmiddelalderen* (Aarhus, 1994).

Trevor Johnson is Lecturer in History at the Faculty of Humanities, University of the West of England, Bristol, and author of a dissertation on the recatholicization of the Upper Palatinate (University of Cambridge, 1992), due to be published by Cambridge UP. He has co-edited *Popular Religion in Germany and Central Europe 1400–1800* (London, 1996).

Beat Kümin is a research fellow of Magdalene College, Cambridge, and author of *The Shaping of a Community: The Rise and Reformation of the English Parish* c. *1400–1560* (Aldershot, 1996). He is co-editing *The Parish in English Life 1400–1600* (for Manchester UP) and a contributor to P. Blickle (ed.), *Gemeinde und Staat im Alten Europa*.

Karin Maag is a postdoctoral research fellow, funded by the Social Sciences and Humanities Research Council of Canada, and author of *Seminary or University? The Genevan Academy and Reformed Higher Education, 1560-1620* (Aldershot, 1995). She is co-editing the conference proceedings of 'The Reformation in Eastern and Central Europe'.

Peter Marshall is a Lecturer in the Department of History, University of Warwick. He is the author of *The Catholic Priesthood and the English Reformation* (Oxford, 1994) and 'The debate over "unwritten verities" in early Reformation England' in B. Gordon (ed.), *Protestant History and Identity in Sixteenth-Century Europe* (Aldershot, 1996).

William G. Naphy is a Lecturer in Early Modern History at Aberdeen University and author of *Calvin and the Consolidation of the Genevan Reformation* (Manchester, 1994). He is co-editor of Manchester UP's 'Studies in Early Modern European History' and about to publish a collection of documents for the European Reformation.

David G. Newcombe is the research assistant for the British Academy's John Foxe project. He has completed a dissertation on the life and thought of John Hooper (Cambridge University, 1990) and published *Henry VIII and the English Reformation* (London, New York, 1995).

Andrew Spicer teaches history at Stonyhurst College. His publications include 'Ministers in the French and Walloon communities in England, 1560–1620' in A. Pettegree (ed.), *The Reformation of the Parishes* (Manchester, 1993); a book on the French-speaking Reformed community in Southampton 1567–1620 (Ph.D. Southampton, 1994) is in preparation.

Markus Wriedt is a senior research fellow at the Institute for European History at Mainz in Germany. He is the author of *Gnade und Erwählung: Eine Untersuchung zu Johann von Staupitz und Martin Luther* (Mainz, 1991), as well as of several essays on the history and theology of the Reformation.

Abbreviations

AEG	Archives d'Etat de Genève
AHR	*American Historical Review*
ArchGK	Archiv der Grossen Kirche, Emden
ARG	*Archiv für Reformationsgeschichte*
BL	British Library, London
CDRO	City and Diocesan Record Office, Canterbury
CO	*Calvini Opera*
CR	*Corpus Reformatorum*
EHR	*English Historical Review*
EJb	*Emder Jahrbuch*
EKP	Niedersächsisches Staatsarchiv, Aurich, Rep, 234: Emder Kontrakten-Protokolle
f./fos	Folio/folios
HLL	Huguenot Library, London
HRO	Hampshire Record Office
HS	*Proceedings of the Huguenot Society*
HStAM	Hessisches Staatsarchiv, Marburg
HStASt	Hauptstaatsarchiv, Stuttgart
JEH	*Journal of Ecclesiastical History*
KRP	H. Schilling and K.-D. Schreiber (eds), *Die Kirchenrats-protokolle der reformierten Gemeinde Emden 1557–1620* (2 vols, Cologne, Vienna, 1989–92)
LP	J. S. Brewer, J. Gairdner, and R. H. Brodie (eds), *Letters and Papers, Foreign and Domestic, of the Reign of Henry VIII* (21 vols, London, 1862–1932)
PaP	*Past and Present*

PHS	Publications of the Huguenot Society
PRO	Public Record Office, London
SCH	Studies in Church History
SCJ	*Sixteenth Century Journal*
SRO	Southampton Record Office
StAZ	Staatsarchiv, Zurich
STC	Short-Title Catalogue
STAA	Staatsarchiv, Amberg
TRE	*Theologische Realenzyklopädie*
TRHS	*Transactions of the Royal Historical Society*
VCH	*The Victoria History of the Counties of England*
WA Br.	*D. Martin Luthers Werke: Kritische Gesamtausgabe* (Weimarer Ausgabe), Briefwechsel

CHAPTER ONE

Reformations old and new:
an introduction

Beat Kümin

The transitional phase between the later Middle Ages and the early modern period has always enjoyed particular prominence in European historiography.[1] One of the prime foci of attention, of course, was and remains the study of religious change in and around the sixteenth century, where the flood of relevant publications shows no sign of abating. A cursory glance at recent work confirms that traditional forms of piety, contemporary criticism of the church, and the effect of reformed ecclesiastical regimes all continue to attract intense scrutiny in various national contexts and academic disciplines.[2] For once, therefore, new research in the area can hardly be justified with reference to previous scholarly neglect. And yet, once it is acknowledged that the issues addressed involve millions of different individual and collective experiences spanning several decades (if not centuries), the magnitude of the historians' task becomes all too apparent and the need to legitimize further work perhaps less of a priority. Given the countless remaining gaps, however, it is essential to define each particular approach as closely as possible. This shall be the purpose of the following introduction.

Any volume dealing with the period cannot ignore the importance of the theological origins, popular understanding, and political consequences of religious change. It must take note of the detailed course of events

---

[1] This introduction originated as a paper presented to a meeting of the 'European Reformation Research Group' at the University of Warwick in August 1995. I am grateful for the comments and suggestions made by the participants and by the contributors to this volume.

[2] A more or less arbitrary selection would include E. Duffy, *The Stripping of the Altars: Traditional Religion in England 1400–1580* (New Haven and London, 1992); E. Cameron, *The European Reformation* (Oxford, 1991); A. Pettegree (ed.), *The Early Reformation in Europe* (Cambridge, 1992); R. W. Scribner, R. Porter, and M. Teich (eds), *The Reformation in National Context* (Cambridge, 1994); M. Forster, *The Counter-Reformation in the Villages: Religion and Reform in the Bishopric of Speyer 1560–1720* (Ithaca, London, 1992). Primary sources, too, are edited in great numbers: see, for instance, P. Johnston and R. W. Scribner (eds), *The Reformation in Germany and Switzerland: Documents and Commentary* (Cambridge, 1993), and W. G. Naphy (ed.), *Documents for the European Reformation* (London, 1996).

and of the 'grand' theories (such as 'Urban Reformation', 'Princes' Reformation', 'Communal Reformation', 'Erastian Reformation', to name but a few) advanced to conceptualize them.[3] There should also be some attempt to address the 'success' of the various initiatives to change popular beliefs and to explore the effect of new religious doctrines on individual mentality or behaviour.[4] All these aspects, however, are implicit rather than explicit in this particular collection of essays, whose primary aim is to assess the local and practical *impact* of religious change on society as a whole, or on some of its constituent groups. It cannot, of course, aspire to provide a comprehensive survey for the whole of the Continent, but examines a number of key socio-economic issues in selected case studies from Central and North-Western Europe between the late fifteenth and early seventeenth century. The contributions, to be more explicit, approach the topic in five thematic clusters:[5]

1. the state and purpose of the clergy;
2. the size and allocation of church resources;
3. the distribution of ecclesiastical patronage;
4. the provision of education;
5. the organization of poor relief.

But why speak of 'Reformations' in the title? Not in order to diminish the singular importance of the great upheavals in the sixteenth century, nor to deny that – with hindsight – there was some coherence to the 'Reformation' as we know it from our textbooks, which took issue with church tradition and resulted in the division of Western Christendom. And yet, once we adjust the focus, differentiations within the movement appear all too clearly, even within one national boundary and during

---

[3] Bernd Moeller, *Reichsstadt und Reformation* (Gütersloh, 1962; new edn, Berlin 1987) and his *Imperial Cities and the Reformation: Three Essays* (Philadelphia, 1972); H. A. Oberman, 'Stadtreformation und Fürstenreformation' in L. W. Spitz (ed.), *Humanismus und Reformation als kulturelle Kräfte in der deutschen Geschichte* (Berlin, 1981); Peter Blickle, *Communal Reformation: The Quest for Salvation in Sixteenth-Century Germany* (Atlantic Highlands, London, 1992); R. W. Scribner, 'Paradigms of urban reform: *Gemeindereformation* or Erastian Reformation?' in L. Grane and K. Hørby (eds), *The Danish Reformation Against its International Background* (Göttingen, 1990), pp. 111–28.

[4] For assessments of the 'success' of the Reformation and the degree of 'Christianization' of contemporary society see, for instance, J. M. Kittelson, 'Successes and failures in the German Reformation: The report from Strasbourg', *ARG*, 73 (1982), 153–74; K. Thomas, *Religion and the Decline of Magic: Studies in Popular Beliefs in Sixteenth and Seventeenth-Century England* (2nd edn, London, 1971); J. Delumeau, *Catholicism Between Luther and Voltaire* (London, 1977).

[5] See table of contents for details. In what follows, the various essays are referred to by the authors' surnames.

one particular phase.[6] The wider the chronological and geographical perspective, the more obvious the diversity. The use of the plural thus reflects the elementary observation that there was no one monolithic experience of 'Reformation' in Europe during the long period under scrutiny, that attempts at a fundamental redrawing of the ecclesiastical system were undertaken at different times for different reasons, and that the century and a half between c. 1470 and 1630 can be divided into at least three quite distinctive parts: a series of more or less effective challenges to the established Church throughout the close of the Middle Ages,[7] a successful evangelical assault in about the second quarter of the sixteenth century (although – in line with contemporary imperatives – often couched in terms of a re-formatio, a return to a purer state),[8] and a later phase of what used to be called 'Second' or 'Counter-Reformation', and is now more generally referred to as Lutheran, Calvinist, or Catholic 'confessionalization'.[9] Formed as a result of a 'mental and institutional consolidation of each of the Christian creeds, which had drifted apart since the schism, into a semi-stable ecclesiastical complex with corresponding dogma, constitution and religious–moral modes of behaviour',[10] the various confessions became im-

---

[6] These issues are addressed in more detail – for the German context – in B. Hamm, B. Moeller, D. Wendebourg, Reformationstheorien: Ein kirchenhistorischer Disput über Einheit und Vielfalt der Reformation (Göttingen, 1995). Wendebourg rejects Moeller's emphasis on the unity (Lutheran 'Engführung') of the early Reformation movement; Hamm takes an intermediary position, acknowledging internal divisions and variety, but stressing a 'coherent' opposition to medieval church tradition. All, however, refuse to relinquish the singular 'Reformation' altogether (ibid., pp. 50–51, 127). English revisionists have started to use the plural to do justice to their national variety of religious change: C. Haigh, English Reformations: Religion, Politics and Society under the Tudors (Oxford, 1993).

[7] Hussites, Lollards, and humanist reform movements could be named among the most conspicuous. See the survey on 'Visions of Reform' in T. A. Brady, Jr, H. A. Oberman, and J. D. Tracy (eds), Handbook of European History 1400–1660 (Leiden, New York, and Cologne, 1995), ii. xxv–126.

[8] For references to this phase cf. note 2 above. The term reformatio had a wide range of political, ecclesiastical, legal, and social connotations in the late Middle Ages: Cameron, European Reformation, p. 38.

[9] The recent literature in this area is immense. Convenient surveys in H. C. Rublack (ed.), Die lutherische Konfessionalisierung in Deutschland (Gütersloh, 1992), H. Schilling (ed.), Die reformierte Konfessionalisierung in Deutschland: Das Problem der 'Zweiten Reformation' (Gütersloh, 1986), and W. Reinhard and H. Schilling (eds), Die katholische Konfessionalisierung in Europa (Gütersloh, Münster, 1995).

[10] A 'geistige und organisatorische Verfestigung der seit der Glaubensspaltung auseinanderstrebenden christlichen Bekenntnisse zu einem halbwegs stabilen Kirchentum nach Dogma, Verfassung und religiös-sittlicher Lebensform', the classic definition of the formation of confessions by Ernst Walter Zeeden, Die Entstehung der Konfessionen (Munich, Vienna, 1965), pp. 9–10.

portant catalysts of the modernization of European society: the consolidation of rivalling churches served as a 'Leitvorgang', or model, for a much more wide-ranging political and social transformation in each territorial entity.[11] This volume, however, deliberately avoids arranging its contributions in chronological order, mainly to allow a fresh look at similarities and differences of this 'Age of Reformations' as a whole.[12] As for the periods covered, most essays focus on the latter two phases, but there are two test cases of reform attempts in the decades before Martin Luther hammered on the notorious Wittenberg door.[13] All the others, furthermore, sketch the late medieval background as well as early modern innovation. This, it is hoped, will help to assess the balance between continuity and change, or, to explain the second part of the title, what was 'old' and what was 'new' about all the different initiatives.

There is by now nothing original about placing religious change in a social context. So much so in fact that Euan Cameron has warned us about the dangers of 'extreme interpretations, namely that lay people pressed for the Reformation for *purely* socio-economic or, conversely, *purely* pious motives'.[14] This is sound advice, and well worth remembering for an overall assessment of the *impact* too. For analytical purposes, however, it may be legitimate to concentrate on the socio-economic dimension. So what are the current historiographical trends for those areas that are of special interest here? Naturally, it will not be possible to do justice to all the nuances which have emerged over the last few decades, but it can be attempted to recall some of the most salient features.

Starting with the state and purpose of the clergy, it used to be thought that this was the Achilles. heel of the late medieval Church. Priests were seen as ignorant, unchaste, and unruly, and their superiors as negligent absentees with a greater interest in court and politics than the effective

---

[11] H. Schilling, 'Luther, Loyola, Calvin und die europäische Neuzeit', *ARG*, 85 (1994), 5–31, here 8. For terminology and historiography see W. Reinhard, 'Konfession und Konfessionalisierung in Europa' in his (ed.), *Bekenntnis und Geschichte* (Munich, 1981), pp. 165–89, H. Schilling, 'Konfessionsbildung, Konfessionalisierung und konfessionelles Zeitalter – ein Literaturbericht', *Geschichte in Wissenschaft und Unterricht*, 42 (1991), 447–63, H. R. Schmidt, *Konfessionalisierung im 16. Jahrhundert* (Munich, 1992), and cf. part (iii) of Peter Dykema's essay below.

[12] Definitions and periodization vary of course: cf., for instance, J. Lebeau and J. M. Valentin (eds), *L'Alsace au siècle de la réforme 1482–1621: textes et documents* (Nancy, 1985), or S. Ozment, *The Age of Reform 1250–1550: An Intellectual and Religious History of Late Medieval and Reformation Europe* (New Haven, London, 1980).

[13] See Bijsterveld and Dykema below.

[14] *European Reformation*, p. 3.

supervision of the cure of souls. Now, of course, we know that the situation was rather more complex. Human failings and abuses there were, but recent scholarship has also pointed to the existence of diligent bishops and graduate local clergy, it has identified practical and financial rather than doctrinal causes of anticlerical behaviour, and it emphasized structural inadequacies of church organization as a root cause for pastoral problems.[15] As for Reformation change, it is clear that seminaries and academies had a major impact on the training of ministers, who were now – putting it very crudely – expected to move from the direction of ritual to the exegesis of scriptural texts, even though staff shortages, financial restrictions, and individual shortcomings continued to haunt the early modern church. In due course, clergymen are said to have developed from members of an estate into practitioners of a profession, but historians disagree whether they necessarily had *that* much more impact on the beliefs and priorities of their flock.[16] It is also clear that anticlericalism was anything but a preserve of the later Middle Ages. Priests had always stood for values and principles which could be at odds with those of their flock and the towering presence in the pulpits of now ever more educated figures may have widened the gap further.[17]

[15] Ibid., pp. 32–7. Revisionism on these points has been particularly strong in England: P. Heath, *The English Parish Clergy on the Eve of the Reformation* (London, 1969) and P. Marshall, *The Catholic Priesthood and the English Reformation* (Oxford, 1994). There were of course regional (and local) differences: H. Cohn, 'Reformatorische Bewegung und Antiklerikalismus in Deutschland und England' in W. Mommsen (ed.), *Stadtbürgertum und Adel in der Reformation* (London, 1979), pp. 303–30. However, the strong emphasis on anticlericalism as a root cause of the German Reformation in studies such as H.-J. Goertz, *Pfaffenhass und gross Geschrei: Die reformatorischen Bewegungen in Deutschland 1517–29* (Munich, 1987), has also been challenged: Bernd Moeller, 'Die Rezeption Luthers in der frühen Reformation' in Hamm et al., *Reformationstheorien*, pp. 23–4.

[16] See the introduction and contributions to A. Pettegree (ed.), *The Reformation of the Parishes: The Ministry and the Reformation in Town and Country* (Manchester, 1993), R. O'Day, *The English Clergy: Emergence and Consolidation of a Profession 1558–1642* (Leicester, 1979), and K. Maag, *Seminary or University? The Genevan Academy and Reformed Higher Education, 1560–1620*, St Andrews Studies in Reformation History (Aldershot, Brookfield/Vermont, 1995). Discussions of the Reformation impact include Kittelson, 'Successes and failures', and R. van Dülmen, *Entstehung des frühneuzeitlichen Europa* (Frankfurt a.M., 1982), pp. 145–58.

[17] Broad panoramas in H.-J. Goertz, *Antiklerikalismus und Reformation: Sozialgeschichtliche Untersuchungen* (Göttingen, 1995) and P. Dykema and H. Oberman (eds), *Anticlericalism in Late Medieval and Early Modern Europe* (Leiden etc., 1993), but see the terminological concerns voiced in K. Schreiner's review of the latter in *Zeitschrift für historische Forschung*, 21 (1994), 513–21; for an example of a clash between popular and clerical values W. Naphy, 'Baptisms, church riots and social unrest in Calvin's Geneva', *Sixteenth Century Journal*, 26 (1995), 87–97. C. Haigh, 'Anticlericalism and the English Reformation' in his *The English Reformation Revised* (Cambridge, 1987), pp. 56–74, argues that the problem was a consequence rather than a cause of the Reformation.

Moving to the fate of church resources in the period, there is wide-spread acknowledgement of an enormous transfer of wealth out of a variety of motives (ranging from sheer greed to pious conviction) and with consequences which changed landholding patterns beyond recognition.[18] It is clear, however, that lay control over church property could be very extensive well before the sixteenth century, and even confiscations were not unheard of in the late Middle Ages.[19] Nevertheless, the Reformation dissolutions reached an unprecedented scale, and the proceeds were put to variable uses: the English and Danish monarchs sold most of it to their nobility and gentry, some German Protestant princes reallocated parts to educational or charitable purposes, while others used it to enhance their own territorial possessions.[20]

Similar developments took place in the field of ecclesiastical patronage. This was more than just an honorary legal title, for it allowed the owner to promote the careers of family members, servants, or clients, and it gave him some leverage over the administration and religious orientation of the respective churches. Again, lay involvement was a long-standing tradition; during the age of the *Eigenkirche*, clergymen had literally been at the whim and mercy of their secular lords. The Gregorian reform, however, eradicated the most blatant encroachments, and by the eve of the Reformation, ecclesiastical bodies usually appointed to the lion's share of clerical positions. Many monarchs had acquired a decisive say in the designation of members of the church hierarchy, but there was still much to gain for ambitious princes and other powerful individuals. With the suppression of monasteries and other religious bodies a great deal of advowsons came up for redistribution, and the state added huge portions to its existing share, even though there were significant differences in terms of Church dependence between Catholic and Protestant areas.[21]

---

[18] H. J. Cohn, 'Church property in the German Protestant principalities' in E. I. Kouri and T. Scott (eds), *Politics and Society in Reformation Europe* (London, 1987), pp. 158–87, W. G. Hoskins, *The Age of Plunder: The England of Henry VIII 1500–47* (London, 1976).

[19] Extensive control for example in German Imperial Free Cities, Central Switzerland, and England: R. Kiessling, *Bürgerliche Gesellschaft und Kirche in Augsburg im Spätmittelalter* (Augsburg, 1971); C. Pfaff, 'Pfarrei und Pfarreileben' in *Innerschweiz und frühe Eidgenossenschaft* (2 vols, Olten, 1990), i. 203–82; R. Swanson, *Church and Society in Late Medieval England* (Oxford, 1989), pp. 196ff. A general survey in J. Hashagen, 'Laieneinfluss auf das Kirchengut vor der Reformation', *Historische Zeitschrift*, 126 (1922), 377–409.

[20] Cameron, *European Reformation*, pp. 294–9.

[21] For the medieval and canonical background see, for example, M. Bergolte, *Die mittelalterliche Kirche* (Munich, 1992), esp. pp. 18–37, and R. E. Rodes Jr, *Ecclesiastical Administration in Medieval England* (Notre Dame, London, 1977). An example of how

Moving on to the fourth theme, the Church still had a formidable grip on education on the eve of the Reformation (from universities and Cathedral schools down to humble parish institutions), but changes were under way too. Most significantly, perhaps, the efforts made by urban authorities to train their citizens for careers other than the priesthood and those by the humanists to improve human knowledge in general and educational facilities in particular.[22] Still, the Protestant reformers' emphasis on scripture has always been seen as the starting-point for a great educational offensive, or – in Lawrence Stone's phrase – an 'educational revolution'. In fact it was often just a case of adding catechisms to an otherwise fairly conventional curriculum, and the success of many ambitious schemes was hampered by financial constraints and a shortage of teachers.[23] Nevertheless, the overall number of schools increased and it has been asserted that 'by the end of the seventeenth century the Protestant countries were the most literate in Europe'.[24]

Lastly, poor relief used to be a particularly obvious candidate for an illustration of how Protestant values ushered in a new beginning. Indiscriminate medieval alms-giving, supported by a salvation concept based on the performance of good works, was contrasted with rationalized and lay controlled modern methods of distinguishing between worthy and unworthy recipients. This view, however, has long been abandoned. Contemporaries were aware of the limits of medieval poor relief, but given the countless parallels between the measures adopted in Protestant and Catholic countries, Christian humanism now appears as the

---

patronage complicated the introduction of a new religious regime in A. Duke, 'The Reformation of the backwoods' in his *Reformation and Revolt in the Low Countries* (London, 1990), pp. 255–7; a summary of post-Reformation developments: van Dülmen, *Entstehung*, pp. 274–5.

[22] R. H. Fife, *The Revolt of Martin Luther* (New York, 1957), pp. 20–31; P. Dubuis, 'Ecoles en Suisse Romande en moyen âge: quelques jalons' in A. Paravicini Bagliani (ed.), *Ecoles et vie intellectuelle à Lausanne au moyen âge* (Lausanne, 1987), pp. 95–130; J. A. H. Moran, *The Growth of English Schooling 1340–1548: Learning, Literacy and Laicization in Pre-Reformation York Diocese* (Princeton, 1985), pp. 150–84; H. de Ridder-Symoems, 'La sécularisation de l'enseignement aux anciens Pays-Bas au moyen âge et à la Renaissance' in J.-M. Duvosquel and E. Thoen (eds), *Peasants and Townsmen in Medieval Europe* (forthcoming); G. Huppert, *Public Schools in Renaissance France* (Chicago, 1984); A. Renaudet, *Préréforme et humanisme à Paris pendant les premières guerres d'Italie 1494–1517* (2nd edn, Paris, 1953). See also Wriedt below.

[23] L. Stone, 'The educational revolution in England, 1560–1640', *PaP*, 28 (1964) 41–80; for a critical assessment of the education policy of an early Reformation regime: N. Orme, *Education and Society in Medieval and Renaissance England* (London, 1989), esp. ch. 1. A Continental case study in G. Strauss, *Luther's House of Learning: Indoctrination of the Young in the German Reformation* (Baltimore, 1978).

[24] H. Kamen, *European Society 1500–1700* (London, New York, 1984), p. 212.

decisive agent of change, and there is also a recognition of just how many experiments had preceded the formal introduction of the new religion. Inflationary and population pressures, furthermore, ensured that towns in particular came up against pressing socio-economic problems without having too much time to appeal to their religious conscience as the ultimate authority.[25]

Even such a short and superficial survey suffices to make the point that the Age of Reformations could hardly be seen as a full-scale socio-economic revolution. The fact that Marxists termed it a *frühbürgerliche Revolution* implies that there was something preliminary and unfinished about it.[26] The changes may have brought enormous gains for some people, but they tended to be members of rather well-established groups anyway. The Church had indeed been turned upside down, but there was still a distinctive clerical estate and most people continued to pay tithes and other dues, albeit in a somewhat different form and often to different recipients. Reformation-inspired programmes for a fundamental redefinition of secular lordship and property ownership existed, of course, but the rulers of the day made sure that neither Thomas Müntzer nor the participants of the German Peasants' War managed to put them into practice.[27] The trend in recent historiography is thus to flatten the peak of the Reformation(s) as a watershed between the medieval and early modern period, to look, for instance, at fifteenth-century roots of sixteenth-century developments,[28] and to agonize over the share of religious factors in the transformation of the post-Reformation world. Even the once so distinctive behavioural pattern of English puritan élites, perhaps *the* prime example for the virulence of pious motive in early modern European

---

[25] See the summaries in the introduction to P. Slack, *Poverty and Policy in Tudor and Stuart England* (London, New York, 1988), and Cameron, *European Reformation*, pp. 258–60. A long-term survey in J. P. Gutton, *La société et les pauvres en Europe , XVIe-XVIIIe siècles* (Paris, 1974), and more specifically on the question of impact: H. J. Grimm, 'Luther's contribution to sixteenth-century organization of poor relief', *ARG*, 61 (1970), 222–34. An example of municipal relief organization in B. Pullan, *Rich and Poor in Renaissance Venice* (Oxford, 1971); discussion of pre-Reformation parish experiments: M. McIntosh, 'Local responses to the poor in late medieval and Tudor England', *Continuity and Change*, 3 (1988), 209–45.

[26] M. Steinmetz, 'Die frühbürgerliche Revolution in Deutschland (1476–1535). Thesen' in R. Wohlfeil (ed.), *Reformation oder frühbürgerliche Revolution?* (Munich, 1972), pp. 42–55.

[27] T. Scott, *Thomas Müntzer: Theology and Revolution in the German Reformation* (London, 1989); P. Blickle, *The Revolution of 1525* (Baltimore, London, 1981).

[28] See, most recently, Schilling, 'Luther, Loyola, Calvin', 11, 16–21 (with references in note 15), and Dykema below.

society, has been somewhat undermined during the last decade or so: the pioneering study on the Essex village of Terling, which had advanced a distinctive Protestant mentality as an agent of change alongside socio-economic developments has triggered a whole barrage of criticism pointing to medieval precedent and the difficulty of disentangling pious from more worldly motives.[29]

In spite of certain reservations, the sixteenth century must be seen as a time of extraordinary socio-economic pressures, caused primarily by population increases and inflation, which called for extraordinary measures and readjustments in a great number of areas.[30] Nevertheless, in line with the warning cited above, this should not be pushed to the extreme of abandoning any attempt to study the effects of deep-reaching religious change on a society in which the Church, after all, had exercised so many rights and privileges. Heinz Schilling, for instance, considers social, political, and religious factors as 'equally important in principle', but assigns 'a certain leading role to religious and theological structures and tendencies when examining the confessional age'.[31] At the same time though, he points to the 'functional similarities in the political, institutional, and social effects of Calvinism and Lutheranism',[32] which puts him in sharp contrast to the undoubtedly most famous sociologist of religion. Max Weber, of course, had distilled an ideal type of 'Protestant ethic' from a close observation of Calvinist sects (in particular their tendency towards asceticism, discipline, and reinvestment rather than conspicuous consumption) which he believed to predispose them above all other confessions for the requirements of bourgeois capitalist production.[33]

---

[29] K. Wrightson and D. Levine, *Poverty and Piety in an English Village: Terling 1525–1700* (2nd edn, Oxford, 1995); see the postscript for a survey of the debate and a defence of the main thesis. Critics include M. Spufford, 'Puritanism and social control?' in A. Fletcher and J. Stevenson (eds), *Order and Disorder in Early Modern England* (Cambridge, 1985), pp. 41–57, and R. von Friedeburg, 'Reformation of manners and the social composition of offenders in an East Anglian cloth village', *Journal of British Studies*, 29 (1990), 347–85, the latter pointing to a generation conflict.

[30] Kamen, *European Society*, p. 183; Slack, *Poverty and Policy*, pp. 3–7 (with reference to some dissenting voices).

[31] 'The Second Reformation – problems and issues' in his *Religion, Political Culture and the Emergence of Early Modern Society: Essays in German and Dutch History* (Leiden, New York, Cologne, 1992), pp. 247–301, here 250.

[32] Ibid., pp. 271–2.

[33] *The Protestant Ethic and the Spirit of Capitalism*, ed. and trans. C. T. Parsons (London, 1972). Surveys of the colossal debate that the concept provoked in G. Marshall, *In Search of the Spirit of Capitalism: Max Weber and the Protestant Ethic Thesis* (London, 1982), J. Weiss (ed.), *Max Weber heute: Erträge und Probleme der Forschung* (Frankfurt a.M., 1989), and H. Lehman and G. Roth (eds), *Weber's Protestant Ethic: Origins, Evidence, Contexts* (Washington, 1993).

There are thus wildly dissimilar interpretations about the long-term impact of religious change and not a few contradictions. Among the range of 'grand theories' of (for want of a better term) 'modernization' which reflect the role of the Reformation, is the idea that confessionalization in the long run contributed to the 'secularization' of European society. This is normally explained as a consequence of the loss of credibility the confessions suffered due to their close ties to the political sphere, but, as Heinrich R. Schmidt has observed, it is not always crystal clear how the supporters of the concept manage to square this secular trend with their claims of a concurrent Christianization and religious-moral penetration of early modern society.[34] To complicate matters further, some dissenting voices locate the absorption of Christian dogma well before the Reformation, while others yet point to the persistence of pagan, magical, and superstitious practices far into the modern period.[35]

Fairly uncontroversial, in comparison, is Volker Press's observation that the Reformation continued and intensified the 'territorialization' of the various political entities of the Holy Roman Empire, and, by analogy, the big nation states too. The confiscation of ecclesiastical property and the takeover of former church responsibilities such as welfare and moral supervision no doubt provided the princes with important new powers. The development of a distinctly territorial religious identity also helped to distinguish their lands from geographical neighbours.[36] Closely related to this process, however, are a number of other 'modernization' concepts which are more hotly debated. Many historians, for instance, see the reformation of society accomplished through a gradual 'acculturation' of the population by its social élites. As part of the initiative to anchor more narrowly defined religious and moral principles more firmly in the minds of their people, a whole army of well-trained ministers and state officials is said to have descended upon the countryside in order to eradicate the remnants of unacceptable

---

[34] *Konfessionalisierung*, pp. 91–3 (addressing the positions of, for example, Heinz Schilling, Winfried Schulze, and Richard van Dülmen). For another national context see J. C. Sommerville, *The Secularization of Early Modern England: From Religious Culture to Religious Faith* (Oxford, 1992).

[35] P. Blickle, 'Communal Reformation and peasant piety', *Central European History*, 20 (1987), 223–6; Thomas, *Religion and Decline of Magic*.

[36] V. Press, 'Kommunalismus oder Territorialismus? Bemerkungen zur Ausbildung des frühmodernen Staates in Mitteleuropa' in H. Timmermann (ed.), *Die Bildung des frühmodernen Staates* (Saarbrücken, 1989), pp. 109–35; for an example of theoretical reflection of confessional divisions and national identity see A. Milton, *Catholic and Reformed: Roman and Protestant Churches in English Protestant Thought 1600–40* (Cambridge, 1995).

popular practice.[37] While it is clear that the intensification of post-Reformation government rode roughshod over a whole number of areas previously under more or less autonomous communal control,[38] it is questionable whether a simple élite/popular distinction will do justice to the phenomenon. Values, after all, travel both ways in society, and it was often the more privileged groups who struggled most to adapt their lifestyles to the ideals of the new regimes.[39]

But what exactly was the new regime? All the relevant interpretations emphasize – from various perspectives and with various thematic priorities – a trend towards more social control, individual discipline, and central regulation, culminating in absolutist regimes in its most extreme persuasion. This is not the place to introduce them all in due differentiation, but their catch-phrases at least can be recalled. Norbert Elias has observed a long-term process of 'civilization', Max Weber an increasing 'rationalization' of human behaviour, and Gerhard Oestreich a trend towards more and more 'social discipline'.[40] All these tendencies, of course, were relative and far from linear (one would struggle to accommodate early modern religious wars and massacres within them) and again, they should not be seen as starting at the Reformation. Oestreich, for instance, finds the first evidence for measures aimed at better social discipline already in fifteenth-century towns. Historiographical debate about the initiators and effect of this early modern paradigm has been raging for some time: most contributors argue for a state and élite inspired, ultimately successful, drive to curb popular excesses, others are more sceptical and emphasize the fact that any measure of success depended on cooperation from below as well as imposed pressure from above.[41] The jury, one might say, is still out on these matters.

---

[37] Delumeau, *Catholicism between Luther and Voltaire*; Schilling, 'Second Reformation', p. 275.

[38] B. Kümin, *The Shaping of a Community: The Rise and Reformation of the English Parish* c. 1400–1560, St Andrews Studies in Reformation History (Aldershot, Brookfield/ Vermont, 1996), ch. 6.

[39] See the two opposing assessments by R. Muchembled and J. Wirth in K. von Greyerz (ed.), *Religion and Society in Early Modern Europe 1500–1800* (London, 1984), pp. 56–65 and 66–78; for a recent long-term regional study: G. Rooijakkers, *Rituele repertoires: Volkscultuur in oostelijk Noord-Brabant 1559–1853* (Nijmegen, 1994).

[40] Concepts elaborated in N. Elias, *The Civilizing Process* (Oxford, 1994), M. Weber, *Economy and Society*, eds G. Roth et al. (Berkeley, London, 1979) and G. Oestreich, *Geist und Gestalt des frühmodernen Staats* (Berlin, 1969).

[41] See Schmidt, *Konfessionalisierung*, pp. 94–106; an optimistic assessment in van Dülmen, *Entstehung*, pp. 202, 294, more pessimistic is R. Po-chia Hsia, *Social Discipline in the Reformation: Central Europe 1550–1750* (London, New York, 1989), pp. 112, 138, 149. The input from below is emphasized in C. Scott Dixon, *The Reformation and Rural Society: The Parishes of Brandenburg-Ansbach-Kulmbach, 1528–1603* (Cambridge,

There is thus no shortage of secular trends and long-term interpretations, and the present collection of essays does not seek to establish even more. Its purpose is more modest and less speculative, namely to shed light on the *immediate* socio-economic impact of religious change in a comparative perspective. The task confronting the contributors, quite apart from providing an in-depth analysis of each topic in its own right, was to transcend the wide range of heterogeneous subject matter by means of a common focus on three main themes:

- First, to try and identify the peculiar blend between continuity and change in their respective case studies;
- Second, to attempt to disentangle the religious and secular motives promoting socio-economic change, and
- Third, to designate the winners and losers of the process.

The results of the first analysis confirm and reinforce the recent call for a better contextualization of the various Reformations in the traditions of their societies. The evidence for continuity is overwhelming: the contributions provide pre- and post-Reformation examples of lay influence on patronage, poor relief, and the reallocation of ecclesiastical property.[42] They emphasize the persistence of municipal interest in adequate basic education, the stable composition of school curricula (apart from the additional stress on the Bible), the continuing dominance of the clergy in institutions of higher learning, and the rivalry of secular and religious claims over all educational facilities.[43] There are cases of 'territorialization' of churches from the fifteenth, sixteenth, and seventeenth centuries,[44] and complaints about the shortcomings of clergymen and unworthy poor in late medieval as well as post-Reformation cases.[45] Changes, on the other hand, include a loss of

---

1996) and in a long-term quantitative analysis by H. R. Schmidt, *Dorf und Religion: Reformierte Sittenzucht in Berner Landgemeinden der frühen Neuzeit* (Stuttgart, 1995).

[42] See Marshall, Fehler, Cahill, Carter, and Dykema below.

[43] See Wriedt (with a long-term survey of medieval developments and an assessment of Luther's 'innovative' contributions), Maag (the Reformation increases magisterial influence, but ministers remain crucial for the running of the system), and Naphy (the Genevan authorities had wrought control of education away from the pre-Reformation chapter, only to see Calvin's ministers reassert clerical influence a few decades later).

[44] Dykema, Cahill, Johnson. From the later Middle Ages, towns pursue a similar 'Kommunalisierung des Kirchenwesens': K. Frölich, 'Die Rechtsformen der mittelalterlichen Altarpfründen', *Zeitschrift für Rechtsgeschichte*, Kanon. Abt. 20 (1931), 539; U. Weiss, *Die frommen Bürger von Erfurt: Die Stadt und ihre Kirche im Spätmittelalter und in der Reformationszeit* (Weimar, 1988), p. 283; Kiessling, *Augsburg*.

[45] See Bijsterveld, Newcombe, and Fehler below.

social mobility,[46] a huge windfall of patronage and church property rights for princes and lay élites,[47] a completely new job profile for the clerical profession,[48] and the provision of academies and other training facilities to improve their qualification.[49] Former ecclesiastical benefices were sometimes used to fund additional educational efforts, but elsewhere they simply augmented the sovereign's income or paid for his debts.[50] In Reformed areas in particular, the poor witnessed the replacement of alms from intercessory foundations such as monasteries or fraternities with deacons and more centralized institutions.[51] Exile churches were now counting on international assistance (as well as higher contributions from their members), because many congregations had to fund not only their own ecclesiastical and welfare operations, but often those of their host communities too,[52] while – in an ironic historical twist – Lutherans could, by the seventeenth century, perceive *Catholicism* as a new and disrupting religious alternative.[53]

The second theme has puzzled historians for quite some time. Euan Cameron's discussion of Reformation poor relief measures, for instance, struggled to determine 'just how distinctively "protestant" or indeed religious these initiatives were'.[54] Here, our case studies provide some interesting suggestions. Both at Emden and in the English exile communities, the poor relief system reflected socio-economic pressures and concerns about unworthy beneficiaries just like elsewhere, but additional incentives derived from specific 'religious' crises such as the

---

[46] See Ingesman (decline of the lesser gentry in mid-sixteenth-century Denmark) and Marshall (dissolutions of 1536–40, and especially those of 1547, decimate opportunities for lower secular clergy).

[47] Redistribution of patronage rights from monasteries to the crown, and – in a few cases – archbishops (Marshall), from archbishops to the king (Denmark), and from towns and the nobility to the prince (Johnson); on the whole, local patrons were replaced by more distant ones (Marshall); confiscation of ecclesiastical property: Cahill, Carter, Fehler, Ingesman.

[48] See Newcombe below.

[49] Cf. Maag (there was continuity in the practice of sending clerics for training abroad); Naphy (with more clerical control over the academy than in Zurich). See, however, the significant improvements made in (less specialized) clerical education in North Brabant on the eve of the Reformation: Bijsterveld.

[50] Cahill and Dykema illustrate a degree of reallocation for 'social' purposes; Carter and Fehler appropriation by the prince.

[51] See Fehler and Spicer below.

[52] Andrew Spicer's analysis also suggests that the poor relief system of exile churches could serve as a model for their host communities; an intriguing parallel to their influence on the local economy: R. D. Gwynn, *Huguenot Heritage: The History and Contribution of the Huguenots in Britain* (London, New York, 1985), ch. 4.

[53] Johnson.

[54] *European Reformation*, p. 258.

deluge of refugees from the Dutch revolt or the St Bartholomew's Day massacre. Furthermore there was a tendency towards 'resacralization' to the extent that supplementary means of support were provided for those poor with the right kind of religious beliefs.[55] A similar phenomenon can be detected in the field of education, where Luther's ideal school curriculum responded to biblical imperatives and where academies were deliberately devised as bulwarks of their respective confessions. Basic education, on the other hand, continued to be directed and expanded in response to the secular and economic needs of the citizenry.[56] Genuine religious motives were involved both in Count Eberhard's reforms in pre-Reformation Württemberg as well as in those of Maximilian in the Upper Palatinate 150 years later, but while the latter showed the typical ingredients of Catholic confessionalization (an inextricable mixture of recatholicization and territorialization), the former were too personal, unbureaucratic, and temporary to fall into the same category.[57] Unambiguously pure religious motivation, fuelled by a period in Continental exile, marked bishop Hooper's visitation of the diocese of Gloucester in the early 1550s as well as the decision of those inhabitants of Amberg to vote with their feet when their *Landesherr* set out to dismantle their Lutheran heritage.[58] On the other hand, no clear religious strategy emerges behind the exercise of patronage in East Yorkshire, either before or after the dissolution (quite in contrast to the impression gained in the Upper Palatinate), and *Landgraf* Philipp's concessions to the Teutonic Knights cannot be explained by theological reasoning either.[59] The same, of course, applies to Henry VIII's taxation of the English parish clergy, while the reforms of North Brabant reflected the influence of their particular urban environment and military realities rather than grass-roots evangelical pressures.[60] The Lutheran lord who protected a venerated image from 'desecration' by a Catholic pilgrimage in the Upper Palatinate combined a defence of local pride and privileges with at best a very unorthodox form of confessional allegiance, and even in Zurich, one of the centres of Reformed propriety, candidates for the ministry were not necessarily sent to Heidelberg

---

[55] See Fehler (the influx of refugees in the 1550s, however, coincided with a major socio-economic crisis) and Spicer below; cf. R. W. Henderson, 'Sixteenth-century community benevolence: An attempt to resacralise the secular', *Church History*, 38 (1969), 421–8.

[56] Wriedt, Maag, and Naphy below.

[57] Dykema and Johnson.

[58] Newcombe and Johnson.

[59] Marshall, Johnson (where religious preference was, however, intertwined with concerns about local *Herrschaft*), and Cahill.

[60] Carter and Bijsterveld.

or Basle for further training (although these universities dominated), but some of them to the lion's dens of Paris and northern Italy.[61]

Moving to the identification of winners and losers, the picture is not at all homogeneous either. Archbishops were swept away in the Danish Reformation, but gained extended patronage rights in East Yorkshire. At the same time, many gentry clients disappeared together with their episcopal patrons in Denmark, while their English counterparts augmented their estates and power with the spoils of the dissolution.[62] The fate of monastic institutions naturally varied in accordance with the confessional flavour of ecclesiastical reform, and that of the nobility depended on whether they shared their prince's religious convictions. Those who did, could prosper (Maximilian confirmed their privileges even after his recatholicization campaign), others suddenly found themselves in exile.[63] The poor lost some of their peculiar spiritual attributes, but gained through more organized and compulsory contributions,[64] while towns must have balanced the removal of rivalling ecclesiastical privileges with the emergence of new forms of clerical ambition.[65] Education benefited from a reallocation of ecclesiastical resources and further expansion, although in England, for instance, the dissolutions and clerical taxation had adverse effects for universities as well as elementary schools.[66] Unambiguous were the socio-economic fortunes for *two* groups only: princes grasped this extraordinary opportunity to further their attempts at territorialization, while the average church-goer found himself more heavily taxed, more closely supervised (by clergymen, state officials, or his local consistory élite), and – in reformed areas – stripped of the fruits of centuries of pious investment.[67]

General conclusions from a limited sample are necessarily hazardous and have to be treated with caution. It is clear that further in-depth

---

[61] Johnson and Maag.

[62] Cf. Ingesman and Marshall (however, given the crown's increased demands on episcopal incomes, English bishops should hardly be seen as overall winners).

[63] See Johnson below.

[64] Spicer and Fehler.

[65] Naphy, Maag, and Fehler.

[66] Cahill, Dykema, Maag, and Wriedt. Carter illustrates the negative impact on university colleges; for the considerable number of late medieval chantry schools: Swanson, *Church and Society*, p. 304.

[67] The princes' gains emerge from the essays of Cahill (where the level of resources allocated to parishes could not compensate for confiscations and the loss of subparochial dissolutions), Dykema, and Johnson; Fehler, Spicer, and Carter illustrate the fate of the congregations; there was no sudden improvement in the level of pastoral care either (Marshall).

studies are required in a great number of areas, and a balanced assessment would then have to distinguish between different social groups, particular socio-economic and religious contexts, as well as short-term versus long-term effects in each and every case. But with due allowances for these reservations, the following impression emerges from the present collection.

First and foremost, one cannot but be struck by the great diversity and complexity of experiences documented in the essays. Once we leave the level of 'grand theories' and long-term generalizations, the use of the plural 'Reformations' seems hard to avoid. There are few unambiguous trends, few undisputable beneficiaries, and quite a lot of contradictory developments. Increased clerical taxation, for instance, could forge yet closer ties between pastors and parishioners, but at the same time create financial pressures which sowed the seeds of future confrontation.[68] Reformation change could increase lay control in some areas and lead to a 'resacralization' of others in return.

Second, in line with recent historiographical tendencies, the Reformations lose much of their towering position if we examine their impact from a socio-economic perspective. The continuities are striking, be it in lay involvement, education, or territorial differentiation. The late fifteenth and early sixteenth centuries emerge quite clearly as particularly intensive periods of reform before the Reformation: this is where we find municipal advances at the expense of ecclesiastical institutions (Geneva provides an example here), this is where bishops start to modify their visitation proceedings (Stokesley foreshadows Hooper in England), this is where humanists devise their educational and poor relief programmes, and it is also a time with already extensively developed 'national Churches'.[69] Significant efforts at modernization had thus been initiated in various areas (with more or less success), and in that sense a doctrinal Reformation was not 'needed' to set them in motion, although it could restart, modify, or intensify them when it came.[70]

Third, religious motives obviously fuelled many a reforming effort, but all of these were invariably compromised by the socio-economic realities they encountered.[71] Some religious orders could be dissolved,

---

[68] See Carter below, where – on balance – anticlericalism seems to be intensified rather than reduced by the crown's fiscal policy.

[69] See Naphy, Newcombe, and Fehler; F. Oakley, *The Western Church in the Later Middle Ages* (Ithaca, London, 1979), pp. 71–9 (chapter on 'national churches'); for far-reaching socio-economic change just before the Reformation see Ingesman below.

[70] There is a lively debate on the subject: see part (iii) of Wriedt below.

[71] The policy of city magistrates reveals socio-economic priorities even at the height of the Reformation: P. Friess, *Die Aussenpolitik der Reichsstadt Memmingen in der Reformationszeit, 1517–55* (Memmingen, 1993).

others were too powerful to oblige, some ideals could be upheld, others (such as the communal foundation of Lutheran ecclesiology) proved explosive and had to be withdrawn very quickly.[72] In fact, change was often provoked by side-effects or exploitation of religious reform rather than pious motive itself. Poor relief systems, for instance, owed as much if not more to the gap left by the dissolution of intercessory institutions as to a 'Protestant ethic',[73] and the English monarch's appropriation of first fruits and tenths appeared as a 'sacrilege' to Catholics and reformers alike, *defensor fidei* notwithstanding.[74] For the *enforcement* of confessionalization at least, claims for a priority of religious factors do not look well-founded.

Finally, the Reformations almost universally benefited those at the top and burdened those at the bottom of society. Regardless of whether doctrinal change was welcomed or enforced, princes added to their possessions, and parishioners picked up the bill. The gains for local and regional élites meant that social differentiation was accelerated, quite simply as a result of practical changes and regardless of any potential effects on religious mentalities.[75]

In terms of its overall effect on dogma, church organization, and personal piety, the Age of Reformations remains a truly monumental transition. In the field of its socio-economic impact alone, the picture is clearly more ambiguous.

---

[72] Cahill (religious orders); P. Blickle, 'Reformation und kommunaler Geist: Die Antwort der Theologen auf den Verfassungswandel im Spätmittelalter', *Historische Zeitschrift*, 261 (1995), 365–402, and (for Luther's disclaimer) his *Communal Reformation*, pp. 120–3.

[73] The considerable contribution to poor relief by monastic foundations is emphasized in Slack, *Poverty and Policy*, p. 13.

[74] See Carter below.

[75] See Ingesman and Marshall below.

PART ONE

State and purpose of the clergy

CHAPTER TWO

Reform in the parishes of fifteenth- and sixteenth-century North Brabant

Arnoud-Jan A. Bijsterveld

In 1559–61 the Low Countries saw the establishment of three archiepiscopal sees (Utrecht, Mechelen, and Cambrai) and of 18 suffragan dioceses.[1] This was an attempt by Philip II (1555–98) to bring the boundaries of ecclesiastical jurisdiction into line with those of his territories. The reorganization substantially reduced the extent of the immense diocese of Liège, the central part of which constituted a prince-bishopric independent of Habsburg rule. Previously, the see had been responsible for the southeastern part of the present-day Netherlands and the eastern half of Belgium, as well as parts of Germany, Luxemburg, and France.[2] This essay will focus on the northernmost part of the old diocese of Liège, that is on the deaneries of Hilvarenbeek, Cuijk, and Woensel in the archdeaconry of Kempenland. Their territory roughly corresponds to the present-day Dutch province of North Brabant, which borders on Belgium to the south. Throughout the period under scrutiny the major part of this region belonged to the duchy of Brabant, which became part of the Burgundian Netherlands in 1430.

The empirical basis of this study consists of a prosopographical analysis of over 3 000 parish priests who served the almost 200 parishes of North Brabant between 1400 and 1570, with particular emphasis on their geographical origin, social background, education, recruitment, career, residential discipline, and their conduct, especially the observance of celibacy.[3] The relevant information derives mainly from 40 registers

[1] This essay was written during my stay as a Visiting Scholar at Princeton University in 1994–5 on grants from the Netherlands Organization for Scientific Research (NWO) and the Van Coeverden Adriani Stichting. Parts of this text were presented as a paper to the 29th International Congress on Medieval Studies at Western Michigan University (Kalamazoo) in May 1994. I wish to thank Hanneke Vissers for helping to write this paper in correct English, and Guido Marnef and Mathieu Spiertz for their advice.

[2] For the general religious and political history of the Netherlands from 1480 to 1648 see D. P. Blok, et al., *Algemene Geschiedenis der Nederlanden*, vols v–vi: Nieuwe tijd (Haarlem, 1979–80); Jonathan I. Israel, *The Dutch Republic: Its Rise, Greatness, and Fall 1477–1806*, Oxford History of Early Modern Europe (Oxford, 1995), pp. 7–230.

[3] Arnoud-Jan A. Bijsterveld, *Laverend tussen Kerk en wereld. De pastoors in Noord-Brabant 1400–1570* (Amsterdam, 1993).

of revenues of the archdeacon of Kempenland, surviving for the period between 1400 and 1566.[4] These consist of two parts: the first provides an inventory of the parishes with the names of most incumbents, resident or absent, plus the fees they owed in case of absence and for the hiring of a deputy, who is also mentioned. The second part is mainly a list of fines paid by clergymen and laymen for the violation of all kinds of canonical rules. This essay will describe the parochial system (i) and general profile of the parish clergy (ii) during the fifteenth and sixteenth centuries until 1570, when the turmoil of the struggle between Spain and the rebellious Dutch provinces started to disrupt the ecclesiastical structure. It will focus on the changes that occurred in this period and, finally, assess the impact of sixteenth-century religious reform (iii).

(i)

Fifteenth-century North Brabant was a mainly rural and relatively prosperous region. Three trading and industrial towns, 's-Hertogenbosch, Bergen op Zoom, and Breda, linked the rising commercial centres in the north, in the county of Holland and in the bishopric of Utrecht, with the south, that is with the Brabant heartland and its towns: Brussels, Antwerp, Leuven, and Mechelen. With its approximately 17 500 inhabitants in 1500, 's-Hertogenbosch was the second largest town in the northern Netherlands after Utrecht. Bergen op Zoom and Breda numbered between 6 000 and 7 000 inhabitants.[5] Although it depended on the south in many respects, the region certainly had a cultural life of its own, which focused on the towns and the splendid courts of the count of Nassau in Breda and the lord of Glimes in Bergen op Zoom, both loyal officials of successive Burgundian and Habsburg rulers.

Compared with the rest of the diocese of Liège, North Brabant was a region with very vast parishes. Although the deaneries of Hilvarenbeek, Cuijk, and Woensel covered about a fifth of the entire diocese, they accounted for little more than 10 per cent of its parishes in 1559. The boundaries of most North Brabant parishes coincided with those of village communities and rural districts of up to 3 500 inhabitants. The towns of 's-Hertogenbosch, Bergen op Zoom, and Breda contained only

---

[4] The information concerning North Brabant has been edited: G. C. A. Juten (ed.), *Consilium de Beke* (Bergen op Zoom, no date) [= reprint of his 'Kerkelijke beneficiën in het voormalig dekenaat Hilvarenbeek. Consilium de Beke', *Taxandria*, 26 (1919) – 30 (1923)]; G. Bannenberg, A. Frenken and H. Hens (eds), *De oude dekenaten Cuijk, Woensel en Hilvarenbeek in de 15de- en 16de-eeuwse registers van het aartsdiakenaat Kempenland* (2 vols, Nijmegen, 1968–70).

[5] Bijsterveld, *Laverend tussen Kerk en wereld*, pp. 99–100.

one parish church. Technically, there were only three curates to take care of all inhabitants of 's-Hertogenbosch, but the many stipendiary and chantry chaplains connected with the parish and collegiate church of St John seem to have taken an important share in the cure of souls.[6]

Generally speaking, large parishes offered attractive benefices: the high number of communicants ensured a large yield of tithes – a portion of which was generally reserved for the incumbent – as well as high proceeds from customary offerings.[7] Members of the higher clergy, such as the canons of the chapters in Liège and other southern towns, were eager to obtain a North Brabant cure, presumably for financial reasons. The parochial network in North Brabant was fairly flexible. Parishes were split up because of their large territories and as a result of population growth. The phenomenon was particularly prominent after 1550. Once the new diocesan division was implemented, the new bishops set about to improve the ecclesiastical network. At 's-Hertogenbosch for example, the bishop created no less than four parishes to serve the 19 000 inhabitants in 1569. This was in accordance with the stipulations of the Council of Trent (1545–63) which instructed bishops to revise the parochial system and to create new parishes if necessary.[8]

Noblemen, mostly local lords, held the advowsons of about a quarter of the nearly 200 North Brabant parish churches, while ecclesiastical dignitaries and corporations accounted for about 70 per cent. Of the latter, secular chapters, inside and outside the region, nominated incumbents for one in four benefices. In about 45 per cent of parish churches the incumbents or vicars were appointed by the head of an abbey, monastery, convent or other religious house. While the Premonstratensian abbeys held the considerable portion of 20 per cent of all cures, the Cistercians presented to only 4 per cent.[9] The distribution of patronage

---

[6] A. A. J. M. van de Meerendonk, *Tussen reformatie en contra-reformatie: geest en levenswijze van de clerus in stad en meierij van 's-Hertogenbosch en zijn verhouding tot de samenleving tussen ca. 1520 en ca. 1570* (Tilburg, 1967), pp. 14–16.

[7] In the following I do not distinguish between rectors, whose revenues were not appropriated to a monastic or collegiate body, and vicars, who acted as priests in parishes where the revenues were appropriated, although the latter was the case in many North Brabant parishes. As both rectors and vicars enjoyed the income of a benefice and received a portion of the tithe, they are regarded as members of the beneficed parish clergy, as opposed to the curates, who merely replaced them. See Bijsterveld, *Laverend tussen Kerk en wereld*, pp. 42–4, 47–50; cf. Christopher Harper-Bill, *The Pre-Reformation Church in England 1400–1530* (London, New York, 1989), pp. 117–19.

[8] Van de Meerendonk, *Tussen reformatie en contra-reformatie*, pp. 11–16; Bijsterveld, *Laverend tussen Kerk en wereld*, pp. 52–3, 330–31, 390.

[9] Ibid., pp. 54–5 and Table 2.1.

resulted in a very high share of regular clergy among the incumbents. One in four was a regular priest and every seventh a Premonstratensian canon.[10] In comparison to their secular colleagues the religious priests – and especially the Premonstratensians – were better educated and resided far more often in their parishes. The high rate of noble patrons naturally resulted in a high number of presentments of noblemen's relatives and friends, especially in the seigniories of Bergen op Zoom, Breda, and in the petty lordships along the river Meuse in the deanery of Cuijk.[11] Last but not least, we should note that the otherwise mighty bishop of Liège had no right at all to appoint parish priests in the northernmost part of his diocese. He had delegated the institution of all beneficed clergy to the archdeacon of Kempenland and the rural deans who, in their turn, could only consent to the choice made by the holders of advowsons. The distribution of parochial patronage gravely obstructed the serious attempts made by the bishops Erard van der Marck (1505–38) and George of Austria (1544–57) to reform the parish clergy. The latter, for instance, ordered in 1548 that the suitability of new incumbents and curates had to be tested by episcopal examiners.[12] Only after the diocesan reorganization and the decrees of the Council of Trent did the bishops manage to increase their influence on the recruitment of the parish clergy.

The relative wealth of North Brabant parishes has already been mentioned, but even large-scale prosopographical research fails to produce more detailed information about the incomes of individual parish priests. Just bits and pieces of churchwardens' or clerical accounts have survived, which makes it difficult to assess the complex aggregate of the parish priests' resources.[13] Peter Hoppenbrouwers analysed all late medieval financial and fiscal sources for 16 villages in the Land of Heusden, a region in the county of Holland immediately adjoining North Brabant. Although he disposed of medieval property-lists for three parishes – two

---

[10] Ibid., pp. 66–73. For the increasing number of religious clergy among the parish incumbents in England see Robert N. Swanson, *Church and Society in Late Medieval England* (Oxford, New York, 1989), p. 86; for patronage in general ibid., pp. 64–79.

[11] The mechanisms of this type of patronage are described in my article 'Les jeux d'influence et le patronage local de la haute noblesse dans le choix des titulaires de cures en Brabant du Nord (XVᵉ-XVIᵉ siècles)', *Revue du Nord*, 77 (1995), 345–63.

[12] L.-E. Halkin, *Réforme Protestante et Réforme Catholique au diocèse de Liége: Histoire religieuse des règnes de Corneille de Berghes et de Georges d'Autriche, princes-évêques de Liége (1538–1557)* (Liège, Paris, 1936), pp. 244–56, 278–83.

[13] Joseph Avril, 'La paroisse médiévale: bilan et perspectives d'après quelques travaux récents', *Revue d'Histoire de l'Eglise de France*, 74 (1988), 91–113, 106; Bijsterveld, *Laverend tussen Kerk en wereld*, pp. 277–8, 331–2.

of which were situated within the region studied here – he had to concede that he could not arrive at an accurate estimate of the landed property of parish churches or parochial institutions. He concluded, first of all, that the possessions of churches, priests and tables of the poor were very heterogenous and subject to great fluctuation, and secondly, that judging from the existing evidence for landed property, the late fifteenth-century incumbents can be regarded as 'relatively well-to-do'.[14] However, as we shall see below, the political and economic crisis of the 1520s and 1530s, which resulted in inflation and a higher tax burden, was to have a serious impact on the parish priests' financial fortunes.

(ii)

During the fifteenth and the first decades of the sixteenth century about 60 per cent of North Brabant incumbents did not actually reside in their parishes and engaged *deservitores* to discharge their pastoral duties. Other rectors, because of personal infirmity or the parish's size, hired *coadiutores* or assistants. These chaplains or curates who ministered the parochial cure of souls constituted some 40 per cent of the parish clergy. It is not surprising that they differed in many aspects from the incumbents. In general, the careers of curates were characterized by less security, a higher mobility, a smaller radius of action, lower earnings, and significantly poorer chances of acquiring a lucrative prebend or additional office. We may thus consider the incumbents and their deputies as two markedly different and almost exclusive classes within the clergy.[15]

Among the incumbents, two categories may be distinguished. As mentioned above, a quarter of them were regular priests, mostly Premonstratensians, but also Cistercians, members of the knightly or-

---

[14] Peter C. M. Hoppenbrouwers, *Een middeleeuwse samenleving: het Land van Heusden ca. 1360 – ca. 1515* (2 vols, Groningen, 1992), i. 371–3, 541. Cf. the rather negative conclusions of Robert N. Swanson, 'Standards of livings: parochial revenues in pre-Reformation England' in Christopher Harper-Bill (ed.), *Religious Belief and Ecclesiastical Careers in Late Medieval England*, Proceedings of the Conference held at Strawberry Hill, Easter 1989 (Woodbridge, 1991), pp. 151–83.

[15] Cf. L. Binz, *Vie religieuse et réforme ecclésiastique dans le diocèse de Genève pendant le Grand Schisme et la crise conciliaire (1378–1450)* (Geneva, 1973), pp. 330–1, 406; Francis Rapp, 'Les clercs souabes dans le diocèse de Strasbourg à la veille de la Réforme' in Kaspar Elm, et al. (eds), *Landesgeschichte und Geistesgeschichte: Festschrift für Otto Herding zum 65. Geburtstag* (Stuttgart, 1977), pp. 265–79, esp. 267–9; Swanson, *Church and Society*, pp. 27–8, 46–8; Francis Rapp, 'Rapport introductif' in *Le clerc séculier au Moyen Age*, XXIIe Congrès de la S.H.M.E.S., Amiens, juin 1991 (Paris, 1993), pp. 9–25.

ders, and some Wilhelmites. Friars merely served as deputies and in very small numbers. The second category consisted of those who managed to combine their cure with a canonical prebend in one of the many chapters within or outside the diocese of Liège; this group also accounts for a quarter of incumbents. As might be expected, the canons constituted an élite among the parish priests: their social origin was mostly distinguished, their education excellent, but they hardly ever resided in their parishes due to the plurality of their benefices and offices.[16]

There were no clerical seminaries before the Council of Trent.[17] Church authorities demanded but a fair knowledge of Latin and sacramental formulae, as well as some basic familiarity with religious doctrine.[18] Theological reading was not expected at all. This meant, first of all, that pastoral skills could only be acquired in some sort of apprenticeship with an older priest. Second, future priests who desired a more thorough education had to attend the Latin schools and possibly a university, both of which merely provided some general training.

Unfortunately, there are no means to establish the quota of future parish priests who attended local Latin schools in preparation for a university education. This is particularly regrettable in light of the fact that the educational infrastructure in the highly urbanized Low Countries, but also in more rural North Brabant, was fairly good in this period. The Latin school of 's-Hertogenbosch, for example, became quite famous, although Erasmus did not like the teaching he received there.[19] In order to assess the parish priests' schooling, I have thus investigated to what extent (future) incumbents and curates had enrolled in one or more European universities.[20] The most popular institutions were those of Leuven and Cologne and, to a far lesser degree, the *studia* of Orléans, Paris, and Heidelberg.

Generally speaking, we observe a steady increase in the number of parish priests enrolling in a university between 1400 and 1570 (see Figure 2.1). However, the gap between incumbents and deputies is

---

[16] Bijsterveld, *Laverend tussen Kerk en wereld*, pp. 76–7, 203–4, 287.

[17] In North Brabant seminaries were not established before the early seventeenth century; previous attempts failed in the 1570s (ibid., p. 137).

[18] See the demands formulated by Ulrich of Strasbourg (†1277) and quoted by Friedrich W. Oediger, *Über die Bildung der Geistlichen im späten Mittelalter* (Leiden, Cologne, 1953), pp. 55–6; Bijsterveld, *Laverend tussen Kerk en wereld*, pp. 135–6.

[19] Van de Meerendonk, *Tussen reformatie en contra-reformatie*, pp. 26–8.

[20] On the basis of the edited registers of enrollment of Continental universities. For an excellent introduction to these sources and their editions see Jacques Paquet, *Les matricules universitaires*, Typologie des sources du moyen âge occidental lxv (Turnhout, 1992).

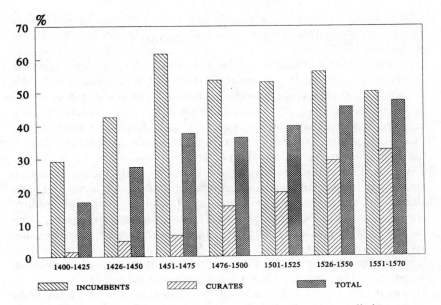

Figure 2.1   Number of North Brabant parish priests having enrolled in a
university, by period

particularly prominent here. After an increase during the first half of
the fifteenth century, no less than 60 per cent of the incumbents of the
third quarter of that century had attended a university. During the
sixteenth century, the figure stabilized at over 50 per cent. As for the
curates, the quota of university students, which had been at a very low
level during the first decades of the fifteenth century, increased slowly
but steadily during the entire period, and reached a percentage of well
over 30 in the decades before 1570.[21]
   The first observation to be made concerns the wide-spread cliché of
the intellectual incompetence of the mass of the parish clergy during the
late Middle Ages and on the eve of the Reformation. According to some
studies of the Dutch parish clergy during the sixteenth century, this
incompetence increased further, but my results suggest a very different
trend.[22] On the eve of the large-scale religious and political tribulations
that swept the Low Countries during and after the 1560s, roughly half
of the parish priests in North Brabant had attended a university. This is

---

[21] All these percentages represent minimal figures!
[22] Reinier R. Post, *Kerkelijke verhoudingen in Nederland vóór de Reformatie van ±
1500 tot ± 1580* (Utrecht, Antwerp, 1954), p. 55; Van de Meerendonk, *Tussen reformatie
en contra-reformatie*, pp. 33–4.

a large figure in comparison to other parts of Western Europe, which may reflect the generally higher educational level in the Low Countries at the time.[23]

It is of course a matter for debate to what extent a high degree of university attendance by the North Brabant clergy can be equated with a high intellectual quality. Enrollment in a university was not necessarily the same as studying there. What we know about contemporary practices suggests that most students only spent some time, from one to two years, at an academic institution. They studied predominantly in the faculty of arts, and most of them left university without even taking a degree. This applies equally to the North Brabant clergy.[24] Almost two-thirds of the students among them attended the faculty of arts alone, and most obtained no degree at all. Only a small élite studied law, theology, and medicine, and these, almost without exception, were the priests who obtained prestigious offices far removed from the ordinary parochial cure of souls.

How then can we assess the usefulness of university education for members of the clerical profession? A period of study in the faculty of arts probably gave a student a better familiarity with the Latin language, as well as an introduction to medieval philosophy and scholasticism. Although this contributed to the clergyman's general knowledge and enabled him to carry out some aspects of the pastoral office more effectively, the curriculum was not primarily aimed at the provision of spiritual or pastoral skills. Theology, from our point of view the most appropriate subject, only played a marginal role. We can thus be fairly optimistic about the parish priests' general degree of education, but there is reason to doubt their pastoral qualification. Nevertheless, we have to recognize the clergymen's readiness to improve their learning. Besides, there was an increase in the number of priests who studied theology after 1550.[25] It was the church authorities, the higher clergy, who failed to respond to this pressure from below and waited

---

[23] Cf. Oediger, *Über die Bildung*, p. 66 and note 3; Post, *Kerkelijke verhoudingen*, pp. 53–5; Peter Heath, *The English Parish Clergy on the Eve of the Reformation* (London, Toronto, 1969), p. 81; Rapp, 'Les clercs souabes', pp. 273–4, and his 'La paroisse et l'encadrement religieux des fidèles (du XIVe au XVIe siècle)' in *L'encadrement religieux des fidèles au Moyen-Age et jusqu'au Concile de Trente: la paroisse, le clergé, la pastorale, la dévotion* (Paris, 1985) pp. 27–43, here 34; Peter Marshall, *The Catholic Priesthood and the English Reformation* (Oxford, 1994), pp. 96–101.

[24] Rainer C. Schwinges, 'Student education, student life' in Hilde de Ridder-Symoens (ed.), *A History of the University in Europe*, vol. i: Universities in the Middle Ages (Cambridge etc., 1992), pp. 195–243, here 196–9; Bijsterveld, *Laverend tussen Kerk en wereld*, pp. 147, 150–1, 189, 197.

[25] Ibid., pp. 191–2: of all parish priests between 1551 and 1570, one out of twelve had studied some theology, which is more than twice as much as in the preceding period.

too long to develop ideas on how a priest should be trained for his profession.[26]

The net increase in the ratio of university-trained priests must be seen against the background of the growing importance of further education in the Low Countries in general. The higher degree of academic interest among the clergy probably owed more to the contemporary opinion that higher education was necessary for certain professions, than to some new moral fervour among the incumbents or curates. Youngsters did not enrol in a university to become parish priests, but to get on in society in general. A clerical career was but one of many opportunities arising out of some years' study at a faculty of arts.[27]

Most historians have been inclined to take either a condemning or apologetic stand towards the so-called abuses of the late medieval clergy and in particular to their failure to observe celibacy. Protestant historians regarded these 'abuses' as signs of Roman decay and decadence, while Catholic writers explained them as understandable lapses of a clergy unfamiliar with the ideals of Trent and the Catholic Reformation. The information in the archdeacon of Kempenland's registers of revenues makes it possible to calculate that between 45 and 60 per cent of all fifteenth-century parish priests failed to observe celibacy at some point during their career.[28] Local research reveals up to 80 per cent non-celibate clergymen. Unfortunately, no precise figures can be established for the sixteenth century, but there are many signs that a considerable share of parish priests continued to ignore the rule of clerical chastity. Sexual debauchery was frequent among all types of priests: whether schooled at university or not, whether incumbent or curate, whether regular cleric or secular priest. This means, first of all, that we cannot in any way link the priests' social status or intellectual ability to their moral behaviour.

Furthermore, it is obvious that clerical 'incontinence' was by no means 'an underground affair', as John Bossy put it. Bossy states that 'efforts at quantification which have been made for dioceses in England

---

[26] To borrow an argument from Heath, *English Parish Clergy*, p. 91. See also Oediger, *Über die Bildung*, pp. 56–7, 64, 67–8.

[27] Hilde de Ridder-Symoens, 'Possibilités de carrière et de mobilité sociale des intellectuels-universitaires au moyen âge' in Neithard Bulst and Jean-Philippe Genet (eds), *Medieval Lives and the Historian: Studies in Medieval Prosopography* (Kalamazoo, 1986), pp. 343–57, esp. 351. Cf. Heath, *English Parish Clergy*, pp. 77–78.

[28] Eric J. G. Lips, 'De Brabantse geestelijkheid en de andere sekse: een onderzoek naar celibaatschendingen bij de Brabantse parochiegeestelijken in de vijftiende en zestiende eeuw', *Tijdschrift voor Geschiedenis*, 102 (1989), 1–30, esp. 26; Bijsterveld, *Laverend tussen Kerk en wereld*, pp. 344–6.

and the rest of Europe suggest a clergy by 1500 continent in practice to a degree of 80 or 90 per cent'. According to him, charges of sexual incontinence against parish priests must be regarded as 'malicious gossip'.[29] This, however, was certainly not the case in North Brabant during the greater part of the period under scrutiny.[30] In the charges filed by ecclesiastical authorities against priests living in concubinage, the names of the women are also mentioned and some of these recur over a period of more than 20 years. Their children populated the parsonages. Moreover, these children seem to have been accepted in local society just as all the others born out of wedlock in those days. Parishioners were apparently ready to make allowances for their curate's failure to observe celibacy, even if he had children. As long as he did not court the maidens and married women of his parish, and as long as he celebrated Mass and administered the sacraments properly, his flock probably restricted itself to mild derision and gossip without taking any further action.[31] How could it have been otherwise in these small parochial communities of some dozens to some hundreds of houses and families?

All the more so, as most parish priests were also part of the parish's network of kin- and friendship: four out of ten priests worked within a radius of less than ten kilometres from their place of birth.[32] In other words, most counted relatives and friends from their youth among their parishioners. The personal ties between pastor and flock were often

---

[29] John Bossy, *Christianity in the West 1400–1700* (Oxford, New York, 1985), pp. 65–6. For a more balanced judgement see Marshall, *Catholic Priesthood*, who, after observing the 'relative paucity of cases of proven or suspected immorality among the parish clergy' in England, explains this by less lay toleration of concubinage and an ecclesiastical atmosphere that 'was notably less conducive to widespread concubinage than it was in parts of the Continent' (pp. 144–5, 150–3).

[30] For a similar assessment see James A. Brundage, *Law, Sex, and Christian Society in Medieval Europe* (Chicago, London, 1987), p. 536, who states that 'clerical incontinence was an open scandal in many parts of Western Christendom'. Cf. Heath, *English Parish Clergy*, pp. 104–8, 118–19, and Harper-Bill, *Pre-Reformation Church*, pp. 48–9.

[31] Bijsterveld, *Laverend tussen Kerk en wereld*, pp. 356–68. For the relationship between priests and parishioners see also Heath, *English Parish Clergy*, pp. 106, 158–63, 191; Binz, *Vie religieuse*, pp. 443–7; M.-C. Gasnault, 'Le clergé dans les paroisses rurales du diocèse de Sens à la fin du Moyen Age' in *L'encadrement religieux*, pp. 317–27, esp. 324; M. Aubrun, *La paroisse en France des origines au XVe siècle* (Paris, 1986), pp. 170–71, 179; Harper-Bill, *Pre-Reformation Church*, pp. 44–53; Robert N. Swanson, 'Problems of the priesthood in pre-Reformation England', *English Historical Review*, 105 (1990), 845–69, esp. 848, 855–61; Andrew Barnes, 'The social transformation of the French parish clergy, 1500–1800' in Barbara B. Diefendorf and Carla Hesse (eds), *Culture and Identity in Early Modern Europe (1500–1800): Essays in Honor of Natalie Zemon Davis* (Ann Arbor, 1993), pp. 139–57; and most impressively, Marshall, *Catholic Priesthood, passim*, esp. pp. 179–88.

[32] Bijsterveld, *Laverend tussen Kerk en wereld*, p. 254. Similarly, Marshall, *Catholic Priesthood*, pp. 195–6.

close and this may account both for his readiness to bend ecclesiastical rules and for the parishioners' tolerance. Together they negotiated a compromise between conflicting norms and values. They reduced the high and 'superhuman' demands of the church to the standards of their own small world, in which loyalty towards relatives and friends and solidarity between villagers prevailed. This is why we see local priests siding with their parishioners in controversial pastoral questions such as irregular marriages or the administration of sacraments to excommunicated members of their flock, in spite of potential conflict with their ecclesiastical superiors.[33]

We have already observed that during the fifteenth and the first decades of the sixteenth century about 60 per cent of incumbents did not actually reside in their parishes.[34] A further 10 per cent alternated periods of absence with periods of residence, which leaves at the most 30 per cent of all incumbents actively engaged in the cure of souls in their parishes.[35] The main cause of the phenomenon was the general habit of pluralism. Dispensations from the duty to reside were not very difficult to obtain for canons or for clerics serving a prelate or secular prince. A 'reasonable cause' was supposed to be study at a university, while illness, minority, the lack of full holy orders, the attractions of a nearby town, or the bad financial situation of a particular benefice could also lead to non-residence.

If we look at the development of absenteeism over time, we observe a rather stable rate up to about 1520. After that year, the figure rose dramatically to some 80 per cent during the 1530s, but decreased again from the 1540s, first gradually and then dramatically, to 30 per cent in the 1550s. During the last decade before 1570, the residence-ratio stabilized at six out of ten incumbents.[36] As a consequence of this drop,

---

[33] For examples see Bijsterveld, *Laverend tussen Kerk en wereld*, pp. 334–7.

[34] For this and the following see ibid., pp. 262–84, and Hoppenbrouwers, *Een middeleeuwse samenleving*, pp. 548–9.

[35] Cf. absenteeism in the French dioceses of Geneva, Rodez, Sens and Langres, which in general shows comparable rates and a similar development: Binz, *Vie religieuse*, pp. 302–3; Nicole Lemaitre, *Le Rouergue flamboyant: clergé et paroisses du diocèse de Rodez (1417–1563)* (Paris, 1988), pp. 170–71, 265; Gasnault, 'Le clergé', pp. 320–1; G. Viard, 'Curés et vicaires en pays langrois au dernier tiers du XVIe siècle', *Revue d'Histoire de l'Eglise de France*, 75 (1989), 93–101, 96–7. For the situation in England see Heath, *English Parish Clergy*, pp. 50–60; Marshall, *Catholic Priesthood*, pp. 177–9.

[36] The same tendencies (although the overall figures of absenteeism were not as high as in North Brabant) are observed in other parts of the diocese of Liège: a rapid increase of absenteeism starting in the early 1520s, a peak in 1526, followed by a continued high rate of absenteeism and a steady decrease during the late 1540s and 1550s (Bijsterveld, *Laverend tussen Kerk en wereld*, pp. 272–3).

the number of curates decreased proportionally: from 70 to 80 per cent of the number of incumbents before 1550, to just 30 per cent afterwards.[37]

What explanations can be found for the rise and fall of absenteeism between 1520 and 1570?[38] The 1520s and 1530s were a period of wars and economic crisis. The resulting increase in inflation and taxes diminished clerical incomes, too. This was presumably the main cause which forced incumbents to leave their parishes to find additional resources elsewhere. In contrast to the fifteenth century, the clergy was no longer fully exempt from princely levies and municipal excise taxes.[39] In addition to this economic and political crisis, we may also have to point to anticlerical voices which became more prominent at that time, especially in the towns.[40] In 1525, the citizens of 's-Hertogenbosch looted two of their convents as a result of a conflict over tax exemptions. Moreover, we observe a major and permanent change in people's attitudes towards popular devotions throughout the Low Countries in about 1520, namely a considerable decrease in the membership of religious confraternities, a slump of the receipts from pious donations, collections, and bequests, and a fading interest in processions.[41] The declining willingness of the faithful to make material sacrifices for spiritual purposes can be accounted for by a combination of religious and socio-economic explanations. Nevertheless, in spite of the waning interest in traditional devotional practices and the fact that Martin Luther's teachings gained their first followers in this period, we cannot speak of a broad anticlerical or Protestant movement which would have made it impossible for parish priests to practise the cure of souls during the 1520s and 1530s.

But what caused the decrease of absenteeism after 1540? First of all, the concerted action of both ecclesiastical and secular authorities to put an end to the nuisance of non-residence. The Regent of the Netherlands, Mary of Hungary (1531–55), sister of Charles V (1506–55), for

---

[37] Ibid., pp. 297–8. The same process is observed in the French diocese of Langres between 1560 and 1573 by Viard, 'Curés et vicaires en pays langrois', 97.

[38] Bijsterveld, *Laverend tussen Kerk en wereld*, pp. 277–84.

[39] Cf. the situation in the neighbouring county of Holland as described by James D. Tracy, 'Elements of anticlerical sentiment in the province of Holland under Charles V' in Peter A. Dykema and Heiko A. Oberman (eds), *Anticlericalism in Late Medieval and Early Modern Europe*, Studies in Medieval and Reformation Thought, li (Leiden, New York, Cologne, 1993), pp. 257–69, here 258–62.

[40] We cannot use the term 'anticlericalism' without referring to its redefinition by Heiko A. Oberman, 'Anticlericalism as an Agent of Change' in ibid., pp. ix–xi.

[41] See Alistair Duke, *Reformation and Revolt in the Low Countries* (London, Ronceverte, 1991), pp. 8–12, 33–6, 46–8, 56–7, 79–82; Koen Goudriaan, 'Het einde van de Middeleeuwen ontdekt?', *Madoc. Tijdschrift over de Middeleeuwen*, 8 (1994), 66–75.

instance, urged the bishop of Liège more than once to eradicate pluralism and to end the unlimited granting of dispensations.[42] There are signs that the obligation to reside was more strictly enforced: during the 1550s and 1560s incumbents were actually compelled to resign if they could not meet their responsibilities. In 1568 the first bishop of the new see of 's-Hertogenbosch, Francis Sonnius (1561–70), sent a letter to all absent incumbents in his diocese ordering them to appear in their parishes and to stay there 'in accordance with the decrees of Trent' or to face deposition.[43] The problem of the poverty of many pastoral benefices, which forced many incumbents to look for resources elsewhere, was also tackled. George of Austria, Bishop of Liège, took measures to augment parish income in 1548, for instance by merging several benefices.[44] This must have made it more attractive for incumbents to reside instead of hiring a curate. Finally, there may have been some change of attitude among the parish clergy themselves, comparable to what we observed with regard to the higher rate of university-trained priests. The consecutive increase and decrease of incumbents' non-residence cannot be explained by economic and political circumstances alone. It also reflected changes in religious and mental attitudes which are difficult to evaluate.

(iii)

Protestantism in North Brabant was mainly an urban phenomenon. From the 1520s onwards many suspects, mostly craftsmen, were brought to trial on the accusation of being Lutherans or heretics in 's-Hertogenbosh, but also in the smaller towns of Bergen op Zoom, Breda, and Eindhoven. At 's-Hertogenbosch, for instance, severe sentences were passed on heretics, and particularly Anabaptists, during the 1530s. Among the first to be charged were parish priests. Winand Quinquius, rector of the parish and dean of the chapter of Eindhoven until his death in 1533, was accused of possessing 'suspect books'. His curate

---

[42] In letters to bishops Erard van der Marck and George of Austria in 1537 and 1549 respectively (L.-E. Halkin, *Réforme Protestante et Réforme Catholique au diocèse de Liége: le Cardinal de la Marck Prince-Évêque de Liége (1505–1538)* (Liège, Paris, 1930), p. 197, and *Réforme Protestante et Réforme Catholique... Corneille de Berghes et Georges d'Autriche*, pp. 281–2; J. Absil, 'L'absentéisme du clergé paroissial au diocèse de Liège, au XVᵉ et dans la première moitié du XVIᵉ', *Revue d'Histoire Ecclésiastique*, 57 (1962), 5–44, here 28–9).

[43] G. van den Elsen and W. Hoevenaars (eds), *Analecta Gijsberti Coeverincx* (2 vols, 's-Hertogenbosch, 1905–7), i. 47–9.

[44] Absil, 'L'absentéisme du clergé paroissial', 38–9.

Godefroi van Itter was charged with delivering unorthodox sermons and being a member of the 'Lutheran and heretic sect'. He wrote a defence addressed to Bishop Erard van der Marck of Liège (†1538), but in 1540 Charles V issued a warrant of arrest for him 'being very notorious because of bad learning'. With the help of the town authorities and the lord of Eindhoven's mother, Van Itter managed to escape to his native village, outside Charles's jurisdiction. It is striking – and indeed typical of this time of turmoil – that the lady was the sister of Cornelius van Bergen, the incumbent bishop of Liège (1538–44)! She and her son could still turn a blind eye on the reform-minded townspeople and parish priests, whom they had appointed. In 1568, however, under William of Orange (lord of Eindhoven 1551–84), Godefroi van den Berghe, rector of the parish and dean of the chapter, had to give account of his 'heretic feelings'. By now, times had definitely changed: the dean lost his benefices and was stripped of his property.[45]

Nevertheless, William of Orange's tolerance in matters of religion is well known. In his town of Breda, Protestantism could take a firm hold during the first years of his lordship (1544–84). In contrast to the trading town of Bergen op Zoom, where Calvinist activity developed only slowly from the 1560s, a considerable part of the population of 's-Hertogenbosch appears to have adopted the 'new religion' by this date. In 1566, 's-Hertogenbosch, Breda and Eindhoven were the scenes of iconoclastic fury. For more than a decade, the Catholics and the Protestants fought over power in the North Brabant towns. After the 'Reconquista' of 1579–82, however, most of the area had returned under firm Spanish domination, with the exception of the towns of Bergen op Zoom and Breda. As a result, the fortunes of Catholicism improved in the southern provinces after 1585. From this point, and especially during the Twelve-Year Truce (1609–21), the Catholic Reformation could take firm roots in 's-Hertogenbosch and most of the North Brabant countryside, until they were reconquered by the States General in the 1620s and 1630s.[46]

---

[45] For the sources quoted in this paragraph see Bijsterveld, *Laverend tussen Kerk en wereld*, pp. 338–40.

[46] T. G. M. Graas, 'De "nyeuwe religie" te 's-Hertogenbosch: de reformatie tot 1629' in A. M. Koldeweij (ed.), *In Buscoducis 1450–1629: kunst uit de Bourgondische tijd te 's-Hertogenbosch. De cultuur van late middeleeuwen en renaissance* (2 vols, Maarssen, The Hague, 1990), pp. 540–9, esp. 546–7; Peter Toebak, 'Het kerkelijk-godsdienstige en culturele leven binnen het noordwestelijke deel van het hertogdom Brabant (1587–1609): een typering', *Trajecta*, 1 (1992), 124–43, and his *Kerkelijk-godsdienstig leven in westelijk Noord-Brabant 1580–1652: Dekenale visitatieverslagen als bron* (2 vols, Breda, 1995).

Although there was a fair amount of criticism about parish organization, patronage distribution and the quality of the clergy in sixteenth-
century North Brabant, it was not strong enough to nurture a widespread Protestant movement. Anticlericalism was directed first and foremost at the regular and higher clergy.[47] The main targets of the early
reformers were neither parishes nor priests, but the wealth and privileges of monastic and collegiate bodies. It is no coincidence that the
paintings of Hieronymus Bosch of 's-Hertogenbosch (c. 1450–1516),
who depicted society's vices so poignantly, never feature secular priests
but only monks and nuns. Yet at the same time, the population seems to
have lost interest in traditional religious practices.

On the whole Protestantism remained marginal, especially in the
countryside. Four factors may have contributed to the eventual 'triumph' of Catholicism in this part of the Netherlands, three of which we
touched upon in our analysis. First, the apparent changes in the parish
priests' profile and attitudes, second, the generally tolerant attitude of
the parishioners towards their pastors, and third, the late but effective
measures the church authorities took to improve the parochial situation
after the crisis of the first decades of the sixteenth century. The last and
decisive factor, however, was the political and military outcome of the
Dutch Revolt.

From an early stage, the parish priests themselves proved to be able
to adapt to the higher standards of lay society and their ecclesiastical
superiors. In no previous age had so many lay people been able to
acquire writing and reading skills as in the first decades of the sixteenth
century. Increasingly, they replaced the clergy in administrative and
educational positions. This higher rate of education and the rapid dissemination of printing could not but result in a more critical attitude
towards religious practice in general and clergymen in particular.[48] If a
priest wanted to remain respected by his parishioners, his schooling had
to be at least as good as theirs. The North Brabant parish priests seem
to have realized this quite early. During the sixteenth century, we ob-

---

[47] Tracy, 'Elements of anticlerical sentiment', p. 257, quotes from a letter of Erasmus
of 1525 in which the humanist states that the people of Holland, Zeeland, and Flanders
harboured a 'more than deadly hatred against the monks'. Tracy mentions three reasons
for this anticlericalism, namely opposition to the tax exemptions all clerical institutions
enjoyed, the abuses of power by particular sections of the clergy, and the involvement of
the mendicants in Charles V's brutal repression of heresy. For the long history of the
antimonastic element in Dutch anti-papism, see Anton van de Sande, 'Decadente monniken
en nonnen: aard en functie van een antipapistisch motief (c. 1500–1853)' in Marit
Monteiro et al. (eds), De dynamiek van religie en cultuur: geschiedenis van het Nederlands
katholicisme (Kampen, 1993), pp. 239–60.
[48] Marshall, Catholic Priesthood, pp. 103–7.

serve a steady increase in the number of university-trained pastors as a result of the growing number of university-trained curates. This is a clear indication of a growing awareness of the need for thorough study among clerics themselves. The shift from law to theology noticeable from 1550 is an additional sign of their acceptance of higher standards. Besides, the drop in absenteeism among incumbents probably attests both to their change in attitude and to the improved financial conditions in the parishes. As for celibacy, we cannot assess to what extent it was observed by North Brabant parish priests during the sixteenth century, but we may assume that a considerable share of them continued to break this rule at some point in their career. The pastors' private life, however, was never a point of serious concern, not for the reformers, nor the parishioners.

In spite of new religious priorities among the well educated and less well educated of the local community, the basic affinity between parishioners and parish clergy does not seem to have been seriously affected. In rural North Brabant, the bonds between parish priests and their flock – based on kinship and village solidarity – were and remained very close.[49] Only in towns were priests occasionally attacked by their parishioners. In 1567, Stephen Langritius, vicar of Bergen op Zoom, was harrassed by a number of women who dragged him through the church by his hair.[50] But even in the turbulent years of the sixteenth century most people remained loyal to their pastors. However, this could change under different political circumstances: Anthony Dhoon, who was appointed vicar of Breda by William of Orange in 1559, alienated his flock because of his sympathy for Spain in the early 1570s, when most of the town's priests sided with Orange. In the 1570s and 1580s, many parish priests had to flee and the cure of souls was disrupted in many places.

After the political, economic, and religious crisis of the 'roaring 1520s', it took some time before church and state authorities took concerted action to improve the situation in the parishes. Although the ecclesiastical network in North Brabant had always been flexible, one is struck by the number of new parishes created after 1550. Church authorities did not only become aware of problems concerning the cure of souls, they also took positive action. Bishop George of Austria's steps to monitor clerical recruitment may have been frustrated by the rigid patronage system and the power of the archdeacons of Liège, but he had some success curbing the extent of non-residence by enforcing the rules more

---

[49] Gerard Rooijakkers, *Rituele repertoires: volkscultuur in oostelijk Noord-Brabant 1559–1853* (Nijmegen, 1994), pp. 151–9.
[50] Bijsterveld, *Laverend tussen Kerk en wereld*, p. 351.

strictly and by ameliorating parochial endowments. The bishops of the new sees could apply pressure yet more successfully. From about 1565, they pursued a rigorous reformation of the parish clergy in the spirit of Trent, which resulted in a new class of better-educated priests.[51] The bishops did not, for instance, refrain from encroaching on patrons' rights which had obstructed episcopal control before. Although these measures came fairly late, the position of the Catholic church could still be saved.

Decisive, however, were the political developments between 1568 and 1648. In spite of the frequent changes of sides the area experienced during the war between Spain, the guardian of Catholic orthodoxy, and the rebellious Dutch provinces in the 1570s and 1580s, the Catholic Reformation could take firm hold in North Brabant from about 1585. At this time the Spanish managed to gain the upper hand both in the east, which belonged to the newly erected diocese of 's-Hertogenbosch, and in most of the west, located in the diocese of Antwerp. When the highest tide of religious confusion ebbed away in the first decades of the seventeenth century, most people had definitively opted for Catholicism and only a minority for the reformed religion. The choice, however, had probably been determined by tradition and popular custom rather than deep spiritual conviction.[52]

After the Twelve-Year Truce (1609–21), a final series of military events overturned the political situation once more. In 1629 the town of 's-Hertogenbosch together with its bailiwick came under the authority of the States General, and in 1637 the town and land of Breda followed suit. From then on, the public practice of Catholic worship was suspended in almost all of North Brabant. The Peace of Westphalia in 1648 confirmed this for the next one and a half centuries, during which the Catholic majority in North Brabant faced a situation of virtual repression by a small number of Protestants: the churches had to be handed over to them and Catholic worship was banished to the conventicles.[53]

---

[51] Mathieu G. Spiertz, 'Succes en falen van de katholieke reformatie' in H. L. M. Defoer et al. (eds), *Ketters en papen onder Filips II* (Utrecht, 1986), pp. 58–74, esp. 61–7; Rooijakkers, *Rituele repertoires*, pp. 116–21, 151, 158; cf. Barnes, 'Social Transformation'.

[52] Toebak, 'Het kerkelijk-godsdienstige en culturele leven', 142; Rooijakkers, *Rituele repertoires*, p. 121.

[53] Rooijakkers, *Rituele repertoires*, describes, most impressively, the popular religious culture and the prevailing oecumenical interaction in this period.

If, in conclusion, we try to assess the importance of genuinely religious factors for the changes observed in this essay, the picture is ambiguous. On the one hand, the existence of anticlericalism, urban Protestantism, and Catholic Reformation fervour cannot be ignored. Developments in the fields of clerical education and absenteeism, however, owed more to socio-economic circumstances and secular trends. Most importantly, the confessional settlement depended on political and military realities rather than on a religious reform movement among the people. This, of course, was by now a common European experience.

CHAPTER THREE

The reforms of Count Eberhard of Württemberg: 'confessionalization' in the fifteenth century

Peter Dykema

At times the historical profession suffers from collective amnesia. A study detailing the ecclesiastical policies of the Württemberg counts, published in 1912, begins with the recognition that prior to the Reformation there existed strong tendencies towards territorial church government throughout Germany. The first footnote goes on to acknowledge the 'current' flurry of research on the theme 'church and state in the late Middle Ages and the Reformation'.[1] Yet, some 80 years later, Ronnie Hsia could observe that in comparison to the sixteenth and seventeenth centuries, 'the expansion of secular authorities at the expense of ecclesiastical autonomy in the territories before the Reformation has received less attention'.[2] Similar remarks about late medieval German territorial church government had already been made by Manfred Schulze, who notes that after decades of perfunctory acknowledgments, the reality of territorial influence has yet to hit home, that is, has yet to make its way into the master narrative of the period 1400–1700.[3] But this may be changing. In a wide-ranging article Heinz Schilling reports how recent studies of politics, religious sociology, and theology continue to break down the wall between the Middle Ages and the Reformation: 'functional similarities between the Protestant and Roman Catholic confessional churches' are forcing historians to re-examine the medieval antecedents to both.[4]

---

[1] Johannes Wülk and Hans Funk, *Die Kirchenpolitik der Grafen von Württemberg, bis zur Erhebung Württembergs zum Herzogtum (1495)* (Stuttgart, 1912), p. 1.

[2] 'The German seventeenth century', *Journal of Modern History*, 66 (1994), 726–36, here 731–2.

[3] *Fürsten und Reformation: Geistliche Reformpolitik weltlicher Fürsten vor der Reformation* (Tübingen, 1991), p. 7 with literature. Schulze addresses the *Fürstenreformation* thesis of confessional historians and shows the fallacy in the line often drawn from 'Luther's Reformation to territorial church government'. He convincingly establishes the need to invert the terms.

[4] 'Luther, Loyola, Calvin und die europäische Neuzeit', *ARG*, 85 (1994), 5–31, esp. 9, see also 16–22.

   This essay is intended as a contribution to this inquiry, appropriate
enough in a volume addressing 'Reformations Old and New'. In particular, the task here undertaken is to measure the social and political
impact of religious change in late fifteenth-century Württemberg as
Count Eberhard the Bearded (1445–96) pursued vigorous ecclesiastical
policies: territorial church reform before the Reformation. For this
purpose, I will address the expansion of Eberhard's ecclesiastical rights
(i) and how he applied these in the foundation of the university at
Tübingen (ii). The argument then turns to the 'confessional' identity of
the territory and the patronage of devotion (iii), specifically, to the
count's support of the Canons and Brethren of the Common Life (iv).
This will lead to an assessment of Count Eberhard's reforms and the
degree to which they represent 'confessionalization' in the fifteenth
century (v).

(i)

During the late Middle Ages, the great monastic houses throughout
Württemberg lost all pretence of independence as they increasingly
came under secular control and jurisdiction. Eberhard exerted influence
over the monasteries by firmly wielding the stewardship rights (*ius
advocatiae*) established by his predecessors over individual houses.[5]
Although canon law limited the duties of the steward to the protection
of the cloister and the exercise of capital justice on the monastery's
lands, secular stewards all over Germany had managed to transform
these responsibilities into effective claims to lordship. More so than
even property ownership, jurisdiction became the criterion for sovereignty.[6] The monasteries in Württemberg continued to appeal to ecclesiastical tradition in asserting their right to choose their own protector
and advocate, but they were quite defenseless against the real authority
of princely power. They had become *landsässig*, little more than subunits
of the territory. A case in point is the Treaty of Münsingen (1482), in
which the abbots of the rich, landowning Benedictine, Cistercian, and
Premonstratensian houses are referred to as 'our' prelates.[7] After Em-

---

[5] Dieter Stievermann, *Landesherrschaft und Klosterwesen im spätmittelalterlichen
Württemberg* (Sigmaringen, 1989), pp. 115–27.

[6] Richard Lossen, *Staat und Kirche in der Pfalz am Ausgang des Mittelalters* (Münster,
1907), p. 78.

[7] The treaty reunified the Württemberg lands, with the agreement of 'unserer prelaten,
ritterschaft und landschaft': Eugen Schneider (ed.), *Ausgewählte Urkunden zur
Württembergischen Geschichte*, Württembergische Geschichtsquellen xi (Stuttgart, 1911),
pp. 65–72, here p. 66.

peror Maximilian raised the Württemberg lands to a duchy in 1495, the 'new' Duke Eberhard I instituted a territorial diet attended by the abbots of the 14 monastic houses within the duchy. While at first glance it would seem their participation secured for them positions of power, it must be emphasized that this was a Württemberg parliament (*Landtag*), not a church council; their presence implied fealty as did their charge to offer advice and counsel (*Rat und Hilfe*). This they were expected to communicate freely to the duke along with other duties appropriate to obedient servants.[8] The prelates were compelled to act as officials of the nascent Württemberg state.

Extending beyond this exercise of lordship over the 14 large landowning monasteries was Eberhard's desire to reform all the religious houses in his territory, including nunneries and mendicant foundations. The development of the observant movement in the Württemberg territories was facilitated by a papal bull of 1459 granting to both Count Eberhard and Count Ulrich (1413–80) of Württemberg–Stuttgart the right to initiate visitations and effect reform; activities then carried out by monastic commissioners in close contact with the territorial lords.[9]

Eberhard's means to gain lordship over and to reform the monasteries in his lands were stewardship rights and papal privileges. Similarly, papal bulls and the execution of accumulated patronage and presentation rights gave him wide influence over the secular and parish clergy, repeatedly allowing him to bypass episcopal authority. While the lion's share of Württemberg lay in the diocese of Constance, portions of the territory were also to be found within the diocesan boundaries of Speyer, Worms, Würzburg, and Augsburg. Its core lands located far from episcopal power bases, Württemberg was never able to dominate any particular bishopric;[10] this helps to explain why its relationship with the papal court grew in importance. The previously noted papal bull of 1459, in addition to allowing territorial visitations of monasteries, also granted Counts Ulrich and Eberhard the right to appropriate

---

[8] From the first *Regimentsordnung* of 1498 the duties of the 'prelaten ... zu dem fürstentumb Wirtemberg gehörig' were quite clear: advice and counsel were to be 'us undertäniger gehorsami zusampt schuldiger pflicht sinen fürstlichen gnaden mitzutailen ganz willig': Wilhelm Ohr and Erich Kober (eds), *Württembergische Landtagsakten 1498–1515* (Stuttgart, 1913), p. 23; see Stievermann, *Landesherrschaft*, pp. 240–60.

[9] Stievermann, *Landesherrschaft*, pp. 135, 264–7. The best work on the observant movement is found in Kaspar Elm (ed.), *Reformbemühungen und Observanzbestrebungen im spätmittelalterlichen Ordenswesen* (Berlin, 1989). The connection between territorial authority and monastic reform is also exemplified by Wilhelm of Hesse's last instructions to his son Philipp: 'Introduce the [observant] reformation!' Cf. the chapter by Richard Cahill in this volume.

[10] In contrast to the Palatinate: Lossen, *Staat und Kirche*, pp. 46–65. For Brandenburg and Saxon influence over episcopal appointments see Schulze, *Fürsten*, pp. 36–45.

parish tithes, a privilege confirmed repeatedly thereafter.[11] Support of
papal politics smoothed the way for the Württemberg counts to amass
further patronage and presentation rights throughout their lands.[12] Of
the 1 100 beneficed clerical positions in Württemberg at the end of the
fifteenth century, Count Eberhard held the right of patronage to over
400: roughly 35 per cent of the total.[13] A fine example of Eberhard's
strategy to eliminate episcopal 'interference' by playing up his own
patronage rights was his decision in 1491 not to present the preacher of
the parish church at Lauffen to the bishop of Würzburg. Based on his
rights as patron of the benefice and as territorial lord, Eberhard declared that by the very act of choosing a candidate he had already
confirmed the preacher into the position, and indeed as firmly as if the
bishop himself had carried out the deed. No further confirmation was
deemed necessary.[14]

(ii)

The founding of the university at Tübingen (1477) offers a chance to
measure the local impact of Eberhard's aggressive *Kirchenpolitik*. Because the legal steps by which the university was founded altered the
status of a parish church and threatened the privileges of a nearby
monastic house, the count required all the means already mentioned
here (stewardship, papal privilege, and patronage rights) in order to
smoothly reorganize the town's ecclesiastical landscape.

Although Eberhard built up Tübingen into the second residence of his
lands during the 1470s and 1480s, it was a monastic house and not the
territorial lord which dominated the local scene prior to the founding of
the university. The Cistercian cloister Bebenhausen, located north of
Tübingen in the Schönbuch forest, was the wealthiest monastic house in
the Württemberg lands and the largest property owner in and around

---

[11] Wülk and Funk, *Kirchenpolitik*, pp. 34–5; Franz-Kuno Ingelfinger, *Die religiös-kirchlichen Verhältnisse im heutigen Württemberg am Vorabend der Reformation* (Stutt-gart, 1939), p. 114.

[12] After the Council of Basel, cooperation between popes and princes became common throughout Europe: John A. F. Thomson, *Popes and Princes 1417–1517: Politics and Polity in the Late Medieval Church* (London, 1980), pp. 153–5.

[13] Wülk and Funk, *Kirchenpolitik*, p. 26; cf. Ingelfinger, *Verhältnisse*, pp. 112–13.

[14] 'So sol er mit und incraft diser unnser ordnung und verschriibung uf das predig ampt bestetiget sin, so kreftigklich als ob er von ainen Bischoff von wirtzburg darauf bestetiget were, und wyter bestetigung nit bedoerffen': HStASt, A602 U10376. Cf. Julius Rauscher, 'Die Prädikaturen in Württemberg vor der Reformation', *Württembergische Jahrbücher für Statistik und Landeskunde* (1908), 152–211, esp. 183.

Tübingen.[15] Holding an impressive array of market rights and clerical privileges, Bebenhausen played a key role in the economic and ecclesiastical constellations of the Schönbuch-middle Neckar region. It received tithes from property up and down the Neckar valley, it held rights of first presentation over dozens of clerical benefices, and it had incorporated nine parish churches, the most significant being the church of St George in neighbouring Tübingen.[16] By 1470 there were 12 benefices associated with this church; the income was collected by the monastic house which in turn paid a parish vicar and chaplains at fixed salaries.[17]

In 1476 Count Eberhard requested and received papal approval for the transfer to Tübingen of his endowed collegiate church at Sindelfingen. At the end of the same year a second bull gave Eberhard permission to found a new university.[18] The count hoped it would serve as 'der Brunnen des Lebens', a fountain of life, to promote piety, reform, and to provide the county with able civil servants. The provost of the Sindelfingen chapter was to become chancellor, the eight transferred canons were to form the nucleus of the new faculty, and the chapter's income was to provide the necessary financial resources.[19]

Because Eberhard's plans would fundamentally affect conditions at St George's, the permission of the church's legal patron, the abbot and chapter at Bebenhausen, was necessary for these proposals to become reality. In the negotiations which followed, Count Eberhard specifically addressed the cloister's concerns: the transfer of the Sindelfingen canons to Tübingen was in no way to compromise Bebenhausen's claims to St George's, including the rights to receive the tithes and appoint the parish vicar.[20] This assurance satisfied the monks and on 11 March

[15] Eugen Neuscheler, 'Die Klostergrundherrschaft Bebenhausen', *Württembergische Jahrbücher für Statistik und Landeskunde* (1928), 115–85; Jürgen Sydow, *Die Zisterzienserabtei Bebenhausen*, vol. ii of *Das Bistum Konstanz*, Germania Sacra xvi (Berlin, 1984), pp. 143–96.

[16] For Bebenhausen's ecclesiastical affiliations throughout Württemberg see the list in Sydow, *Bebenhausen*, pp. 196–222 and the maps on the endpapers.

[17] Reinhold Rau, 'Die Tübinger Pfarrkirche vor der Reformation', *Tübinger Blätter*, 46 (1959), 33–45.

[18] The two bulls are printed in Rudolf von Roth (ed.), *Urkunden zur Geschichte der Universität Tübingen aus den Jahren 1476 bis 1550* (Tübingen, 1877), pp. 1–6, 11–20. For the founding of the university see Waldemar Teufel, 'Die Gründung der Universität Tübingen: Wagnis und Gelingen, Anstöße und Vorbilder' in Hansmartin Decker-Hauff et al. (eds), *500 Jahre Eberhard-Karls-Universität Tübingen* (3 vols, Tübingen, 1977), i. 3–32, and his *Universitas Studii Tuwangensis: Die Tübinger Universitätsverfassung in vorreformatorischer Zeit (1477–1534)* (Tübingen, 1977), esp. pp. 26–37.

[19] Teufel, *Universitas*, pp. 120–2. The quotation is taken from Eberhard's letter approving the statutes of the university: Roth (ed.), *Urkunden*, pp. 30–8, esp. p. 31.

[20] *Regesta Episcoporum Constantiensium* (5 vols, Innsbruck, 1895–1941), v. #14912. See also Roth (ed.), *Urkunden*, pp. 3, 14, and 27.

1477 all the parties concerned witnessed a public reading of the two papal bulls. The university offered its first lectures shortly thereafter.

Although Bebenhausen's right of patronage over the office of parish vicar at St George's remained intact in a strictly legal sense (the abbot continued to present the nominees to the bishop of Constance, in keeping with Eberhard's promise of 1477), in fact the cloister's patronage rights came to be reduced to simply putting forward candidates who had already been named by Count Eberhard to serve as university professors. After the resignation in 1477 of the last Bebenhausen appointment, the parish vicar Konrad Braun, each of the next four vicars, Johannes Heynlin, Johannes Vergenhans, Konrad Scheferlin, and Martin Plantsch (who served until 1531), were chosen first and foremost to teach theology.[21] Because the university endowment did not yield sufficient support, these men received the bulk of their income from their salary as parish vicar: a salary raised considerably in 1479 to 120 guilders, clearly to enhance the attractiveness of the dual position.[22] Shortly thereafter the responsibilities of the parish vicar were explicitly broadened to include administrative and court duties. Along with the chancellor, the vicar was given the task to ensure the smooth implementation of the university bylaws and to serve as a mediator between the university, the city, and the count whenever problems arose.[23] Serving no function at the university in the original statutes, the office of parish vicar was quickly reshaped to serve the needs of the new institution, while the income from the parish office was used to supplement the salary of a professor and administrator as the same person filled each of these roles.

Bebenhausen's loss of patronage rights becomes even more evident by examining the situation of the ten altar chaplains assigned to the parish. The investiture protocols for the diocese of Constance clearly show that prior to 1477 the abbot and convent of Bebenhausen presented all the candidates for the chaplain posts at St George's. However, from 1477 onwards, the new collegiate chapter executed the right to nominate

---

[21] Johann Haller, *Die Anfänge der Universität Tübingen 1477–1537* (2 vols, Stuttgart 1927–9), ii. 25, 132.

[22] Teufel, 'Die Gründung', p. 9. In southern Germany, the average salary for a parish vicar of an incorporated church was 50 guilders: Martin Brecht and Hermann Ehmer, *Südwestdeutsche Reformationsgeschichte: Zur Einführung der Reformation im Herzogtum Württemberg 1534* (Stuttgart, 1984), p. 31.

[23] 'Item Wir setzen vnd wöllent, das der Cantzler diser vniuersitet och der Kirchher zu Tuwingen in irem vfniemen sweren söllent ain sonder ufsenhen zuhaben vnd mit flys darob zesinde, das dise ordnungen gehalten werdent. ... Vnd ob sich irrungen begebent zwüschent vnser herrschafft vnd der vniuersitet oder der vniuersitet vnd den von Tuwingen, so wöllet wir sie darinn fur mitler vnd tedingßlüt haben': from the 1481 bylaws in Roth (ed.), *Urkunden*, p. 74. For incorporated parishes, *Kirchherr* referred to the vicar.

these clerics as part of its cooptation rights.[24] Prior to 1477, the office
of parish vicar and the ten chaplaincies at Tübingen's parish church had
been filled by clerics nominated by the monks at Bebenhausen. A year
later, the Cistercians held the right of first presentation to only one
office, the parish vicar, an office which served primarily to augment the
income of a theology professor. St George's was no longer a simple
parish church in the pocket of a nearby monastery but a collegiate
church in a territorial residence city. Whatever legal rights remained
with the cloister, the real patron of this church was now Count Eberhard.

The foundation of the university affected Bebenhausen not only in
regard to patronage rights but also through a shuffling of the urban
topography and fierce new competition at the city's marketplaces. In
1477 Count Eberhard firmly requested that Bebenhausen vacate its
oldest tithe warehouse (*Pfleghof*) in the city in order to make room for
university expansion; a demand issued in his role as steward and advocate for the cloister. For the next 25 years Bebenhausen sought to regain
economic rights lost in the move; a severe loss as many of the cloister's
market privileges were specifically tied to the forfeited property.[25] The
stakes were raised because university faculty and students enjoyed privileges similar to those held by the monks. Bebenhausen's commercial
activities were restricted even as new competition came into being.[26]

As the young university developed further financial needs, Eberhard
and his advisors orchestrated a series of revenue enhancing measures
which recast the legal relationship between university, collegiate church,
and patron. The goal of these steps, legal and fiscal independence, was
achieved in 1486 as Eberhard cut his own legal ties and presented to the
university all rights to patronage and income from those parish churches
and benefices which had been incorporated into the university.[27] With

---

[24] Manfred Krebs (ed.), *Die Investiturprotokolle der Diözese Konstanz aus dem 15.
Jahrhundert*, supplement to *Freiburger Diözesan-Archiv*, 66–73 (1939–54), 856–8. On
the chapter's right of cooptation (self-nomination, *Selbstergänzungsrecht*), see Johann
Baptiste Sproll, 'Verfassung des St. Georgen-Stifts zu Tübingen und sein Verhältnis zur
Universität in dem Zeitraum von 1476–1534', *Freiburger Diözesan-Archiv*, 3 (1902),
105–92; 4 (1903), 141–97; esp. 3 (1902), 142, 160, 178.

[25] Sydow, *Bebenhausen*, p. 160; cf. Haller, *Die Anfänge*, i. 41–3; ii. 11–15. For the
economic function of monastic properties in Württemberg cities see Stievermann,
Landesherrschaft, pp. 216–20. Bebenhausen was not the only monastic house which
gave up property. Blaubeuren and the Augustinian friars were also summoned to provide
space for the university: ibid., pp. 274–5.

[26] For the privileges held by the university and the university community see Haller,
Die Anfänge, i. 43–4, 47–8, 91; ii. 15–16.

[27] 'Vnnd wir verzyhen vnns für vnnser erbenn vnnd nachkomen zu den vorgemelten
Kirchen vnnd pfrunden mit iren Zugehörungen als vorstett all vnnser gerechtikait, die
wir daran oder dartzu gehapt haben': from the announcement of Eberhard's gift pub-

no legitimate heir, Eberhard knew that at his death the rule of the territory would pass to his nephew Eberhard the Younger, who showed little interest in the university; a measure of independence was thus deemed crucial. In fact, Eberhard continued to play a large role in hiring professors and administering finances at the university until his death in 1496. The income from the incorporated parishes had never been appropriated by Eberhard, but rather used for 'pious purposes': building up the university.[28] For the churches affected, however, the result remained that parish finances flowed away from the villages and toward the university.

Through Count Eberhard's investment and support Tübingen achieved the status of a territorial residence as county, and later ducal, power emanated from a new focal point: the university. Eberhard combined the application of his patronage rights with an adept use of the influence he held over cloister Bebenhausen in order to achieve his ecclesio-political objectives. Not only through the training of civil servants and an educated clergy, but even in the very foundation of the university territorial interests were pursued. As such the university became a tool in the development of a Württemberg territorial church.

(iii)

The efforts of Count Eberhard to expand territorial authority into the ecclesiastical sphere were more numerous and more successful than those of most other German princes. His strategy, however, was by no means unusual. The growth of territorial power at the expense of ecclesiastical independence is a fact of the fifteenth century.[29] Focusing on the forms taken by that power in one revealing case, this investigation has thus far considered the legal and institutional factors most commonly assessed in studies on state and church in the late Middle

---

lished in Roth (ed.), *Urkunden*, pp. 78–80. Already between 1479 and 1482, other parish churches had been incorporated into the Tübingen collegiate chapter.

[28] Haller, *Die Anfänge*, i. 29–30, 77–80. For the attempts to attain fiscal solvency for the university see Teufel, 'Die Gründung', pp. 9–10, and *Universitas*, pp. 120–5. Compare Richard Cahill's conclusions on Philipp of Hesse and the theme of piety and power below.

[29] For the Palatinate see Lossen, *Staat und Kirche*, and Henry J. Cohn, *The Government of the Rhine Palatinate in the Fifteenth Century* (Oxford, 1965), pp. 140–9. For other territories see Schulze, *Fürsten*, pp. 13–45, and Hans Erich Feine, *Kirchliche Rechtsgeschichte: Die katholische Kirche* (5th edn, Cologne, 1972), pp. 497–9. Cities too made deep inroads into ecclesiastical privileges: for one example see Rolf Kießling, *Bürgerliche Gesellschaft und Kirche in Augsburg im Spätmittelalter: Ein Beitrag zur Strukturanalyse der oberdeutschen Reichsstadt* (Augsburg, 1971).

Ages (jurisdiction, patronage rights, conflict and cooperation with the ecclesiastical hierarchy). Too often neglected, however, is the particular relationship between political ideology and the formation of religious culture. This issue is crucial for an understanding of the motivations behind territorial initiative in ecclesiastical affairs and the ramifications of such activity for religious change, its reception, and its lasting impact on society. Here it will be useful to probe the boundaries and comparative limits of 'confessionalization', a concept which has recently opened up fruitful areas of research into the religious and political life of early modern Germany.[30]

As it has been defined, confessionalization refers to a 'process' whereby competing religious parties, in an atmosphere of mutual critique and competition, came to adhere to confessional creeds, organized themselves in institutional churches, and imposed their identity on society, forming new 'confessional' cultures: Roman Catholic, Lutheran, and Reformed. Most often the catalyst and agent in this process was the nascent territorial state seeking to ensure unity of belief and practice within its borders. Thus an historical category both integral and parallel to early modern state building, confessionalization affected public as well as private life, promoting societies in which religious creed and political power combined in the formation of socially disciplined subjects.[31]

By definition, confessionalization requires confessions and, at a later stage, confessional churches: separate religious entities which defined themselves over against one another and evolved in contention with the churches in neighbouring territories. These confessional groups and churches, it is argued, developed after the Peace of Augsburg 1555. The period 1517–55, the 'German Reformation' strictly defined, is described as a time of upheaval, flux, and confessional incubation, but not yet institutionalization. At most a prologue to the process of confessionalization proper.[32] Thus anyone seeking to compare territorial influence

---

[30] A good introduction is provided by Heinrich Richard Schmidt, *Konfessionalisierung im 16. Jahrhundert* (Munich, 1992). The author's lamentations about the lack of research (pp. 55–6) must be revised in light of the substantial contributions of the last ten years. See the literature cited by Hsia, 'The German seventeenth century', and Schilling, 'Luther, Loyola, Calvin'.

[31] Schmidt, *Konfessionalisierung*, p. 1; Heinz Schilling, 'Die Konfessionalisierung im Reich: Religiöser und gesellschaftlicher Wandel in Deutschland zwischen 1555 und 1620', *Historische Zeitschrift*, 246 (1988), 1–45, esp. 5–6 [English translation in his *Religion, Political Culture and the Emergence of Early Modern Society* (Leiden, 1992), pp. 205–45, here 209]; Wolfgang Reinhard, 'Reformation, Counter-Reformation, and the early modern state: a reassessment', *Catholic Historical Review*, 75 (1989), 383–404, 390.

[32] Schmidt discusses various proposals for periodization in the confessionalization process: *Konfessionalisierung*, pp. 110–15.

in ecclesiastical affairs during the late Middle Ages with the confessionalization process in early modern Europe is faced with two hurdles. The word itself, 'confessionalization', presupposes 'confessions' and these did not yet exist in the late Middle Ages.[33] Second, the literature on confessionalization has already identified the 1520s through to the 1540s as a preparatory period during which the foundations for the confessionalizing process were laid; hence the late fifteenth century is at least three generations removed. To these problems Heinz Schilling's recent article opens a window of opportunity: the 'roots' of confessionalization may reach farther back than the decade of the 1520s.[34] While not insisting to find a fully developed 'confessional' identity in late medieval Württemberg, we can trace the beginnings of a territorial identity in the religious sphere; not only princely sovereignty over ecclesiastical institutions, but also the early development of a distinctive religious culture. This regional religiosity helped to fuel a drive towards unity and self-definition analogous to the cultural formation which in the confessional age would be sustained by creeds, catechisms, and polemical theology.

In the fifteenth century, one expression of this identity had its focus at the princely court: the patronage of devotion. Princes took seriously their self-understood duties as the spiritual as well as secular fathers (*Landesväter*) of their subjects, and it fell upon them to ensure true faith, right worship, and Christian obedience within their lands.[35] This religious concern to promote piety and upright living, which at the same time sought to augment good government by preserving order and discipline, led territorial lords to patronize the publication of vernacular catechetical literature based on the Ten Commandments,[36] and to heartily support the observant monastic movement.[37] Eberhard's attention to monastic reform has already been noted, and he too was concerned with the comportment of his subjects, issuing discipline ordinances in

---

[33] See, however, the dissenting opinion of Winfried Eberhard, *Konfessionsbildung und Stände in Böhmen 1478–1530* (Munich, 1981), esp. pp. 9–40. Eberhard explicitly acknowledges the religious heterogeneity of the Empire in the late Middle Ages, a point often ignored and even denied in the debate over confessionalization.

[34] 'Luther, Loyola, Calvin', pp. 9, 16–18, 27.

[35] In describing this supervision, Schulze's image of the 'territorial diocese' is certainly preferable to Schmidt's use of 'regional administrative bodies of the universal church' ('Gebiets-Verwaltungs-Körperschaften der universalen Kirche': *Konfessionalisierung*, p. 14), but is to be distinguished from the later Lutheran concept of the *Notbischof*; see Schulze, *Fürsten*, pp. 194–7.

[36] Robert J. Bast, *Honor your Fathers: The Emergence of a Patriarchal Ideology in Early Modern Germany, 1400–1600* (Leiden, forthcoming).

[37] Schulze addresses in detail the support offered to the observant movement by Saxon princes in *Fürsten*, pp. 129–91.

1479 and 1495.[38] But the unique feature of Eberhard's ecclesio-religious policy, and the aspect which interested him most during the last 15 years of his life, was the active presence of the Brethren of the Common Life in Württemberg. The semi-monastic houses of this communal movement were to bear the fruit of the count's religious vision for his territory: or so it was hoped.

(iv)

Eberhard's preference for the simple piety of the Common Life movement, a branch of the *Devotio Moderna*,[39] became manifest as he energetically supported the establishment of the Brethren in Württemberg after 1477. Their first foundation was at the collegiate church St Amandus in Urach, Eberhard's primary residence, and was followed by chapters at five additional churches over which the count held patronage rights: Herrenberg (1481), Dettingen (1482), the castle parish church in Tübingen (1481–82), Tachenhausen (1486), and finally Einsiedel in the Schönbuch forest (1492).[40] So fervent was Eberhard's belief that the Canons and Brethren would bring about the improvement in divine worship he deemed necessary, that he later would come to regard the introduction of the Common Life in Württemberg and specifically the founding of St Peter's at Einsiedel as among his finest achievements;[41] a pride reflected in other documents of the time.[42] The settlement at Einsiedel came to hold first rank among the Common Life houses, for it was there that Eberhard's

[38] Klaus Graf, 'Geschichtsschreibung und Landesdiskurs im Umkreis Graf Eberhards im Bart von Württemberg (1459–1496)', *Blätter für deutsche Landesgeschichte*, 129 (1993), 165–93, esp. 179–80; Stievermann, *Landesherrschaft*, pp. 148–9.

[39] John Van Engen, *Devotio Moderna: Basic Writings* (New York, 1988), see esp. the introduction.

[40] Wilfried Schöntag, 'Die Kanoniker und Brüder vom gemeinsamen Leben in Württemberg', *Rottenburger Jahrbuch für Kirchengeschichte*, 11 (1992), 197–207, esp. 200–1.

[41] Along with the establishment of the university at Tübingen and the reunification of the Württemberg territories in 1482: Dieter Mertens, 'Eberhard im Bart und der Humanismus' in Hans-Martin Maurer (ed.), *Eberhard und Mechthild: Untersuchungen zu Politik und Kultur im ausgehenden Mittelalter* (Stuttgart, 1994), pp. 35–76, esp. 51–2.

[42] At the occasion of Württemberg's elevation to a duchy in 1495, the humanist Jacob Wimpheling praised Duke Eberhard for the blossom of religious life during his reign, noting explicitly the role of the university and the chapter at St Peter's ('... quo nova religio et foelix achademia floret', and, 'Quo nova religio. Commendatur dux a duobus egregiis nuper ab eo institutis. Unum est in obsequio christi, ordo scilicet Sancti Petri novus in scheinbacho', the second being the university): *Ad illustrissum Principem Eberardum, Wyrtenbergensem Theccensemque ducem* (Strasbourg, 1495), pp. a iii, b i.

political and religious visions merged. St Peter's was to serve as a model for the pious restructuring of society, an ideal ordering of the social groups in the territory based on an understanding of the *ecclesia primitiva*: the Christian community at the time of the apostles. In seeking to tease out an early form of 'confessional' identity from Eberhard's Württemberg, it is these two factors which come to the fore: devotion centred on the common life and the patronage of this devotion with an eye towards promoting territorial consolidation.

As in other houses of the Common Life movement, the residents of St Peter's were to live in spiritual harmony, but not in obedience to a monastic rule. The house was to be a voluntary community structured on the three estates of medieval society. A prior and 12 canons made up the clerical branch; the number set intentionally to prompt reflection on Jesus and his twelve disciples. Men of noble or knightly birth comprised the second group, 12 in number plus an elected master who was responsible for administration of the chapter and discipline over the lay members. The third estate was represented by 12 citizens from the free cities of the Württemberg territory. These 38 residents, who would likely have found the stringent rules of the existing orders too severe, were to participate together in worship to God, obey his commandments, and be responsible to the Upper German Chapter of the Canons and Brethren of the Common Life.[43]

The statutes of St Peter's exhort all the members, clerical and lay, to treat one another as true brothers and fellow servants of God, so that there would be no difference between noble and non-noble, cleric and layman, rich and poor.[44] Although spiritual equality may have been the

---

[43] 'Doch inen die strengkait ander gestifter orden zu schwäre wäre': see the extensive citation from the statutes found in W. M. Landeen, 'Das Brüderhaus St. Peter im Schönbuch auf dem Einsiedel', *Blätter für württembergische Kirchengeschichte*, 60–61 (1960–61), 5–18, 7–8, and his 'Gabriel Biel and the Devotio Moderna in Germany', *Research Studies of Washington State University*, 27 (1959), 135–213; 28 (1960), 21–45, 61–95, here 27 (1959), 206–07. The HStASt possesses two manuscript copies of the St Peter's statutes. The spelling in each is distinctive as is the order of the text. Landeen's citations and the description provided in 'Das Brüderhaus' (p. 7 note 3) correspond only to the document now catalogued as HStASt A522 U6/7 (not A522 B1a as he states). Although citing folios, Landeen's curious numeration in fact is based on counting only those pages with text, beginning with the front cover as 'folio 1'. Because his quotations themselves are accurate and his articles are available, I continue to cite Landeen along with HStASt A522 U6/7, where the citation above appears at f. 5ʳ⁻ᵛ. Landeen reported the 1493 printed version of the statutes had been lost, but for the few surviving copies see Wolfgang Leesch and others (eds), *Monasticon fratrum vitae communis*, Teil ii: *Deutschland* (Brussels, 1979), pp. 55–6.

[44] 'Es sollen all Brüder, gaistlich und laien, us göttlich und brüderlich lieb mit ainander früntlich und fridlichen wandeln als warlich Brüder und kinder ains himelschen vaters, kainer sich über den andern erheben': HStASt A522 U6/7, f. 14ʳ; Landeen, 'Das Brüderhaus', 11–12.

desired religious atmosphere, the statutes also guaranteed the particular privileges of each estate. Indeed, it is the distinctive feature of St Peter's that the estates remained separate from each other within the broader framework of community. Eberhard was explicit in his preamble to the statutes: there were three estates in his lands, and therefore these three groups should come together in community at Einsiedel.[45] St Peter's was not to be a monastery where social standing was dissolved under monastic vows, but a community of worship which reflected the stratified society of the territorial lands. Only during worship in the common chapel and when taking meals in the refectory were all the canons and lay brothers together, and even then sitting in segregated groups according to estate and age. Each estate had its own dormitory and enjoyed distinct privileges. For example, the noble members of the house were allowed to hunt in the Schönbuch forest, wear finer clothing than the non-noble lay brothers, and engage a squire, as long as he had a good reputation and was approved by the lay master.[46]

The founding of St Peter's and especially the distinctive features of its charter provide clues to what Klaus Graf has called 'territorial discourse' (*Landesdiskurs*) in late fifteenth-century Württemberg. Printed on the title page of the 1493 statutes is the announcement that the collegiate house at Einsiedel was to be inhabited by 'priests, nobles and free citizens of the provinces Württemberg and Swabia'.[47] Whereas in 1493 Württemberg was still a county (a conglomeration of lordships, purchased and annexed territory on its way to becoming, but definitely not yet, a leading power in the empire), Swabia was one of the traditional duchies of the Holy Roman Empire bolstered by a near-mythic heritage.[48] In case the 12 lay noble positions at St Peter's could not be filled with suitable candidates from Württemberg's second estate, the statutes stipulated that members of the nobility from all of Swabia were encouraged to apply: Swabia, but no other region of the empire.[49] Throughout the statutes, the stated purpose of St Peter's is to further the praise of God and to benefit 'the nobles in Swabia, our cities and

---

[45] 'Nach dem wir in unser Herrschaft dreierlei stend habend, Gaistlichen, Adel und Ritterschaft, Stett und gemain Volck, wann wir dann ... ufrichten einen stift und Convent, in denen von den dreien obgenannten ständen gott dem Herrn truwlich gedient werd': HStASt A522 U6/7, f. 5^{r-v}; Landeen, 'Das Brüderhaus', 8, and 'Gabriel Biel', 207.

[46] Landeen, 'Das Brüderhaus', 9, 10, 14.

[47] Graf, 'Geschichtsschreibung', 186.

[48] See Graf, 'Geschichtsschreibung', 186–8, for Swabia as 'Fatherland' and its associations with the Hohenstaufen imperial dynasty.

[49] 'Ob man die in der herschafft Wirtemberg nit funde sunst die im lannd in Swaben sitzend unnd wonend unnd sunst nit von dehainem anndern land': cited in Graf, 'Geschichtsschreibung', 188; HStASt A522 U6/7, f. 5^v.

subjects'.[50] At the time of St Peter's foundation, the Württemberg nobility was struggling to maintain independence and may have looked askance at membership in Eberhard's most personal endowed chapter. Their resistance to the count's attempts to integrate them more firmly into the territory helps to explain why Eberhard was willing to extend the entrance invitation to nobles throughout Swabia. But the liberal use of 'Swabian' language reveals all the more Eberhard's search for rhetorical forms which would enhance Württemberg claims to leadership in the Swabian League; a place of first rank based on the prominence of historical Swabia.[51]

Although Württemberg lands were slowly coalescing into the form of an early 'modern' state, the images used to justify the territory's increasing political influence were drawn from the past and grafted onto the forms of devotion promoted at St Peter's. Likewise, the Canons and Brethren, reflecting their roots in the *Devotio Moderna*, based their understanding of community on older forms: the primitive Christian church in the apostolic age.

In any discussion of the religious motivations for the Common Life movement, the role of Gabriel Biel must be addressed.[52] A leading figure in the expansion of the Brethren of the Common Life into central and upper Germany, Biel was prior of the house at Urach after 1479, became theology professor at the University of Tübingen in 1484, and served as the first prior of St Peter's at Einsiedel from its foundation in 1492 until his death in 1495. The phrase in the St Peter's statutes drawing the allusion from the 12 clerics and the prior to Christ and his apostles finds its intellectual foundation in a concise defence of the common life written by Biel shortly after 1468.[53] Separating the movement from all monastic orders, Biel applies the term *ordo* to any disciplined and upright way of living, and, speaking for the clerical adherents of the common life, he contends 'we both live out and display the "order" of the apostles and disciples of Christ and of the holy mother church at the time of its origins, whose model and way of life are described in Acts'.[54] The plain goal of the movement is neither to create

---

[50] 'Dem adell im land zuo Swaben unnd unnsern stetten unnd unndertanen nutz': cited in Graf, 'Geschichtsschreibung', 189.

[51] Graf, 'Geschichtsschreibung', 188–92.

[52] Landeen, 'Gabriel Biel', beginning at p. 149; Heiko A. Oberman, *The Harvest of Medieval Theology: Gabriel Biel and Late Medieval Nominalism* (Cambridge, Mass., 1963).

[53] *A Treatise on the Common Life*: appendix to Landeen, 'Gabriel Biel', 28 (1960), 79–95.

[54] 'Dicimus nos habere vel gerere ordinem apostolorum vel discipulorum Christi vel sancte primitiue matris ecclesie de cuius ordine vel modo viuendi scribitur Actis': ibid., 79–80.

a new religious order nor resuscitate an old one, but rather 'to serve and protect the integrity of the clerical life through reputable, disciplined living and the common life'.[55] This agenda, to reform the secular clergy according to standards understood to be in place during the apostolic age, found a frequent echo throughout the German fifteenth century; the common life was no monopoly of the *Devotio Moderna* and its various branches.[56] Still, contemporaries saw something fresh and distinctive in the structure and goals of St Peter's, something in addition to the common life shared by the three estates. The role of the clerics, neither monks nor secular canons nor even canons regular but rather 'secular canons regular', evoked effusive praise for the 'new order of St Peter'.[57] Gabriel Biel had helped to develop this vision for a semi-religious common life and had worked to enact it in Württemberg. He must be acknowledged as Count Eberhard's intellectual partner in the shaping of a Württemberg 'confessional' identity.

Together Count Eberhard the Bearded and Gabriel Biel raised up the Canons and Brethren of the Common Life, with their goal of disciplined living in the service of God, as a central pillar, an axis around which the religious and political life of the territory was meant to revolve. A symbolic capstone to this edifice was the burial of Duke Eberhard in 1496 on the grounds of St Peter's, wearing the blue robe of the lay brethren. Yet the death of this territorial lord signalled as well the move to other interests as Eberhard's reforms began to unravel quickly. Biel, also buried at St Peter's, had died a year before in 1495, and it was not long before the religio-political constellation in Württemberg shifted dramatically.

After the short reign of Eberhard's nephew, Eberhard II, the succession passed in 1498 to Ulrich (1487–1550), yet another nephew of Eberhard the Bearded. In the following years Duke Ulrich further consolidated territorial power but ignored Eberhard's reforms: support of the Common Life chapters ceased, the goals of St Peter's were left unpromoted, observance in the monastic houses was no longer sharply controlled through territorial visitations. Ulrich continued to gather and

---

[55] 'Honesta conuersatione [et] cohabitatione seruare et saluare cupimus vite clericalis integritatem': ibid., 94.

[56] Kaspar Elm, 'Die Bruderschaft vom Gemeinsamen Leben: Eine Geistliche Lebensform zwischen Kloster und Welt, Mittelalter und Neuzeit', *Ons geestelijk Erf*, 59 (1985), 476–82, 488–90; Bernhard Neidiger, *Das Dominikanerkloster Stuttgart, die Kanoniker vom Gemeinsamen Leben in Urach und die Gründung der Universität Tübingen: Konkurrierende Reformansätze in der württembergischen Kirchenpolitik am Ausgang des Mittelalters* (Stuttgart, 1993).

[57] Neidiger, *Das Dominikanerkloster Stuttgart*, pp. 119–20, citing Konrad Summenhart, Wimpheling, and the abbot Trithemius ('ordinis Sancti Petri nova religio'); cf. ibid., p. 9.

exercise patronage rights and by 1514 he presented clerics to 44 per cent of all benefices within the duchy, yet his personal interests and investments went towards the cultivation of an elaborate court life rather than to religious endowments.[58]

The singular nature of Eberhard's vision, and its swift demise after his death, can best be shown, once again, through the example of the semi-religious Brethren chapters. Independent since their establishment,[59] the chapters drew most of their new members from other houses in the middle-Rhine region. This became the point of conflict in complaints articulated by the territorial estates, who insisted in 1514 that all clerical positions in the land be filled by native sons.[60] In a second series of complaints the estates called for an end to the independent status enjoyed by the houses, a proposal embraced by the duke. Armed with a papal bull, Ulrich was able to reactivate his full patronage rights over the Württemberg Canons of the Common Life. In 1517, five of the six houses were converted into secular chapters, a portion of their income being appropriated by Ulrich and used to pay off debts and to further staff the musical troup active at his court. Only St Peter's, the burial site of Duke Eberhard, was left untouched. Given the praise directed toward St Peter's creative and visionary charter at the time the house was founded, it is ironic to note the primary reason given for the dissolution of the semi-religious chapters: the common life practiced by the canons was novel and alien.[61]

Whereas Eberhard used his patronage as a benefactor and supporter of the Common Life, Ulrich acted as a lay appropriator, shifting ecclesiastical finances to serve other purposes. His officials took inventory of the property belonging to each house and lowered benefice incomes,

---

[58] Hans Wülk, 'Staat und Kirche in Württemberg nach dem Tode Graf Eberhards im Bart (1496) bis zur Einführung der Reformation', *Württembergische Vierteljahrshefte für Landesgeschichte*, 26 (1917), 1–41.

[59] Eberhard had ensured that each house enjoyed the fiscal and ecclesiastical liberties characteristic of the Rhineland and Upper German settlements. Freedom from taxation in the present and future was guaranteed, the chapter was given the right to name new members, episcopal authority was strictly limited, while the territorial lord renounced his patronage rights, including rights to income. See Schöntag, 'Die Kanoniker', 198–201; for houses in Hesse see Landeen, 'Gabriel Biel', 27 (1959), 157–69. Eberhard's close working relationship with Gabriel Biel may help to explain why the count allowed the Common Life houses so much independence while he tightened his patronal control elsewhere in the territory.

[60] Wilfried Schöntag, 'Die Aufhebung der Stifte und Häuser der Brüder vom gemeinsamen Leben in Württemberg: Ein Vorbote der Reformation?', *Zeitschrift für Württembergische Landesgeschichte*, 38 (1979), 82–96, esp. 84–6.

[61] 'Novum et alienum modum vivendi presbyterorum et clericorum in communi viventium': cited by Schöntag, 'Die Aufhebung', 90. Cf. n. 57 above.

diverting remaining funds into the territorial coffers.[62] Although his purposes were different, Ulrich used papal permission and patronage rights, like Eberhard before him, to bend ecclesiastical institutions to his desires. The territorial prince continued to exercise his influence in the ecclesiastical sphere.

The house of St Peter's at Einsiedel was closed down in 1534 at the outset of the Reformation in Württemberg and Duke Eberhard's body was transferred to the collegiate church at Tübingen. But already long before this it was clear that the goals of St Peter's were never realized, never embraced by the estates of the land. According to an undated report by Konrad Brun, the last prior of the chapterhouse, there was strife between members of the three estates and the necessary income was always lacking.[63] In 1534 only five persons were living 'the common life', all priests.[64] Eberhard's experiment for a territorial common life had failed. It was a personal vision which found no resonance among the independent-minded nobles and which never reached out to the general populace.

(v)

As did other princes of his day, Eberhard acted as a powerful and watchful shepherd over his flock, exercising influence in the ecclesiastical administration as well as working to mould proper worship and discipline. In Eberhard's understanding of *Landesvater* there were no internal religious issues (*innere kirchliche Angelegenheiten*) which did not fall under his responsibility. In this sense, the assumptions of those who ruled did not essentially change from the fifteenth to the seventeenth centuries. To practice good government meant to shape the tenor of religiosity in the territory, when necessary by manipulating the ecclesiastical landscape using the legal and political means available. For the territorial lord concerned to promote the common good, support of religious reform was of immediate benefit: discipline and morality ensured order and right worship which, in turn, brought God's grace and blessings to shine upon the land. Piety and power politics were not

---

[62] Schöntag, 'Die Aufhebung', 91–6. Schöntag draws interesting parallels between Ulrich's appropriation of the chapter income and his later secularization and appropriation of monastic holdings as he introduced the Reformation into Württemberg in 1534.

[63] The chapter is 'bisher allein bei dem Stand der Priester geblieben, denn die drei Stände haben sich übel miteinander können vergleichen, das Einkommen hat es auch nicht mögen ertragen': cited in Leesch et al. (eds), *Monasticon fratrum*, p. 60.

[64] Ibid., p. 61.

mutually exclusive, indeed the prince was compelled to play a leading role.

Eberhard employed many of the same strategies which today are associated with princes in the confessional age. He carried out visitations, exercised jurisdiction over ecclesiastial institutions, expanded the application of his patronage and stewardship rights, and gradually closed off the territory to outside influence. Yet functional similarities do not necessarily indicate unbroken continuity. The sojourn of the Brethren of the Common Life in Württemberg exemplifies the contingency inherent at this most early stage of 'confessionalization', prior to the increased competition of the sixteenth century and the concomitant pressure to define territorial religion over against rival confessions or threatening neighbours.

In the distinctive environment of the fifteenth century, Eberhard and his advisors had the luxury to compose a personal model of reform for his lands. Drawing its inspiration first from the observant movement and then from the Brethren of the Common Life, Eberhard's plan for territorial devotion was focused on monastic or semi-monastic centres, out from which piety, right worship, and discipline would radiate, enhancing the common good. Permanent cultural formation and religious change foundered on Eberhard's death, but also because he never garnered the support of the populace for his policies: the clerics were recruited from outside the territory, the knights remained aloof, and the commoners came to resent the experiments carried out at the expense of their parish churches. Too tenuous to survive his death and not uniformly applied throughout the territory, Eberhard's reforms cannot be labelled confessionalization as such. But they represent more than a passing instance of territorial influence in church affairs. His reforms epitomize the beginning of vigorous territorial participation in the formation of devotion for religious and political ends; an early chapter in a long story which begins in the fifteenth century and reaches well into the eighteenth.

CHAPTER FOUR

John Hooper's visitation and examination of the clergy in the diocese of Gloucester, 1551

D. G. Newcombe

There is an old saying meant to convey certainty (or, perhaps, inevitability): 'as sure as God is in Gloucester'. Bishop John Hooper would not have recognized its meaning when he took up residence in his diocese in the spring of 1551. The diocese, as we shall see, was hardly on the cutting edge of the Reformation. When, in 1549, he left the comfortable surroundings of Zurich and the circle that had gathered around Heinrich Bullinger, it was, no doubt, with the promise of a chance to put his reformed ideas into practice in England. He arrived in London that summer with instant access to the most powerful men in the government of Edward VI: he lived in the duke of Somerset's household and was on friendly terms with the earl of Warwick. And, soon after his return, he served the government well by testifying against Bishop Bonner at the trial that led to his deposition. It was an act that would come back to haunt Hooper when Bonner regained his position under Queen Mary, but, for the time being, Hooper enjoyed the patronage of the mighty.

Hooper's credentials as a reformer were well established long before he came into his diocese. He had published three books while in exile, his Lenten sermons before the king in 1550 and the prolonged and unsatisfactory dispute over the wearing of vestments demonstrated his commitment to a reformed church. All had earned him the epithet, 'the future Zwingli of England' – an appellation he would not have been dissatisfied with at all.[1] Hooper was a force to be reckoned with and, although we have no contemporary accounts of the attitudes of those who waited for him to arrive in Gloucester, the vast majority of the clergy must have viewed his appointment with apprehension.[2]

---

[1] A. Pettegree, *Foreign Protestant Communities in Sixteenth-Century London* (Oxford, 1986), p. 30.

[2] There have been several published accounts of the life of John Hooper. W. M. S. West in his series of articles for the *Baptist Quarterly* ['John Hooper and the origins of

It was no secret that Hooper hoped to transform his diocese and create a church in the image of that he left behind him on the Continent. The model in Zurich valued a learned ministry highly and the education of the clergy in Gloucester was always pivotal to his plan. There are a number of points in Hooper's Visitation Articles which point to this Zurich influence, most notably Hooper's insistence on regular examinations of the clergy in quarterly sessions and his demand that the clergy spend more time in personal study. However, Hooper realized (even as the leaders of the Zurich reformation had) that he could not expect the average run of ministers to be ready or willing to participate in anything as intellectually challenging as the *Prophezei* that he admired during his exile.[3] His first order of business, therefore, was to discover what kind of material he had to work with in order to effect change. He undertook to explore the parameters of the clergy's knowledge by means of a general examination the likes of which had not been seen before.

While the clergy normally expected to be examined at ordination and at institution to a benefice, these tests merely ensured that they understood both their duties and rudimentary Latin.[4] More searching inquiries were very rare. When Bishop John Stokesley became bishop of London in 1530 he had severe misgivings about the suitability of the curates in his diocese and undertook an examination for which we have only partial returns. Limited though our evidence is, the results must have been alarming to a man of Stokesley's academic character: only 11 of the 56 examined were thought to be sufficiently educated to perform their duties competently and without further study.[5] Unprecedented when compared to medieval visitations (which concentrated on issues related to fabric, morality, and sacraments), Stokesley's examination of his curates foreshadowed Hooper's efforts in Gloucester in terms of emphasis and expectations. However, Stokesley's agenda was limited

---

Puritanism', *The Baptist Quarterly*, 15 (1953–4), 346–68; 16 (1955–6), 22–46 and 67–88] provides much important information but is justly criticised for a rather partisan theological point of view. E. M. Hunt, *The Life and Times of John Hooper, Bishop of Gloucester* (Lewiston, 1992), adds little to our knowledge of Hooper. My own, as yet unpublished dissertation is, perhaps, the most complete review of Hooper's life and thought: D. G. Newcombe, 'The life and theological thought of John Hooper, Bishop of Gloucester and Worcester, 1551–1553' (Ph.D. Cambridge, 1990).

[3] For more on the reformation and the education of the clergy in Zurich see Bruce Gordon, *Clerical Discipline and the Rural Reformation: The Synod in Zürich, 1532–1580*, Zürcher Beiträge zur Reformationsgeschichte xvi (Berne, New York, 1992), especially pp. 177–84.

[4] M. Bowker, *The Henrician Reformation* (Cambridge, 1981), pp. 127–8.

[5] P. Heath, *The English Parish Clergy on the Eve of the Reformation* (London, 1969), pp. 73–4.

and set in a far different political and religious climate – 'reform' meant something quite different to the bishop of London in 1530 than it did to the bishop of Gloucester in 1551. Hooper's visitation and examination of the clergy in Gloucester represents one of the few bits of contemporary evidence that gives us even a partial glimpse at the state of the clergy on the ground in the period immediately following the official Reformation in England. For that reason, if for no other, it is important to understand the results of that survey properly.

(i)

When he finally arrived in his diocese, John Hooper was appalled at conditions there. Gloucester was in the grips of a disabling inflation which many, Hooper's wife among them, feared would lead to rebellion.[6] Terrible as the economic suffering was, it was typical that Hooper should perceive the problem as essentially spiritual. The diocese of Gloucester was not known as being particularly sympathetic to new religious ideas. True, there had been some small Lollard presence in the Cotswolds and in the Forest of Dean, but this was never as important as has been thought.[7] Indeed, it has been argued that as late as 1548, 'in remote parts [of the diocese] men had barely heard of the [reform] movement so far as doctrine and ritual were concerned'.[8] This despite the fact that many of the deaneries had been under the episcopal guidance of Hugh Latimer while he was bishop of Worcester and before the diocese of Gloucester had been created in 1541. During his brief administration (1535–39), Latimer had been particularly concerned to fight superstition and had preached fierce sermons against relics, the pope, other bishops, and prelates in general. His assertion that all ecclesiastics were thieves and deserved hanging if only enough rope could be found, was not received with universal approval.[9]

---

[6] H. Robinson (ed.), *Original Letters relative to the English Reformation* (Cambridge, 1846–7), i. 108.

[7] K. G. Powell, 'The social background to the Reformation in Gloucestershire', *Transactions of the Bristol and Gloucestershire Archaeological Society* [hereafter *TBGAS*], 92 (1973), 99.

[8] F. D. Price, 'Gloucester diocese under Bishop Hooper 1551–1553', *TBGAS*, 60 (1938), 52. See also K. G. Powell, 'The beginnings of Protestantism in Gloucestershire', *TBGAS*, 90 (1971), 141–57, and K. G. Powell, *The Marian Martyrs and the Reformation in Bristol* (Bristol, 1972), pp. 1–8.

[9] G. E. Corrie (ed.), *Sermons and Remains of Hugh Latimer* (Cambridge, 1845), pp. 309–17. Dr Sherewood of Dyrham parish accused Latimer of uncharitableness in a very bad tempered letter which Corrie includes in the above volume. See also Powell, 'Beginnings', 148–9.

As for the mid-sixteenth-century laity, Caroline Litzenberger recently demonstrated that they were 'not so quick to switch to Protestantism'.[10] Hooper's verdict on the subject was much more sanguine, but it seems clear that there was no great groundswell in favour of the new religion in the diocese. There were, of course, some rather peculiar beliefs at large within the diocese, but these were the idiosyncratic exception rather than the rule.[11] What is more, the evidence from wills is ambiguous and their interpretation causes countless methodological problems.[12] The picture which begins to emerge is of a diocese which, in so far as it cared about reform, was sitting determinedly on the fence.

The root of the problem, from Hooper's point of view, was in the leadership at both diocesan and local levels. The diocese had been administered indifferently by its first bishop, John Wakeman until 1549.[13] The clergy, when not openly hostile, acquiesced in the changes brought about under Edward VI and it is difficult to identify with any precision the sympathies of the majority. On the one hand, there were notoriously conservative elements in the diocese such as John Harpsfield, later archdeacon of London and known for his ruthless treatment of Protestants under Mary.[14] On the other hand, clergy like John Parkhurst, later bishop of Norwich, had clearly Protestant sympathies and chose to live in exile after 1553.[15] Yet among the mass of the clergy there are few clues to go on. The number of deprivations in 1554 (most presumably

---

[10] Caroline J. Litzenberger, 'Responses of the laity to changes in the official religious policy in Gloucestershire (1541–80)' (Ph.D. Cambridge, 1993), p. 130. For a useful general discussion of the religious situation in Gloucester see pp. 104–30.

[11] One man from Wotton-under-Edge, for instance, offered the apparently sincere religious defence when questioned about his manifold adulteries: 'I knowe the law is for me to have children by adulterie; I wolde wisshe Moses lawe to be agayne'. Gloucestershire Record Office, 6/62. See also Powell, 'Social Background', 100.

[12] For a full discussion of the problems involved in the interpretation of wills see E. Duffy, *The Stripping of the Altars* (New Haven, 1992), pp. 504–23, and C. Burgess, 'Late medieval wills and pious convention: testamentary evidence reconsidered' in M. A. Hicks (ed.), *Profit, Piety and the Professions in Later Medieval England* (Gloucester, 1990), pp. 14–33. Litzenberger makes the point that, in Gloucester, the 'majority of lay people making wills opted for the safe middle ground of neutral will preambles': 'Responses', p. 130.

[13] Price, 'Gloucester diocese', 51–2.

[14] For biographical detail see A. B. Emden, *A Biographical Register of the University of Oxford A.D. 1501–1540* (Oxford, 1974), pp. 267–8. Interestingly, Harpsfield was examined for his D.Th. by Cranmer (among others) during Cranmer's trial in 1554. See D. M. Loades, *The Oxford Martyrs* (London, 1970), p. 135, and J. Foxe, *The Acts and Monuments of John Foxe*, J. Pratt (ed.), (London, 1870), vi. 511–20.

[15] Emden, *Oxford*, pp. 433–4.

for marriage) tells us little.[16] Most of those who can be traced beyond the 1551 visitation appear to have adjusted admirably to the various changes in religious policy under the Tudors: the clergy in Gloucester were, above all, survivors.[17] But as far as Hooper was concerned, there were few ministers in the diocese who would be assets in implementing his programme of reform. He wrote to Cecil in April 1551 that 'as for the success and going forthward of God's word ... every day the number doth increase and would do more and more, in case [there] were good teachers amongst them for the furtherance thereof'.[18] If he looked at the potential for Protestant education among the laity with optimism, Hooper was not so hopeful about his clergy.

Complaints about the ignorance of the clergy are a commonplace throughout the sixteenth century,[19] and it has been alleged that it was the clergy of Gloucester's shortcomings which inspired William Tyndale to translate the Scriptures into English.[20] In part, dissatisfaction with the intellectual quality of the clergy may be explained by the increase of literacy and education among the laity, yet if, as it has been asserted, the 'clergy of the 1540s and 1550s did not meet the new standards of learning required of them' by bishops such as Hooper,[21] this does not necessarily imply that they were ignorant. Few of the clergy were illiterate.[22] There were, however, worrying gaps in their education, in particular their grasp of Scripture seemed tenuous and Hooper's examination in Gloucester appears to confirm this. Of course, prior to the Reformation, the bible had been a less essential text in many parishes than the service book and it is hardly surprising that men had difficulty reciting passages from it when required to do so.[23]

---

[16] Marriage cannot be seen as proof of reformed ideas. There were 66 deprivations in Gloucester in 1554–5, but not all of these were men with reforming tendencies. See H. E. P. Grieve. 'The deprived married clergy in Essex, 1553–61', TRHS, 4th Series 22 (1940), 153. See also J. Oxley, The Reformation in Essex to the Death of Mary (Manchester, 1965), pp. 179–85, and R. O'Day, The English Clergy: The Emergence and Consolidation of a Profession 1558–1642 (Leicester, 1979), pp. 25–7.

[17] See D. M. Palliser, 'Popular reactions to the Reformation during the years of uncertainty, 1530–70' in C. Haigh (ed.), The English Reformation Revised (Cambridge, 1987), p. 112.

[18] A. Townsend (ed.), The Writings of John Bradford, M.A. (Cambridge, 1853) ii. 395.

[19] Cf. D. M. Barrat, 'Conditions of the parish clergy from the Reformation to 1660 in the dioceses of Oxford, Worcester, and Gloucester' (D.Phil. Oxford, 1950), p. 39.

[20] J. F. Mozley, William Tyndale (London, 1937), pp. 10–11.

[21] O'Day, Emergence, p. 28.

[22] Barrat, 'Conditions', p. 61. For levels of illiteracy in Tudor England see D. Cressy, Literacy and the Social Order (Cambridge, 1980), pp. 104–74.

[23] Heath, Parish Clergy, pp. 6–7: 'It is more likely that [their] acquaintance with [their] faith was derived from the service book than directly from the Bible.'

But the clergy in the diocese of Gloucester were no worse than elsewhere in England. Despite Tyndale's attacks in the 1520s, few were scandalously ignorant. Gloucester, as much as any diocese outside of London, had benefited from the general rise in the number of educated clergy since the fifteenth century and, while the number of graduates does not necessarily indicate relative learning or ignorance,[24] it does provide a useful guide for comparison between dioceses.[25] Of the 311 clergy listed in the examination results of 1551, 63 (or 20.3 per cent) appear to have been (or claim to have been) graduates.[26] This percentage is not out of line with the evidence from other dioceses in the early to mid-sixteenth century.[27]

As suggested, the number of graduates is not always the best indicator of the quality of the clergy. Forty-one of the graduate clergy in Gloucester took Hooper's examination in 1551 (the others were either non-resident or excused for some other reason) and of these 15 (or 36 per cent) failed. Some of these failures were spectacular, although they do not always ring true. Richard Bonde, with a bachelor's degree in canon law, failed to answer five of the nine questions, having particular difficulty with the Ten Commandments and the Lord's Prayer.[28] John Prynne, a doctor of canon law, was examined by Hooper in London and found 'indoctus', although this result might be explained by his advanced years.[29]

In some respects, Gloucester was better off than other dioceses. While it has been noted that 'graduates were always prone to be non-resid-

---

[24] Among those who Stokesley found unsuitable were six M.A.s, two of whom were barred from serving in the diocese of London. Heath, *Parish Clergy*, pp. 73–4. Even during Archbishop Whitgift's time, when the numbers of graduate clergy were increasing, a degree was no guarantee of learning. Whitgift complained that 'the University giveth degrees and honours to the unlearned and the church is filled with ignorant ministers being for the most part poor scholars'. J. Strype, *The Life and Acts of Whitgift, D.D.* (Oxford, 1822), i. 610.

[25] Barrat, 'Conditions', p. 42.

[26] The figures for Gloucester were generated by consulting Emden, *Oxford*, and J. and J. A. Venn, *Alumni Cantabrigienses* (Cambridge, 1922–7). Others, not listed in these sources but who claimed to be graduates, have come to light in the Gloucester Diocesan Records.

[27] O'Day, *Emergence*, p. 233. Twenty per cent of the clergy were graduates in Canterbury and Durham dioceses during the 1520s and 1530s; 15.3 per cent in Norwich between 1523–8; 33 per cent in London between 1522–30. Surrey was unusual with 34.1 per cent between 1520–30 but fell off to 14.3 per cent during the reign of Edward VI. See also Heath, *Parish Clergy*, pp. 70–92.

[28] For biographical detail see Emden, *Oxford*, p. 57.

[29] Prynne held a number of positions, often concurrently, during his life. He died in 1558 while serving as treasurer and subdean of Lincoln Cathedral. Emden, *Oxford*, pp. 465–6.

ent',[30] in Gloucester only 18 graduate clergy (or 28.5 per cent of all graduates) were non-resident as compared to 63 cent of the graduates in Lancashire, for instance.[31] What is more, graduate clergy tended to be spread fairly evenly throughout the deaneries, Campden having the most with 13. There were good reasons for graduates to stay in the diocese: poor though the see was, there were some very comfortable livings. Bishop's Cleeve was valued in the *Valor Ecclesiasticus* at £84 6s. 8d., Cirencester at £59 3s. 10d., Berkeley at £32 14s. 8d., Tetbury at £35 15d., and Standish at £44 2s. 8d. The average income a clergyman might expect in Gloucester was about £12 a year and well in line with other dioceses in England.[32] But the median value of the livings was closer to £9 per year and this led, inevitably, to pluralism and its attendant problem of neglect. Fifty-seven parishes of the 379 listed in the examination results had non-resident clergy and were served by poorly paid curates of questionable ability. These curates were generally among those who did poorly when examined by Hooper.

One problem that Hooper did not have was a lack of bodies. Despite the decline in numbers seeking ordination in the middle of the century,[33] only one parish in Gloucester was vacant in the diocese at the time of the visitation of 1551 (a situation which would be radically different at the turn of the century). Clearly this was because of the large pool of former monastics available in the diocese. Although it is difficult to know for sure, as many as 66 clergy listed in the results may have been former religious.[34] Many of these served as curates (whose stipends we have no way of knowing) or in the poorest of the livings in the diocese and were among the least educated.[35]

---

[30] Bowker, *Henrician Reformation*, p. 119.

[31] C. Haigh, *Reformation and Resistance in Tudor Lancashire* (Cambridge, 1975), p. 29.

[32] Heath, *Parish Clergy*, p. 173; Bowker, *Henrician Reformation*, p. 134; F. Heal, 'Economic problems of the clergy' in R. O'Day and F. Heal (eds), *Church and Society in England: Henry VIII to James I* (London, 1977), pp. 99–117. See also M. Zell, 'Economic problems of the parochial clergy in the sixteenth-century' in R. O'Day and F. Heal (eds), *Princes and Paupers in the English Church, 1500–1800* (Leicester, 1981), pp. 19–43.

[33] M. Bowker, 'The Henrician Reformation and the parish clergy' in Haigh (ed.), *English Reformation Revised*, pp. 75–93.

[34] This figure has been arrived at by consulting G. Baskerville, 'The dispossesed religious of Gloucestershire', *TBGAS*, 49 (1927), 63–97, as well as checking names on the 1551 examination list against D. S. Chambers (ed.), *The Faculty Office Registers 1534–1549* (Oxford, 1966). It is extremely difficult to identify with precision all of the religious in Gloucester for any number of reasons, not the least of which is the frequent use of aliases during the period.

[35] This tends to bear out Zell's point that 'clerical poverty in the second half of the sixteenth century appears to have been less a consequence of an over-abundant supply of ministers, than of a relatively large number of under-endowed livings': 'Economic problems', p. 32.

This then, in brief, was the raw material that Hooper had to work with when he took over his diocese. The profile of the see of Gloucester at the time of his arrival in 1551 was not profoundly different to the profiles of other dioceses. If Hooper was to effect any change, he was going to have to work with these men, many of them uneducated, some hostile and suspicious, and few of them overtly sympathetic to Hooper's theological vision.

(ii)

Hooper began his visitation on 4 May 1551. He brought with him 50 articles of religion, 31 injunctions, 27 interrogatories to be asked of the clergy and 61 interrogatories to be put to the laity. In addition he brought nine questions which comprised his examination of the clergy.[36] The articles were the chief instrument by which Hooper could hope to introduce change into his diocese. They go beyond anything seen previously, following those of Ridley of 1550, but anticipating the Forty-Two Articles of which Hooper had seen a draft.[37]

The 50 articles Hooper brought to Gloucester set out his theological vision and instructed all his clergy not to 'teach or preach any manner of thing necessary for the salvation of man other than that which is contained in the book of God's holy word'.[38] To facilitate this, Hooper 'collected and gathered out of God's holy word a few articles, which I trust shall much profit and do ye good'.[39] The injunctions and interrogatories provided a more practical guide to how this broadly Zwinglian vision was to be put into effect on the ground. Particularly interesting among the injunctions are those which deal directly with the educational standard Hooper expected of his clergy.

Other bishops had for some time enjoined their clergy to read and study the New Testament and even commit some passages to memory.[40]

---

[36] C. Nevinson (ed.), *Later Writings of Bishop Hooper* (Cambridge, 1852), pp. 118–51.

[37] 'Four-fifths of his articles consist of an anticipation of the coming Articles of Religion, the rest follow Ridley': W. H. Frere and W. M. Kennedy (eds), *Visitation Articles and Injunctions* (London, 1910), i. 137. See also C. Hardwick, *A History of the Articles of Religion* (London, 1876), pp. 76–113.

[38] Nevinson (ed.), *Later Writings*, p. 120.

[39] Ibid., p. 119.

[40] Cf. Shaxton's Injunctions for Salisbury Diocese (1538) in Frere and Kennedy (eds), *Articles*, ii. 55, and Lee's Injunctions for York Diocese (1538) in ibid., p. 44. Even Hooper's arch-enemy, Bishop Bonner, had enjoined his clergy to read and memorize Scripture and required that they be ready to be examined by him when he commanded it: ibid., p. 83.

In addition, the Royal Injunctions of 1547 commanded not only that the clergy study the New Testament in Latin and English (as well as Erasmus' *Paraphrases*) but that bishops examine their clergy to see 'how they have profited'.[41] Hooper went further. Injunction 6 expected the clergy to be 'learned and exercised in the Testaments of God, the New and the Old', and commanded that the clergy 'study every quarter of the year such books as I here in these injunctions appoint to be studied and learned; so without the book that every quarter unto me, or to mine assigns, they make rehearsal of the contents of every book in Latin or English'.[42] Injunction 7 took the process a step further and ordered meetings of the clergy in the deaneries to be held four times a year, when theological questions and disputes were to be discussed and settled in the presence of either the bishop or his deputies.[43] The episcopal presence at these meetings was not only a way of ensuring that theological disputes did not get out of hand – it is clear that Hooper was intent on keeping a close eye on the educational progress of his clergy in an unprecedented way. No other episcopal injunctions prior to Hooper's lay out such a detailed plan for the oversight of the clergy's continuing education.

His articles and injunctions were not greeted with universal approval in the diocese and a few consistory court cases appear to have resulted from Hooper's visitation. These are useful in understanding the problems that Hooper faced, but perhaps the clearest picture of the clergy is to be found in the results of the examination. The findings, however, must be treated with care for several reasons. The most important is that the earliest surviving copy of the original document is an eighteenth-century transcription.[44] Two other copies of the transcription are available: a hand-copied folio which was used (and presumably made) by the editor of the Parker Society's edition of Hooper's later works and kept in the British Library,[45] and a typescript copy in the Hockaday Collections at the Gloucester Public Library.[46] We have no way of knowing whether these copies are correct or complete. Another reason for caution is that there have been three analyses (two published) of the

---

[41] Ibid., p. 123.

[42] Ibid., p. 281. The books assigned were (by quarter): the epistle to the Romans, Deuteronomy, the Gospel of Matthew, and Genesis.

[43] Ibid. It is not clear whether Hooper expected to examine the clergy on Scripture at these meetings or at some other time, but it would make sense that these quarterly meetings would be used for both purposes.

[44] *A True Copy of Bishop Hooper's Visitation Booke, made by him, A.D. 1551, 1552*: Dr. William's Library, Morice MS. 31.L/3.

[45] BL, Additional MS. 21, 251.

[46] Gloucester Public Library, 'Hockaday Collections', vi, no. 2.

results and none of them agree in all aspects, nor do any of them concur with the interpretation presented here.[47] As only one of the previous attempts made any effort to describe the methods used in interpreting the data (and even here the comments are incomplete),[48] it is difficult to know why the various analyses disagree.

The examination was divided into three sections of three questions each. The first section examined the clergy on the Ten Commandments. They were asked, first, how many commandments there were; second, where they were to be found in Scripture; and third, to recite them from memory. The second section concerned the Apostle's Creed and the clergy were asked to identify the articles of the Christian faith, to recite them, and to use scriptural authority to 'prove' them. Finally, they were asked to recite the Lord's Prayer, identify who its author was and tell where it was to be found in Scripture.[49] The examination was given at the time of the visitation and was oral. Whether Hooper supervised it personally (as he was visiting all of the deaneries) or delegated some of it to deputies is not clear, but it may be that other examiners were appointed.

The organization of the results makes it difficult to determine whether a minister was thought to have passed the examination successfully; accuracy in any analysis of these results suffers from the irregularity with which the results were recorded. In some cases, a single comment was all that was noted: John Parkhurst, for instance was found to be 'a man of notable intelligence and learnedly answered all articles from memory.'[50] On the other hand, hopeless cases, such as Richard Sheffarde, the vicar of Frampton, were often reported to be 'painfully ignorant'.[51] In the majority of cases the results were recorded by section and it is not always clear which questions were considered to be satisfactorily answered and which were not. A typical example of a satisfactory entry is that of Rhys Jones, rector of Leckhampton:

---

[47] Nevinson (ed.), *Later Writings*, p. 151. Nevinson's analysis is very brief and gives very little detail of the variety of results in the document. J. Gairdner, 'Bishop Hooper's visitation of Gloucester', *EHR*, 19 (1904), 98–100. Frere and Kennedy seem to have relied on Gairdner's analysis. The third analysis is the unpublished work done by Hockaday in the 'Hockaday Abstracts', volume 33, and the 'Hockaday Collections' cited above, both in the Gloucester Public Library. Both F. D. Price, 'Gloucester Diocese', and Gairdner appear to have consulted Hockaday's work.

[48] Gairdner, 'Visitation', 98–100.

[49] Nevinson (ed.), *Later Writings*, p. 151.

[50] 'Vir insigniter doctus et docte respondet ad omnes articluos supra memoratos': 'Hockaday Collections', vi, no. 2, p. 24.

[51] 'Vir penitus ignorans': ibid., p. 93.

Rizeus Jones Rector examinatus de Preceptis dicit quod dicem [sic]
sunt numero scripta vicesimo capite Exodiac memoriter eadem
recitare valet prout ibidem continentur. Etc.

The results were entered by parish, not by incumbent, and therefore,
out of a total of 379 entries, a number of parishes had no recorded
results. Some 37 parishes had clergy who lived outside the diocese,
accounting for 35 individual priests as two of the non-residents held
two benefices apiece within the diocese of Gloucester in addition to
those they held outside the diocese. Three parishes had clergy who were
judged to be too infirm or decrepit to be examined. Two more parishes
had incumbents who had either resigned or retired to a benefice outside
of the diocese and were not examined. One minister simply did not
appear and one parish was vacant. In addition, 23 churches were looked
after by pluralists, whose examination results were recorded under one
of their other benefices. One further priest did not participate for
reasons which were not recorded. When all 'no result' entries are totalled,
we find that 311 clergy were examined.

Of the 311 results, 79 were judged satisfactory without detailed
comment and a further 12 appear to have answered all areas satisfactorily
or 'fairly well'.[52] This represents 29.3 per cent of the clergy who took
the exam. Only a very few respondents failed completely: seven were
found utterly ignorant without any detailed comment, while one more
was recorded as unsatisfactory in all areas (representing only 2.5 per
cent of the clergy examined). The remaining 212 results show clergy
who failed to answer one or more of the nine questions satisfactorily. It
is this large number which has given the impression that 'a truly astonishing state of affairs' existed among the clergy in Gloucester.[53] But there
are a variety of ways to look at the results. All of the previous analyses
counted the number of unsatisfactory responses to each question and
appear to have assumed that failure in any part of the examination was
evidence of ignorance. None stopped to investigate the results any
further, let alone wonder whether there might be good reasons that the
clergy at the time might have had difficulty. Instead, they preferred to
point up those areas which seemed most notable or shocking (for example, the number of respondents who could not recite the Lord's Prayer).
Looked at in this manner, the results do present a very sorry picture
indeed. Nine clergy were unable to give the number of the Commandments, a further ten could not recite the Lord's Prayer – surely a basic

---

[52] Litzenberger counts 65 satisfactory results, but is not entirely clear how she arrived
at this figure: 'Responses', pp. 115–17.

[53] Price, 'Gloucester Diocese', 101.

expectation of any minister. Yet this paints too grim a picture of the clergy in Gloucester.

Of the unsatisfactory results, 43 clergy were judged to have failed because of one unanswered question,[54] while a further 124 missed just two.[55] Two questions in particular were major stumbling blocks for the clergy of Gloucester: the recitation of the Ten Commandments and proving the Creed from Scripture. Yet these results do not prove that the vast majority of clergy in Gloucester were ignorant, or that they were unfamiliar with the Bible.

That so many should have had trouble reciting the commandments is hardly surprising. The commandments were not yet commonly used in services of worship and even if they could not recite them, they still knew where they were to be found in Scripture. Further, the examination is not clear whether the minister was expected to answer in English or in Latin, or both. The historian John Strype believed that Latin and English were required for some questions, but the Royal Injunctions of 1547 seem to indicate that either would be acceptable. Conceivably, some clergy might be able to recite the commandments in one or the other but not both and yet be judged 'ignorant'.[56]

The second major problem for most of the clergy was proving the Creed from Scripture. It is difficult to know just what was meant by this or what was expected in the way of an answer. It is quite possible that many who were confronted with this had never faced such a question before and did not understand what was required of them. What can be said is that unfamiliarity with Scripture is not proved by a failure to answer this question, as most of the clergy were able to answer correctly when asked for specific chapters of the Bible in other parts of the examination. As no model answer is provided, the passing or failing of this question must have been an entirely subjective decision on the part

---

[54] Forty-one were unable to 'prove' the Creed from Scripture and two more were unable to recite the Ten Commandments as written in Exodus 20.

[55] One hundred and nineteen were unable to recite the commandments or prove the Creed; three were unable to prove the Creed or cite the chapter in which the Lord's Prayer is found; one was unable to prove the Creed and, oddly, did not know who the author of the Lord's Prayer was; and one more did not know the author of the Lord's Prayer nor where it was to be found in Scripture.

[56] Christopher Haigh comments that 'the Gloucester figure has often been used to argue that parish clergy were uneducated or stupid; they show rather that priests did not yet know the English Bible': *English Reformations* (Oxford, 1993), p. 314. I would not go so far. While the Gloucester results do not demonstrate that the clergy were stupid or uneducated, it is not clear at all that Hooper was testing knowledge of the English Bible. Strype's horrified comment that 'some could say the Pater Noster in Latin, but not in English' is unsubstantiated and he provides no clues as to where he got this information: *Memorials of Cranmer* (London, 1840), i. 312.

of the examiners. How strict they were is open to question. We know that some of the clergy were later discovered to be illiterate at the quarterly meetings Hooper set up to keep an eye on their progress (a fact that the visitation failed to reveal), but these had already done poorly on the examination in the first instance. This sheds very little light on the judgements made in 1551 with regard to the two major stumbling blocks.

The results reviewed with these factors in mind do not show a diocese made up of grossly ignorant clergy. In fact, the examiners themselves were only moved to single out seven of their colleagues as hopelessly ignorant. There were, to be sure, a number of cases very much on the borderline. Some of these, at least, made creative efforts to answer the questions. Thomas Taylor of North Cerney, for instance, was unable to prove the Creed from Scripture, but he claimed that he was content to believe it, because it was promulgated by the authority of the king.[57] William Pye, vicar of Lee, replied that the Lord's Prayer was given by Christ at the time of His Passion when He commanded His disciples to watch and pray.[58] John Dumbell, clearly unprepared for the examination, when asked where the Lord's Prayer was to be found, ventured that it was to be found in his Lord the King's book of Common Prayer.[59] The vast majority of the clergy, however, did not make fools of themselves.

Despite some ridiculous responses sprinkled throughout the results, the number of what have been called 'absolute dunces' in the diocese, even when counted unsympathetically, represented less that a tenth of the total number.[60] While individuals within the diocese may have demonstrated appalling ignorance, this is hardly an accurate description or indictment of the diocese as a whole. By and large, the clergy in Gloucester were adequately prepared for and adequately performed the tasks expected of vicars and curates, even if there were few Zwinglian Protestants among them. Clearly there were few enough 'learned' men in the diocese, but there were fewer still who could be condemned for their utter ignorance. The fact is that we hear few complaints from their parishioners, and most of the clergy who were charged to appear before

---

[57] 'Quia satis erit sibi credere propterea quod traditus [sic] aucthoritate Regia': Gairdner, 'Visitation', 111.

[58] 'Tempore Passionis suae mandavit discipulis sius dicens, "Vigilate et orate"': Gairdner, 'Visitation', 120.

[59] 'Scit esse Domini Orationem propterea quod tradita sit a Domino Rege, ac scripta in libro Regio de Communi Oracione': 'Hockaday Collections', vi, no. 2, p. 64.

[60] Gairdner, 'Visitation', 99.

the consistory courts did so, not for ignorance, but for sharp practice.[61] That so many should have answered as well as they did, in a diocese which was hardly at the centre of the Reformation and which had neglectful leadership since its foundation in 1541, is probably more remarkable than the few who, like William Ayds, curate of Oxenhall, answered nothing correctly.[62] At worst the clergy of Gloucester could be accused of mediocrity but not ignorance, even if their new bishop chose to focus on the few cases which only served to confirm his already strong views on the ignorance of the clergy.

---

[61] See, Newcombe, 'Hooper', pp. 233–89, and Litzenberger, 'Responses', pp. 104–30.

[62] 'Nihil directe respondere valet': G. Baskerville 'Elections to Convocation in the Diocese of Gloucester under Bishop Hooper', *EHR*, 44 (1929), 32.

PART TWO
Church resources

CHAPTER FIVE

The sequestration
of the Hessian monasteries

Richard Cahill

It is often assumed that rulers in sixteenth-century Europe converted to the new teachings of Wittenberg and Zurich in order to pad their pockets with the wealth of the church.[1] Scholars of the English Reformation have used terms such as 'plunder' and 'sacrilege' to describe the expropriation of church property.[2] Similar phenomena in the German principality of Hesse, however, have received more gentle press,[3] even though the sequestration[4] of monasteries was a radical and rapid endeavour, lasting little over one year. What effect did this 'Great Transfer' have upon the Hessian society and economy? To what extent did this dissolution of the monasteries influence parish life at the local level? This essay attempts to answer these questions by examining the process of sequestration in the 1520s, and then analyzing the use of the

---

[1] For an introduction to this topic in Germany, based on extensive secondary literature, see Henry J. Cohn, 'Church property in the German Protestant principalities' in E. I. Kouri and Tom Scott (eds), *Politics and Society in Reformation Europe* (London, 1987), pp. 158–87.

[2] See W. G. Hoskins, *The Age of Plunder: The England of Henry VIII 1500–47* (London, 1976), p. 122, and Patrick Carter's essay in this volume.

[3] For example Eckhart Franz, 'Die hessischen Klöster und ihre Konvente in der Reformation', *Hessisches Jahrbuch für Landesgeschichte*, 19 (1969), 147–233; David B. Miller, 'The dissolution of the religious houses of Hesse during the Reformation' (Ph.D. Yale University, 1971); Wolf Struck (ed.), *Quellen zur Geschichte der Klöster und Stifte im Gebiet der mittleren Lahn* (3 vols, Wiesbaden, 1956–84).

[4] The term 'sequestration' is used to signify both the dissolution of the religious communities and the expropriation of their former wealth. In addition to being anachronistic (the term was not used in pre-Napoleonic times), the term 'secularization' is avoided because it conveys a contemporary connotation of a division between the profane and the sacred. Many sixteenth-century German rulers referred to themselves as ruling 'by God's Grace' and thought of themselves as 'Christian princes'. It thus seems inappropriate to speak, as Midelfort does, of 'general questions of the secular control of morals and of Church property': H. C. Erik Midelfort, 'A Protestant monastery in Hesse?' in Peter Newman Brooks (ed.), *Reformation Principle and Practice* (London, 1980), p. 75. For the legal distinctions of the terminology see Hans Lehnert, *Kirchengut und Reformation: Eine kirchenrechtsgeschichtliche Studie* (Erlangen, 1935).

former monasteries' wealth. Glances at the dissolution in England shall help to assess the developments in a comparative perspective.

(i)

The practice of sequestration of church property by princes was ancient. In the eighth century Charles Martell used ecclesiastical wealth to promote the 'Christianization' of the heathen Hessians.[5] From Martell until Napoleon, rulers have made strategic use of the church's capital.[6] So it was in Hesse. Since the primogenitor of the princely household was St Elizabeth, the Hessian Landgraves viewed themselves as natural guardians of the church, and beneficiaries of her wealth. In the fifteenth century, Hessian princes exercised considerable power over and concern for the monasteries of their land. They carried out visitations and reforms in the 1480s and 1490s. In 1491, Landgrave Wilhelm lifted the ban against the sale of property to clerics, which allowed monasteries to increase their holdings.[7] When Wilhelm died young of syphilis in 1509, he instructed his then five year old son, Philipp of Hesse, that 'all of the monasteries in our principality should be brought to the reformation'.[8] In other words, Philipp was to complete his father's initiative.

Of the three commodities which monasteries provided, namely *caritas*,[9] clergy, and credit, Philipp was initially interested only in the last. In his war against the Imperial Knights (1522–3), he borrowed large sums of money from the monasteries in his lands.[10] After reaching his credit

---

[5] Timothy Reuter, '"Kirchenreform" und "Kirchenpolitik" im Zeitalter Karl Martells: Begriffe und Wirklichkeit' in Jorg Jarnut, Ulrich Nonn, et al. (eds), *Karl Martell in seiner Zeit* (Sigmaringen, 1994), pp. 35–59.

[6] For a general introduction and further literature see Peter Landau, 'Kirchengut' in *TRE*.

[7] Walter Heinemeyer, 'Territorium und Kirche in Hesse vor der Reformation', *Hessisches Jahrbuch für Landesgeschichte*, 6 (1956), 138–63.

[8] 'Alle Klöster im Fürstentum sollen zur Reformation gebracht werden': 'Testament Landgraf Wilhelms des Mittleren (29 Jan. 1508)' in Hans Glagau (ed.), *Hessische Landtagsakten* (Marburg, 1901), p. 9, no. 1. 'Reformation' here is doubtlessly used in the sense of 'observant reform'. See Euan Cameron, *The European Reformation* (Oxford, 1991), pp. 41–3.

[9] I choose to use the Latin 'caritas' rather than 'charity' in order to avoid modern connotations of the word. Cf. C. S. Lewis, *The Screwtape Letters* (New York, 1982), p. 121.

[10] In 1522, for example, he borrowed 500 Gulden from the Abbot of Haina, and 600 from the St Martin's Chapter in Kassel: Eckhart Franz (ed.), *Kloster Haina Regesten und Urkunden* (2 vols, Marburg, 1970), ii. 554, no. 1368. Johannes Schultze (ed.), *Klöster, Stifter und Hospitäler der Stadt Kassel und Kloster Weißenstein* (Marburg, 1913), p. 430, no. 1176.

limit, Philipp demanded more for the sake of Hesse's national security, and the religious houses complied with his request. For example, in response to Philipp's demand for 1 000 Gulden, the Chapter of St Martin's Church in Kassel declared that the loan they had granted him the previous year need not be repaid. They also paid an additional 400 Gulden to the Landgrave.[11] It was strangely appropriate that Philipp put down the revolt of vocal opponents of monasticism with funds from monastic institutions.

The attitude of the Imperial Knights exemplified and paralleled a fairly widespread anticlericalism in Hesse, which was bolstered in the 1520s by the new teaching of Luther.[12] In March 1522, the Abbot of Haina wrote: 'In Hesse, due to the teaching of Martin Luther, there are uprisings and unrest everywhere, especially against the clergy, so that the country priests are no longer safe in their houses and are often fleeing to the city.' The Abbot himself had been attacked three times on the open road.[13] In 1523, Philipp informed the Archbishop of Mainz that he was no longer able to guarantee the safety of his clergy (Sendpriester) on Hessian roads.[14]

Evidence of anticlericalism in the early 1520s can also be found in the refusal of peasants to pay their feudal and spiritual dues. In 1523, a parish priest, Mutianus Rufus, wrote to the Hessian chancellor complaining that the people of Gerstungen were so negatively influenced by 'the foolish speaking and spiteful pamphlets' that they refused to continue to pay their annual dues.[15] In the holdings of the monastery of Haina, to cite another example, the parishioners of Armsfeld refused to pay the abbey its traditional one sixth of the harvest in 1522.[16]

---

[11] Schultze (ed.), *Kassel*, p. 431, no. 1182.

[12] For example, in July 1521, the official of the neighbouring Count of Hanau wrote to the Abbot of Haina, recommending that he grant the peasants their own altar in the new chapel of the monastery. If the Abbot would not, he warned, the Lutheran movement might take the day: Franz (ed.), *Kloster Haina*, p. 546, no. 1351.

[13] Abbot Dietmar von Haina to Abbot Gerhard von Altenberg (19 March 1522): Franz (ed.), *Kloster Haina*, pp. 550-1, no. 1362.

[14] HStAM, Bestandteil 3, no. 2086. Although the records are not very complete, some monks left their monasteries in the early 1520s. By May 1522, at least two monks had left the monastery of Haina: Franz (ed.), *Kloster Haina*, p. 552, no. 1364.

[15] 'Die Reden törichter Leute und gehässige Flugschriften' : HStAM, Bestandteil 22a; quoted by Friedrich Küch, 'Landgraf Philipp und die Einführung der Reformation in Hessen', *Zeitschrift des Vereins für hessische Geschichte und Landeskunde*, N. F. 28 (1904), 210-42.

[16] Franz (ed.), *Kloster Haina*, p. 550, no. 1360. Also, a conflict over agricultural property between the abbey and a certain Theis Lober was only resolved at law: ibid. p. 558, no. 1379.

At Marburg, evidence of a decisively evangelical anticlericalism surfaces in the city's articles of complaints to the Landgrave in May 1525.[17] The parishioners bemoaned that 'this city is over burdened with clergy',[18] and unlike earlier city grievances, which contained one or two complaints against the clergy's economic privileges, no less than 12 of 34 articles in 1525 were directed against the men in holy orders.[19] They first requested the Landgrave to install a good pastor and chaplains so 'that the holy Gospel and Word of God will be profitably proclaimed in Marburg'.[20] The evangelical tenor of these grievances is obvious.

The Landgrave was to develop similar attitudes himself. Philipp became a Lutheran in the summer of 1524 and wasted little time before he publicly attacked monasticism as unbiblical.[21] There is no evidence that Philipp's conversion to the new teaching was simply a ploy to strip the Church of its assets. In fact the course of events suggests that he exercised a certain restraint. The Peasants' War of 1525 provided the perfect opportunity for Philipp to take over the wealth of the monasteries under the pretense of military threat, but he resisted the temptation.

Still, claiming that monks and nuns might flee from their monasteries with valuable items, Philipp ordered an inventory of all monasteries, parishes, and chapters in Hesse in February 1525.[22] All documents and silver goods were either to be evacuated or brought under lock and key by the prince's officers. The Landgrave's orders were carried out that spring. In July 1525, the Swabian League suggested to its members, whose resources were being exhausted by the repeated dues to the League, that they raise additional funds from silverware and monstrances of the chapters, parishes, and monasteries in their lands.[23] Philipp fol-

---

[17] 'Beschwerdeartikel der Stadt Marburg, September 1525' in Friedrich Küch (ed.), *Quellen zur Rechtsgeschichte der Stadt Marburg* (Marburg, 1918), p. 289ff, no. 212.

[18] 'Ist dise staidt mit geistlichen personen zuviel belestigt': ibid.

[19] For early complaint articles see ibid., pp. 181–8 (1486), pp. 244–6 (1514), and pp. 271–7 (1523).

[20] 'Das heilig evangelium und wort gottis eintrechtlich zu Marburg verkunidigt werde': ibid., pp. 289–95, no. 212.

[21] He did so in a letter to the Franciscan Nikolaus Ferber which was published as a pamphlet several times in 1525. Günther Franz, Walter Köhler, et al. (eds), *Urkundliche Quellen zur hessischen Reformationsgeschichte* (Marburg, 1954), ii. 5. Cf. Hans Schneider, 'Die reformatorischen Anfänge Landgraf Philipps von Hessen im Spiegel einer Flugschrift', *Hessisches Jahrbuch für Landesgeschichte*, 42 (1992), 131–66.

[22] For an example see Franz et al. (eds), *Urkundliche Quellen*, ii. 8–9. Most of the extant inventories are in HStAM, Bestandteil 22 a 8 and 9. For a list of the various published results of these inventories see Eckhart Franz, 'Die hessischen Klöster und ihre Konvente', 150, note 19. In England, the compiling of inventories immediately preceded confiscation. See Peter Marshall's essay in this volume.

[23] 'Bey irn gaistlichen stifften, capitteln, cläster und pfarren, under inen gesessen, an munsteranzen und anderen gezierden von sibler aufzubringen.' League's suggestion dated

lowed its advice, and collected more than twice his dues, namely 10 700 Gulden worth of coinage and precious religious objects. This amounted to 84 per cent of the total wealth of silver and gold of the Hessian monasteries.[24] In the account books of the Kassel treasury an entry for 1527 reveals the sad fate of medieval silver craftsmanship. The mint master reported the production of 1 312 Gulden coins from the monasteries' treasures.[25]

When Philipp drew upon the monasteries' wealth during the Peasants' War he was not acting in a novel, nor distinctly evangelical way. As the military campaigns of 1519 and 1522–3 show, he had set precedents well before he became a follower of the new teaching.[26] Many Catholic members of the League carried out similar actions in their territories and other Catholic princes also used the wealth of the monasteries in their territories. In some cases, they replaced the abbots with their own officials, or even abolished the convent. In Pomerania as early as 1522 and 1523, the Catholic Duke Boleslav X sequestrated the monastery of Belbuk.[27] Even the Emperor Charles and his brother Ferdinand did not refrain from taking over ecclesiastical property.[28] In Württemberg, for example, Ferdinand brought the monasteries under his government's control and had the pope approve of it in exchange for a third of the income which the religious houses generated.[29] In the summer of 1525, Margraves Casimir and Georg von Brandenburg advised Philipp to take control of the monasteries until a future church council would decide their fate, but Philipp rejected this suggestion.[30] In

---

18 June 1525: HStAM, Bestandteil 3, no. 140. Philipp had been a member of the League since 1519: ibid., Bestandteil 3, no. 123.

[24] Franz et al. (eds), *Urkundliche Quellen*, p. 152.

[25] Franz Gundlach, *Die Hessischen Zentralbehörden von 1247 bis 1604* (3 vols, Marburg, 1932), ii. (Urkunden und Akten) 88.

[26] It is interesting to note that 1519 was the first time that Hessian Monasteries were actually taxed by the prince. The clergy, like the nobility, were until this time traditionally exempt from such taxes. See Günter Hollenberg (ed.), *Hessische Landtagsabschiede 1526–1603* (Marburg, 1994), p. 42.

[27] K. Körber, *Kirchengüterfrage und Schmalkaldischer Bund*, Schriften des Vereins für Reformationsgeschichte xxx (1913), pp. 32ff.

[28] Henry Cohn notes that 'since all the leading secular rulers in Germany, with the notable exceptions of the Austrian Habsburgs and Bavarian Wittelsbachs, sooner or later adopted the Reformation, they all benefited to some extent from a policy of secularisation': Cohn, 'Church Property', p. 158. Such a statement gives the false impression that the Hapsburgs did not benefit from sequestrating church wealth.

[29] When the abbots complained in 1525, Ferdinand allowed them to lease their monasteries back for 4 000 Gulden a year. The prelates in turn collected this sum from all the religious houses: Gustav Bossert, *Das Interim in Württemberg* (Halle, 1895), pp. 134–5.

[30] Philipp to the Margraves Casimir and Georg of Brandenburg (23 October 1525): Franz et al. (eds), *Urkundliche Quellen*, p. 12, no. 11.

the end, it was not the Peasants' War, but the Recess (concluding statement) of the Imperial Diet of Speyer (1526) which provided Philipp with the legal justification to carry out the Reformation of his territories. Although Philipp had not consulted his estates since 1518, he now felt the need to seek wider support for his plans. He dealt with his two most likely opponents, the clergy and the nobility, separately. An assembly of all Hessian religious leaders in October 1526 at Homberg produced the first Hessian Church Ordinance.[31] Although it was never promulgated, the document provides us with a glimpse of how Philipp and his men planned the sequestration of the monasteries. The last of the 34 chapters (which Luther called 'such a heap of laws'[32]) dealt with this topic. It denied the biblical basis for monasticism, forbade new recruits, suggested what to do with those who wished to leave, claimed that the vows could be broken with good conscience, and pronounced on many other topics.

> Finally, if some, affected by the spirit of blindness so strongly, that they, in opposition to God's Word, as servants of men, wish to remain in the monasteries, they should be tolerated temporally, but with expressed conditions that they do not read the Mass, nor cry out, as thus far, nor ring the bells. Also, we do not want them to give the sacrament to anyone, nor listen to confession, neither public nor private, nor go around outside their monasteries with crucifixes, nor bury the dead. In short, we want them to stay in their corner and in no way involve themselves in the leadership of our Church.[33]

Philipp's statements make it clear that this corresponded to his own convictions. We have seen above how, in 1525, he had criticized monasticism in response to the Franciscan prior of Marburg,[34] and in his autograph memorandum of 1527 he repeated the same ideas.[35] Philipp wasted no time in implementing his plans for the monasteries. In February 1527, he issued orders for yet another inspection of the monasteries. This time his commissioners were to install a warden (*Vogt*) in each monastery to ensure that no goods were misappropri-

---

[31] The document was written after the synod by a committee which included Franz Lambert of Avignon: *Reformatio ecclesiarum Hassiae* (1526), printed in Emil Sehling (ed.), *Die Evangelischen Kirchenordnungen des XVI. Jahrhundert* (Tübingen, 1965), viii. 43ff. Some of the older literature refers to the so-called Homberg Synod as a diet (*Landtag*). It was not. See, for example, Wilhelm Schmitt, *Die Homberger Synode und ihre Vorgeschichte* (Homberg, 1927).

[32] 'So ein hauffen gesetze': Luther to Philipp (7 January 1527): WA Br, iv. 157, no. 1071.

[33] Latin text in *Reformatio ecclesiarum Hassiae*, chapter xxxiv, paragraph 189.

[34] See note 21 above.

[35] See Küch, 'Einführung', pp. 238–9 (Beilagen 1–5).

ated, to copy all the letters of feudal tenure, to command the priors to provide a copy of the last six years of financial records within six weeks, and to lock up all remaining silverware, chalices, and monstrances.[36]

Perhaps Philipp and his men were anticipating that most monks and nuns would leave of their own volition, as had been the case with the entire Carmelite monastery in Kassel the year before.[37] Since this did not prove to be the case during the visitations of March and April 1527, Philipp issued yet another set of instructions for visitations in June. Whereas the February instructions had dealt exclusively with the wealth and property of religious houses, those of June were also concerned with religious life at the parish level. Preachers and ceremonies had to be examined and, if need be, removed, while poor relief measures and primary schools were established.[38] The last and longest part of the instructions dealt with the monasteries. 'Most importantly, the Gospel should be proclaimed and preached in the cloisters.'[39] Monks were to be informed that if they chose to leave, the state would pay them a lump sum and an annual pension. Priors who are 'unreasonable and ungodly' were to be removed; if able preachers were among their ranks, they were to be installed as priors. Those who wished to remain in the monasteries had to obey the (new) wardens.[40] Still, even after this second set of visitation instructions, things did not proceed as smoothly as Philipp had hoped. Although most Hessian religious houses did not resist Philipp's instructions, some were reluctant. The mother superior of St Georgenberg refused to allow a preacher into the cloister grounds because 'he even had a housewife'.[41] More threatening to Philipp's plans, however, was the response of some of the nobility and knights. For this reason Philipp called the first meeting of the estates of Hesse since his minority. But this was not a genuine diet (*Landtag*) since neither representatives of the cities nor the clergy were invited.[42] The nobility and the monasteries had enjoyed a mutually beneficial relation-

---

[36] HStAM, Bestandteil 22 a 1; Franz et al. (eds), *Urkundliche Quellen*, pp. 27–8, no. 39.

[37] Schultze (ed.), *Kassel*, pp. 286–7, no. 740.

[38] On 30 August 1527 Philipp issued another order which called for the introduction of poor chests throughout the land: Franz et al. (eds), *Urkundliche Quellen*, p. 42, no. 63.

[39] 'Für allen dingen soll in monche- und nonneclöstern das evangelium verkündiget und geprediget wereden': HStAM, Bestandteil 22 a 1; Franz et al. (eds), *Urkundliche Quellen*, pp. 27–8, no. 39.

[40] 'So gar unvernünftig und impii': Franz et al. (eds), *Urkundliche Quellen*, pp. 37–8, no. 57.

[41] 'Er [hait] auch ein husfraue': ibid., pp. 38–9, no. 58.

[42] See note 31 above.

ship for centuries and the recess of 15 October 1527 testifies to Philipp's endeavours to make the sequestration attractive to the nobility. Many of its members were patrons of monasteries while others depended on the cloisters to provide a home for their unmarried daughters. Indeed, Philipp's own father had deposited two of his illegitimate daughters in Hessian nunneries. The recess specified that any monks or nuns who came from the nobility would be offered a generous compensation for leaving their institution.[43] Two cloisters (and their lands) were to be put under direct control of the nobles, to provide for their unmarried kin. Furthermore, 30 poor knights were to receive yearly income of grain or produce (*naturalia*). Any net annual gains from the property of all the monasteries was to be put in a common chest, under the control of the nobles and the cities.[44]

Although some of these promises were never fulfilled, they secured enough of the nobility's support for Philipp to continue and complete his programme of sequestration. By the end of 1527, Philipp had succeeded in dissolving almost all of the religious houses in his territory. The sequestration in Hesse was one of the earliest of the Reformation throughout Europe and became a paradigm for other Protestant princes.[45]

And yet it is interesting to note the marked difference between the dissolution of the Hessian monasteries and those in England. Quite apart from the discrepancies in procedure (Philipp manipulated his estates even more blatantly than Henry VIII) and administration (no Court of Augmentation was set up in Hesse[46]), perhaps the most interesting point of comparison is the way in which the former church property was used. The effect of the sequestration on Hessian society and economy shall now be examined in greater detail for the three case studies of Marburg, Kassel, and Haina.

(ii)

The Franciscan prior of Marburg, Nikolaus Ferber, who had attempted in late 1524 to dissuade the Landgrave from his newly found faith in the Lutheran Gospel, was the most strident opponent of the Reforma-

---

[43] The Recess was issued in Philipp's name alone, since the cities and clergy were not present.

[44] Hollenberg (ed.), *Hessische Landtagsabschiede*, p. 64, no. 2.

[45] Compare, for example, Duke Ulrich's sequestration of the cloisters of Württemberg. See Martin Brecht, *Südwestdeutsche Reformationsgeschichte* (Stuttgart, 1984), pp. 215ff.

[46] See Walter C. Richardson, *History of the Court of Augmentations 1536–1554* (Louisiana, 1961), and P. A. Cunich, 'The administration and alienation of ex-monastic lands by the crown: 1536–47' (Ph.D. Cambridge, 1990).

tion in Hesse.[47] At the so-called Synod of Homberg in 1526, where most of the clergy showed little resistance to the Prince and his theologians, Ferber was the most (and virtually only) outspoken antagonist.[48] When the visitations and sequestration began in 1527, the Franciscans showed no signs of compliance. The other religious orders in Marburg, the Dominicans and the Brethren of the Common Life, accepted the financial incentives to depart from their monasteries. The Franciscans did not; first, they refused to leave their monastery in exchange for money, then, in an act of corporate defiance, all Hessian Franciscans abandoned their friaries in May 1528 and left the territory refusing the Landgrave's gold.[49] No other order in Hesse responded to the sequestration in this manner.

Although the departure of the Franciscans from Marburg was atypical, their property was used for the same purposes as that of their religious brethren. Philipp's special plan for Marburg emerges from a memorandum of January 1527.[50] The Landgrave had moved his court and residence from Kassel to Marburg a few weeks earlier and he planned to mould his new capital into a model of the Reformation for all of Hesse.[51] Philipp's intention to use the wealth of monasteries to fund education in Hesse was manifest in September 1526, when he wrote to Luther and Melanchthon.[52] With determined energy, the project took less than a year to fulfil. In the summer of 1527, the lectures began at the *Philipps-Universität*, as it was later called. Its staff, students, and classes were housed in the former monasteries of Marburg. Thus, one of the major impacts of the sequestration on Hessian society was the creation and funding of the first university in the territory; the first evangelical university in the world.[53] The importance of having a do-

---

[47] It was in response to Ferber's letter that Philipp wrote the first public defense of his faith. As mentioned above, Philipp's letter was published as a pamphlet and in two of the known editions, Ferber's letter was published along with Philipp's. See Irmgard Bezzel (ed.), *Verzeichnis der im deutschen Sprachbereich erschienenen Drucke des 16. Jahrhunderts* (Stuttgart, 1983–4), H 2819–23. See also Schneider, 'Die reformatorischen Anfänge', 159.

[48] See Schmitt, *Die Homberger Synode*, p. 77.

[49] There were also Franciscans in the towns of Hofgeismar, Grebenstein, Frankenberg, and Grünberg.

[50] Philipp wrote, 'Item die universitet hie anczurichten': Franz et al. (eds), *Urkundliche Quellen*, p. 26, no. 37.

[51] See note 66 below and cf. Peter Dykema's essay in this volume for Count Eberhard's remodelling of late fifteenth-century Tübingen.

[52] WA Br, iv. 112–15, no. 1035. Philipp's plans for a university are also evident in Eobanus Hessus' letter to Adam Krafft, Philipp's court preacher from September 1526: Franz et al. (eds), *Urkundliche Quellen*, p. 19, no. 27.

[53] On the university see, for instance, W. Heinemeyer, T. Klein, and H. Seier (eds), *Academia Marburgensis: Beiträge zur Geschichte der Philipps-Universität Marburg*

mestic institution of higher learning (*Landesuniversität*) for the training
of new clergy and jurists is evident. From the annual income which the
former church property produced, nine per cent was allocated to the
university (see Figure 5.3 below),[54] and the Recess of the assembly of
October 1527 subsequently 'legitimized' Philipp's initiative.

Life at the parish level was affected greatly by the closures of the
monasteries and the creation of the university. In 1525, the city of
Marburg had complained to Philipp about the overabundance of clergy
in the city, but within three years their numbers dropped dramatically.[55]
The availability of fewer churches must have also been noticed by the
common person in the parish; the church of the Dominicans was turned
into a grain warehouse,[56] while the chemistry and philosophy depart-
ments of the new university were housed in the Franciscan church and
monastery. The church of the Brethren of the Common Life was transformed into a lecture hall and a 'modern' urban problem was solved by
using St Kilian's as a car park for city wagons. Only the two largest
buildings, the main parish church and St Elizabeth's, the oldest Gothic
church in Germany, continued to be houses of worship.

Examining the patronage of these two remaining churches in Marburg
allows us to discuss the only monastic order in Hesse whose property
was not sequestrated by the prince, namely the Teutonic Knights.
Marburg was the seat of the regional general (*Landkomtur*) of the
Hessian administrative province (*Ballei*), and no other religious order in
the city could rival their financial, political, and pastoral importance.[57]
They were the administrators of the hospital which St Elizabeth had
founded, and they held the rights of patronage of the only two churches
still open for worship. Their great influence in the city reflected their
political and economic strength in the Empire as a whole and the
Hessian *Ballei* in particular, which consisted of four districts (*Komtureien*)
and five outposts (*Kastnereien*) – a substantial source of revenues.[58]

(Marburg, 1977); among the first foreign scholars at the institution were Patrick Hamilton and John Frith.

[54] This figure includes a scholarship fund which exists to this day.

[55] Twelve Brethren of the Common Life (*Kugelhaus*), 12 Dominicans, and 17 Franciscans
had left the city by the summer of 1528. If the secular clergy in Marburg numbered less
than ten, which is likely, then Marburg lost over 80 per cent of its clergy.

[56] Today a small parking lot next to the church, which is now the University Church,
bears the name 'Grain Market' (*Kornmarkt*).

[57] The Teutonic Knights had their own system of provinces which did not always
coincide with territorial boundaries. For a general introduction to the order see Udo
Arnold, *Zur Wirtschaftsentwicklung des Deutschen Ordens im Mittelalter*, Quellen und
Studien zur Geschichte des Deutschen Ordens xxxviii (Marburg, 1989).

[58] The Emperor had granted the *Deutschmeister* of the order the imperial status of a
spiritual prince (*Geistlicher Reichsfürst*) in 1494. See Bernhard Demel, 'Von der

In 1525, Philipp informed Daniel von Lehrbach, the *Landkomtur* of the Teutonic Knights, that he was sending a preacher, Johann de Campis, to Marburg with instructions to proclaim to the people in the parish church on every Sunday and Saint's Day 'the Word of God and the Holy Gospel, uncontaminated and pure'.[59] By 1525 this phrase had taken on explicitly evangelical meaning.[60] Whether it was Lehrbach's resistance or the call to be Philipp's chaplain (*Feldprediger*) during the Peasants' revolt which caused De Campis' departure from Marburg is uncertain.[61] When Philipp's court theologian, Franz Lambert, drafted a new evangelical ordinance after the Synod of Homberg the following year, Lehrbach, like most of the Hessian clergy, did not publicly oppose it.[62] After the synod, Philipp presented yet another evangelical preacher, Hybernius Winter, to the parish church in Marburg, but even though there was again no recorded resistance from the Knights, Winter, too, remained less than a year, before he married a former nun and left.[63] By May 1527, when Philipp's men replaced the parish priest with two evangelical pastors,[64] the Landgrave had clearly usurped a de facto 'right of presentation' to the church from the Teutonic order. Nevertheless, Lehrbach thought it prudent not to upset the prince and even accommodated his guests in the Knights' quarters, when the Landgrave sponsored some tournaments later that summer.[65]

Philipp was obviously pleased with the course of events in the city. His instruction for the visitation of June 1527 required that all of Hesse

---

katholischen zur trikonfessionellen Ordensprovinz: Entwicklungslinien in der Personalstruktur der hessischen Deutschordensballei in den Jahren 1526–1680/81' in Udo Arnold and Heinz Liebling (eds), *Elisabeth, der Deutsche Orden und ihre Kirche* (Marburg, 1983), p. 196.

[59] 'Dem volk das wort gottes und das heilig evangelium lauter und rein': Franz et al. (eds), *Urkundliche Quellen*, p. 7, no. 3.

[60] Compare C. Augustijn, 'Allein Das Heilig Evangelium: het mandaat van het Reichsregiment 6 maart 1523', *Nederlands Archief voor Kerkgeschiedenis*, 48 (1968), 150–65.

[61] I can find no evidence in the documents for Hütteroth's claim that Lehrbach as patron gave approval to De Campis' installation: Oskar Hütteroth, *Kurhessische Pfarrgeschichte* (2 vols, Eschwege, 1927), ii. 5.

[62] Gerhard Müller, *Franz Lambert von Avignon und die Reformation in Hessen* (Marburg, 1958); Johann W. Baum, *Franz Lambert von Avignon nach seinen Schriften und den gleichzeitigen Quellen* (Strasbourg, Paris, 1840; reprint: Geneva, 1971); Schmitt, *Die Homberger Synode*.

[63] Philipp gave him 5 morgens (slightly more than 10 acres) of land in Kassel: Hütteroth, *Pfarrgeschichte*, ii. 5.

[64] Namely, 'einem Amando, gnant, einem verlaufenen monich, und sunst einem magistro von Fulda mit wib und kinde [Adam Krafft]': Franz, et al. (eds), *Urkundliche Quellen*, p. 36, no. 56.

[65] The games were 'Rennen und Stechen': HStAM, Bestandteil 106 b, D.O. Rechnungen no. 3, Jg. 1526–7.

follow the example of Marburg,[66] and the radical change in the Hessian Church met with surprisingly little resistance.[67] It was only when the prince's long fingers reached for the money box that the Knights finally reacted.

In late 1527, Philipp installed a warden in their house at Marburg, despite repeated opposition from the *Landkomtur*. The official, who happened to be Philipp's illegitimate stepbrother, was to monitor the finances of the house. The conflict between the Teutonic Knights and the Landgrave, however, was only temporary. Unlike the other orders in Hesse, the Knights were not only part of an international organization but also a military force upon which Philipp depended in times of need. It was a perceived threat in 1528[68] which seems the most likely reason for the favourable settlement that the Knights obtained from Philipp.[69] It stipulated that the warden was to be removed from their house in return for their agreement to pay the salaries of two preachers in Marburg and one in the town of Kirchhain. The Knights were also subjected to the same annual tax to fund the new university as all other clergy (60 Gulden).

In the summer of 1529, the preachers of Marburg reported to Philipp that the house of the Teutonic order was a den of prostitution and that people there were taking communion while drunk.[70] The preachers, who had recently implemented a 'sign-in communion' in the parish church,[71] recommended that Philipp forbid the Knights from saying mass and offering communion, but to little effect. Due to the order's strong position, it was not until 1539 that Philipp terminated the Catholic religious cult in the church of St Elisabeth by removing the patroness' shrine and scattering her sacred bones. Here is a clear example of pre-

---

[66] 'Jeden pharherr oder prediger [soll] angesagt werden, dass er es mit den ceremonien, messen und allen andern halt, wie es zu Marpurg in der phar gehalten': Franz et al. (eds), *Urkundliche Quellen*, p. 37, no. 57.

[67] This seems to suggest that it was commonly assumed that the territorial lord had the 'right' to intervene in ecclesiastical affairs. Cf. Peter Dykema's essay above.

[68] This was the 'Pack Affair': in 1528 the councillor of ducal Saxony, Otto von Pack, led Landgrave Philipp to believe that his prince, Georg of Saxony, and other Catholic princes were planning to attack Hesse and other areas where the new teachings of Luther were being institutionalized. See Kurt Dülfer, *Die Packschen Händel Darstellung und Quellen* (Marburg, 1958).

[69] HStAM, Bestandteil 3, no. 1772.

[70] 'Nicht wenige hurerei getrieben werde': Franz et al. (eds), *Urkundliche Quellen*, p. 90, no. 139.

[71] In an effort to insure the piety of those partaking in the Lord's Supper, the priest began to register each parishioner who desired to take communion. This practice became common in several Protestant Churches and continues to this day in several Lutheran bodies in North America; for an examination of the practice in England see J. P. Boulton, 'The limits of formal religion', *London Journal*, 10 (1984), 135–54.

Reformation religious ritual remaining in place despite the official Reformation of the entire territory of Hesse.

The most common response to the prince's attempts to sequestrate the monasteries was some form of compliance.[72] In Kassel, Philipp's capital for most of his reign, the first dissolution occurred in February 1526, when the Carmelite convent – of its own volition – relinquished its buildings and its 24 monks into the care of the Landgrave. This was exactly one year before the visitation orders which led to the dissolution of the vast majority of Hessian religious houses and may provide evidence of the impact of the new religious teaching at the parish level. In his official letter of release, the sub-prior of the Carmelites reported that their move was due to a decline in offerings and donations.[73] The mendicant orders may have also suffered from the consequences of a proclamation against their ownership of branch-houses (*termini*) in 1524,[74] and there are indications of general economic decline in the chapters and orders of Kassel in the early 1520s. The number of letters of credit issued by St Martin's, for example, dropped from five in 1519 and three in 1520 to two in 1521 and one in 1522. For the 12 years from 1510 to 1522 the average number of letters per year was 2.7, while no letters of credit were recorded at all after 1523.[75]

What might explain the decline in monastic support in the early 1520s? As early as 1522, a letter to Duke George of Saxony from one of his officers contained the information that there were 'many Lutherans' at Philipp's court in Kassel, even though the prince himself intended to remain in his old faith for the time being.[76] It is likely that Lutheran

---

[72] Out of more than 40 religious houses, only a few offered serious opposition to the will of the Landgrave, namely the Franciscans, the Teutonic Knights (see above), and Haina (see below).

[73] 'Das uns und unserm convent dy opfer, almuszen (darauff unser orden gestifft ist) nidderfellig werden, das wir und hinfurther mit liebs fudung [=Nahrung] nicht konnen noch mogen enthalten': Schultze (ed.), *Kassel*, p. 286, no. 740.

[74] Christoph Ludwig Kleinschmidt et al. (eds), *Sammlung fürstlich hessischer Landesordnungen und Ausschreibungen* (8 vols, Kassel, 1767–1816), i. 48.

[75] Based on HStAM, 22 a 1 f. 156ff. This decline would deserve further analysis, especially in a comparative perspective. Some recent studies have argued that late medieval piety was flourishing, rather than in decline, during the early sixteenth century. See, for instance, the recent 'revisionism' with regard to the English Reformation: C. Haigh, *English Reformations: Religion, Politics, and Society under the Tudors* (Oxford, 1993), esp. part I.

[76] 'Befinde an s. f. g. hofe vil Martinianer, aber s. f. g. bestehet uf der prube, leset ime das iczige irrige wesen nit gefalln, sagt, wolle in dem glauben, darinne er geborn un uferzogen, bleyben bys son lange bebstliche heyligkeyt, Rom. Ksl. mt. samt Cristlichen

ideas spread in the city and the court due to the Carmelites. Members of the order served as the traditional spiritual councillors to the Landgraves, and in the early 1520s Johann de Campis, who had studied and then taught in Wittenberg, became the reader (*Lesemeister*) in their monastery. Philipp appointed him to be the preacher at the Hessian court before 1525 and then commissioned him to preach in Marburg, as mentioned above.[77] It was under De Campis's influence that the Carmelites surrendered their monastery and church.

Fortunately for Philipp's budget, the Carmelites turned over their buildings and forfeited any rights to their property before he promised to compensate departing monks with a pension. Philipp gave the church of the Carmelites to one of the parishes in Kassel whose own building was dilapidated and no longer safe for use. Although the Landgrave seems to have gained the income of the monastery's former branch in Spangenberg, the financial impact of sequestration of the Carmelite monastery at the local level in Kassel was minimal. As for pastoral provision, the city gained one church, but lost 23 clergy.[78]

Since Philipp had made De Campis a canon at St Martin's Chapter in late 1525, it is not hard to imagine that it was his influence there which lead the 12 canons to accept the sequestration of their chapter without opposition. Unlike the Carmelite monastery, St Martin's had a vast array of endowments, properties, and benefices. It maintained a boys' school and 13 altars; the most venerated treasure was a piece of the authentic cross of Christ, which Landgrave Ludwig I had brought with him from Jerusalem in 1429.[79] After the sequestration Philipp determined that the income of the chapter's 12 benefices should support five Protestant pastors, a school for boys, and an ecclesiastical building fund. Thus the entire wealth of St Martin's was used for the benefit of the Hessian State Church.

The Cistercian monastery of Haina was the largest and wealthiest monastery in Hesse. It is, therefore, an especially interesting case study. How did its monks respond to Philipp's attempts at sequestration? How did its dissolution affect Hessian society and economy?

---

konigen, geystlichen und weltlichen churfursten und fursten, auch stenden der heyligen Cristenheyt eyn ander bessers vorordenen.' Sittich von Berlepsch to Georg of Saxony (25 Feb. 1522): Felician Gess (ed.), *Akten und Briefe zur Kirchenpolitik Herzog Georgs von Sachsen* (2 vols, Leipzig, 1905; Reprint: Cologne, Vienna, 1985), i. 282, no. 308.

[77] For this he was given a half acre of garden in the Neustadt of Kassel as a life long, tax free, fief: Hütteroth, *Kurhessische Pfarrgeschichte*, pp. 4–5.

[78] Schultze (ed.), *Kassel*, p. 286, no. 740.

[79] Ibid., pp. 289–440, several documents.

Unlike the Franciscans of Marburg, who fought then fled, or the Carmelites of Kassel, who complied willingly, the prior and monks of Haina persisted in their opposition to sequestration. The Recess of October 1527 claimed that the majority of monastics were fleeing their cloisters, but this was not true. Only a fraction (less then 20 per cent) of the Hessian monks had left their monasteries, even though many had been offered 'early retirement' by Philipp's visitors by this time. In Haina, for example, no more than 8 of the 36 regulars (22 per cent) had left the monastery prior to November 1527.[80] Of these eight, we know the fate of only three: two became evangelical pastors, the third was given the former Haina property (Hof) at Wildungen. It seems likely that those monks who favoured the new teachings left the monastic life willingly, while those opposed to the changes resisted the dissolution of their convent.

Philipp had taken control of the monastery in Haina before the 1527 Recess,[81] but afterwards the incentives to take 'early retirement' became imperatives.[82] On 14 November 1527, only 14 of the 40 members of the convent (both monks and lay brothers) signed formal acknowledgements that monasticism was unchristian, but virtually all the monks accepted the cash sum and/or a pension which the Landgrave 'offered' them.[83] However, eight of the 40 refused to disband,[84] and set up a convent in exile at Mainz, under the leadership of prior Flakenberg. From there they challenged Philipp in the Imperial Chamber Court (Reichskammergericht). Their efforts continued until 1539, when Philipp and the monks finally reached an agreement.[85] In exchange for with-

---

[80] HStAM, Bestandteil 22, a 1, no. 2: 'Register belangende die ausgegangene Moniche und Nonnen'. Cf. Franz (ed.), Kloster Haina, pp. 576–8, no. 1410.

[81] This is evident from the letter of Abbot Andreas von Altenberg, which lists the prince's actions and condemns them as 'allem gescriebenen geistlichen und weltlichen Recht widerstreite': ibid., p. 575, no. 1409ª. Since this letter was written on the same day as the Recess (15 Oct. 1527), the actions it describes must have taken place earlier.

[82] Ibid. and Hollenberg (ed.), Hessische Landtagsabschiede, p. 67, no. 2.

[83] Eckhart Franz, 'Die hessischen Klöster und ihre Konvente', 190–3. Midelfort's total of 36 monks ('A Protestant monastery?', p. 76) comes from his miscounting (recte 31) the document printed in Franz (ed.), Kloster Haina, no. 1415, pp. 575–9. This document from October–November 1527 only includes those monks and lay brothers who happened to be present, while Franz's list in 'Die hessischen Klöster' is comprehensive, including all 40 monks and lay brothers.

[84] In England the monks and nuns were never formally required to disband nor denounce their order's rule: see Joyce Youings, The Dissolution of the Monasteries (London, 1971), p. 13. In Hesse, on the other hand, Philipp's visitors seemed to require all monks to sign a formal statement renouncing monasticism. Such statements exist in the HStAM, Bestandteil 22.

[85] Franz (ed.), Kloster Haina, pp. 649–51, no. 1497. Some monks continued their legal efforts to no avail until 1558: ibid., pp. 658–72.

drawing all claims to the (former) properties of the convent, Philipp
allowed the monks to live at Haina's *terminus* in Frankfurt. They were
to receive the income of its other properties in that city. The prince also
gave them a generous annual pension of 200 Gulden each.[86] Only five
of the 40 monks (13 per cent) became Protestant pastors, a figure which
lies below the Hessian average of 20 per cent.[87] One fifth of the monks
of Haina became employees of the Landgrave, half of whom remained
in the buildings of the former monastery (see Figure 5.1).[88]

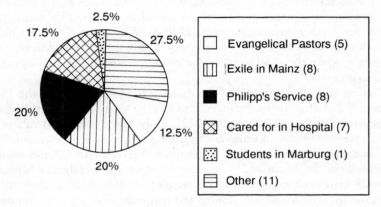

Figure 5.1   Fates of the 40 monks of Haina[89]

The dissolution of the monastery of Haina, like all the others had an
impact on more than just the lives of the former monks. What did
Philipp do with the sequestrated property and the money it produced?
The state gained a net sum of approximately 27 427 Gulden from the
former monastery of Haina and some of its *termini*. Of this amount, 71
per cent was used to fund hospitals, just over one per cent supported

---

[86] Ibid., pp. 649–51, no. 1497.

[87] Eckhart Franz, 'Die hessischen Klöster und ihre Konvente', 159.

[88] Although they were allowed to remain in the building, they were not allowed to
continue their monastic life; this contrasts with the situation in Kent: see Sibylle Schüler,
Die Klostersäkularisation in Kent (Paderborn, 1980), p. 100. For an interesting comparison of lifestyle of the Haina inhabitants before and after the Reformation see Midelfort,
'A Protestant monastery?'.

[89] Figure 5.1 is based on HStAM, 22 a 1 Pak. 2, fos 87–94. Cf. Franz (ed.), *Kloster
Haina*, p. 575, no. 1410. Three of the former monks defy simple classification: one,
Wilhelm Dolberg, first studied at Marburg and then became a pastor. Another, Johann
Hundsdorf, joined the secular clergy and was later in Philipp's service at the Haina
hospital. The third, Konrad Fleck, studied at Marburg, became the pastor of the parish
of Haina, and then worked in the hospital. In the figure, the author has counted each of
these three in only one of their later activities.

the local parish, and 16 per cent went to the new university in Marburg, whereas only 12 per cent fell into the coffers of Philipp's government (see Figure 5.2).

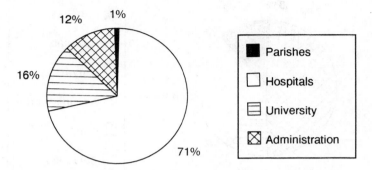

Figure 5.2   Reallocation of Haina's wealth[90]

Philipp soon mortgaged most of the small properties which the monastery had held. A total of all the receipts from May 1528 alone equals 858 Gulden, eight Gulden more than Philipp gave out in the original cash compensations to the monks of Haina.[91] If one adds all the monastery's assets, which Philipp then leased or sold as fiefs, the total exceeds 13 000 Gulden.[92] It seems that since Philipp was in a legal conflict with the exile convent of Haina, he was especially careful to see that its wealth benefited the common good.

However, the philanthropic use of Haina's wealth is not representative of the larger picture. An analysis of the reallocation of all confiscated monastic income throughout northern Hesse produces a rather different, yet still 'favourable' picture (see Figure 5.3). Administration

---

[90] The pie chart is based on the aggregate value of the properties transferred at the time of the sequestration, as calculated by W. D. Wolff, *Die Säkularisierung und Verwendung der Stifts- und Klostergüter in Hessen-Kassel unter Philipp dem Grossmütigen und Wilhelm IV* (Gotha, 1913), pp. 368–9. Wolff's work is limited to northern Hesse and not very explicit about its methodology, but no other scholar has yet attempted to calculate the entire process. His sum total represents only the values which he assigns to Haina itself (22 900 Gulden), its *terminus* in Fritzlar (1 537 Gulden), and its *terminus* in Singlis (2 990). Of these 27 427 Gulden, 291 Gulden went to the parishes, 19 321 to the hospitals, 4 390 to the University of Marburg, and only 3 425 to the state's budget.

[91] Franz (ed.), *Kloster Haina*, pp. 595–7, no. 1435.

[92] This sum is reached by adding the figures in Franz (ed.), *Kloster Haina*, pp. 609–10, no. 1453; pp. 612–18, no. 1457–9; pp. 594–5, no. 1434. Wolff, *Die Säkularisierung*, pp. 368–9, places the value at 19 475 Gulden, because he includes an approximated value of *naturalia*.

takes up the largest single part, but social and religious purposes still amount to over 50 per cent:

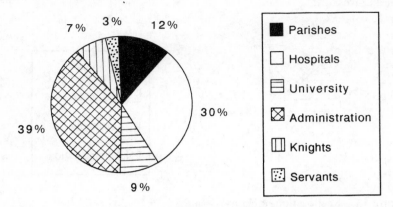

Figure 5.3   Use of the total net wealth of sequestrated Hessian religious houses[93]

Bound by the Recess of 1527 to use the income to benefit the 'common good', the Landgrave conveniently defined this to include military de-fence.[94] Since Philipp was preparing against potential Catholic attacks in 1528, he thought that he could act with good conscience. In 1529–30, his plan to re-instate Duke Ulrich of Württemberg gave him further reason to continue to use sequestrated income.[95]

Philipp's autograph memorandum of January 1527 provides evidence that the Landgrave was planning to establish some hospitals in his

[93] Wolff, *Die Säkularisierung*, pp. 368–84 (most of the transactions date from the period *c.* 1527–40). The overall pattern is clear, but the exact figures are a matter of interpretation: Midelfort, 'A Protestant monastery?', p. 75, cites Karl E. Demandt, *Geschichte des Landes Hessen* (2nd edn, Kassel, 1972), pp. 226–7, as a 'recent study' showing that roughly 60 per cent of former monastic revenues were used for philan-thropic purposes, while the other 40 per cent went to the prince's administration. However, Demandt's study, first published in 1959, seems to be based on Wolff's figures also. Eckhart Franz, in his otherwise very helpful article 'Die hessischen Klöster und ihre Konvente', 169, provides no detailed information: 'Genaue Gesamtzahlen können allerdings hier noch nicht gegeben werden.' He cites the disarray of the 'Kammer-Akten' as being the prohibitive factor. Miller, 'Dissolution of religious houses' also made no attempt to present a total fiscal picture. Nor does Kersten Krüger's otherwise useful book *Finanzstaat Hessen 1500–67* (Marburg, 1980) clarify this complicated question.

[94] In Figures 5.2 and 5.3, the category 'administration' includes military expenses of the Hessian state.

[95] Such newly acquired wealth must have also proved useful when Philipp lost 10 000 Gulden at the Diet of Augsburg while gambling with the advisor of Archduke Ferdinand: Franz et al. (eds), *Urkundliche Quellen*, pp. 164ff.

territory.[96] Yet it was only after a few years of enjoying the monasteries' wealth that Philipp decided to use the halls of Haina and three other locations for this purpose. They were to serve the medical needs of the rural population and the psychiatric needs of the territory. While hospitals for burghers and nobles already existed in Hessian cities, these country institutions were the first form of rural health care, and Haina became the first psychiatric hospital in Germany. One of the major effects of sequestration for Hessian society was the creation of 'country hospitals'.[97]

In conclusion, it is true that all the wealth of the former monasteries fell into the prince's hand, as it did in England or Württemberg, but the difference was the way in which the resources were put to use. Based on the evidence of Figure 5.3, a substantial amount of Philipp's newly acquired wealth benefited 'useful' social and religious purposes such as education, health care, and pastoral provision. Henry VIII and Duke Ulrich, in contrast, used the proceeds to finance wars and general government expenditure, rather than schools and hospitals.[98] In Hesse the sequestrated cloisters continued to provide the three commodities for which they had been founded: *caritas*, clergy, and credit. *Caritas* took the new form of hospitals, run by the state. Many of the former monks became clergy of the new Hessian Church, trained in evangelical theology in the buildings of former monasteries at Marburg. As for credit, Philipp no longer needed to make formal requests to the cloisters, for he had acquired 100 per cent of their capital. Still, unlike many of his peers, he made sure that it was not only himself who shared in the spoils of the old religion.

---

[96] 'Item zu gedenken der spitel halben': ibid., pp. 25–6, no. 37. Midelfort is evidently unaware of this document: 'It is not clear how long he had harboured such plans': 'A Protestant monastery?', p. 76. His account gives the impression that Philipp founded the hospitals several years after sequestrating the monasteries as a means of justifying his actions.

[97] See Karl Demandt, 'Die Hohen Hospitäler Hessens: Anfänge und Aufbau der Landesfürsorge für die Geistesgestörten und Körperbehinderten Hessens (1528–91)' in Walter Heinemeyer and Tilman Puender (eds), *450 Jahre Psychiatrie in Hessen* (Marburg, 1983), pp. 35–134.

[98] Youings, *Dissolution of the Monasteries*, and J. J. Scarisbrick, *Henry VIII* (London, 1968), p. 511; Brecht, *Südwestdeutsche Reformationsgeschichte*, p. 222; V. Ernst, 'Die Entstehung des württembergischen Kirchenguts', *Württembergische Jahrbücher für Statistik und Landeskunde*, 2 (1911), 386–96.

CHAPTER SIX

The fiscal Reformation: clerical taxation and opposition in Henrician England

Patrick R. N. Carter

In November 1534, following the break with Rome, the English parliament imposed two new taxes upon the clergy in perpetuity: the first fruits and tenths (the former a sum equal to a full year's income payable by every cleric upon institution to a benefice, and the latter an annual levy upon all beneficed clergy).[1] These were granted 'for the more suretye of contynuance and augmentacion of his Highnes royall astate, beinge not onely nowe recognysed (as he alwayes yn dede heretofore hathe bynne) the only supreme hede in erthe nexte and ymmediately under God of the Churche of Englande, but also their moste assured and undouted Sovereigne liege lord and Kynge'.[2] This preamble to the first fruits statute, with its fulsome praise of Henry VIII, left no doubt of the broader significance of the royal taxes intended to replace pre-Reformation papal annates, first suspended and then abolished in 1534. For the introduction of first fruits and tenths cannot be dismissed simply as financial opportunism, although the chief motive behind their imposition was unarguably fiscal. Demands for payment of first fruits and tenths were closely tied to the developing doctrine of the royal ecclesiastical supremacy. As a result, the new tax regime implemented in 1534 was to have important consequences for the crown, clergy, and laity, and swiftly became a focus of popular opposition to the religious policies pursued in England during the 1530s.

Royal taxation of the church did not originate in the break with Rome. Throughout the later Middle Ages English monarchs had regularly

---

[1] On clerical taxation during the English Reformation see F. Heal, 'Clerical tax collection under the Tudors: the influence of the Reformation' in R. O'Day and F. Heal (eds), *Continuity and Change: Personnel and Administration of the Church of England, 1500–1642* (Leicester, 1976), pp. 97–122, and P. R. N. Carter, 'Royal taxation of the English parish clergy, 1535–58' (Ph.D. Cambridge, 1994).

[2] 26 Henry VIII, c. 3: *Statutes of the Realm* (11 vols, London, 1830–52), iii. 493–4.

asserted the right to tax their clerical subjects, although the level and incidence of such fiscal demands varied considerably. Under Edward I the costs of war compelled the crown to require ever-increasing sums from the church, culminating in the king's demand of 1294 for a half of all incomes for one year.[3] Provincial clerical convocations continued to make regular grants to his successors, who also commonly retained a portion of papal taxes levied within the realm. The advent of the Tudors brought no change in the importance of clerical tax revenue to royal finances; the pre-Reformation peak came with the subsidy secured by cardinal Wolsey in 1523, estimated to be worth £120 000 over five years. By comparison, papal taxes throughout the later fifteenth and early sixteenth century were negligible. The last clerical subsidy granted by the English church to the papacy raised £14 000 in 1502 for a crusade against the Turks, while annates from bishops and abbots averaged only £2 200 per annum during the early sixteenth century.[4] The developments of 1534 in clerical taxation thus grew out of medieval precedents; their chief novelty lay in their magnitude and their association with the doctrine of the royal supremacy.

The English crown's increased taxation of the clergy after 1534 carried both fiscal and political rewards, despite promoting discontent with royal religious policies. Anxious to secure a reliable income sufficient to support royal ambitions without continual recourse to parliamentary taxes, Henry VIII and his councillors found first fruits and tenths a welcome fresh source of revenue. Initially worth nearly £50 000 per annum, the new taxes rapidly fell in value following the dissolution of the monasteries which reduced the clerical tax base considerably. After 1540, however, this decline was partially reversed by the granting of regular clerical subsidies voted by convocation (as during the 1520s) but now confirmed by parliament.[5] In total, clerical taxation during the two decades between the introduction of first fruits and tenths in 1534 and the renunciation of royal ecclesiastical revenues by Mary Tudor in

---

[3] M. Prestwich, *War, Politics, and Finance under Edward I* (London, 1972), pp. 186–91, G. L. Harriss, *King, Parliament, and Public Finance in England to 1369* (Oxford, 1975), pp. 49–52, and especially J. H. Denton, *Robert Winchelsey and the Crown, 1294–1313* (Cambridge, 1980).

[4] W. E. Lunt, *Financial Relations of the Papacy with England, 1327–1534* (Cambridge Mass., 1962), pp. 156–68, 305, 444–5, J. J. Scarisbrick, 'Clerical taxation in England, 1485–1547', *JEH*, 11 (1960), 41–54, and M. Kelly, 'Canterbury jurisdiction and influence during the episcopate of William Warham, 1501–1532' (Ph.D. Cambridge, 1965), appendix ii ('An introduction to clerical taxation under archbishop Warham').

[5] Combined annual first fruits and tenths receipts: £46 053 [1535], £51 770 [1536], £42 830 [1537], £43 616 [1538], £33 844 [1539]. During the three years 1542–44 total annual receipts for first fruits, tenths, and subsidies averaged £48 938. Compiled from BL Lansdowne MS 156, fos 137^r–139^v, 150^r–151^r, 156^r–159^r.

1555 yielded almost £750 000. While these receipts amounted to no more than a small fraction of the total royal fiscal profits of the Reformation, clerical tax receipts nonetheless comprised a crucial component of crown finances, particularly when the realm faced the crippling costs of foreign wars during the 1540s.[6]

As well as replenishing royal coffers, first fruits and tenths were important symbols of the relationship between the English church and crown following the break with Rome.[7] During the early 1530s royal political and fiscal demands upon the church were closely intertwined. In 1531, by encouraging fears of a general prosecution for *praemunire*, Henry VIII succeeded in extracting from the clergy a limited recognition of his title as supreme head of the English church, together with a substantial subsidy.[8] There was a similar link three years later: parliamentary approval of the first fruits statute in November 1534 coincided with a restatement of the declaration of the royal ecclesiastical supremacy, without its earlier restricting clause ('quantum per Christi legem licet'). Analogous to the feudal dues demanded of new tenants and officials by their lords, the very act of paying first fruits was invested with considerable symbolic significance. As an expression of the new relationship between church and crown, payment of the taxes was enhanced by the replacement of the standard papal term 'annates' by 'first fruits', for the latter derived from the thankofferings to God required under the Mosaic law. The transformation of a papal levy into a perpetual royal tax reflected Henry VIII's elevated status as the *dominus in capite* of the English church and her property, both spiritual and temporal.

The economic consequences of increased taxation for parish clergy varied greatly according to individual circumstances. The burden did not fall equally upon all. As taxes upon benefices rather than individual clergy, first fruits and tenths did not affect curates and stipendiary clergy, although the inclusion of a poll tax in clerical subsidies from 1540 once more brought unbeneficed clergy within the ranks of clerical taxpayers. Wealthier pluralists were able to survive on the profits of one

---

[6] During the early 1540s crown revenue from ex-monastic lands, by comparison, averaged approximately £220 000 *per annum*. See P. A. Cunich, 'The administration and alienation of ex-monastic lands by the crown: 1536–47' (Ph.D. Cambridge, 1990), pp. 203–5.

[7] The best recent study of the royal supremacy, although it makes only brief mention of clerical taxation, is R. Rex, *Henry VIII and the English Reformation* (London, 1993).

[8] The fiscal importance of *praemunire* proceedings is examined in J. A. Guy, 'Henry VIII and the *praemunire* manoeuvres of 1530–1', *EHR*, 97 (1982), 481–503. For a different interpretation of events cf. G. W. Bernard, 'The pardon of the clergy reconsidered', *JEH*, 37 (1986), 258–82.

benefice while discharging the first fruits of another, but their poorer colleagues faced considerable hardships. The imposition of first fruits discouraged clergy from resigning one benefice in favour of another, since it might be several years before the lost income would be re-couped. Although permitted to compound for the sum due, and thereby pay in several instalments, prospective incumbents nonetheless faced a considerable reduction in income (in addition to obligatory payments to archdeacons, registrars, and patrons incurred in the course of securing presentation and induction to their livings). The dilemma for new in-cumbents was presented in a sermon delivered at Paul's Cross in 1547: 'I pray you to loke yf there be any provyso howe the prestes shall lyve for that yere'.[9] The plight of poor clergy was particularly acute. John Rote, an ex-monk in Northampton, was assigned a vacant vicarage in the town (valued at only £7 *per annum*) in lieu of a pension. In their report the local commissioners strongly recommended that Rote's first fruits be remitted 'leste the pore man shuld bege in the meantime'.[10] An allowance for incumbents whose livings did not exceed eight marks (£5 6s. 8d.) in annual value to pay nothing for their first three years offered some comfort to the poorest beneficed clergy, but did nothing to lift the burden for the majority. Prior to the Reformation payment of papal annates had been largely confined to the ranks of the higher clergy, while medieval assessments for royal tenths and other subsidies usually included generous allowances. Both the costs of necessary repairs and curates' stipends (taxed separately) were generally deducted from in-cumbents' incomes. By contrast from 1535 royal first fruits were paid by all new incumbents (however mean their benefice), while annual tenths affected all beneficed clergy immediately. Furthermore, these taxes were based upon a rigorous new assessment which more accur-ately reflected clerical incomes.

Since most parish clergy depended upon the laity for their livelihoods, whether through tithes, offerings, or cash stipends, the dramatic in-crease in the level of clerical taxation had serious repercussions for laymen as well. First fruits made the task of securing an incumbent more difficult; many of the reassessments of decayed benefices were undertaken at the suit of parishioners unable to attract suitable clergy without some tax relief. When clerical incomes were threatened, the burden ultimately fell upon parishioners, as in the Northampton parish of St Gregory, where it proved impossible to secure an incumbent owing

---

[9] PRO SP 1/228, fos 55ᵛ–56ʳ; S. Brigden, *London and the Reformation* (Oxford, 1989), p. 379. The preacher was John Feckenham, chaplain to Bishop Bonner of London and later abbot of Westminster.

[10] BL Cottonian Cleopatra E IV, f. 238ᵛ.

to high taxes and declining income, 'without the further charges of the said parissheners to be contributories to the salarie and here [hire] of the saide priste'.[11] Yet if clergy and laity were joined by a common concern with the damage to clerical livings caused by excessive taxation, first fruits and tenths also fostered friction between them. Facing a serious loss of income because of taxation and attacks upon sources of casual revenue such as pilgrimages, clergy sought to enforce their remaining rights through vigorous prosecution of tithe suits and demands for full fees for pastoral services. The link between parochial offerings and payment of taxes was acknowledged in 1553 when the deadline for annual tenth collection was pushed back from 1 April until 31 May. Many parish clergy relied upon Easter offerings for the coin with which to pay their tenths, but as this income was tied to a moveable feast they frequently failed to meet their obligation to the king.[12] Some parishioners and relatives of clergy were more directly affected by royal demands for first fruits, since they acted as sureties for new incumbents compounding for first fruits. In the event of default the crown did not hesitate to proceed against the sureties to recover arrears. Laymen could not afford to ignore changes in clerical taxation during the 1530s, for ultimately any reduction in clerical incomes merely increased financial demands upon parish coffers.[13] Patrons and parishioners were thus forced to share the burden imposed upon the clergy in 1534.

Unlike his fellow princes in Hesse and some other continental states, Henry VIII made no serious attempt to devote any of the profits of the fiscal Reformation in England to either educational or pious purposes.[14] On the contrary, the introduction of first fruits seriously threatened the finances of the universities, where fellows of colleges found themselves liable for the new taxes. In the spring of 1535 Oxford colleges were suing for reductions in their assessments, alleging decay and insupportable charges. Balliol, amongst other colleges, claimed to be in 'extreme povertye'; a decline in rental income had led to a decrease in the number of fellows, and unless the looming burden of taxation were lessened, the situation would deteriorate further.[15] At Cambridge the crisis was claimed to be

---

[11] PRO E 347/17/1.

[12] 7 Edward VI, c. 4 (*Statutes of the Realm*, iv/i. 168): 'for that the Persons Vicars and Curates within this Realme for the most parte bee not hable to paye their Tenthes before that they shall have receyeved the profites of their Benefices whiche yerely growethe and rennethe to them at the feast of Easter, whiche feast in many yeres fallethe after the first daye of Aprill'.

[13] Contributions from churchwardens' funds grew steadily under Henry VIII, particularly during the late 1530s: B. Kümin, 'Parish finance and the early Tudor clergy' in A. Pettegree (ed.), *The Reformation of the Parishes* (Manchester, 1993), p. 54.

[14] See R. Cahill's essay in this volume.

[15] PRO E 344/12, fos 220v–221r.

equally grave. The royal visitors informed Thomas Cromwell in October 1535 that 'we found the nombre of felowes decreased for that (as they said) they that were chosen felowes were not able to pay the kings first frutes'. Corroborating the colleges' complaints, the visitors recommended that Cromwell, as chancellor, should consider some relief for the university.[16] Both Oxford and Cambridge embarked upon an intense lobbying effort, writing to the king and queen and enlisting the support of the visitors. In July 1535 Cambridge wrote to Anne Boleyn beseeching her assistance: the university protested that the inevitable consequence of the new taxes upon the university would be 'the greate losse and decay of larnynge and goodde lettres and the fynall damage of the publique and commonwealth of this realme'. This letter was followed two weeks later by similar petitions from Oxford.[17]

This concerted campaign to secure some relief bore fruit in early 1536, when parliament passed an act exonerating the universities (together with Eton and Winchester) from payment of first fruits and tenths upon their incomes, although fellows presented to other benefices remained liable for the taxes. In gratitude Cambridge addressed an effusive letter of thanks to the queen for promoting their suit.[18] While an early draft of the 1536 statute declared that the king's generosity was founded upon his 'muche more estymyng thincrease of godly larnyng and spiritual treasure than any purchase of worldelye riches whiche is transitory' and made no mention of any obligations to be laid upon the universities in return, the final version stipulated various acts to commemorate this royal benevolence.[19] In addition to the provision of annual masses for the king (and obits following his death), each university was to appoint and pay one lecturer, to be known henceforth as the 'King Henry VIII lecturer'. At Cambridge a lecturership in Greek was created, funded through quarterly assessments from the colleges, while Oxford colleges contributed a total of twenty marks (£13 6s. 8d.) for the salary of a *praelector theologicae*, in compliance with the requirements of the statute.[20] The universities thus escaped the potentially

---

[16] PRO SP 1/98, f. 110[r].

[17] D. Wilkins, *Concilia Magnae Britanniae et Hiberniae* (4 vols, London, 1737), iii. 811–12; *LP* ix, no. 13, 4; BL Cotton. Faustina C III, f. 481[r].

[18] 27 Henry VIII, c. 42 (*Statutes of the Realm*, iii. 599–600); *LP* x, no. 345, 130; Cambridge University Archives Luard 163 (letters patent of *inspeximus* confirming the exoneration). The university paid 23s. in fees to obtain the letters patent (M. Bateson (ed.), *Grace Book B part II* (Cambridge, 1905), p. 208).

[19] PRO SP 1/101, f. 354[r].

[20] See D. H. Leader, *A History of the University of Cambridge*, vol. i: The University to 1546 (Cambridge, 1988), pp. 333–5, and G. D. Duncan, 'Public lectures and professorial chairs' in J. McConica (ed.), *The History of the University of Oxford*, vol. iii: The Collegiate University (Oxford, 1986), p. 343.

crippling burden of royal taxation upon college incomes, at relatively little cost to themselves, apart from flattering Henry VIII's reputation as a patron of scholarship.

In marked contrast to the success of the universities in escaping from demands for first fruits, a parallel attempt to exempt chantry priests who ran schools failed. The promoters of the proposal argued that these chantry schoolmasters deserved favourable treatment: 'for that theyr offices industryes and labours [are] no less paynfull then necessarye to the contynuance of a publyque or a comenwelth'. The supporters of these schools lacked the political influence enjoyed by Oxford and Cambridge, however, and any exemption of such chantry priests would have set an unwise precedent, while not gaining the same recognition which followed from Henry's benevolence to the universities.[21]

Attempts by English monarchs to treat the church and clergy as their other subjects in matters of taxation provoked considerable opposition. During the later Middle Ages the church fought to restrict royal taxation. The efforts of Edward I during the 1290s to tax both temporalities and spiritualities faced determined resistance from the English clergy and hierarchy (fortified by the papal bull *Clericis Laicos*), but threats of outlawry and a papal retreat eventually compelled the church to capitulate to royal demands.[22] Although in practice the crown's direct right to tax the clergy came to be tolerated, levies (especially upon the poorer parish clergy) remained deeply unpopular; Wolsey's subsidy in the mid-1520s met with 'more untowardenes than towardenes', according to archbishop Warham.[23] It is scarcely surprising, therefore, that the introduction of first fruits and tenths should fan the flames of popular discontent with the fiscal and religious policies pursued by the crown during the 1530s. Both clerics and laymen feared the consequences of the new taxes upon clerical purses and parish coffers, and moreover recognised their place in the planned destruction of the old religion.

Opposition to the new taxes was detected as early as March 1535, when levying of first fruits and tenths had scarcely begun. Martin Bassett, vicar of the impoverished St Clement's in Cambridge, complained to an acquaintance in a local tavern that his benefice was 'veary small in valewe and not able to fynde hym by reasons of the great payments that he sholde make yerely to the kyng'. Emboldened by

---

[21] PRO SP 1/104, fos 151ʳ–154ʳ; SP 1/108, fos 12ʳ, 251ʳ; SP 1/110, f. 102ʳ; S. E. Lehmberg, *The Reformation Parliament, 1529–1536* (Cambridge, 1970), p. 230.

[22] Prestwich, *War, Politics, and Finance*, pp. 86–7, and Denton, *Winchelsey*, pp. 55–99.

[23] PRO SP 1/234, f. 242ʳ; G. W. Bernard, *War, Taxation, and Rebellion in Early Tudor England: Henry VIII, Wolsey, and the Amicable Grant of 1525* (Brighton, 1986), pp. 102, 105.

wine, Bassett went on to declare that 'raither than the kyng shold have this money paide to hym and his successors accordyng to the Acte [of 1534] yt were better that the kyng had no hed above his shoulders nor none that shold succede hym'. When challenged by his companion, the vicar declared that 20 000 men in England were of like mind. Unfortunately for the bibulous Bassett, his friend did not number among them, and the vicar was promptly reported to the mayor of Cambridge who despatched him to Cromwell for examination (although he appears to have escaped with nothing more than a stern warning).[24]

Simmering popular discontent with religious changes, including attacks upon monastic foundations and increased taxation of the parish clergy, boiled over in October 1536. At Louth in Lincolnshire the diocesan registrar John Frankish, who had arrived to examine assembled local clergy on the valuations of their benefices, was attacked and his baggage looted. Amongst the papers burned by the crowd was a volume listing the values of livings; Frankish also served as diocesan collector of the new clerical tenth (a fact which probably fuelled local clerical anger).[25] Studies of the Lincolnshire revolt and the Pilgrimage of Grace which followed have acknowledged the importance of taxation as a grievance but fail to appreciate the significance of first fruits and tenths in combining the twin concerns of the rebels with the subversion of true religion and the weakening of the commonwealth. Laymen regarded the introduction of first fruits and clerical tenths as a dangerous constitutional innovation, for they were direct taxes granted in perpetuity. They also linked the imposition of heavier royal taxes upon the clergy to a general royal attack upon the church; the rebel leader Robert Aske declared that 'in all parts of the realme mens herts much grogs [grudge] with the supression of the Abbeys and the furst fruts by reason the same wold be the distruccion of the holl relegion in Ingland'. To these fears were added other more purely economic concerns as well, for it was widely believed that increased taxation and royal collection of monastic rents and revenues would lead to a shortage of specie, crippling commerce.[26]

[24] PRO SP 1/92, f. 187[r].

[25] For events at Louth see M. Bowker, 'Lincolnshire 1536: heresy, schism, or religious discontent?' in D. Baker (ed.), Schism, Heresy, and Religious Protest, SCH ix (Cambridge, 1972), pp. 195–212.

[26] PRO E 36/118, f. 32[v] (examination of Robert Aske); M. L. Bush, 'Tax reform and rebellion in early Tudor England', History, 76 (1991), 379–400, '"Up for the Commonweal": The significance of tax grievances in the English rebellions of 1536', EHR, 106 (1991), 299–318, and his '"Enhancements and Importunate Charges": An analysis of the tax complaints of October 1536', Albion, 22 (1990), 403–19.

Apart from those clergy punished following the Pilgrimage of Grace, only one priest is known to have suffered in part for his criticism of clerical taxation. In 1538 George Croft, a wealthy West Country pluralist and royal chaplain, denied the royal supremacy, upheld the primacy of the papacy, and was punished accordingly. He was certainly an acquaintance of Sir Geoffrey Pole, and was implicated in the Exeter conspiracy.[27] Some of Croft's criticism of the Henrician church was directed toward royal taxation of the clergy, characterizing the first fruits statute as 'a very oncharitable law'; during examination in the Tower he admitted denouncing the payment of first fruits as 'a greyvous joyke' or deceit. His interrogators displayed a determined interest in discovering the extent of clerical discontent, demanding to know how common such views were in Croft's circle.[28] As a result of his opposition to the supremacy, manifested through hostility to royal demands for first fruits, Croft was tried for treason and executed. His exemplary punishment, while attributable in large measure to association with Pole and his supporters, remained a stern warning of the potential price of hostility towards royal taxation of the church. Henry's prerogative to raise revenue from the clergy was inextricably bound with his supreme headship, and criticism of the former could conveniently be construed as a coded comment upon the latter.

The cries raised against first fruits and tenths were not confined to 1536. Many lesser clergy no doubt shared the view of Thomas Cruch, vicar of Walberton, Sussex, who grumbled that following the introduction of clerical tenths 'the kyng had soe myche of the prysts withyn this Realme, that he cowde never spend hyt well yn good use'.[29] While displaying a woeful if understandable ignorance of the frailties of royal finances, Cruch was certainly not alone in his views. Nor were such sentiments confined to the lower parochial clergy. Dr Richard Benger, a prosperous and conservative Kentish cleric, was equally vocal in his criticism of the subsidy voted by convocation in 1540.[30] During a

---

[27] At the time of his arrest Croft possessed five rectories in Dorset, Somerset, Oxfordshire, and Devon, and had been a royal chaplain since 1531. He also held several posts in Chichester cathedral during the 1520s and early 1530s: A. B. Emden, *Biographical Register of the University of Oxford, 1501–1540* (Oxford, 1972), p. 150. See also M. H. Dodds and R. Dodds, *The Pilgrimage of Grace and the Exeter Conspiracy* (2 vols, London, repr. 1971), ii. 297–328.

[28] PRO SP 1/138, f. 211r; SP 1/139, f. 21v.

[29] PRO SP 1/131, f. 111r.

[30] PRO STAC 2/8, f. 77r. Benger was rector of two Kent parishes, Brasted and Woodchurch, as well as canon of Wingham. He had already developed a reputation for outspoken criticism of the new order in religion. On an earlier occasion, standing before a warm fire, he mischievously suggested to a chaplain of Archbishop Cranmer that it would be a fine thing to roast those of the 'new learning' over such flames. Benger's case

heated exchange with archbishop Cranmer, Benger allegedly 'marveiled of suche payments as were graunted to the kyngis grace considering the excidyng somes of money which his grace had receyvid of the houses suppresid'. Although later denying these specific words, he admitted saying that 'yf all the goodes of thabbeis came to the kingis handes, that then he the kingis grace should have no nede to have the said twoo dymys [that is, the recent clerical subsidy]'. In his view excessive taxation of the clergy was a sin, and Henry would surely be damned for 'taking godds part'. Benger added a personal rebuke of the archbishop, who should have been a firm opponent of the taxes and guardian of the welfare of his clergy, 'for so were the Archebisshopps herebefore wonte to be'. He repeated Ezekiel's denunciation of the false prophets who had neglected the welfare of Israel, leaving God's chosen people defenceless: 'O Israel, thy prophets are like the foxes in the desert. Ye have not gone up into the gaps, neither made up the hedge for the house of Israel to stand in the day of the Lord'. This portrayal of Cranmer as a negligent prophet clearly stung, and unfavourable contrasts between Henry's primate and early defenders of clerical liberties like Becket and Winchelsey were neither politic nor wise.[31] While some lesser clergy might escape serious punishment for grumbling about contributing to the crown's coffers, Benger faced charges of treason for his outburst. Astonishingly, he was acquitted by a jury in Kent, to the evident displeasure of the archbishop and council. The reluctance of the laity of Kent to condemn Benger may have been an early warning of the hostility of a large portion of Kentish society to Cranmer and his policies, which emerged later in the so-called 'prebendaries' plot'.[32] At the same time, it perhaps betrays a deeper lay unease with the increasing fiscal demands made by Henry upon the church.

Conscious of a growing coalition between conservative clergy and laity, the crown attempted to isolate clerical grievances and undermine any sympathy which might exist in lay society for the parish priests' plight, arguing that 'this matier of the tenthe touchethe only prests and men of religion'.[33] Such a division between secular and spiritual grievances was implicitly challenged, however, by the leading citizens of

---

is discussed in detail in G. R. Elton, *Policy and Police: The Enforcement of the Reformation in the Age of Thomas Cromwell* (Cambridge, 1972), pp. 317–21, and P. Clark, *English Provincial Society from the Reformation to the Revolution: Religion, Politics and Society in Kent 1500–1640* (Hassocks, 1977), pp. 61–2.

[31] Benger was alleged to have quoted from Ezekiel 13.5: 'Non ascenditis ex adverso, neque opposuistis murum pro domo Israel, ut staretis in proelio in die Domini'. The precise text was a source of some controversy during his later examination by Cranmer.

[32] Clark, *English Provincial Society*, pp. 57–66.

[33] PRO SP 1/114, f. 23v.

Coventry who argued in 1547 that the high assessment of the vicarage of Holy Trinity and the resulting excessive sums due for clerical taxes prevented them from finding anyone prepared 'to be owre pastor to feede us gostly with gods worde, and to minister unto us the holy sacraments as to Christis flocke behovyth'. The laity attributed the decay of livings and the consequent need to alleviate the burden of taxation to the recent changes in religion. The prohibition of pilgrimages to the image of the rood at St Gregory's church in Northampton meant that the parish could 'gett no prist to mynster and serve the cure', since first fruits for a new incumbent would be £10, while the living was estimated to be worth no more than £3. In Coventry and Northampton the high level of clerical taxation, compounded by worsening economic conditions and the financial consequences of changes in religious policy, aroused the anger of parishioners who believed that the provision of services in their local parish churches was being adversely affected.[34]

A similar point was made by the London mercer Henry Brinklow, albeit in a more forthright manner and from a reformer's perspective. In his 1543 *Complaynt of Roderyck Mors* he vigorously attacked the extension of the old papal annates to all beneficed clergy: 'All men must so often pay, pay, that a man if he toke not good hede wold thynk, that the latyn papa were translated into English ... I think the kyngs grace could be as well content to scrape out this uncharytable pay pay, as he was to put out of his realme that Romyssh papa'. Taxation of the clergy, especially the levying of first fruits, was 'cleane contrary to the word of God, and playn robbry, if men durst so call it'. Citing Deuteronomy, St Paul had urged the adequate maintenance of ministers: 'The elders that rule well, are worthy of double honoure, most specially they which labour in the worde and teachinge. For the scripture sayeth: thou shalt not moosel the mouth of the oxe that treadeth out the corne'. The exaction of first fruits violated this injunction and tarnished the purity of the English Reformation. Brinklow angrily demanded: 'shall not he then do a Christen preacher wrong, and breake Gods commandment, that moselyth hym for the space of whole xij monthes, though he never so diligently treade out the corne of Gods word, that the peple may eate and digest it'.[35] Whether articulated by conservatives or reformers, clerics or laymen, the arguments against first fruits and tenths (and

---

[34] PRO E 347/17/1 (petition to Lord Chancellor Wriothesley from the mayor and citizens of Coventry, 1547; and return of a commission concerning the valuation of St Gregory, Northampton, 1546).

[35] J. M. Cowper (ed.), *Henry Brinklow's Complaynt of Roderyck Mors*, Early English Text Society, Extra Series xxii (London, 1874), pp. 39–40.

clerical subsidies) shared much in common. Clerical taxation was tanta-mount to sacrilege, representing a misdirection of the resources and wealth of the church from their rightful purposes to the king's own use and thereby undermining the protection and promotion of true religion (howsoever defined).

Local lay opposition to clerical taxation was certainly encouraged by the clergy. Anticlerical polemics commonly accused conservative priests of stirring their flocks to revolt, spreading sedition, and fulminating against the suppression of abbeys, the exaction of first fruits, and the spread of the 'new learning'. One tract depicted the parson's heart as 'full of malice sorow greef displeasure and rancor', and claimed that his sole pastoral objective was to foster hostility to the changes among his flock.[36] Ever cunning and dissembling, he would encourage grumbling in the tavern, skilfully steering the conversation towards the poverty of his parishioners, which he then attributed solely to the changes in religion:

> What marvaile is it then saieth master parsone thoughe we have no money how many thousande poundes by yere goeth now to Lon-don for the rents of abbey lands, for first fruicts, for tenths, for lones subsidies benivolences fyvteenes and such other ... which alle heretofore good neighbours was woont to be spent here in the cuntre for victualls among us.[37]

The threat to the rural economy posed by the new taxes upon the clergy, combined with the seizure of monastic incomes, had been one of the principal grievances of the revolts of 1536. The anonymous author of this tract claimed that the ignorant laity were easily led astray by such crafty clerics intent upon fomenting rebellion and restoring 'the liberties of their malignant church'. Similar concerns were voiced in an anonymous memorial addressed to Cromwell, which pointed out the potential problems in permitting the bishops to retain responsibility for collecting the new clerical tenth. They might be tempted to use the money to further the cause of reestablishing the papal authority in England.[38] A conservative episcopate may have had some misgivings about the new taxes (although the role of the hierarchy in the collection

---

[36] In the anonymous 'Treatise on the Evils of the Realm' (c.1542–50), BL Royal MS 17 B XXXV, f. 6ʳ. During the 1549 rising in the West Country, the council strove to counter rumours being spread among the populace by 'popish priests': J. Cornwall, *Revolt of the Peasantry 1549* (London, 1977), p. 88.

[37] BL Royal MS 17 B XXXV, f. 9ʳ⁻ᵛ.

[38] PRO SP 1/99, f. 227ʳ. The same writer argued the necessity of using ecclesiastical revenue in the crown's possession for charitable purposes, for the good of the common-wealth: 'for els it wilbe thought that al theyse tenths, primitiae fruts and suppresyd lands be taken only of covetyse and not of charytye'.

of royal taxation was long established), but the fear of funding papal restoration was groundless. Of far greater danger was the ammunition the new exactions provided to digruntled parish clergy anxious to undermine the changes of the 1530s while countering the threat increased taxation posed to their economic welfare.

As with attacks upon lucrative ceremonies and the assault upon the abbeys, first fruits, clerical tenths, and other exactions weakened the economic status of the clergy and became a focus for discontent during the later 1530s. The payment of taxes by clergy to the crown without the consent of the provincial convocations reinforced the king's position as supreme head of the church. While isolated grumbling might safely be overlooked, the revolts of 1536 and the trials of Benger and Croft demonstrate that the crown did not always tolerate criticism of its ecclesiastical policies – policies in which taxation was an integral part. Squeezed between rising prices and an increasing burden of taxation, clergy feared for their economic survival and endeavoured to enlist the laity in their cause. Lay opposition, in turn, centred on the consequences of clerical impoverishment for parish life, while those sympathetic to reform lamented the diversion of financial resources from the provision of pastors and preachers to the crown's coffers. The concerns expressed by laymen for the economic survival of the parochial clergy, while encouraged by conservative clerics attempting to undermine the new order, highlight the fears among the parishioners that the Henrician Reformation threatened much more than their parish priest's purse. The political, social, and religious consequences of increased clerical taxation were considerable but ambiguous; the imposition of first fruits and tenths prompted many clergy to assert their rights more vigorously, creating friction with lay parishioners over questions of tithes and customary payments. At the same time, however, the existence of clear empathy between clergy and laity lends credence to the arguments of those critics of previous Protestant historiography intent upon undermining the place of popular anticlericalism in the origins of the English Reformation.[39]

Assessing the abolition of papal annates and the subsequent imposition of royal first fruits and tenths, the eighteenth-century ecclesiastical historian Jeremy Collier observed that 'even tho' the person was chang'd, the burthen continued, and the church had only the liberty of paying

---

[39] Especially C. Haigh, 'Anticlericalism and the English Reformation' in his *The English Reformation Revised* (Cambridge, 1987), pp. 56–74.

her money to another hand'.[40] Such a neat summation is misleading, however, for it overlooks the ample medieval precedents for royal as well as papal taxation of the English church, while underestimating both the significance of the doctrine of the royal supremacy for fiscal theory in early modern England and the harshness of the tax regime introduced in 1534. For the crown the changes in taxation which accompanied the Henrician Reformation brought increased control over the clergy and also considerable revenue, while clergy and laity faced economic burdens which hindered the progress of reform and stirred resentment against royal policies. Despite the measure of leniency displayed towards the universities, the consequences for the reputation of reform were serious. During the later years of the reign of Henry VIII increased clerical taxation directed resources away from the educational and pastoral work of the English church and the advancement of reforms, towards costly military campaigns in France and Scotland. This diversion of ecclesiastical revenues drew charges of sacrilege, uniting reformers and conservatives alike in criticism of the fiscal Reformation of the 1530s.

---

[40] J. Collier, *An Ecclesiastical History of Great Britain* (2 vols, London, 1708–14), i. 503.

PART THREE
Ecclesiastical patronage

Episcopal patronage and social mobility in late medieval and Reformation Denmark

Per Ingesman

Since the establishment of history as a modern academic discipline at the end of the nineteenth century, Danish historiography has been characterized by a strong materialist emphasis.[1] Great stress, therefore, has been laid on the fact that the Danish Reformation of 1536 was a social, economic, and political, as well as – or perhaps even more than – a religious or theological event. In his famous dissertation of 1879 on the relationship between crown and nobility in the sixteenth century, the founding father of modern Danish historiography, Kristian Erslev, frankly set out to study 'the state revolution of 1536 and its consequences to royal and noble power'.[2] And if a revolution is defined as a fundamental change in the distribution of economic wealth and political power, brought about by violent means, it is difficult to deny that the Danish Reformation was one.

The religious changes were carried out by King Christian III (1534–59). Because of his well-known Lutheran sympathies, the Council of the Realm had refused to elect him as successor after the death of his father, King Frederick I (1523–33). Civil war broke out between Christian and adherents of his cousin, King Christian II (1513–23), whom his father had deposed ten years earlier. When after two years of war Christian stood victorious in Copenhagen, he immediately carried out a *coup d'état* against the Council of the Realm. The Council consisted of the seven Danish bishops, together with a number of leading noblemen, but Christian III and his advisers decided to proceed against the bishops alone. They were placed under arrest and the noble members of the

---

[1] The authors thanks Ken Farnhill (Cambridge) and the editor who willingly undertook the task of improving the language of the original draft. Their joint effort did a lot to enhance the style of the argument.

[2] Kr. Erslev, *Konge og Lensmand i det sextende Aarhundrede: Studier over Statsomvæltningen i 1536 og dens Følger for Kongemagt og Adelsvælde* (Copenhagen, 1879).

Council were faced with an ultimatum: either they gave their consent to the deposition of the bishops – or they would be imprisoned themselves! The nobility consented, and in a series of documents set up over the next few months the Reformation was given a legal facade: The bishops were declared solely responsible for the civil war, because of this alleged crime against the realm they were deprived of their position, and as compensation for the damage they had caused to the king their estates were handed over to the crown.[3]

The consequences of the events of 1536 were no less revolutionary than the way they were undertaken. The Council of the Realm was the only political body of later medieval and early modern Denmark, so the removal of the bishops at a stroke deprived the church of its part in political power. But it lost its economic position, too, as the King took over the estates of the bishops and of the landowning monasteries. In both cases the nobility was to benefit, politically, because it became the only counterpart to the king in the government of the realm, and economically, because the crown gradually sold off the greater part of the confiscated ecclesiastical property. Reducing the powerful medieval church to a mere branch of early modern state administration, the Reformation left the nobility as the only group in Danish society with landed wealth, privileges, and political power.

The *consequences* of the Danish Reformation, however, have not been at the centre of recent historiography. Most socio-economic research has concentrated on the *background* of the events, trying to identify developments in later medieval society which made the revolution of 1536 possible. This emphasis reflects an important trend in Danish historiography since the 1960s, namely the concern with the social and economic changes following the so-called 'late medieval crisis'.[4]

From the end of the fourteenth to the beginning of the sixteenth century Danish society went through a process of social, economic, and political restructuring after the devastating effects of the Black Death around 1350. The period was thus characterized by an extraordinarily high degree of social mobility. It is perhaps most easily recognized

---

[3] For recent surveys of the Danish Reformation in English see Leif Grane and Kai Hørby (eds), *Die dänische Reformation vor ihrem internationalen Hintergrund: The Danish Reformation against its International Background* (Copenhagen, 1990), and Ole Peter Grell (ed.), *The Scandinavian Reformation: From Evangelical Movement to Institutionalisation of Reform* (Cambridge, 1995).

[4] An up-to-date introduction to research on Denmark in the later Middle Ages, with a comprehensive bibliography, in Per Ingesman and Jens Villiam Jensen (eds), *Danmark i Senmiddelalderen* (Aarhus, 1994).

among the secular élites of nobility and gentry.[5] An examination of the leading noble families at the time of the Reformation shows that none of them had belonged to the leading aristocracy at the time of the Black Death. And while prominent noble families disappeared, often under obscure circumstances, new families rose to take over their position. Plenty of examples show how families which were at best part of the lower gentry at the end of the fourteenth century worked their way up into the richest and most influential circles at the beginning of the sixteenth. The most remarkable feature, however, is that to a great extent the gentry was 'open' at its lower end, too; that there were frequent and easy crossings of the borderline between peasants and burgesses on the one hand and gentry on the other.[6]

An important role in this process was played by the benefices of the church, especially the bishoprics and the canonries in the cathedral chapters. Canonries offered an opportunity for people of non-gentry or non-noble origin to reach a position in society where they would, in many ways, be equal to the aristocracy. Bishoprics were of even greater importance as instruments of social mobility. Some bishops definitely were of humble origin, and even if the majority had a gentry background, they did not come from the most prosperous families. A typical bishop of the later Middle Ages, therefore, was a man who had made his way up, and then enabled his relatives, his friends, and his clients to follow his lead.[7] This is where patronage comes into the picture.

---

[5] Although I have used the English terms 'nobility' and 'gentry' it is important to remember that in Denmark there were no formal dividing lines between the two. They were one group: the *adel*, the class of people owning land without having to pay tax on it, in return for the obligation of doing military service for the king. And yet, there were enormous social, economic, and political differences between the higher-ranking 'nobility', and the lower-ranking 'gentry'. The nobility had rich possessions; from 100 up to 1 000 tenant farms, it received from the crown the important fiefs with castles and local administrative functions, and it had political influence, perhaps even a seat in the Council of the Realm. The gentry, on the other hand, or at least the lower part of it, resembled the class of yeomen. Poor gentry families often owned but a small manor house with no more demesne land than that of a wealthy yeoman or humbler tenant. In the aftermath of the agrarian crisis they were constantly under pressure to sell their estates to the nobility or the church. One of their means of survival was to enter into client relations to bishops or noblemen.

[6] Erik Ulsig, *Danske Adelsgodser i Middelalderen*, Skrifter udgivet af Det historiske Institut ved Københavns Universitet ii (Copenhagen, 1968); Troels Dahlerup, 'Lavadelens Krise i dansk Senmiddelalder', *Historisk Tidsskrift*, 12th series 4 (1969–70), 1–43; Troels Dahlerup, 'Danmark' in *Den nordiske Adel i Senmiddelalderen: Struktur, funktioner og internordiske relationer*, Rapporter til det nordiske historikermøde i København 1971 9–12 August (Copenhagen, 1971), pp. 45–80. An English summary in Troels Dahlerup, 'Heraldry and Social Change in Late Medieval Denmark' in *Genealogica & Heraldica Copenhagen 1980* (Copenhagen, 1982), pp. 35–42.

[7] Dahlerup, 'Danmark', pp. 52–4.

In this paper I will discuss episcopal patronage as one of the means promoting the high degree of social mobility in later medieval Denmark. The argument is based on two substantial studies, one on the estate administration of the Danish archbishops of Lund in the later Middle Ages, the other on the composition of the cathedral chapter of the archbishop in the same period (c. 1400–1536).[8] We shall start by looking at the role of patronage in ecclesiastical careers in general (i), before concentrating on the forms of patronage exercized by the bishops (ii). In conclusion we will return to the Danish Reformation, discussing the events of 1536 against their late medieval background, in particular the possible influence of episcopal patronage, with the social structures it created, on the course of the Reformation, and the impact of religious change on the system of patronage and social mobility in general (iii).

(i)

It is difficult to assess the precise role of patronage in late medieval ecclesiastical careers. To a certain degree this is due to the nature of the phenomenon itself, but it also reflects the nature of the surviving Danish source material. There is normally little information on the early careers of clergymen, even in the case of otherwise well-documented prelates. Prosopographical studies of important clerical groups like bishops or cathedral canons are of great value, of course, but in the main we have to base our conclusions on individual examples.[9]

I am, therefore, going to start with a case study of a man who went virtually from the bottom to the top of late medieval society: the Danish archbishop Birger Gunnersen (1497–1519). A detailed account of his remarkable career can be found in a foundation deed of 1512, in which the archbishop established a chantry in his cathedral church at Lund. As beneficiaries of the prayers to be said, this comprehensive document mentions everybody who had helped the future archbishop in the course of his life. The deed thus informs us about the main stages in the career

---

[8] Per Ingesman, *Ærkesædets godsadministration i senmiddelalderen*, Skånsk senmedeltid och renässans xii (Lund, 1990), and 'Den lundensiske kapitelsgejstlighed i senmiddelalderen' (Ph.D. Aarhus University, 1985).

[9] In England, of course, the record survival is much better: see Ralph A. Griffiths (ed.), *Patronage, the Crown, and the Provinces in Later Medieval England* (Gloucester, 1981), especially ch. 8, and R. B. Dobson (ed.), *The Church, Politics, and Patronage in the Fifteenth Century* (Gloucester, New York, 1984).

of Birger Gunnersen, while at the same time shedding light on the role of his patrons.[10]

The source does not contain any precise dates, but knowing that Birger began his university studies in 1464, we are able to set up an approximate chronological framework for the early part of his life. Birger was born around 1445, or perhaps a couple of years earlier, as the son of a parish clerk in the countryside of Northern Hallandia. He went to school in the nearby town of Varberg, probably at the beginning of the 1450s. Around the middle of that decade he proceeded to a cathedral school, not that of his own diocese in Lund, however, but that of Roskilde on Zealand. And finally he spent five years abroad, at the acclaimed cathedral school of Skara in Sweden. That must have been around 1460, and prepared him to start his studies at the university of Greifswald in May 1464.

How did a poor boy like Birger finance his education? In his deed Birger mentions three families that accommodated him during these years: one in Varberg, one in Roskilde, and one in Skara. Although it is well known that late medieval and early modern city households often made some extra money by letting out rooms,[11] I doubt that this was the case here. To allow a poor school boy to live in the family home must have been an act of charity. And it was, of course, precisely for that reason that Birger many years later named the members of those three families among the benefactors for whom prayers were to be said in his chantry.

One of the interesting insights provided by our document is the fact that it was only a small step from benefactor to patron. We do not know much about schools or school attendance in later medieval Denmark,[12] but it is amazing that Birger was educated in faraway Skara. I see only one possible explanation: that we have here the first example of Birger being patronized by a high-ranking churchman. As benefactors in Skara, Birger mentions two bishops, Bengt and Brynolf, alongside a man – a bailiff of bishop Bengt – in whose house he was living.

---

[10] The document [hereafter *Sanctuarium Birgerianum*] has been edited in *Samlinger til den Danske Historie*, 1 (3/1779), 1–89.

[11] Often it was women who exercised this function in the household economy: see Grethe Jacobsen, 'Women's work and women's role: Ideology and reality in Danish urban society, 1300–1550', *Scandinavian Economic History Review*, 31 (1983), 3–20, esp. 18, and her *Kvinder, køn og købstadslovgivning 1400–1600: Lovfaste Mænd og ærlige Kvinder*, Danish Humanist Texts and Studies xi (Copenhagen, 1995), pp. 209–10.

[12] The best account is in Bjørn Kornerup, *Ribe Katedralskoles Historie: Studier over 800 Aars dansk Skolehistorie* (vol. i, Copenhagen, 1947); for England cf. Nicholas Orme, *English Schools in the Middle Ages* (London, 1973).

The reference to Brynolf must be a mistake,[13] but apart from this detail the story makes very good sense: we know that bishop Bengt of Skara was an exile in Denmark from 1452 to 1457, where he must have met young Birger as a schoolboy in Roskilde. On his return to Skara he brought Birger with him and placed the young Dane in the house of one of his bailiffs. After his death in 1460, his successor must have taken over as patron. And so, many years later, Birger with gratitude mentions these two bishops of Skara, 'who did us much good for about five years when we went to school there. God reward them for that!'[14]

Birger was clearly a promising schoolboy, but also very poor. Continuing his studies abroad, he chose the German university that lay closest to Denmark: newly founded Greifswald, only a few sailing hours away on the other side of the Baltic Sea. When he registered, his fees were waived because of poverty – one of the ways in which universities themselves helped students of humble origins. And in Greifswald, it seems, his housing problems were solved in exactly the same way as in his school years: he stayed in the house of a family whose members – as an old man in 1512 – he gratefully remembered for their favours.

In four years Birger took his masters degree, enabling him to act as a teacher himself in 1469. This, however, was not the ultimate aim of a young Dane who went to a foreign university in the later Middle Ages. The intention was to return to Denmark to enter the service of church or state,[15] and that was precisely what Birger did in due course. From now on, patronage assumes centre stage. Birger first became head of the cathedral school at Lund, then a scribe in the royal chancery, and finally chancellor to her majesty the queen. And on every single occasion he gives the name of a high ranking person who promoted him: the archdeacon of Lund called him from the university to become a school master at home, the chancellor of the king sent for him to be a clerk in the royal chancery in 1474, and the king himself made him chancellor to his queen in 1477.

The king, of course, was the most important patron of later medieval Denmark, and service to him was richly rewarded. For an ecclesiastic the reward took the form of benefices: those rectories, canonries, and, finally, bishoprics that the king could bestow on his servants and clients. In his 1512 description, Birger does not even attempt to conceal

---

[13] Bengt Gustavsson was bishop of Skara 1449–60, but the name of his immediate successor was Johannes, not Brynolf. Archbishop Birger presumably confuses him with Brynolf Gerlaksson, bishop of Skara 1478–1505.

[14] *Sanctuarium Birgerianum*, p. 21.

[15] Jan Pinborg, 'Danish students 1450–1535 and the University of Copenhagen', *Université de Copenhague: Cahiers de l'Institut du Moyen-Age Grec et Latin*, 37 (1981), 70–122.

this, listing the granting of benefices along with other favours he enjoyed by King Christian I (1448–81) and his Queen, Dorothea of Brandenburg: 'They did us great honour and virtue, and provided us with benefices and prelacies. And they loved us and did us much good in many ways. May God and the Virgin Mary reward their souls for that and give them eternal rejoicing in heaven without ending'.[16]

Surviving documents show how Birger advanced through the hierarchy of the Danish church. To begin with he was awarded a number of rectories in the countryside, then he became the incumbent of the large and beautiful church in the important town of Kalundborg, close to a royal stronghold, and finally, around the middle of the 1480s, he was appointed archdeacon at the rich cathedral of Roskilde, royal burial place and a centre of worship for the kings of Denmark. Canonries in three other cathedral chapters, Lund, Viborg, and Ribe, were added in due course.[17]

The death of King Christian I in 1481 had no negative consequences for the career of Birger Gunnersen. Until her death in 1495 he served as chancellor to the queen dowager, whereafter King John (1481–1513) made him chancellor to *his* Queen, Christine of Saxony. In 1497, eventually, came the promotion to archbishop of Lund. On this point Birger is eager to tell us that he was elected in accordance with the rules of canon law by the cathedral chapter, of which he was a member himself. But we know enough about political realities in late medieval Denmark to be quite sure that this was a pure formality, for it was the will of the king that decided the case. No doubt, therefore, the promotion of Birger Gunnersen to the archbishopric of Lund in 1497 was the final reward for more than 20 years of loyal service to the kings and queens of Denmark.

In the history of the medieval church it is not unusual to find bishops and archbishops, even cardinals and popes of humble origins. In England, for instance, the career of Cardinal Thomas Wolsey – son of an Ipswich butcher – has a striking resemblance to that of his Danish contemporary Birger Gunnersen.[18] Lacking noble birth, wealth, and power, such men clearly owed their rise to their intellectual abilities. But how widespread was the phenomenon, and what role did patronage

---

[16] *Sanctuarium Birgerianum*, p. 22.

[17] On the career of Birger Gunnersen see Henry Bruun, *Poul Laxmand og Birger Gunnersen: Studier over dansk politik i årene omkring 1500* (Copenhagen, 1959), pp. 12–16, and Ingesman, *Ærkesædets godsadministration*, pp. 262–5.

[18] Peter Gwyn, *The King's Cardinal: The Rise and Fall of Thomas Wolsey* (London, 1990), especially ch. 2 on his early career.

play in it? Was Birger Gunnersen an atypical example, or is it just that in *his* case we see openly and clearly what the surviving sources normally fail to reveal? Let us reassess the evidence.

There is no doubt at all that late medieval Danish bishops were normally royal clients, with a common background in the chancery of the king. And the reason is quite obvious: because of their political importance, as *ex officio* members of the Council of the Realm, it was vital for the king to have his own men appointed. He assured this by means of pressure on cathedral chapters and cooperation with Rome. In fact the relations between pope and king were so intimate that the *curia* normally refused to accept a candidate without royal approval.[19]

As for the deans and canons of cathedral chapters, there is at least one good reason to believe that patronage was of crucial importance in their ecclesiastical careers. Looking at the biggest and richest chapter of late medieval Denmark, that of Lund, we find that only one third of the members were of gentry origin, the majority being people with a peasant or urban background.[20] How should these clergymen have acquired their schooling, their university degrees, and their benefices, if not by some form of patronage by kings, nobles, or other influential personalities?

In the ecclesiastical sphere, the most important catalysts of social mobility were the bishops. Often of humble social origin themselves, they soon became major patrons in their own right. This process must now be examined in greater detail.

(ii)

Late medieval bishops were normally powerful landlords as well as spiritual leaders, allowing them to exercise both ecclesiastical and secular patronage. The former, unfortunately, cannot be examined in detail due to the scarcity of surviving episcopal records. Unlike in England, there are no bishops' registers to illuminate the study of the church in this period. Ecclesiastical preferment, however, seems to be the less important part of episcopal patronage, as many advowsons were held by other dignitaries.

For a start, the pope claimed rights of provision to deaneries and canonries in the whole of Western Christendom. The king, in turn, exercised the advowson to two canonries in each Danish institution, a

---

[19] Dahlerup, 'Danmark', pp. 52–4, and his 'Kirke og samfund i dansk senmiddelalder' in Ingesman and Jensen (eds), *Danmark i Senmiddelalderen*, pp. 282–91, esp. p. 282.

[20] Ingesman, 'Den lundensiske kapitelsgejstlighed'.

privilege which the pope extended – during a royal visit to Rome in 1474 – to the two highest-ranking posts in every Scandinavian chapter. The canons themselves, finally, insisted on the right to elect their own dean and to approve the appointment of any new colleague. We do not really know how these opposing claims came to be reconciled, but it seems that the patrons reached some form of *modus vivendi*, allowing everyone a share in the process. Two observations suggest that the bishops' influence on the composition of Danish cathedral chapters was limited. First, episcopal relatives are only rarely found among their members. In Lund, for instance, a mere three examples are known from a period of 150 years. Second, there were not many episcopal servants, either: of the 145 canons of the cathedral chapter of Lund in the period 1400–1536, only about 10 seem to have been promoted as a reward for their services as chancellors, secretaries, or chaplains of the archbishops.[21]

With regard to parish churches, the lack of sources makes conclusions even more difficult. Even here, however, we find several conflicting patrons. Normally the king, nobles, or monasteries appointed to the churches in villages where they owned all or most of the land. Furthermore, the king claimed rights of presentation to all parishes in boroughs, as a result of their royal foundation. The bishops, therefore, had to be content with the remaining few churches, and local peculiarities reduced their influence further. Most importantly, for some unknown reason, the king presented to nearly *all* parishes in one of the seven Danish dioceses, Odense.[22] There are no detailed studies of parochial patronage, but we do know that the king used rectories – just like canonries – as rewards for his ecclesiastical servants, for instance for scribes in their early chancery careers. Birger Gunnersen, who obtained parochial benefices in the diocese of Odense and the borough of Kalundborg, can serve as an exemple. Numerically speaking, parish advowsons might well have been the single most important form of the bishops' ecclesiastical patronage, but the sources prohibit any quantitative analysis.

Let us now turn to the use of relatives and clients in the administration of episcopal estates, in other words to the secular patronage of Danish bishops in the later Middle Ages. The sources are more abundant here, and the topic has been addressed in a number of recent studies.[23] For

---

[21] Ibid. On Danish relations with the papacy see Johs. Lindbæk, *Pavernes forhold til Danmark under kongerne Kristiern I og Hans* (Copenhagen, 1907).

[22] Dahlerup, 'Kirke og samfund', p. 283.

[23] Troels Dahlerup, 'Nepotisme som administrativt system: Ribe stift i senmiddelalderen' in Carsten Due-Nielsen et al. (eds), *Struktur og funktion: Festskrift til Erling Ladewig*

obvious reasons, historians have been especially attracted by examples of outspoken nepotism in episcopal administration. Not least has their attention been drawn to those dramatic situations where the death of a bishop gave rise to a violent struggle between the relatives of the deceased, unwilling to give up their lucrative positions, and the new bishop, trying to establish himself firmly in his diocese. One such feud, sparked by the accession of Birger Gunnersen after the death of archbishop Jens Brostrup (1472–97) shall serve as the starting-point.

In contrast to Birger Gunnersen, Jens Brostrup was descended from a gentry family, albeit one of very modest means. We are not quite sure who his father was, perhaps a squire who rented a manor from the bishop of Roskilde in 1429. This would square with the fact that members of his mother's family were well-known clients of the bishops for three generations. The career of Jens Brostrup was not very different from that of Birger Gunnersen, and royal patronage played the same crucial role in it. Having started his university studies in Rostock in 1447, Jens Brostrup went to Cologne in 1448, where he became a *baccalaureus in decretis* in 1455. Back in Denmark he worked his way up through the royal chancery, reaching the top in 1468 or 1469, when he was made chancellor to the king. That he was richly provided with benefices goes without saying. A brilliant career as a royal servant culminated in the promotion to archbishop of Lund in 1472.[24]

The appointment to the see of Lund at a stroke made Jens Brostrup one of the wealthiest men of later medieval Denmark, being rivalled – apart from the king himself – only by the bishop of Roskilde. As a feudal remnant from the high Middle Ages, the archbishopric possessed the entire island of Bornholm in the Baltic Sea, with its strong castle, several towns, and about 800 peasant holdings. On the mainland, Jens Brostrup owned estates comprising between 2 000 and 3 000 holdings spread all over Scania, Hallandia, and Blekingia. The most distant properties, in Blekingia, in eastern and in southern Scania, were controlled by local officials. As for the rest, a huge complex of about 1 000 tenant farms around Lund were administered directly by the episcopal palace, while the more marginal estates tended to be enfeoffed in smaller parts, of about five to fifty tenant farms each.[25]

Petersen (Odense, 1994), pp. 61–72; Elisabeth Hertzum Becker-Christensen, 'Roskildebispernes forleningspraksis i senmiddelalderen' in Aage Andersen, Per Ingesman et al. (eds), *Festskrift til Troels Dahlerup*, Arusia – Historiske Skrifter v (Aarhus, 1985), pp. 177–89; Ingesman, *Ærkesædets godsadministration*.

[24] On his background and career see ibid., pp. 222–8.

[25] The structure of the estates and their administration are described in full detail in ibid., part I. An average Danish farm – held either by a yeoman or a tenant – comprised about 40 acres of land.

For a man like Jens Brostrup, himself a former client, it must have been almost natural to use his position to favour his relatives. And so he did: he made his brother captain of two of the episcopal castles, gave him a number of smaller fiefs, and entrusted several others to his two nephews and a nephew-in-law. He used the son-in-law of his maternal cousin as captain of one of the castles, adding the lordship of a small manor on his retirement. And finally, he appointed the same cousin, being a widower in his old days, and after him yet another nephew as archdeacons in the cathedral chapter. The consequences for the family of the archbishop are quite obvious. The Brostrups, previously with no land and no connections at all in the archdiocese, soon prospered in their new environment: the archbishop bought a gentry estate for the family in the vicinity of Lund and nephews and nieces married into the local nobility, establishing strong ties to some of the leading noblemen of the archdiocese. A solid foundation for a further step up the social ladder was laid.[26]

And yet, with the death of Archbishop Jens in 1497, the position of the Brostrup family was suddenly threatened. A conflict broke out with the new archbishop that was to last for several years. The Brostrups themselves soon capitulated – a characteristic expression of their weak position after the death of their patron. The struggle, however, was carried on by those noblemen with whom the deceased archbishop had established such close connections. From the start it was the son-in-law of Jens Brostrup's brother who emerged as the leading figure, among other things refusing to pay the traditional tribute for the fiefs he held from the archbishopric. But a more mighty man stood behind him: Poul Laxmand, court master of the realm and uncontested leader of the local nobility. Soon a triangular political contest developed, with the archbishop, the court master, and the king as the most prominent figures. The fight went on until 1502, when two noblemen struck down Poul Laxmand in the middle of Copenhagen. The aftermath is very revealing: instead of punishing the murderers, King John accused Poul Laxmand of treason, had him condemned *post mortem*, and confiscated all his land as a compensation for the harm he was said to have done to the crown. Later on he sold a great deal of it – to no-one else than archbishop Birger Gunnersen, who used it as an endowment for his magnificent chantry in the cathedral church![27]

For the Brostrups, the death of Archbishop Jens and the defeat of its noble protectors proved a catastrophe. Within a few years the family

---

[26] On the family of the archbishop see ibid., pp. 222–4.

[27] The strife is treated in detail by Bruun, *Poul Laxmand og Birger Gunnersen*.

disappeared from the archdiocese under circumstances just as obscure as those under which it had arrived a generation before.

Historians have interpreted the conflict between Birger Gunnersen and the heirs of his predecessor as a fight of principles against nepotism and aristocratic influence in the church. Jens Brostrup represented the secularized and corrupt bishop of noble origin, who cared only for the well-being of his own family, while Birger Gunnersen appeared as a man of 'clean hands' with a heroic mission to win church lands back from the nobility. In my opinion, this is too stark a contrast.[28]

Undoubtedly, there was nepotism in the estate administration of Jens Brostrup. If you study it more closely, however, the relatives of the archbishop – with his brother as the sole exception – were *not* in fact the most privileged persons. Several people without family relations to the archbishop, notably the most important estate officials, held more and bigger fiefs than for instance the episcopal nephews. Furthermore, the fact that there are no relatives of Birger Gunnersen in his episcopal administration does not mean that patronage and clientelism did not play a role during his term of office. The system remained basically unchanged, with new gentry administrators simply replacing the friends and relatives of Jens Brostrup. The existence of nepotism in episcopal administration is undeniable, but in my opinion it was only part of a broader patronage pattern and not even its most common form: apart from the episcopacy of Jens Brostrup, evidence of nepotism in the estate administration of the Danish archbishops is really very scarce.

Perhaps one of the reasons for this is the background of the Danish primates themselves. All of them shared two common features, at least until 1523. The first is the fact that the majority were 'outsiders', that is, people coming from other parts of Denmark to a diocese where they had no relatives or friends.[29] Second, although the greater part of them seem to have been of gentry origin, only one archbishop came from a very wealthy and well-established family. Most were *homines novi*, people rising from obscure roots to high positions – and that is, of course, exactly why patronage played such a major role in their careers. For the appointments they then made in their own right, this background had two potential consequences: *either* that the archbishop

---

[28] Ingesman, *Ærkesædets godsadministration*, pp. 228–30, 265–8.

[29] The following list provides the names and years of office of the archbishops of Lund in the later Middle Ages, with the diocese of origin in brackets: Jakob Gertsen 1392–1410 (Roskilde), Peder Mikkelsen Kruse 1410–18 (Lund), Peder Lykke 1418–36 (Roskilde), Hans Laxmand 1436–43 (Lund), Tue Nielsen 1443–72 (Viborg), Jens Brostrup 1472–97 (Roskilde), Birger Gunnersen 1497–1519 (Lund), Jørgen Skodborg 1520–1 (Ribe), Didrik Slagheck 1521–2 (Münster), Johan Weze 1522–3 (Utrecht), Aage Jepsen Sparre 1523–32 (Lund), Torben Bille 1532–6 (Lund).

would be especially eager to promote his own and not so well-to-do relatives (for example Jens Brostrup), *or* that he did not have very many relatives to support (as in the case of Birger Gunnersen). We can certainly observe very widespread episcopal patronage indeed, but with only few instances of outspoken nepotism. To a certain degree this holds true for the other Danish dioceses as well, although nepotism seems to have been more widespread there, no doubt because the bishops were more likely to come from local gentry families.[30]

Another reason for the limited extent of nepotism in the archbishopric must have been the fact that episcopal clients exercised so many important administrative functions that it was neither possible nor wise for a bishop to let the group be dominated totally by nephews and other relatives. To a certain degree we find in Denmark that same form of 'bastard feudalism' that K. B. McFarlane has described for England.[31] A late medieval bishop needed retainers to do military service, he needed men trained in law and administration to take care of his estates and legal rights, and normally he would find those people primarily among the gentry of his diocese. Danish bishops of the later Middle Ages, therefore, were patrons of large groups of gentry clients. In a way patronage was just the most appropriate contemporary administrative system.[32]

(iii)

In 1536 King Christian III deposed the Danish bishops, confiscated their estates, and replaced them with Lutheran 'superintendents', who were royal officials on a fixed salary without any kind of secular power. The Reformation stripped the bishops of what had enabled them to act as patrons on a grand scale: their estates and their power to confer benefices. The benefices in the cathedral chapters and elsewhere were now all in the gift of the king, and the former episcopal estates were either sold off to the nobility or put together with the old crown lands, traditionally administered by the nobility in the form of large fiefs. From a socio-economic perspective, the Danish Reformation had royal servants and noblemen as its winners, episcopal clients and lower gentry as its losers.

---

[30] See for instance Dahlerup, 'Nepotisme som administrativt system'.

[31] For an introduction to the concept and the research carried out by McFarlane and his students see Michael Hicks, *Bastard Feudalism* (London, 1995), and R. H. Britnell and A. J. Pollard (eds), *The McFarlane Legacy: Studies in Late Medieval Politics and Society*, The Fifteenth Century Series i (Stroud/New York, 1995).

[32] Compare Dahlerup, 'Nepotisme som administrativt system'.

As Troels Dahlerup has pointed out, the Danish Reformation meant if not 'the fall of the gentry' then at least a serious crisis for that large part of their members whose livelihood depended on the administration of church properties, especially those of the episcopal sees. It was thus only the upper part of the landowning class, the nobility, who benefited from the Reformation. To the lowest strata of the aristocracy, the lower gentry, it could mean extinction. Instead, a smaller, richer, and more influential aristocracy emerged on the other side of the Reformation. The relatively 'open' society of the later Middle Ages gave way to a society with a considerably wider gap between the aristocracy and the ordinary people, a society with far less social mobility than before.[33]

However, it was not solely a result of the Reformation. The elimination of the bishops dealt a serious blow to the social structures created by episcopal patronage, to what might be called the local patronage communities. But the Reformation only added the finishing touches to an ongoing process of social change within the aristocracy, in which the bishops themselves played a role. According to Troels Dahlerup their patronage system, with its corresponding social structures, was in decline from around 1500, as a consequence of the system itself: due to episcopal promotion, a number of gentry families became even more powerful and, to a certain degree, succeeded in monopolizing the episcopal sees.[34] Therefore, the bishops' social profile rose during the last pre-Reformation generations, and well-to-do episcopal relatives began to push out members of previous client families. Besides, estate administration showed a tendency towards rationalization and centralization, so that a lot of smaller fiefs simply disappeared. The traditional possibilities of making a living for the lowest strata of the gentry vanished with them.[35]

No wonder, therefore, that we do not find widespread support for the bishops and the old church from gentry circles in the history of the Danish Reformation. To a certain degree, the opposite is the case: from around 1520 the Danish gentry joined the nobility in complaints against the church, among other things criticizing bishops and prelates for not letting the gentry be in charge of church estates 'as they used to do in the old days'.[36] And some former gentry clients of the archbishops were so desperate, it seems, that they even joined a local peasant rising in the

---

[33] Dahlerup, 'Lavadelens Krise', 'Danmark', and 'Heraldry and Social Change'.

[34] Perhaps best seen in Ribe: see Dahlerup, 'Nepotisme som administrativt system'. But the post-1523 archbishopric provides another good example: Both Aage Jepsen Sparre and Torben Bille came from leading noble families of the archdiocese.

[35] Dahlerup, 'Danmark', pp. 53–4, 68, 69–70.

[36] 'Udkastning til tvende K. Christian den Andens Anordninger om Kirke- og Skolesager', *Danske Magazin*, 6 (1752), 359–67, esp. 363.

archdiocese in 1525, participating in attacks on episcopal castles and noble manor houses.[37]

Ten years later the Reformation was carried out virtually without protest. The Danish Reformation was not followed by those local risings that we find for instance in England ('The Pilgrimage of Grace', 1536) or in Sweden ('Dackefejden', 1542). This, of course, reflects the fact that in Denmark social and economic unrest, civil wars and peasant uprisings, took place *before* the Reformation, not afterwards. But a change from 'symbiotic' to hostile relationships between church and gentry during the last generation before the Reformation must be taken into account too. One of the reasons why episcopal power fell so easily in Denmark is that the bishops lacked supporters willing to fight for their cause. And the explanation for that could well be that Danish bishops, on the eve of the Reformation, had forgotten about the importance of fostering their clients.

---

[37] Dahlerup, 'Lavadelens Krise', 38–40.

CHAPTER EIGHT

The dispersal of monastic patronage in East Yorkshire, 1520–90

Peter Marshall

The sudden and ignominious collapse of English monasticism at the end of the 1530s brought with it the most significant transfer of property since the Norman Conquest. The pattern whereby monastic estates passed to the crown, and were in large part subsequently alienated by a hard-pressed Henry VIII and his equally impecunious children, has been clarified by a number of important local studies, and in the process several myths have been overturned. Henry did not use his windfall profligately to endow a host of court favourites; nor did the sales facilitate the emergence of a new class of parvenu landowners. Rather, the bulk of the lands were sought and secured by the established landed families.[1] Historians have not failed to notice that the property expropriated from the stricken religious houses comprehended more than manors, liturgical furnishings, and the lead from church roofs. The dissolution of 1536 and subsequent surrenders of 1537–40 brought into the king's hands a host of monastic advowsons, and effected a transfer of ecclesiatical patronage the scale of which can hardly be exaggerated.[2] In dissolving the religious houses, the monarch had at a stroke, and by a huge margin, confirmed his position as the single

---

[1] J. A. Youings, 'The terms of disposal of the Devon monastic lands, 1536–58', *EHR*, 69 (1954), 18–38; T. H. Swales, 'The redistribution of the monastic lands in Norfolk at the Dissolution', *Norfolk Archaeology*, 34 (1966), 14–44; C. Kitching, 'The disposal of monastic and chantry lands' in F. Heal and R. O'Day (eds), *Church and Society in England: Henry VIII to James I* (London, 1977), pp. 119–36.

[2] In Essex, for example, 41.4 per cent of advowsons were owned by religious houses in 1536, in Worcester diocese 42.6 per cent, in the dioceses of Canterbury, Chichester, and Lincoln the religious made over one third of all presentations to livings: J. E. Oxley, *The Reformation in Essex to the Death of Mary* (Manchester, 1965), p. 263; D. M. Barratt, 'The condition of the parish clergy between the Reformation and 1660, with special reference to the dioceses of Oxford, Worcester, and Gloucester' (D.Phil. Oxford, 1949), p. 353; P. Ayris, 'Thomas Cranmer's register: a record of archiepiscopal administration in diocese and province' (Ph.D. Cambridge, 1984), p. 221; S. J. Lander, 'The diocese of Chichester, 1508–58: episcopal reform under Robert Sherburne and its aftermath' (Ph.D. Cambridge, 1974), p. 200; M. Bowker, *The Henrician Reformation: The Diocese of Lincoln under John Longland 1521–1547* (Cambridge, 1981), p. 39.

greatest ecclesiastical patron in the realm. Yet to date there has been little systematic attempt to assess the ramifications of the dissolution in terms of the ownership and exercise of parochial patronage. The following discusssion, which takes as its focus the East Riding of Yorkshire, will attempt to delineate the part played by the religious houses in the provision of priests for the parishes before 1536, and to assess the implications of the dispersal of their patronage, not least for the implementation of religious policy and the quality of pastoral care.

The archdeaconry of the East Riding was one of five archdeaconries constituting the massive archdiocese of York, and contained 165 parishes in the early 1530s. It thus provides a convenient case study to assess the dynamics of the patronage exercised by the religious houses in the early part of the sixteenth century. Twenty-seven houses possessed the right to nominate parish clergy in the area (see Map 8.1). Of these, almost half (13) were situated within the Riding itself, and a further 10 were within 20 miles of its boundaries. Of the remainder, Guisborough Priory was located near the North Sea coast in the North Riding, and Bardney Abbey some 40 miles south of the Humber in Lincolnshire. Indeed, only two of the houses exercising patronage within the Riding were more than a day's ride away.[3] The extent to which monastic patronage had a firmly local focus is underlined by the fact that, with the exclusion of the friaries, only two East Yorkshire houses, the Benedictine nunneries of Thicket and Nunburnholme, possessed no advowsons in the Riding.

There was, of course, no even spread of patronage among the religious. Twelve houses had the advowson of a single church. Some of these – Drax, Nostell, Pontefract, and Whitby – were North or West Riding houses with considerable patronage elsewhere in the diocese, but others – Ellerton, North Ferriby, Nunkeeling, Swine, Wilberfoss, Yedingham – were small local houses nominating the priest of the parish in which they were situated. At the other end of the scale, six houses possessed five or more advowsons. Of these only two, Bridlington (12 advowsons) and Kirkham (7), were situated within the archdeaconry itself. Their prominence reflects the very considerable influence over advowsons in the East Riding exercised by the Augustinian canons, traditionally more involved in the affairs of the secular church than the Cistercians or Benedictines.

---

[3] Alnwick (Northumberland), which owed its advowson of Leconfield to a patronal connection with the Percys, and Durham Priory, which presented to Brantingham, Eastrington, and the five vicarages subject to the collegiate church of Howden. I am greatly indebted to Mr J. S. Johnston for drawing the map.

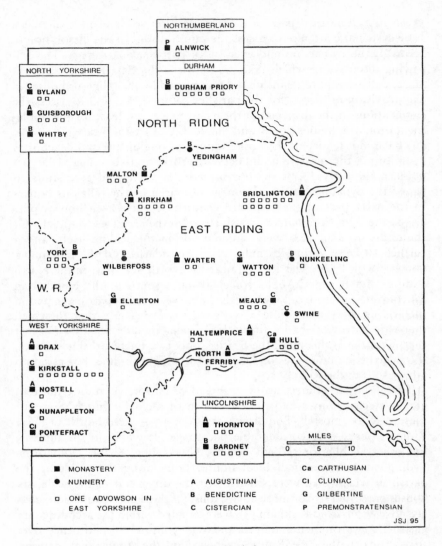

Map 8.1 Monastic patronage in East Yorkshire

Taken together, the religious houses enjoyed a commanding position over the patronage of benefices with cure of souls, with over half the advowsons in the Riding in their hands (see Table 8.1). Of the 84 advowsons held by the religious, all but 14 were of appropriated livings. In most of these a vicarage had been ordained, but 12 remained as perpetual curacies, employing a stipendiary priest who enjoyed no ten-

Table 8.1   Ownership of advowsons in the archdeaconry of the East
Riding, pre-1536

Patron	No. advowsons	% advowsons
Archbishop of York*	4	2.4
Other ecclesiastics	30	18.2
Crown	3	1.8
Other lay patrons	29	17.6
Collegiate churches	14	8.5
Religious houses	84	50.9
Unclear	1	0.6
Total	165	100.0

*includes 3 advowsons held by Cistercian Abbey of Meaux where collation reserved to the archbishop.

ure of his living. In fact, sole concentration upon advowsons of parishes underestimates the full scale of patronage of the secular clergy open to the religious houses. As across much of northern England, the parish system sat rather uneasily on the East Riding, where many parishes were geographically extensive and a significant proportion of the population worshipped regularly in dependent churches and in chantry chapels which provided some rudimentary cure of souls. There were at least 107 of these in sixteenth-century East Yorkshire, of which between 57 and 60 were situated in parishes subject to a religious house.[4] Possession of appropriated churches was, of course, important to the finances of the religious houses, but at the same time it reduced the attractiveness of the parishes in their gift. The *Valor Ecclesiasticus* of 1535 gives clear annual values for 149 East Riding parishes, of which 71 belonged to religious houses. The average value of an East Riding vicarage in 1535 was £9 1s. 3d., and though monastic vicarages tended to be slightly better endowed than those appropriated to colleges or ecclesiatical dignities, averaging £9 15s. 2d., neither sum would have been regarded by contemporaries seeking preferment as an irresistible enducement. Rectories in the gift of religious houses were markedly more valuable than the vicarages, averaging £12 12s. 4d., but none of the really important benefices in the archdeaconry had monastic patrons. Almost

---

[4] P. Marshall, *The Face of the Pastoral Ministry in the East Riding, 1525–1595*, Borthwick Paper lxxxviii (York, 1995), p. 3. Nomination of curates in these chapelries normally pertained to the monastic appropriator.

invariably, these were in lay hands: Bainton (worth over £35 *per annum*) belonged to the Slavin family, Settrington (over £42) to the Bigods, Cottingham (most valuable of all at £106 13s. 4d.), was presented to in the 1530s by the Duke of Richmond.[5]

Any attempt to discern clear patterns and priorities in the monastic exercise of advowsons is destined to encounter severe difficulties, as the historian struggles to infer motives from the bare record of presentation in episcopal registers. Claims that monastic patronage was generally used for the advancement of clerks with legal experience or political influence which could be mobilized in the monastery's favour are suggestive, but difficult to establish with any degree of certainty.[6] All kinds of pressures may have influenced monastic choices, both from inside and outside the houses themselves. The chance survival of a collection of 175 letters sent to the Prior of Durham in the early fifteenth century reveals how an influential monastic patron might be bombarded with requests from external sponsors, anxious to advance a particular protégé or acquire *carte blanche* to nominate to a particular benefice.[7] In the absence of comparable evidence for any of our monastic patrons in the sixteenth century, it would be wise to avoid dogmatic assertions about the priorities discernible in the exercise of monastic patronage, but a study of the presentations made to East Yorkshire benefices in the half-generation preceding the dissolution may shed some light on the matter.

As Table 8.2 reveals, the discrepancy between the volume of patronage in theory available to the religious houses, and that actually exercised, is quite striking. One tempting explanation for this would be that the poorer monastic benefices attracted fewer ambitious careerists and were therefore occupied by clerks more likely to stay longer in the parish. In fact, however, a comparison of the lengths of tenure of monastic and non-monastic appointees reveals no obvious distinction. A more persuasive explanation for the imbalance is the clear tendency of some religious houses to alienate their own patronage through the making of grants of next presentation. This represented a formal alienation of the right to present a clerk to the archbishop when the next vacancy arose, while still retaining ultimate ownership of the advow-

---

[5] N. A. H. Lawrance (ed.), 'The clergy of the Archdeaconry of the East Riding, Harthill Deanery', Borthwick Institute, York, typescript, 2 vols, Add MS 152-3 [hereafter *Fasti Hartill*], pp. 7, 75, 82, and *Fasti Parochiales*, vol. v: *Deanery of Buckrose*, Yorkshire Archaeological Society Record Series [hereafter: YASRS] cxliii (1985) [hereafter *Fasti Buckrose*], p. 41.

[6] A. H. Thompson, *The English Clergy and their Organization in the Later Middle Ages* (Oxford, 1947), p. 105; Bowker, *Henrician Reformation*, p. 45.

[7] R. B. Dobson, *Durham Priory 1400–1450* (Cambridge, 1973), pp. 144–72.

Table 8.2   Presentations in the East Riding, 1520–35

No. of parishes for which presentations can be reconstructed*	116	
Advowsons of these held by religious houses	66	(57.0%)
Advowsons held by other patrons	50	(43.0%)
Total presentations, 1520–35	131	
Presentations made by religious houses	58	(44.3%)
Presentations by other patrons	71	(54.2%)
Patron unclear	2	(1.5%)

*This figure excludes the perpetual curacies, the parishes in the gift of Beverley Minster, for which no institutions were recorded in the archbishops' registers in this period, and a few others for which records are incomplete.

son.[8] In the period 1520–35 at least 11 presentations were made to East Riding livings under grants of next presentation from monasteries. In each case the grantor was a fairly wealthy house with a number of benefices at its disposal: Bridlington made three grants, Kirkstall, Kirkham, and St Mary's, York, two each, and Malton and Warter, one. Like Durham Priory in the fifteenth century, such houses were undoubtedly susceptible to the attention of would-be patronage brokers. One group clearly benefiting from monastic alienations were educated clerks and their influential ecclesiastical patrons. In 1521, for example, John Coltman, a well-connected pluralist who in 1535 became sub-treasurer of York Minster, was presented to the rectory of Foxholes, the most valuable East Riding living in the gift of a monastery, by John Chapman MA, notary public of York, under a grant from St Mary's Abbey.[9] In 1523 Chapman presented to another of St Mary's rectories, that of Huggate, his candidate on this occasion being Edward Kellet MA, a York prebendary who was later to become precentor of the cathedral.[10] Chapman clearly acted regularly as a middleman in such cases: at some point he also acquired from Malton Priory the next presentation to another valuable rectory, Langton, a grant which was exercised posthum-

[8] R. O'Day, 'The law of patronage in early modern England', *JEH*, 26 (1975), 256.

[9] N. A. H. Lawrance (ed.), *Fasti Parochiales*, vol. iii: *Deanery of Dickering*, YASRS cxxiv (1967) [hereafter *Fasti Dickering*], p. 38; K. J. Allison (ed.), *Victoria History of the County of York, East Riding* (6 vols, London and Oxford, 1969–1989) [hereafter *VCH*], ii. 197.

[10] *Fasti Harthill*, p. 155; J. Le Neve, *Fasti Ecclesiae Anglicanae 1300–1541*, vol. vi: *Northern Province*, compiled by B. Jones (London, 1963), pp. 13, 63.

ously by his executor, William Mooke, in 1535.[11] Similarly active was
the Subdean of York, William Clyfton, who in 1539 presented fellow-
prebendary Thomas Teshe to Beeford under a grant obtained from
Bridlington Priory, and in 1534 and again in 1540 had the nomination
to Bridlington's rectory of Sproatley. In 1534 he had also presented to
Kirkstall's vicarage of Kilnsea, and in 1557 he exercised the same right
at Leven by a grant from the provost of Beverley Minster.[12] Prominent
York ecclesiastics like Chapman and Clyfton were well placed to act as
middlemen between the religious houses prepared to sell or grant next
presentations and the ambitious, usually graduate clergy looking for a
first step on the ladder of preferment or an additional benefice to add to
their collection. In similar fashion, the Archdeacon of York, Hugh
Ashton, presented to Kirkham's rectory of Burythorpe in 1520, and the
Dean of York, Brian Higden to Kirkstall's vicarage of Owthorne in
1537.[13] In such cases the monasteries' role may well have been an
essentially passive one, reacting to offers and entreaties from outside
agents, though doubtless also conscious of the potential advantages of
accommodating important suitors.

The decision to make a grant of next presentation may not always,
however, have conformed to this model. In April 1524 Kirkham Priory
granted the next vacancy of Burythorpe to William Dayvell and
Christopher Lassells esq., and in 1540 Dayvell exercised his grant on
behalf of William Newton. The monks of Kirkham pensioned in 1538
included an Edmund Newton, and by the mid-1550s one of this name
was acting as William Newton's curate at Burythorpe. It is at least
conceivable that Edmund Newton, perhaps a novice at the time, may
have alerted a kinsman in secular orders to the willingness of his house
to alienate its right of presentation, and that William Newton arranged
for a third party to purchase the grant and present him in due course
when the living fell vacant, Edmund Newton being in the end rewarded
with a curacy after the dissolution.[14] A similar process may have lain

---

[11] *Fasti Buckrose*, p. 28.

[12] Le Neve, *Fasti Northern Province*, p. 17; N. A. H. Lawrance (ed.), 'The clergy of
the Archdeaconry of the East Riding, Holderness Deanery', Borthwick Institute typescript, 2 vols, Add MS 154–5 [hereafter *Fasti Holderness*], pp. 19, 81, 85, 144. The
Dissolution Acts of 1536, 1539, and 1547 all confirmed the rights of monastic and
collegiate grantees. Grants of next presentation thus remained valid, and could be
exercised legally after the disappearance of the religious houses and colleges: H. Gee and
W. J. Hardy (eds), *Documents Illustrative of English Church History* (London, 1896),
pp. 261, 287, 345.

[13] *Fasti Holderness*, p. 97; *Fasti Buckrose*, p. 7.

[14] Borthwick Institute, York [hereafter BI] Adm 1540/1; C. Cross and N. Vickers,
Monks, Friars, and Nuns in Sixteenth-Century Yorkshire, YASRS cl (1995), p. 299; A.
G. Dickens, *Reformation Studies* (London, 1982), p. 107.

behind the presentation in 1540 of Henry Morwyn to another Kirkham living, Kirby Grindalythe, by John Burnande and John Donnyngton. A Richard Morwyn was ordained subdeacon in 1525, and pensioned at Kirkham in 1538.[15] Two Bridlington cases may also fit the pattern. The James Todde presented to Carnaby in 1539 may have been a kinsman of the Bridlington monk, Robert Todde, who was licensed to take a benefice in August 1537. He was almost certainly a kinsman of the William Todde of Ripon, who along with John Dyghton of Batley had acquired the next presentation and exercised it on his behalf.[16] The family connections seem even more obvious in the case of Reginald Charder, presented to the rectory of Thwing in 1528 by Edward Charder and Robert Charder, who had acquired the right from a monastic community which in 1537 included Mathew Charder.[17] On this occasion the previous incumbent, William Tate, had resigned, and was later assigned a pension of 10 marks, an indication that the line between playing the system and outright simony could be a very fine one.[18]

What all these cases suggest is that access to monastic parish patronage was available to a wide variety of would-be patrons of East Riding livings. Some sought grants of next presentation on behalf of a distinct candidate, though others may have regarded them as an investment. There are examples of lay people acquiring more than one grant, and of grantees reassigning (presumably selling) the right to a third party.[19] Of the 46 presentations definitely made under grant of next presentation from religious houses in the period 1520–90, there are 10 for which the date of initial grant can be determined. These show that the median period between grant and presentation was 15 years. The implication is, the Thwing case notwithstanding, that the traffic in these grants was generally not an overtly simoniacal procedure linked to impending vacancies by death or resignation.

Of course, the great majority of presentations pertaining to the religious houses were not alienated, but exercised directly. In such cases, however, it would be unwise to assume that communities always acted with a free hand, or sought out the candidate who reflected communal monastic priorities. It was the practice of some sixteenth-century English houses, for example, to make grants of mere nomination, which

---

[15] *Fasti Buckrose*, p. 20; Cross and Vickers, *Monks, Friars, and Nuns*, p. 304.

[16] Ibid., p. 259; *Fasti Dickering*, p. 19.

[17] Ibid., p. 91; Cross and Vickers, *Monks, Friars, and Nuns*, p. 256. Mathew was only ordained subdeacon in February 1537, so was unlikely to have been a member of the community in 1528; the continuing association of Charders with Bridlington is nonetheless intriguing.

[18] *Fasti Dickering*, p. 91.

[19] Ibid., p. 35; *Fasti Holderness*, p. 44; *Fasti Harthill*, p. 92; BI Adm 1549/6.

involved no formal registration with the bishop.[20] In many, perhaps most, cases, the true patron, whether he was an outside petitioner, or a vocal advocate within the cloister, remains forever hidden. Yet it may be safe to assert that in many ways the religious houses' exercise of their patronage in the decades before the dissolution should be considered paradigmatic of their relationship with society as a whole. Influential laymen and clerics were able to direct monastic patronage to the benefit of their own clients, in a manner which should probably not be regarded as overtly exploitative or parasitic. Rather, as with the distribution of offices, stewardships, and hospitality, it reflects the monasteries' awareness of the currents of influence and connection in their localities, and their desire to negotiate them successfully.[21] On the other hand, there were good reasons for monasteries to keep a check upon who obtained the vicarages of their appropriated livings. Potential disagreements over the division and collection of tithe, or the extent of monastic obligations to the vicar, could be arrested if the latter were himself a member of the community. With papal license, regulars might serve parish churches, and in the East Riding the Augustinian houses in particular were apt to follow this practice, Haltemprice presenting a string of its own canons to Kirkella and Wharram Percy; Ellerton, North Ferriby, Guisborough, and Drax following a similar pattern in some or all of their appropriated benefices.[22] In those parishes where a vicarage had not been ordained, a regular rather than a secular stipendiary may often have been used to serve the cure, as also in some of the dependent chapels within appropriated parishes.[23] It was perhaps in finding chaplains for these stipendiary posts that the religious houses had the freest hand, as well as a useful social function to perform. In the 1520s, the diocese of York, like other parts of the country, was producing record levels of priests, the great majority of whom had neither the talent nor the connections to come to the attention of a patron of a

---

[20] R. N. Swanson, *Church and Society in Late Medieval England* (Oxford, 1989), p. 75.

[21] On the Yorkshire gentry's role as monastic stewards see G. W. O. Woodward, 'The Benedictines and Cistercians in Yorkshire in the sixteenth century' (Ph.D. Trinity College, Dublin, 1955), pp. 99–107, and B. English, *The Great Landowners of East Yorkshire 1530–1910* (Hemel Hempstead, 1990), pp. 40–41. It is revealing that Sir Marmaduke Constable, granted a next presentation of Roos by Kirkham Priory in 1528, was steward of Kirkham's manor of Whitwell: BI Adm 1538/15; J. Caley and J. Hunter (eds), *Valor Ecclesiasticus temp. Henrici VIII* (6 vols, London, 1810–34), v. 104.

[22] *Fasti Harthill*, pp. 5, 110, 133, 176, 254, 270; *Fasti Buckrose*, pp. 70–1.

[23] Ibid., pp. 3, 53; *Fasti Harthill*, pp. 84, 163, *Fasti Dickering*, p. 45; *VCH*, i. 294. In 1536 the Abbot of Whitby petitioned Cromwell for a relaxation of visitation injunctions 'for certain of my brethren to go into the country to say mass every Sunday at certain chapels in our parish': *LP*, x. 239.

benefice.[24] A house like Bridlington, which in addition to its 12 bene-fices was responsible for the cure of souls at 9 chapels, could provide much-needed opportunities for the hard-pressed lower clergy.

All of this begs the question of how seriously monastic patrons took the provision of pastoral care in the parishes nominally in their charge. One local observer, the East Riding gentleman Francis Bigod, later to play an idiosyncratic and quixotic part in the Pilgrimage of Grace, lambasted the religious houses for their self-serving disregard for the welfare of souls. In his *Treatise Concernynge Impropriations of Bene-fices* (?1535), Bigod attacked the system of monastic appropriation as an 'intollerable pestilence' leading to 'the undoynge of all men'. The artificial poverty of appropriated livings made it impossible to attract educated, preaching clergy to serve them, and though he insisted that he had nothing to say about the actual patronage of such livings, Bigod clearly regarded the whole involvement of monks with the cure of souls as an aberration.[25] It is debatable, however, whether Bigod's order of priorities – a graduate preaching clergy expounding Protestant doctrine – should be accepted as the benchmark of adequate pastoral care, or would have been accepted as such by more than a tiny minority of East Riding parishioners in 1535. In fact, in the absence of episcopal visita-tion records for the diocese of York in the pre-Reformation period, it is impossible to judge whether the laity fared better or less well in parishes where the advowson belonged to a religious house, though the intract-able and clearly long-standing problems of decayed fabric manifested by some formerly appropriated East Riding churches in the later six-teenth century hint that monastic appropriators may have been less conscientious than other rectors in their duty of maintaining the chancel in good repair.[26] One test that can be applied is to examine the number of graduates presented. In the period 1520–35, at least 21 presentations of graduates were made to East Riding benefices, of which only 5 were made by the religious houses. Lay patrons presented 8 graduates, and secular churchmen 4, despite their much smaller share of overall pat-ronage. Yet it is highly improbable that this statistic signals any lower commitment to pastoral care on the part of the monasteries: graduates

---

[24] J. A. H. Moran, 'Clerical recruitment in the diocese of York: data and commentary', *JEH*, 34 (1983), 19–54.

[25] A. G. Dickens (ed.), *Tudor Treatises*, YASRS cxxv (1959), pp. 42–57, quotes at pp. 42, 49.

[26] J. S. Purvis, *The Condition of Yorkshire Church Fabrics 1300–1800* (York, 1958), pp. 16–18. There is pre-Reformation visitation evidence from other parts of the country suggesting that laypeople were sometimes unhappy about regulars serving cures when the latter resided in their monastery, rather than the parish: P. Marshall, *The Catholic Priesthood and the English Reformation* (Oxford, 1994), p. 184.

were naturally attracted to the richer benefices, largely in the hands of the crown and other lay patrons. Presentation to the most desirable monastic benefices was, as we have seen, often formally granted to other patrons. Graduates were in any case more likely to be absentees or pluralists once they were appointed, with the parish left in the care of a curate. The needs of parishioners were perhaps unlikely to be a decisive influence on the exercise of monastic patronage, but it seems that vacancies were filled by at least minimally qualified candidates and notorious scandal probably seldom ensued. Margaret Bowker's observation that the monasteries' patronage gave them greater power than any pope or bishop to effect reform at the parochial level, and that the opportunity was missed, is in one sense uncontroversial, but is problematic if intended as an unimpeachable indictment of the religious orders.[27] The deployment of monastic advowsons performed a number of functions, and satisfied, at least in part, a number of constituencies. Francis Bigod notwithstanding, it does not seem to have been an occasion of widespread lay dissatisfaction on the eve of the monasteries' dissolution.

The fall of the East Riding monasteries, recently described by Claire Cross, was swift but hardly painless.[28] A number of monks were deeply implicated in the Pilgrimage of Grace and its epilogue in East Yorkshire, the rising led by Francis Bigod and John Hallom. These included the Prior of Bridlington, William Wood, executed at Tyburn in June 1537, whose house with its large estates and 20 appropriated livings came, by a novel interpretation of the terms of attainder, directly into the hands of the crown. The last of the East Riding monasteries disappeared with the surrender of Meaux in December 1539, and the crown's position as a patron of ecclesiastical livings had been transformed. In 1535 the king owned only 3 of the 165 advowsons in the Riding. After 1540 he became easily the largest patron, a position enhanced when the 1547 Chantries Act brought in the 13 advowsons held by the great collegiate church of Beverley Minster (see Table 8.3).

The crown now presided over a vast reservoir of ecclesiastical patronage, which in theory could have been used to ensure support for its religious policies at the parish level in a region which throughout the later sixteenth century manifested religious recalcitrance and conservative sym-

---

[27] M. Bowker, *The Secular Clergy in the Diocese of Lincoln 1485–1520* (Cambridge, 1968), p. 67.

[28] C. Cross, *The End of Medieval Monasticism in the East Riding of Yorkshire,* East Yorkshire Local History Series xlvii (Beverley, 1993).

Table 8.3   Ownership of advowsons in the East Riding, 1550

Patron	No. advowsons	% advowsons
Archbishop of York*	14	8.5
Other ecclesiastics	32	19.4
Crown	85	51.5
Other lay patrons	33	20.0
Unclear	1	0.6
Total	165	100.0

*includes one advowson nominally in hands of the crown, where archbishop had right of nomination.

pathy.[29] Yet Henry and his successors were never able to take full advantage of this opportunity, partly due to their own policy of piecemeal alienation, partly due to the monasteries' own legacy in massively accelerating the rate at which they granted next presentations in the years and months preceding their closure. This tendency forms part of that national phenomenon of which historians of the dissolution have long been aware: the proliferation, particularly from 1537, of grants to laymen under the convent seal of pensions and annuities, fees and nominal offices in the monastery, and leases of land on favourable terms.[30] Cromwell's circular letter to the heads of religious houses in March 1538, denying that any general dissolution was intended and ordering such anticipatory alienations to stop, can be taken as confirmation that the government had by this point decided to seize all monastic endowments, and it was probably understood as such by the letter's recipients.[31] In such circumstances the desire of abbots and priors to curry favour with their influential lay neighbours was heightened, as was the determination of importunate suitors to salvage what they could from the floundering wreck of monasticism. In East Yorkshire, the impossibility of dating most grants of next presentation makes it difficult to trace the process precisely, but it seems certain that at least five, and possibly 11, houses granted next presentations to benefices at a time when their dissolution seemed likely

[29] H. Aveling, *Post-Reformation Catholicism in East Yorkshire 1558–1790*, East Yorkshire Local History Series xi (Beverley, 1960).

[30] J. Youings, *The Dissolution of the Monasteries* (London, 1971), pp. 57–61; D. Knowles, *The Religious Orders in England*, vol. iii: *The Tudor Age* (Cambridge, 1959), p. 353; J. H. Bettey, *The Suppression of the Monasteries in the West Country* (Gloucester, 1989), pp. 70–72.

[31] *LP*, xii/1. 573.

or imminent. Kirkstall alienated presentation to Owthorne in November 1537 and to Kilnsea in August 1538.[32] Durham Priory granted a presentation to Eastrington in February 1538, and Guisborough to its rectory of West Heslerton in October.[33] Thornton Abbey's actions in regard to its vicarage of Humbleton in Holderness seem almost frenetic: in 1538 Robert Hall acquired the living via a grant from the abbey, and only two years later Edward Brown presented Thomas Tompson as vicar, again by monastic grant.[34]

The motivation of those abbots and priors prepared to relinquish direct control of their patronage remains a perplexing question. Clearly, it was not in all, if in any, cases an act of gratuitous defiance. Indeed, in some instances the alienation of patronage looks more like part of the process of expropriation than an assertion of independent action on the part of heads of houses. In August 1538, for example, Kirkstall granted the next presentation of Kilnsea to Cromwell's visitor, Thomas Legh, almost certainly at his insistent request.[35] In March 1536 Legh had written to the Prior of Guisborough demanding 'one advocation' of the parish church of Barningham in the North Riding. His postscript that 'in so doing you shall deserve thanks and such pleasure as I may do you', with its nicely judged combination of conventional pleasantry, offer of sponsorship, and thinly veiled threat, epitomizes the pressures heads of houses were under at the time of the first sequestrations.[36]

It would seem, however, that most grants of next presentation made in the run-up to the dissolution were not given to particularly influential national or local figures. Of a possible maximum of 21 such grants,[37] only three were made to individuals identified as gentlemen. By contrast, seven grants were acquired by small syndicates of two or three laymen or clerks of lower social status, the teaming of grantees carrying the strong implication that the grants in question had been purchased.[38]

---

[32] BI Adm 1560/12 and 1577/9.

[33] BI Adm 1549/6; *Fasti Buckrose*, p. 19.

[34] *Fasti Holderness*, p. 72.

[35] BI Adm 1577/9.

[36] J. W. Clay (ed.), *Yorkshire Monasteries Suppression Papers*, YASRS xlviii (1912), p. 25.

[37] This figures represents grants made by monasteries where the date of presentation was 1540 or later; the median date of these presentations is 1547.

[38] A point made by R. O'Day, *The English Clergy: The Emergence and Consolidation of a Profession 1558–1642* (Leicester, 1979), p. 110. There is no evidence what sums were paid by grantees in East Yorkshire, though a letter in 1536 from the Prior of Holy Island to Cromwell's servant, Anthony Bellasis, suggested a grantee might be compensated with 20 nobles, £10 or 20 marks [*sic*] for returning the next presentation of Giggleswick (West Riding): *LP*, xi. 877. In late sixteenth-/early seventeenth-century Worcestershire, sums paid seem to have varied from £40 to £100: Barratt, 'Condition of the parish clergy', p. 382.

In a number of cases it seems clear that the grantees were acting as proxies for kinsmen or friends who had little prospect of gaining access to the patronage system in any other way. In 1546, for example, John Benisonne was presented to the vicarage of Ganton by William Benisonne, John Benisone, and Henry Noble by virtue of a grant from Bridlington Priory.[39] To this extent, the spate of grants in 1537–9 can be viewed as monasteries realizing their assets, essentially little different from the sales of timber and church plate, and granting of leases for cash down which Cromwell was so eager to prevent. Yet there are indications that a number of houses adopted a more astute and strategic approach, and that in some cases presentation rights over monastic livings may have involved reciprocal obligations. The right to the next presentation of Westow, for example, was acquired from Kirkham Priory by Thomas Vavasour gent. and Thomas Wirral, probably in the late 1530s. When the grant was exercised in 1546, their candidate was William Bekfelde, a former canon of the house.[40] The Thomas Ellys presented by Alice Midgley to Aldborough in 1547 by grant from the abbot and convent of Kirkstall was almost certainly the Thomas Ellys pensioned at that house in 1539.[41] In some other cases of former religious subsequently found beneficed in livings which had belonged to their house one suspects the issuing of grants, records of which have not survived. Even in cases where no formal alienation of patronage rights may have taken place, the fact that at least 14 former monks and canons came to occupy beneficed or unbeneficed posts formerly in the gift of their abbey or priory in the East Riding suggests that in some cases there may have been a tacit understanding or arrangement between the pre- and post-dissolution patrons.

We can do no more than conjecture as to the precise nature of such transactions. Did grantees collude with grantors out of regard for religious houses and their inmates, and a desire to see them well-settled in

---

[39] *Fasti Dickering*, p. 42. The degree to which monastic patronage may have operated in a general sense to facilitate social mobility is a nicely balanced question. As Per Ingesman's essay in this volume demonstrates, in Denmark the changes in the patronage structure brought by the Reformation resulted in a much less 'open' church. To an extent, a similar case can be argued for East Yorkshire: grants of next presentation opened control of benefices to the yeoman class, while posts in the larger monastic parishes provided a wealth of opportunities for the humbler stipendiary clergy. On the other hand, relatively lowly figures in society continued to acquire grants of next presentation long after the dissolution, and though it is likely that the successors of the monks may in some cases have been less assiduous in providing assistant clergy for the parishes in their charge, it was undoubtedly the 'Protestant' dissolutions of 1547, rather than those of 1536–40, which decimated opportunities for the lower secular clergy.

[40] *Fasti Buckrose*, p. 61; Cross, *End of Medieval Monasticism*, p. 41.

[41] *Fasti Holderness*, p. 4; *LP*, xiv/2. 567.

the world, or was more tangible inducement being offered? Either way, the result was significantly to delay the crown's ability to exercise control of its newly-won livings, some of them, like Foston, Langton, and West Heslerton, among the more valuable in the Riding.[42] There were at least nine former monastic benefices in the East Riding to which the crown was unable to present its candidate until the 1570s. At Kilnsea, the crown's first post-dissolution presentation was in 1590, and at Willerby in 1599, a full 62 years after the disappearance of the original patron, Bridlington Priory.[43]

Yet the vicarious, not to say posthumous, influence of the religious houses was not the sole factor in the long-term inhibiting the crown from exploiting to the full its newly acquired control over the bulk of benefices in the East Riding. In the decades following the dissolution, a considerable number of advowsons were granted away by the crown itself. Advowsons were, of course, often sold along with monastic estates, but this was not an automatic process.[44] In East Yorkshire at least, the crown seems to have been relatively slow to part with monastic lands, a tendency mirrored by its attitude to advowsons.[45] Of 87 advowsons acquired by the crown in 1536–40, at least 47 seem to have been retained throughout the half-century following the dissolution. Of the remainder, some confusion surrounds the fate of the dozen monastic perpetual curacies, appointments to which were not, of course, recorded in the episcopal register. Given that these positions had nothing to offer the incumbent but a curate's stipend, it seems virtually certain that the crown showed little interest in them, and that the patronage would have devolved in most cases on the farmer of the benefice.[46] A similar pattern is apparent with the other unbeneficed clerical positions formerly in the monasteries' gift, and presentation to stipendiary posts in chapelries seem to have passed relatively quickly into lay hands.[47] Of the more valuable benefices, a number filtered into the hands of local gentry. Sir Ralph Ellerker acquired Kirkella in 1545, and Sir John

---

[42] In 1535 Foston was calculated to be worth £15 8s. 6d., Langton, £17 4s. 6d., West Heslerton, £21 6s. 8d.: *Fasti Dickering*, p. 30; *Fasti Buckrose*, pp. 16, 26.

[43] *Fasti Holderness*, p. 81; *Fasti Dickering*, p. 93.

[44] In 1545, for example, a grant to Thomas Raynmore of the rectory of Scarborough explicitly excluded the advowson: *LP*, xx/1. 465 (25).

[45] In England as a whole *c.* 75 per cent of monastic lands had been alienated by 1558, but in the East Riding most of it still belonged to the crown: English, *Great Landowners of East Yorkshire*, p. 43.

[46] See, for example, J. T. Cliffe, *The Yorkshire Gentry from the Reformation to the Civil War* (London, 1969), p. 269; *Fasti Buckrose*, p. 30; *VCH*, iii. 195.

[47] *VCH*, i. 135, 294, 297; ii. 20, 103, 147, 161, 206; iii. 196.

Ellerker was granted North Cave in 1549.[48] Elizabeth granted Seamer to Sir Henry Gate in 1560, and around the same time Thomas Spencer acquired Yedingham.[49] By 1570 Sir John Constable had secured Sproatley.[50] Another group of advowsons went to important laymen from outside the Riding, whose descendants tended to hang on to them throughout the sixteenth century. Sir Richard Gresham, a former mayor of London and assiduous speculator in monastic property, purchased the advowson of Swine in 1546.[51] Thomas Manners, Earl of Rutland, 'founder' of the Augustinian Priory of Warter, was granted its vicarages of Lund and Warter in 1541, and the Earl of Northumberland was granted that of Wressle in 1558.[52] Sculcoates was granted to Elizabeth's favourite, Sir Christopher Hatton, in 1586.[53] A couple of advowsons went to ecclesiastical corporations outside the diocese. In 1541 the new Dean and Chapter of Durham were re-endowed with Durham Priory's living of Brantingham, and in 1547 Scalby was granted to the Dean and Chapter of Norwich.[54] By far the greatest beneficiary of livings alienated by the crown, however, was the Archbishop of York, a figure whose patronage in the Riding was negligible before the dissolution (see Table 8.1). In the first half of the 1540s, Archbishops Lee and Holgate received from Henry VIII eight former monastic advowsons in East Yorkshire in addition to three others (Rowley, Scrayingham, and Etton) which had come into the crown's hands through other channels. The motivation behind these grants had little to do with any desire to augment the spiritual authority of the archbishop. Instead it was part of a process whereby under a series of exchanges in 1542–5, the prelate was forced to hand over valuable episcopal manors and was compensated with the income in tithes from impropriated benefices.[55] The

---

[48] Clay, *Suppression Papers*, p. 116; *VCH*, iii. 33. Ellerker's patronage of Kirkella seems initially to have come via a grant of next presentation from the king: BI Adm 1554/16. Sir Ralph provides an example of how an important local gentleman with limited patronage of his own could take advantage of the traffic in next presentations: in the 1540s he acquired a grant of Brantingham from the Dean and Chapter of Durham as well as of Hilston from its lay patrons: BI Adm 1557/17; *Fasti Holderness*, p. 58.

[49] *Fasti Dickering*, p. 81; *Fasti Buckrose*, p. 75.

[50] *Fasti Holderness*, p. 144.

[51] Clay, *Suppression Papers*, p. 157; W. G. Hoskins, *The Age of Plunder: The England of Henry VIII 1500–1547* (London, 1976), pp. 137–9.

[52] *LP* , xvi. 678; *Fasti Harthill*, p. 270.

[53] *VCH*, i. 303.

[54] *Fasti Harthill*, p. 34; *Calendar of Patent Rolls, Edward VI* (6 vols, London, 1924–9), i. 59.

[55] C. Cross, 'The economic problems of the see of York: decline and recovery in the sixteenth century', *Agricultural History Review*, 18 (1970), 64–83; F. Heal, *Of Prelates and Princes: a Study of the Economic and Social Position of the Tudor Episcopate* (Cambridge, 1980), pp. 117–18.

crown's loss of parochial patronage to the Archbishop in the 1540s was recouped in 1547 with the dissolution of the collegiate churches. The treatment of these advowsons showed a similar pattern to those of the monasteries: nine (or possibly eight) were still in the crown's hands in 1590.

In the late 1550s, however, the crown's attitude to its recently acquired monastic advowsons had undergone a marked transformation, a reflection of Queen Mary's determination to return to the church the assets that had been stripped from it by her father. A statute of 1555 declared the crown's intention to restore first fruits, tenths, and the income from the crown's remaining impropriated livings, though at this stage reserving all patronage rights.[56] By 1558, however, Mary and Pole had embarked on a thorough-going policy of returning advowsons to the bishops as compensation for the diversion of spiritual revenues towards the costs of the French war. Under these arrangements Archbishop Heath received the advowsons of no fewer than 54 livings in the East Riding.[57] For a short period at the end of 1558 and beginning of 1559, the Archbishop of York possessed unprecedented control over the appointment of clergy in his diocese, but the experiment had little chance of surviving into the next reign. The act of Elizabeth's first parliament in 1559 restoring first fruits, tenths, and impropriated benefices to the crown explicitly revoked the Marian grants of patronage, and Elizabeth reverted to her father's policy of occasional alienations (see Table 8.4).[58]

Arguably the most significant prospect the dispersal of monastic patronage opened up was the chance for patrons to use their newly-acquired advowsons to advance clerks who shared their religious position. To Robert Burton, writing in the 1620s, it was axiomatic that patrons would tend to behave in this way: 'if the patron be precise, so must his chaplain be: if he be papistical, his clerk must be so or else be turned out.'[59] Yet in later sixteenth-century East Yorkshire there seems to be remarkably little indication of patrons systematically placing priests in livings for ideological reasons, to advance or hinder the cause of reformation. The patrons who might seem to be best placed to promote Protestant ministers, and who had good reason for doing so were, of

---

[56] *Statutes of the Realm* (11 vols, London, 1830–52), iv. 275–8. See R. H. Pogson, 'Revival and reform in Mary Tudor's church: a question of money' in C. Haigh (ed.), *The English Reformation Revised* (Cambridge, 1987), pp. 139–56.

[57] *Calendar of Patent Rolls, Philip and Mary* (4 vols, London, 1936–9), iv. 399–400, 401, 402, 420, 437, 438, 439, 449, 450.

[58] *Statutes of the Realm*, iv. 362.

[59] R. Burton, *The Anatomy of Melancholy*, cited in C. Hill, *Economic Problems of the Church from Archbishop Whitgift to the Long Parliament* (Oxford, 1956), p. 55.

Table 8.4   Ownership of advowsons in the East Riding, 1590

Patron	No. advowsons	% advowsons
Archbishop of York	14	8.5
Other Ecclesiastics	31	18.8
Crown	61	37.0
Other lay patrons*	58	35.2
Unclear	1	0.6
Total	165	100.0

*figure includes presentation to 10 perpetual curacies, very probably in lay hands by the later sixteenth century.

course, the archbishops of York, and in the judgement of A. G. Dickens, the Henrician exchanges 'materially increased their power over their clergy and over the whole ecclesiastical system of the North'.[60] Yet, as W. J. Sheils has noted, the impropriated benefices acquired by the archbishops were rarely well-endowed enough to attract ambitious graduates, and the finances of the archdiocese could not realistically entertain the rediversion of rectorial income into support of the minister.[61] The Elizabethan archbishops did what they could to further reform in East Yorkshire, but their collection of advowsons proved an uncertain instrument. During the vacancies of the see in 1568–70, 1576–7, and 1588–9, presentments to archiepiscopal livings were made by the crown. Moreover, by no means all archiepiscopal nominees turned out to be reliable Protestants. Archbishop Young's presentee as vicar of Easington in Holderness was discovered at the visitation of 1567 to be saying communion for the dead, and in 1586 Grindal's candidate in the impoverished living of Skipsea was accused of failing to provide sermons.[62]

A handful of lay patrons did show some apparent concern for the spiritual qualities of their nominee: in 1565 Robert and Benedict Cholmeley used a grant of next presentation from the Duchess of Suffolk to present the graduate preacher Robert Paley to Burton Agnes, a former appropriation of St Mary's Abbey, York, and a strongly conservative area, where as early as the 1560s some Catholic parishioners

[60] Dickens, *Reformation Studies*, p. 339.

[61] W. J. Sheils, 'Profit, patronage, or pastoral care: the rectory estates of the archbishopric of York, 1540–1640' in R. O'Day and F. Heal (eds), *Princes and Paupers in the English Church 1500–1800* (Leicester, 1981), p. 98.

[62] Dickens, *Reformation Studies*, p. 163; BI V.1586/CB f. 143ʳ.

were moving into full recusancy.[63] In 1582 the 'Puritan' President of the Council in the North, the Earl of Huntingdon, used his influence with his aunt, Lady Winifred Hastings, patron of Rowley, to ensure the presentation of a learned minister to that rectory.[64] Yet most of the leading gentry of the Riding seem to have shown little interest in using their patronage to insinuate either 'hot' Protestants or crypto-Catholics into the established church.[65] The complex background to a presentation at Settrington illustrates the point. In 1561 the patrons, Lord and Lady Strange, made a grant of next presentation to Thomas Clifford of Brakenburgh in Lincolnshire, who in turn alienated the grant to Christopher Monckton of Londesborough and Sir William Babthorpe of Osgodby. Babthorpe was a leading East Riding Catholic who in 1581 played host to the Jesuit Edmund Campion. Yet he sold his right of presentation to Settrington to the Duke of Norfolk, who in 1568 used it to present Matthew Hutton, Dean of York, and later Archbishop, an exemplar of godly Protestantism and scourge of papistry.[66] Similarly, the Catholic Mathew St Quintin sold a next presentation of Harswell to Sir John Gates, who exercised it in 1582.[67] Conversely, another notorious papist, Sir Thomas Metham, acquired a grant to present John Gill to Middleton-on-the-Wolds in 1571. His motives for doing so are unknown to us, but perhaps more remarkable is the fact that the patron making this grant to Metham, described at the time as 'a most wilful and obstinate Papist' with two sons among the exiles at Louvain, appears to have been the crown itself.[68] There is in fact little evidence that the crown followed any more thoroughly consistent a policy with regard to the candidates it placed in its livings than the monasteries had done. In Elizabeth's reign a number of advanced Protestants were presented by the crown, but visitation records suggest that royal nominees were as likely to be reported for disciplinary offences as any other part of the clerical body in the East Riding.[69]

---

[63] *Fasti Dickering*, p. 13; Sheils, 'Rectory estates of the archbishop', p. 99.

[64] C. Cross, *The Puritan Earl: The Life of Henry Hastings Third Earl of Huntingdon 1536–95* (London, 1966), p. 265.

[65] This may have been starting to change by the early decades of the seventeenth century: in the 1630s the Stricklands of Boynton placed several 'Puritan' ministers in the six East Riding benefices in their possession: Cliffe, *Yorkshire Gentry*, pp. 268–9.

[66] Ibid., p. 173; *Fasti Buckrose*, p. 64.

[67] *Fasti Harthill*, p. 127.

[68] Cliffe, *Yorkshire Gentry*, pp. 171–2; *Fasti Harthill*, p. 198.

[69] R. A. Marchant, *The Puritans and the Church Courts in the Diocese of York 1560–1642* (London, 1960), pp. 259, 269, 318; BI V.1567–8/CB, fos 30^r, 165^r; V.1571–2/CB, f. 65^r; V.1578–9/CB, fos 43^v, 35^v, 37^r, 200^r; V.1586/CB, fos 162^{r-v}; V.1590–91/CB, f. 134^r; W. J. Sheils (ed.), *Archbishop Grindal's Visitation, 1575: Comperta et Detecta Book* (York, 1977), pp. 71, 85.

If the crown was on occasion prepared to sell its rights of presentation, it is perhaps unsurprising that some lesser lay patrons took a distinctly commercial rather than religious interest in their recently acquired patronage. Puritan propagandists in Elizabeth's reign did not hesitate to assert that patrons regularly sold benefices to would-be incumbents, or bestowed them on their servants in lieu of wages.[70] In East Yorkshire, at least three Elizabethan incumbents were forced into public denials that they had acquired their living through simoniacal means. In 1567, the rector of Langton, Henry Bilton, protested strongly that 'he did not come to his benefice by convention or paction of simony', but suspicion is aroused by his being presented by a notary, who seems to have acquired the next presentation from a grantee of Malton Priory.[71] In another former monastic benefice, Lund in Harthill deanery, the vicar, Oswald Nelson, was charged with simony in 1576. Patron of the benefice was the Earl of Rutland, whose grandfather had been granted the advowson by Henry VIII in 1541. Nelson's explanation in court of his nomination sheds interesting light on the dynamics of securing a patron: he claimed to have been presented by the earl without any payment 'at the request of one Mr Fawether of Hull, being this repondent's kinsman'.[72] A more clear-cut case of simony seems to have taken place at Patrington, a living formerly in the gift of Beverley Minster. Here the parishioners reported to the Ecclesiastical Commission in 1571 that their rector, Thomas Langdale, was the beneficiary of 'certain simoniacal pactions and covenants'. More specifically, it was alleged that the post-dissolution patron, Ralph Crayke, had sold the advowson to Sir John Constable on the condition that Constable's nominee would let the rectory back to Crayke for a 'reasonable rent', which in this case was believed to be considerably below the true value of the benefice. Langdale admitted that such a covenant had been made, and that he had let the rectory to Crayke, but claimed, somewhat implausibly, that he had been presented without conditions, 'simply for his service done to the said Sir John'.[73]

Preaching before the queen in the early 1580s, Archbishop Sandys was firm in his conviction that the great transfer of parish patronage from monasteries to the laity had served for little other than to perpetuate abuses inherent in the old system: 'the chiefest benefices were by the

---

[70] Hill, *Economic Problems of the Church*, pp. 211–12.
[71] BI V.1567–8/CB, f. 155[r]; *Fasti Buckrose*, p. 28.
[72] *LP*, xvi. 678; BI CP G 1817.
[73] BI HC CP 1571/1.

pope long since impropriated unto monks which devoured the fruits
and gave a silly stipend unto a poor Sir John to say mass; and as they
left it so we found it still.'[74] By this time it had become something of a
Protestant cliché that from the point of view of advancing the Word of
God lay patrons were little, if at all, better than the papistical institutions they had replaced, advancing unlearned clerks for a variety of
secular considerations, and showing little or no regard for the material
or spiritual welfare of the parishes in their gift.[75] The root of the
malaise was regularly perceived to be the continuation of the system of
impropriations, and the consequent anomaly whereby the spiritual income of tithes went to the support of laymen. In 1605 William Crashaw,
curate of St John's church in Beverley, had the East Riding clearly in
mind when he wrote that 'my small experience doth show that in one
corner of one county of this kingdom, wherein there are some 150
parishes or parochial chapels, almost 100 of them are impropriate'. The
great bulk of the income from these benefices, Crashaw noted ruefully,
went not to the support of 'painful and able ministers', but to 'the
feeding of kites and cormorants'.[76] To all these critics the removal of
patronage from the monasteries represented a missed opportunity – to
do away with impropriations and have a properly funded preaching
ministry, the policy Francis Bigod had advocated on the eve of the
Henrician dissolutions. Yet it was precisely the right to tax the parishioners that made the possession of former monastic appropriations and
their attendant advowsons an attractive prospect to both crown and
lesser laity, as well as, increasingly, an essential aspect of the finances of
the archbishop. In such circumstances, the aspiration to replace the
priests appointed by the monks with learned and godly ministers was,
in the short to medium term at least, never a realistic one, even if it had
been shared by all lay patrons. Whether the transfer of so much patronage to the laity really had a deleterious affect on the standard of
pastoral care in the East Riding is a nicely poised question. Certainly
there were far fewer clergy in the parishes of the East Riding in the
1590s than in the 1520s, but this is likely to be symptomatic of a

---

[74] J. Ayre (ed.), *The Sermons of Edwin Sandys*, Parker Society (Cambridge, 1851), p.
155.

[75] See, for example, H. Robinson (ed.), *Original Letters Relative to the English Reformation*, Parker Society (Cambridge, 1847), ii. 546, and works by Crowley, Brinkelowe,
Becon in C. H. Williams (ed.), *English Historical Documents* (London, 1967), v. 310,
330–32, 953; Hill, *Economic Problems of the Church*, pp. 65–6, 211–14.

[76] D. J. Lamburn, 'Petty Babylons, godly prophets, petty pastors, and little churches:
the work of healing Babel' in W. J. Sheils and D. Wood (eds), *The Ministry: Clerical and
Lay*, Studies in Church History xxvi (Oxford, 1989), pp. 239–40.

falling-off in recruitment and of the changed priorities of Protestantism rather than of the negligence of new patrons.[77]

There is evidence that the lay rectors who had replaced the monks were often careless of their responsibilities towards church fabrics, and a very marked rise in the number of recorded tithe suits in the East Riding might suggest that lay impropriators were more relentless in pursuit of their rights than their monastic forebears, or, alternatively, that lay people were more reluctant to pay their tithes to an obviously non-spiritual end, a claim made by the Elizabethan rector of Wickersley in the West Riding, Michael Sherbrook, in his nostalgic tract, *The Fall of Religious Houses*. Although, in contrast to some other parts of the country, Yorkshire monasteries do not seem to have habitually farmed their rectories to laymen, perhaps a more pertinent explanation for the rising level of litigation is the sharp inflation besetting the country from the 1540s which made it incumbent upon all manner of tithe-owners to press for full payment in kind.[78] There is no doubt that the parishes of East Yorkshire witnessed massive change in the half-century following the dissolution of the monasteries: the transformation of the interiors of their churches, the imposition of Protestant forms of worship, the huge shrinkage of the clerical body, and the beginnings of its transformation into a largely graduate preaching ministry. Little of this, however, can be directly attributed to the disappearance of the religious houses, or the conscious will of a new coterie of patrons.

It would be facile though to propose that the confiscation and dispersal of so much monastic patronage was ultimately an act of little significance. Before 1535 the greater part of the patronage of parochial livings in East Yorkshire, as in much of the country, was in the hands of the church. Thereafter, it was overwhelmingly under lay control, a critical realignment, indicative of so much that had changed in the relationship between church and state in England. Moreover, the transfer of patronage to the crown consequent upon the dissolution in the East Riding seemed to represent an extreme intrusion of external state power into the heart of the local community, as patrons with local roots and responsibilities were replaced by a distant authority less open to pressure and persuasion from interested parties. The relative reluctance of the crown, at least up to the 1590s, to part permanently with its

---

[77] A survey in 1526 noted the names of nearly 600 secular clergy resident in the East Riding: W. Brown and T. M. Fallow (eds), 'The East Riding clergy in 1525–6', *Yorkshire Archaeological Journal*, 24 (1917), 62–80. A survey in 1592 provided only 146 names: Lambeth Palace Library, Cart. Misc. xii, no. 9 (BI Microfilm 35).

[78] Purvis, *Condition of Yorkshire Church Fabrics*, pp. 16–18; Purvis (ed.), *Select Sixteenth-Century Causes in Tithe from the York Diocesan Registry*, YASRS cxiv (1949), p. viii; Dickens (ed.), *Tudor Treatises*, pp. 114–15.

advowsons in East Yorkshire, reinforces this impression. As Margaret
Bowker has noted, as potential patrons the religious houses were acces-
sible and non-peripatetic. The crown, by contrast, was expensive to
approach and had large numbers of its own servants to reward.[79] Yet a
seismic relocation of influence from locality to centre may in some ways
have been more apparent than real. Around 40 per cent of the crown's
windfall of advowsons had been permanently granted away by 1590,
and more was to follow in the succeeding decades. The beneficiaries
were sometimes absentee southerners, but more often they had strong
local interests and connections, as in the case of the archbishop of York,
or East Riding (often recusant) gentry families like the Ellerkers and
Constables. The traffic in next presentations, much of it initiated by the
monasteries themselves in their final phase, facilitated manipulation of
the patronage system by predominantly local figures normally excluded
from its operation. The fact that all but five of the monastic livings
acquired by the crown were valued in 1535 at less than £20 a year
meant that the great bulk of the crown's new presentations were made
by the Lord Keeper of the Great Seal. As Rosemary O'Day has shown,
successive Elizabethan Lord Keepers largely had to rely on recommendations from local bishops, courtiers, and gentry. The crown's reluctance to make formal grants of next presentation thus masked the
contingent nature of many of its presentations.[80] The power, as well as
the desire, to fracture the monasteries' influence over the parish churches
in East Yorkshire came overwhelmingly from outside, but in this, as in
other aspects of the dissolution, there was no shortage of people on
hand able and willing to pick up the pieces.

---

[79] Bowker, *Henrician Reformation*, p. 122.

[80] O'Day, *The English Clergy*, ch. 9, and 'The ecclesiastical patronage of the Lord
Keeper, 1558–1642', *TRHS*, 5th Series 23 (1973), 89–107.

CHAPTER NINE

Patronage, *Herrschaft*, and confession: the Upper-Palatinate nobility and the Counter Reformation

Trevor Johnson

The utility of investigating early modern religious change within its broader social, political, and economic context has become a common-place for historians of the Reformation since the 1960s, inspired in particular by the pioneering work of Bernd Moeller.[1] An important instance of the many possible contextualizations which can be applied to religious change is the impact of reform on the relationship between the church and its property. Adoption of the Reformation inevitably entailed the secularization, or transfer into lay (above all, princely) hands, of ecclesiastical capital and revenues, of which the dissolution of the English monasteries in the 1530s is one of the best-known examples. In Germany, however, as Henry Cohn has argued, secularization was 'the fate ... not only – and not even principally – of monastic lands, but of church property in the wider sense, embracing also the lands and whole government of bishoprics ... the property of parishes in town and country, patronage to benefices, religious and charitable endowments, schools and universities, and by extension the ecclesiastical jurisdiction that had controlled all such property'.[2] Plucking one item from Cohn's list, and taking as its focus a regional case study, the following essay concentrates on the theme of lay, especially noble, patronage to bene-fices and its relationship to religious change, instanced here not by a shift from late-medieval Catholicism to Protestantism, but from Protest-antism to post-Tridentine Catholicism.[3]

---

[1] B. Moeller, *Imperial Cities and the Reformation* (Philadelphia, 1972). For a recent appreciation of Moeller's seminal approach in this respect see J. Bossy, 'The German Reformation after Moeller', *JEH*, 45 (1994), 673–84.

[2] H. J. Cohn, 'Church property in the German Protestant principalities' in E. I. Kouri and Tom Scott (eds), *Politics and Society in Reformation Europe* (London, 1987), pp. 158–87, esp. p. 158.

[3] In the pre-Reformation Holy Roman Empire, as elsewhere, the right to present clergy

The region which will be examined is the small south-east German territory of the Upper Palatinate, previously Protestant but in the 1620s reconverted to Catholicism after its invasion and annexation by Elector Maximilian I of Bavaria. Although Maximilian's recatholicization was eventually successful, in the early years it encountered a degree of passive resistance and obstruction, led in the main by the Upper Palatinate's largely Lutheran landowning nobility. Patronage to ecclesiastical benefices represented merely one aspect of an entire apparatus of formal and informal local power at this élite's disposal (the nexus of authority encapsulated in the German term *Herrschaft*), but it gained prominence at a critical juncture in the recatholicization, since for the confessionally motivated among the nobility it appeared to offer the prospect of protecting Lutheran clergy (and therefore Lutheran worship) from expulsion by the Catholic authorities. With the introduction of the Counter Reformation, as previously with the arrival of Protestantism, lay patronage found itself subject to the dramatic new tensions of the confessional age. As a result, it might be asked how the venerable insititution was affected by the process. The nature of this particular dispute also prompts the question as to which was uppermost in noble assertions of traditional patronal rights, the 'political' desire to defend familial property, jurisdictional autonomy, social power, and local identity against the encroachments of the newly installed, 'proto-absolutist' Bavarian regime, or the 'religious' wish to use all available means to articulate and defend individual conscience and confessional allegiance. A similar question of political or religious motivation can be asked of the policies of the Bavarian state itself.

Prior to its invasion by Bavaria in late 1621, the Upper Palatinate, a cluster of lands bordering Bavaria and Bohemia, had belonged to the

---

to benefices, termed the *ius patronatus*, was held in the main by diocesan bishops and ecclesiastical institutions, especially monastic houses. However, it was also extensively owned by secular corporations (such as town councils) or passed down, as a form of property, through generations of individual lay families. Often such lay patronage derived from a princely or noble ancestor's foundation or donation of the church or chapel to which the benefice in question was attached. Under the *ius patronatus*, medieval decretalists had distinguished between a number of 'spiritual' components (*collatio, concessio*, and *institutio*) reserved to the diocesan ordinary and a temporal component (*praesentatio*) which belonged to the patron. The hereditable character of the patronage right, its description as an 'honour' or as a 'burden' of obligations, and the powers it could confer over the disposal of parochial income as well as over clerical appointments were much debated issues amongst late medieval canon lawyers. For a survey of the medieval developments and discussion of post-Reformation reconfigurations of patronage rights see J. Sieglerschmidt, *Territorialstaat und Kirchenregiment: Studien zur Rechtsdogmatik des Kirchenpatronatsrechts im 15. und 16. Jahrhundert* (Cologne, Vienna, 1987).

dominions of the Palatine electors, whose rule was usually delegated to a *Statthalter*, or regent, resident in the local capital at Amberg. From 1556 the official religious confession of the territory (as of the Palatinate as a whole) had oscillated confusingly between Evangelical (Lutheran) and Reformed (Calvinist) variants as successive electors sought to impose their own adopted faith on their population.[4] The return to Catholicism in the 1620s, in the wake of the Bavarian invasion precipitated by Elector Frederick V's reckless Bohemian adventure, marked nothing less than the fifth confessional *volte-face* in the region in the space of some 60 years. The general population's bewilderment, not to mention frustration, at such dramatic change was neatly crystallized in the outburst of a blacksmith of the town of Waldeck, who interrupted a church service in February 1627 with the despairing cry: 'Oh, my God! We have gone astray! I was born and bred a Lutheran. When the Calvinist and Zwinglian religion arrived in the Palatinate, I had to change my faith. Now the Papists have come too, saying their religion is the true one because it is the oldest. We have really gone astray!'[5]

Despite the confusion which inevitably attended each swing of the confessional pendulum, there is compelling evidence that the evangelical faith had come to enjoy a substantial measure of support in the region. In marked contrast to the experience of the Upper Palatinate's counterpart on the Rhine, the Reformation had already been espoused as a popular movement in the 1540s, above all amongst the citizenry of Amberg, before its formal adoption by the prince. Thereafter, the gradual consolidation of a distinctive Lutheran identity, particularly among the towns and the nobility, was clearly demonstrated by the force of local resistance to the imposition of Calvinist institutions, policies, and personnel during the administrations of Frederick III (1559–76), Johann Casimir (1583–92), Frederick IV (1592–1610), and Frederick V (1610–19). In 1563, for example, in the presence of Elector Frederick III himself, the noble-dominated Upper-Palatinate diet voiced its objection to any future adoption of Reformed doctrine and usages, playing the

---

[4] Older literature on the Reformation in the Upper Palatinate is dominated by the trilogy of studies by J. B. Götz, *Die religiöse Bewegung in der Oberpfalz von 1520 bis 1560* (Freiburg, 1914), *Die erste Einführung des Kalvinismus in der Oberpfalz, 1559–76* (Münster, 1933), and *Die religiösen Wirren in der Oberpfalz, 1576–1620* (Münster, 1937). For a more recent treatment of the Palatinate as a whole in the Reformation period see Volker Press, *Calvinismus und Territorialstaat: Regierung und Zentralbehörden der Kurpfalz, 1559–1619* (Kiel, 1970).

[5] STAA, Subdelegierte Registratur 1827 (22 February 1627). For a similar example see H. Cohn, 'The territorial princes in Germany's Second Reformation, 1559–1622' in M. Prestwich (ed.), *International Calvinism, 1541–1715* (Oxford, 1985), pp. 135–65, esp. p. 157.

traditional card of a threat to withhold taxation. In justification for its opposition, the diet cited the endangered personal salvation of its individual members and (an accurate prediction, this) the dire political repercussions of any breach of the Religious Peace of 1555, particularly given the territory's exposed position in the midst of hostile Catholic neighbours.[6] In the 1590s, resistance escalated into anti-government riots in Amberg and the murder of Calvinist officials. After 1595, under the regency of Prince Christian of Anhalt, the architect of Frederick V's ambitious foreign policy and a forceful exponent of administrative centralization, open hostility to the Calvinist 'Second Reformation' subsided, but local attachment to a home-grown Lutheranism, as much as to traditional political autonomy, was far from eliminated.[7]

Despite the obvious strength of Lutheranism, it would seem that Maximilian of Bavaria was, from the outset, keen to oversee a full-scale restoration of Catholicism in his newly-won territory.[8] The project's success depended in the first instance on an assumption of legal and political authority, a factor which materialized gradually, but seemingly inexorably, over the decade following the invasion. By an imperial decree of 1621, all previous oaths of homage were dissolved and fealty was henceforth to be owed to the emperor, with Maximilian as his imperial commissioner. In 1623, the Bavarian ruler was invested with the electoral rank stripped from the banned Frederick V and was provisionally granted the Upper Palatinate as security for the war-debt of 12 million Gulden owed him by the emperor. Finally, in 1628, Ferdinand II formally granted the Upper Palatinate to Bavaria (effectively this was a sale, as in return the war-debt was written off). Incorporation of the Upper Palatinate fulfilled a longstanding claim by the Bavarian branch of the Wittelsbach family against their Palatine cousins and coupled a considerable enhancement of dynastic, political, and diplomatic leverage to the economic and strategic benefits of additional territory, popu-

---

[6] K.-O. Ambronn, 'Amberg und die oberpfälzischen Landstände bis zu ihrer Auflösung 1628' in K.-O. Ambronn, A. Fuchs, and H. Wanderwitz (eds), *Amberg 1034–1984: Aus tausend Jahren Stadtgeschichte* (Amberg, 1984), pp. 75–90.

[7] 'Die Maßnahmen des Fürsten Christian stießen aber auf die tief verwurzelte Identifikation der Oberpfälzer mit einer eigenen Tradition, die sich mit der Autonomie des Landes verbunden hatte': V. Press, 'Die "Zweite Reformation" in der Kurpfalz' in H. Schilling (ed.), *Die reformierte Konfessionalisierung in Deutschland: Das Problem der 'Zweiten Reformation'* (Gütersloh, 1986), pp. 104–29, esp. p. 119.

[8] For recent studies of the Counter Reformation in the Upper Palatinate see W. Ziegler, 'Die Rekatholisierung der Oberpfalz' in H. Glaser (ed.), *Um Glauben und Reich: Kurfürst Maximilian I* (2 vols, Munich, 1980), i. 436–47, M. Popp, 'Kirchengeschichte Ambergs zwischen Rekatholisierung und Säkularisation' in Ambronn et al., *Amberg 1034–1984*, pp. 137–52, and, for further references, T. R. Johnson, 'The recatholicisation of the Upper Palatinate, 1621–*c*. 1700' (Ph.D. Cambridge, 1992).

lation, and revenue. However, whilst Maximilian was scarcely immune to temporal considerations, he was also the quintessential Counter-Reformation prince, combining daring political ambition with militant championing of the Catholic cause and an extravagant personal piety. Maximilian's pilgrimages to local Bavarian shrines and participation in the festivals of the Munich Jesuit college were the public manifestations of a genuinely ascetic devotional ardour, to which his hair shirts and discipline (found among his affects after his death) or the dedication to the Virgin written in his own blood (posthumously discovered in the pilgrimage chapel at Altötting) were mute witnesses. For Maximilian, toleration of heresy within his domains was unthinkable.[9]

Nevertheless, as Walter Ziegler has noted, the implementation of the policy of recatholicization was gradual, with the timing and extent of each incremental turn of the confessional screw mirroring Maximilian's own creeping legal and political grip on the territory.[10] In 1623, for example, the placement at the disposal of the Jesuits of a few of the territory's churches marked the beginning of the return of Catholic influence. In 1624, the Calvinist School in Amberg was closed and the first Reformed clergy were dismissed. In 1625, Protestant government officials were replaced by Catholics. The year 1626 saw a wave of mass expulsions of evangelical clergy. In 1628, Protestant books were confiscated and burnt, whilst a deal was struck between Pope Urban VIII and the emperor whereby for a 12-year period (subsequently extended) the revenues of the Upper Palatinate's medieval monasteries, secularized at the Reformation, were to remain available for secular purposes, save for a third of the total, the so-called *pia tertia*, which was allocated to the task of recatholicization. When Maximilian was granted the Upper Palatinate, the arrangement was transferred to him. Cession of the territory also finally allowed Maximilian to culminate the project with the issue in the same year of a decree, the *Religionspatent*, requiring the conversion or emigration of all Protestants within six months. It is impossible to determine with any accuracy how many Upper-Palatinate subjects chose to emigrate rather than convert to Catholicism as a result. However, although their numbers appear to have been small relative to the total population, their social standing would have given their departure a disproportionate significance. Over ten per cent of the

---

[9] On Maximilian's character and piety see P. J. Steiner, 'Der gottselige Fürst und die Konfessionalisierung Altbayerns' in Glaser (ed.), *Um Glauben und Reich*, i. 252–63, B. Hubensteiner, *Vom Geist des Barock: Kultur und Frömmigkeit im alten Bayern* (Munich, 1967), R. Bireley, *Maximilian von Bayern, Adam Contzen S.J. und die Gegenreformation in Deutschland, 1624–35* (Göttingen, 1975), and A. Kraus, *Maximilian I: Bayerns Großer Kurfürst* (Graz, etc., 1990).

[10] Ziegler, 'Rekatholisierung'.

citizenry of Amberg, for example, including most of the capital's economic and political élite, were among the Protestant emigrés.[11] Of the
nobility who had declared one way or the other by 1630, 93 families
had emigrated (including that of the former territorial marshal and
speaker for the nobility and the estates in the Upper-Palatinate diet,
Hans Friedrich Fuchs of Winklarn), whilst a roughly equal number had
converted.[12] By 1630, the vast majority of the remaining population had
conformed and were, at least nominally, once again within the fold of
the Catholic church.

Maximilian's gradualist approach to the task of recatholicization was
partly determined by wider diplomatic considerations, but it also reflected his appreciation of local political realities. This can perhaps best
be seen in the caution with which the Bavarian ruler approached the
conversion of the Upper-Palatinate nobility, in the course of which the
patronage question was briefly brought to the fore. Maximilian was
evidently appraised of the Lutheran sentiments of many of the landed
élite and the resistance which they had mounted against the Calvinist
policies of the later-sixteenth-century Palatine electors and must have
feared that they would now prove equally restive when confronted with
a Catholic regime. Warning notes were sounded as early as November
1621, just after the Bavarian invasion, for, when summoned to swear
the new act of homage, many nobles procrastinated and some, like the
magistrate of Auerbach, Hans Jacob von Schlammersdorf, emigrated
immediately rather than abandon their allegiance to Frederick V.[13] The
nobles' ability to exert their local *Herrschaft*, in effect to intimidate
their tenantry on their estates, raised the spectre of large tracts of the
country becoming hotbeds of Lutheran resistance. At the same time,
Maximilian depended upon the nobility, the class which filled the ranks
of the local rural magistracy, to secure stability and order. Collectively,
the nobility had their teeth drawn in 1628, when Maximilian abolished

---

[11] Emigrations from Amberg at the time of the recatholicization are analysed in A.
Fuchs, 'Amberger Exulanten: Zur Emigration in der Stadt Amberg während der
Gegenreformation', *Oberpfälzer Heimat*, 23 (1979), 97–104. In Amberg, which had a
population of slightly under 5 000 at the time of the *Religionspatent*, at least 136
families or individual members of converted families, perhaps 500 people in all, left the
town between 1627 and 1630. Adding the families of Protestant clergy, schoolmasters,
scholars, and officials, Fuchs arrives at a figure of 745 emigrants, or 15 per cent of the
population and 10.6 per cent of the town's citizenry. The emigrants included three
former mayors and seven other former councillors, all three of the town's qualified
physicians and its last remaining book printer. The 63 emigrants whose capital can be
assessed owned 25.63 per cent of the citizenry's total taxable wealth.

[12] Ziegler, 'Rekatholisierung', p. 440.

[13] F. Lippert, *Geschichte der Gegenreformation in Staat, Kirche und Sitte der Oberpfalz-
Kurpfalz zur Zeit des dreißigjährigen Krieges* (Freiburg, 1901), pp. 18–25.

the Upper-Palatinate diet. The Bavarian ruler was no more prepared to tolerate the presence of a potentially ideologically hostile and financially obstructive representative assembly in his new territory than his sixteenth-century predecessors had been in their Bavarian heartland.[14] Individually, however, the vital role of the nobility in the social order was recognized, and in 1629 their personal privileges and freedoms were renewed.[15]

It is, however, the period before the forced conversions, emigrations, and abolition of the diet that concerns us here, for it was chiefly during the mid-1620s that a section of the nobility demonstrated, through their manipulation of patronage rights, a command of resources sufficient to at least slow the pace of recatholicization and compel Maximilian and his officials to re-examine their strategy. The question of noble patronage arose when the Bavarian regime began to target the Protestant clergy in post, a group which had been either tolerated or appointed by the old, Reformed regime. The first steps were piecemeal. In January 1625, for example, the town preacher at Amberg, Johann Widmann, was denounced as a Calvinist by the Amberg Jesuits. Although Widmann had allegedly sworn solemnly in the pulpit (raising two fingers in the time-honoured gesture) that he had never subscribed to Reformed propositions, the Jesuits claimed to have discovered evidence to the contrary in the shape of a 41-page confession, dated 1609, and other documents bearing his signature in the archives of the Calvinist church council (*Kirchenrat*). Described as 'seditious and refractory', Widmann was dismissed and expelled. Ignoring an appeal from the town council to replace him with a Lutheran, Maximilian appropriated the town's traditional right of appointment to the high-profile post ('times', he wrote ominously, 'have changed'), left it vacant, and decreed that the remaining ministers in the capital could be assisted by the Jesuits. By the end of the year the Jesuit superior could boast that his priests were now saying mass in all four of the capital's major churches.[16] In June 1625, the remainder of the Reformed clergy played into the government's hands by choosing to make a stand on the issue of emergency baptism, or, as it

---

[14] On the struggles between the Bavarian dukes and their diets in the sixteenth century see S. Weinfurter, 'Herzog, Adel und Reformation: Bayern im Übergang vom Mittelalter zur Neuzeit', *Zeitschrift für Historische Forschung*, 10 (1983), 1–39.

[15] Ziegler, 'Rekatholisierung', p. 440.

[16] STAA, Oberpfälzisches Religions- und Reformationswesen (hereafter ORuR) 555; Lippert, *Gegenreformation*, pp. 66–8; M. Högl, *Die Bekehrung der Oberpfalz durch Maximilian I* (Regensburg, 1903), p. 11. On the Jesuit contribution to the recatholicization of the Upper Palatinate see W. Gegenfurtner, 'Jesuiten in der Oberpfalz: Ihr Wirken und ihr Beitrag zur Rekatholisierung in den oberpfälzischen Landen (1621–50)', *Beiträge zur Geschichte des Bistums Regensburg*, 11 (1977), 71–220.

was termed, the *Jachtaufe*. The Calvinist ban on this traditional and popular practice had further alienated the Evangelical Protestants from their Reformed counterparts, a division on which the recatholicizers doubtless aimed to capitalize. On 16 June 1625, Maximilian issued a decree authorizing all subjects of the Upper Palatinate to perform the rite if an infant was otherwise in danger of dying unbaptized and forbidding Calvinist clergy from fining them for doing so.[17] Parish clergy were required to read out the instruction from their pulpits on 20 July, with secular officials present to insure compliance or to read out the instruction themselves if the clergy refused. Having set the trap, Maximilian must have been gratified to see the Reformed ministers rushing headlong into it. In the event, over a quarter of the pastors either altered the text of the mandate or refused to read it out and, as a result, were ordered to leave their posts.[18]

On 23 September 1625, Maximilian pressed home the attack by issuing his first general order for the dismissal of non-Catholic clergy. Ministers were to be removed and replaced by Catholic priests wherever 'a slight pretext and opportunity' arose, but, in order not to alarm or antagonize the population, officials were to take care that 'this does not give the appearance of a thorough reformation of the Upper Palatinate in the matter of religion'.[19] Since the ministers tried to continue their work, organizing informal conventicles, a second order followed, on 26 April 1626, expelling the dismissed pastors from the territory. In theory, Lutheran clergy were exempt, although magistrates blurred the distinction. In September 1626, the elector complained that some Calvinists were still in their livings, while only a few parishes had seen

---

[17] The text of the decree is given in Lippert, *Gegenreformation*, pp. 58–9.

[18] Högl, *Bekehrung*, p. 12. Lippert gives a figure of 55 clergy (out of some 200) refusing to read out the mandate: *Gegenreformation*, p. 59. Typical was the case of Mathias Kregel, a chaplain at Tännesberg. Kregel had already been brought to the attention of the Bavarian authorities in March 1625, when he had presumed to 'blaspheme against the most holy Mass and to liken other most praiseworthy ceremonies to conjuring tricks'. Besides this 'scabious' preaching and his refusal to read out the *Jachtaufmandat*, he kept to the old calendar and, according to the magistrate of Treswitz, had not even been legitimately installed. The elector ordered his expulsion on 28 December. In June 1627, he was arrested while visiting Treswitz, but managed to escape from custody: STAA, Subdelegierte Registratur 1802.

[19] Similar phrases abound in other decrees issued at this time. When it came to the introduction of the Gregorian calendar, for example, both Maximilian and his officials on the ground were keen to ensure that this was done gradually, and for ostensibly practical, 'political' reasons, in order to avoid giving the impression that it was part of a policy to impose religious change throughout the territory, a 'reformation', as the authorities in Amberg put it, which would be 'odious' in the eyes of the Lutheran populace ('es möchte das werckh von dem *odioso nomine reformationis* ... zue salviern sein'): STAA, Geistliche Sachen 587 (15 November 1625).

Catholic priests and many remained vacant, placing 'many thousands of souls in mortal danger'. The Amberg officials replied that they had not delayed 'in removing all the preachers (except those of the nobility), either on account of their crimes or on any other political pretext, or because they belonged to the Calvinist ... sect'.[20]

A key qualification was placed in parentheses in this report: 'except those of the nobility', referring to the *Adelsprädicanten*, the incumbents of parishes where noble families enjoyed the *ius patronatus*. By November 1626, when the new Bavarian regime was considering the problem posed by such clergy, they estimated that 30 of a total of perhaps 160 parishes were currently subject to the patronage of Upper-Palatinate noble families, supplemented by a number of subordinate or 'filial' chapels and other benefices.[21]

As with other aspects of the traditional privileges of this class, noble patronage was clearly regarded as a special case, to be approached with circumspection. As much a pragmatist as a zealot, Maximilian was unwilling to antagonize a powerful group upon whose cooperation the grass-roots governability and peace of the region depended. At the same time, concessions here threatened to derail the recatholicization, as reports of a number of incidents associated with the *Adelsprädicanten* confirmed. On 22 April 1626, for example, the new Catholic magistrate of the district of Nabburg reported to the Bavarian administrators in Amberg a disturbance which had taken place the previous day during the celebration of a wedding in the village of Willhof. The church at Willhof was a filial chapel of the parish of Altendorf, where the incumbent, a Protestant pastor, had recently died. Seizing the opportunity presented by the sudden vacancy, the Catholic dean of Nabburg had appointed Caspar Degenmayer, parish priest of Schwarzhofen, as priest-in-charge at Altendorf. However, patronage over Willhof was also claimed by a local nobleman, Albrecht Gerhard von Löschwitz, who employed a judge and a Protestant minister in the neighbouring village of Altfalter. The tension surfaced when a villager, Georg Rauch, planned to celebrate his marriage in Willhof. On the day of the wedding, Father Degenmayer arrived to perform the ceremony, only to discover that the church had been locked up on the orders of the judge of Altfalter. The verger and the churchwarden refused to hand over the keys, whilst the

---

[20] Högl, *Bekehrung*, pp. 12–15; Lippert, *Gegenreformation*, pp. 58–65.

[21] Högl, *Bekehrung*, pp. 16–17. With shifting jurisdictions and parish amalgamations and divisions, the total number of parishes was constantly fluctuating. Adolf Schosser gives a figure of 160 parishes and 30 additional benefices for the territory in 1650: 'Der oberpfälzische Diözesanklerus im Jahrhundert der Rekatholisierung', *Jahresbericht des Vereins zur Erforschung der Regensburger Diözesangeschichte*, 14 (1940), 28–40, esp. 30.

villagers ridiculed and threatened the priest. Pleading that 'even though he was in black he was not the Devil' and having vainly suggested conducting the service in the cemetery, Degenmayer beat a retreat. However, no sooner had he left than the judge ordered the church to be reopened and a horse was sent to bring the Protestant pastor over from Altfalter. As soon as he arrived the wedding went ahead.[22] The Bavarian officials at Amberg immediately ordered the interrogation of the bridal party and witnesses. The judge of Altfalter was questioned in the capital and, despite the intercession of von Löschwitz, received a fine of 30 *Reichstaler* and was required to pay court costs.[23] Here it was the noble claim of patronage over a filial chapel which had resulted in the humiliation of a Catholic cleric: his subjection to the mockery of villagers, the denial of his authority, and the triumph of his Protestant rival.

Noble patronage was also able to create safe havens for Protestant clergy who had already been removed once from more exposed benefices. In June 1625, Johannes Apiarius, the pastor of Ammerthal near Amberg, was one of a number of preachers accused of reviving the *Institutionswerk*, the Calvinist programme of catechetical instruction and moral discipline, despite a ban which had been imposed by Maximilian three years previously. Apiarius was removed from Ammerthal, but, against the orders of the government, was immediately reinstated in his former parochial post at Hohenkemnath by the local lord.[24]

The principal fear of the Bavarian authorities was not that noble patronage could provide outdoor relief for clergy on the run, but that the patronage and protection of Protestant pastors by a significant section of the territory's élite could, as with other aspects of their *Herrschaft*, exercise considerable influence on the religion of their ten-

---

[22] STAA, Subdelegierte Registratur 889 (22 April, 16 May 1626).

[23] Albrecht von Löschwitz outlined his version of the affair in a letter to Amberg. He conceded that the reported events had taken place, but justified the actions of his judge by claiming that the latter had been misinformed by the bridegroom on the day before the wedding that the parish of Altendorf was still vacant and that therefore the Protestant minister at Altfalter should perform the service. When Degenmayer turned up, he was refused admission to the church because he could not produce any authorization from either the district official or the dean. Although the Protestant pastor had been sent for, he had not been told of the presence in the village that morning of his Catholic rival and did not learn of it until a letter of complaint from Degenmayer arrived after the wedding. Had the preacher known, von Löschwitz claimed, he would have delayed the wedding until the problem had been cleared up. Von Löschwitz thus couched the affair in terms of a series of misunderstandings and jurisdictional confusion, arguing that the blame, if any, rested not with his judge, but with the wedding-party ('diesen beschehenen Irthumb und Mißverstand die Uhrsach am meisten an den hochzeitern gelegen'): STAA, Subdelegierte Registratur 889 (10 May 1626).

[24] M. Weigel, J. Wopper, and H. Ammon (eds), *Ambergisches Pfarrerbuch* (Kallmünz, 1967), p. 5.

ants. The relationship between noble patronage and local religious identity can be illustrated in the case of the village of Pertolzhofen. Throughout the sixteenth century the village's patrons, the noble von Pertolzhofen family, although Lutheran, had protected its greatest treasure, a life-sized *Gnadenbild* or miraculous image of the Virgin, the *Schöne Maria*. The survival of the image was noted during Calvinist visitations in 1580, 1596, and in 1616, when the officials reported in dismay that pilgrims were still frequenting the shrine in pursuit of sacred healing. Following the Bavarian takeover in 1621, a local magistrate noted that in the past Pertolzhofen's Virgin had been extremely popular with 'Lutherans'. As evidence of a lively shrine-folklore, he recounted a story of two villagers of nearby Obermurach who had vowed an annual gift to the shrine in return for the recovery of their sick children. The miraculous cures duly took place, but, as time went by, the peasants forgot their promise. Immediately the children suffered relapses and their illnesses persisted until the flow of donations resumed.[25] It is striking that a Lutheran noble family should have exercised their patronal rights over a church in order to shelter and promote a traditional Catholic pilgrimage. The harmony between patrons and pilgrims points to a devotional style in which evangelical orthodoxy counted less than local religious identity.

In the case of Pertolzhofen, the alliance of local religion and noble patronal autonomy proved an obstacle not only to Calvinist iconophobia, but also to the much more image-friendly attentions of Counter-Reformation Catholicism, as evinced by events at the shrine during the recatholicization. In 1625, a Catholic secular cleric, Johannes Wolf, was appointed parish priest of the neighbouring village of Oberviechtach. The following year, threatened by the plague and presumably at Father Wolf's instigation, Oberviechtach vowed an annual pilgrimage to the Pertolzhofen *Schöne Maria*. Relating the events in a subsequent report, Wolf confirmed the picture already described of a shrine still resorted to by 'Lutherans'. This augured well and, on 15 June, the day of St Vitus, Wolf set off to fulfil the vow at the head of some 300 of his parishioners. Close to Pertolzhofen, he halted the procession and sent two envoys ahead to ask the Lutheran patron, Hans Thomas von Pertolzhofen, for access to the church for half an hour. They promised that neither mass nor sermon would be held: the pilgrims wished merely to fulfil their vow by depositing a gift at the shrine. However, the envoys met with a hail of abuse and threats from the noble, who had already prepared his men to resist any attempted entry into the village by the pilgrims. Von

---

[25] R. Weiss, 'Die Wallfahrt zur Schönen Maria von Pertolzhofen', *Oberpfälzer Heimat*, 32 (1988), 78–98, here 82–4.

Pertolzhofen warned them that 'the *Pfaff* [priest] could stay outside, or he would dust his pillows for him. If he wanted to keep life and limb he should not come; he would see him dead'.[26] Undeterred, Wolf marched his people towards Pertolzhofen, but the bridge over the river Murach, just outside the village, was barred by von Pertolzhofen's contingent. There followed a confrontation between the priest and the lord, the latter threatening the former with a stick. Denouncing the behaviour of the noble as neither Lutheran nor Calvinist but 'Turkish', the priest turned to the pilgrims and ordered them, now that they were within sight of the shrine, to kneel down. He then conducted a brief open-air service, accompanied by laughter and blasphemies from von Pertolzhofen. Wolf thanked the noble for the 'honour' which he had thereby done to the emperor, the elector, and his parishioners, at which von Pertolzhofen exploded, crying that he asked nothing of the emperor or the elector, being himself a 'privileged person'. The priest blessed all present and then led his group back to Oberviechtach. A Whitsun pilgrimage the following year was also resisted and it was not until January 1628 that the church at Pertolzhofen was opened by force under the orders of the elector (in the lord's absence) and Wolf was finally able to take his flock there and say mass. In the correspondence which followed the first incident, von Pertolzhofen defended his patronal rights, of which he claimed to have ample documentation. He stressed that he had refused to allow the pilgrims to enter his church because it was not a filial of Oberviechtach, but of nearby Niedermurach, and argued that Oberviechtach and its priest had designs on Pertolzhofen. Wolf, he wrote, should pay more attention to his own filial at Gaisthal, which he had allegedly never visited, and leave Pertolzhofen alone.[27]

As in the case of von Löschwitz, von Pertolzhofen had not raised a Lutheran banner, but had instead based his actions on an appeal to inherited *Herrschaft*. Nevertheless, Maximilian and his officials feared that the pockets of noble patronal parishes would prove to be bastions of Protestantism and that, protected by their patrons, the surviving pastors would be able to frustrate the efforts of their Catholic counterparts. By 1626, conversions to Catholicism in the territory as a whole were still few and far between. In Amberg, for example, they numbered 24 in 1622 and no more than 74 in 1625. Even with the introduction of

---

[26] 'Der Pfaff möge draußen bleiben oder er wolle ihm die Kissen ausstauben, er wolle Leib und Leben bei ihm lassen, er soll nicht kommen, tot müsse er ihn haben': Weiss, 'Die Wallfahrt zur Schönen Maria', 87.

[27] Following the publication of the *Religionspatent* in 1628, the 63-year-old Hans Thomas von Pertolzhofen refused to convert to Catholicism and emigrated to Regensburg: Weiss, 'Die Wallfahrt zur Schönen Maria', 86–90.

more Catholic clergy, and in particular with the restoration of a secular clergy under diocesan control to support the groups of regulars (Jesuits, Capuchins, and Benedictines) which had hitherto been operating alone, the regime feared that their good work would be jeopardized if they were unable to monopolize the pulpits.

Confirming such fears, in December 1626 the Amberg Jesuits complained that there was an exodus from the capital every Sunday, as Ambergers flocked to the nearby rural parishes where Protestant preachers were still maintained by the nobility. It had been suggested that the town gates should be closed on Sundays to prevent this, but, in a telling expression of pessimism, the authorities argued that if this were done the people would still boycott the Catholic ceremonies and simply hold informal Protestant services at home instead.[28] As we have seen, in the autumn of 1626 the Bavarian officials informed Maximilian that all Protestant preachers had been removed with the exception of those employed by the nobility, where aristocratic claims to patronage represented an obstacle. Now, however, the officials thought they had detected an exposed flank. Prior to the Reformation, most of the noble parishes, they claimed, had not actually been independent parishes as such, but rather 'simple beneficies' (*simplicia beneficia*) or filials of other 'mother' churches. Consequently if all these filials were once more 'reassigned to their mothers', that is to say rejoined to their original parishes, the nobility would in fact retain only a very few parishes in which they could claim a *ius patronatus* from past tradition. And yet, even shifting the goalposts in this way did not represent a complete solution to the problem. The officials stressed that the few remaining noble parishes would still impede the success of the Catholic clergy. They were unsure whether the noble ministers could be expelled *en masse*, on the technicality that because they had been appointed under the previous regime they could all be classed as Reformed (and thus bereft of rights under the terms of the Peace of Augsburg), or whether only those who could be removed under the pretext of the amalgamation of filial and parish churches or of their inability to provide proof of patronal rights should be removed. Again Maximilian prevaricated, ordering that all the preachers were to be expelled under the umbrella of Calvinism, except those who had been appointed by the nobility and examined in Amberg prior to 1625, on whom Maximilian promised a resolution in the near future. Once again his approach reveals caution in the face of an out-and-out confrontation with the nobility.

---

[28] 'Sie wurden nichts desto weniger den alhiesigen Gottesdienst fahren lassen, und sich zu haus mit ihren postillenten behelffen': STAA, Subdelegierte Registratur (16 December 1626).

The following year (June 1627), the complaints were repeated 'that the nobility's preachers ... are preventing people from converting and making them dependent on them'. The scale of the problem had evidently diminished and the local officials only singled out the three noble parishes of Lintach, Ammerthal, and Theuern, all of which lay close to the capital. 'As long as they are tolerated', the report nevertheless continued, 'we can only hope for poor results'.[29] Now, however, Maximilian had finally resolved to bite the bullet. On 2 September, the government wrote to ten nobles, including the patrons of the three parishes close to the capital, asking them to send their pastors to the chancellery in Amberg the following day at three in the afternoon to receive their dismissals in person. These were presumably the only remaining recalcitrant cases. The clergy were to vacate their parishes within a fortnight on pain of fines and corporal punishment. In the case of the three nearest parishes to the capital, the immediate response was negative. Instead of the ministers, a joint letter arrived from their three noble patrons, Hans Joachim Mendl of Lintach, Sebastian Wolf Portner of Ammerthal, and Hans Georg Portner of Theuern, asserting their traditional privilege of appointing to the benefices in question.[30] The government pronounced the immediate suspension of the pastors from all parochial duties. On 5 September, the Amberg Secretary, Bartholomäus Schäffer, described his attempt that morning to install a Catholic priest, Peter Jäckhlin, in the parish of Lintach.[31]

Arriving a little after seven o'clock, Schäffer rode straight to the vicarage and asked for the Protestant minister. The latter emerged, half-dressed, and when Schäffer asked him to hand over the key to the church, replied that it was always kept by his lord, Hans Joachim Mendl, in the castle. Among a large group of bystanders was the verger, who said that his key to the church had been taken from him the day before by Mendl, because the latter was concerned about the threat to his minister. Schäffer then asked the Protestant cleric to fetch the key from Mendl. After a quarter of an hour he still had not returned and a messenger was sent to the castle asking for the key. Mendl himself then appeared. Schäffer explained his mission to install and hand over 'temporal possession' of the parish to the Catholic cleric. Mendl replied that he knew of the government's order, but 'was not giving up the key, because he was the patron of this place and could not easily allow himself to be dispossessed of that of which his forebears had had

---

[29] STAA, ORuR 558 (25 June 1627).

[30] Ibid. (3 September 1627).

[31] Ibid. (5 September 1627). The report is quoted in Lippert, *Gegenreformation*, pp. 79–80.

undisturbed possession for many years'.[32] That very morning, he said, he had sent a letter of complaint to Elector Maximilian in Munich and would not surrender the key until he received a decision from the capital. Schäffer advised him to cooperate:

> If he then had something legitimately to claim concerning his ... alleged *ius patronatus*, he could pursue it properly in the appropriate places and, if he had due proof, nothing would be taken away from him. For now, because the parish of Lintach was in fief to the abbey of Kastl, Your Electoral Highness would allow him nothing of it, but it would be seen whether his forebears by chance previously possessed it, by whom and by what law and title, for if they once wrongly availed themselves of it ... then it had never been his own right, and if they had previously been undisturbed, there was a different opinion now, and for Catholics there were different laws and practices when dealing with spiritual property; he could therefore not be dispossessed of something which neither he nor his forebears had ever legally owned.[33]

At this point, according to Schäffer, the noble called out to the villagers, and told them he was not being rebellious but was simply defending his and his descendants' rights, that he had always been a good vassal and that it was 'astonishing' that he had not been given the chance to put his case.[34] Schäffer accused him of not recognizing the Bavarian officials in Amberg as representatives of the elector or as plenipotentiaries. Mendl again refused to hand over the key, 'crying out to the villagers that he was protesting against violence'. Schäffer took the cue and appealed to this audience in his turn, reading out the electoral order installing Jäckhlin as the new priest and threatening to punish anyone who tried to prevent him from opening the church. Mendl withdrew to his castle, while Schäffer went to the verger's house in the cemetery, requisitioned

---

[32] 'Also gebe er die schlissel nicht von handen, weilen er dis orths *Patronus*, und sich des ienigen, welches seine voreltern lange iahr in ruhiger Possession hergebracht, also leichtlich nicht könne depossessionire lassen': STAA, ORuR 558 (5 September 1627).

[33] 'Habe er hinnach an seinem ... vermainten *iure patronatus* etwas rechtmessig zu praetendirn, könne ers gehörigen ortten gebührlich suechen, werde ihme auf genuegsamen *demonstrationes* nichts benommen werden, diser Zeit, weilen die Pfar Lintach dem Stifft Castel zu lehen gehe, gestehe E. Churfl. Dhl. ihme daran nichts, ob gleichwol etwa seine Voreltern solches anhero gehabt, werde es sich jedoch zeigen *a quibus, quo iure et titulo*, dan da sie sich dessen ain mahl unbillich bedient und ungleich an sich gebracht, seye es jedoch an ihme selbst nie recht gewest, ob sie auch anhero dabei ruhig gebliben, auch habe es ieziger Zeit ain andere meinung, und seye bei den Catholl. mit geistlichen guetter umbzugehen ain anderes Recht und manir, er könne dessen solcher gestalt ihme zu praejudiz nicht depossessionirt werden, welches er oder seine Vorfahren niemahls rechtmessig possidirt haben': ibid.

[34] 'Es bedunckhe ihme verwünderlich sein, das man dergleichen *processum ab executione* anfange': ibid.

an axe from the frightened man and had the church door broken open so that the priest could say mass. A homily was preached, albeit to a small congregation: 'no one from Lintach came to church', reported Schäffer, 'except for some young children, and 20 men and women from the neighbouring hamlet'.[35]

The dispute dragged on. A month later, the Catholic priest complained that his Protestant predecessor was still in residence. When Jäckhlin moved on to Illschwang at the end of October, a new Catholic priest, Daniel Landanus, was appointed. Landanus too had complaints. Although the Protestant pastor had now moved out, he had handed over the parish register to Mendl, who refused to release it. Mendl was also accused of boycotting the church and holding unofficial Protestant services in his castle instead. The noble was said to have taken a chalice and various vestments from the church and was continuing to have the bells rung at his pleasure without first telling the priest. All this was setting a 'bad example'. In April 1628, Landanus repeated the accusations against Mendl, adding that he was having problems with a Lutheran schoolmaster, who had spoken out against Catholicism and disturbed his parishioners, 'who anyway look more to the noble than to God and their conscience'. Mendl had banned his retinue in the castle from attending Catholic services in the village, even locking the castle gates on Sundays and holidays. Mendl and his wife, according to Landanus, 'also said to my face only yesterday that I need not say any more Masses for their conversion ... as they would sooner go begging than convert to our Christian Catholic religion'. True to his word, Mendl subsequently chose to emigrate from the Upper Palatinate rather than convert.[36]

Like the interrupted nuptials at Willhof or the frustrated pilgrimage at Pertolzhofen, the incident of breaking-and-entering at Lintach testified to the fact that a powerful section of the Upper-Palatinate élite was determined to use its traditional prerogative to resist the recatholicization. There were similar incidents in noble parishes at Theuern, Trausnitz, and Tiefenbach, where a musket-shot was fired when the Jesuit superior arrived to say mass.[37] By the end of 1627, however, it would appear that one way or another the Protestant clergy previously sheltered by the nobility had finally been expelled. The first phase of the recatholicization, the removal of non-Catholic clergy, had at last been completed.

The way lay open for Elector Maximilian to issue, on 27 April 1628, his *Religionspatent*, requiring the conversion or emigration of the entire

---

[35] Ibid.

[36] Ibid.

[37] Lippert, *Gegenreformation*, pp. 78–83.

population within six months. Again the population was not treated with equality, as the nobility were granted the privilege of a two-month extension to the conversion deadline, in order for those who would be emigrating to settle the sales of their estates. The elector again stressed to his officials the importance of monitoring the nobility's reaction to the *Religionspatent*. In November 1628, for example, an irritated Maximilian reminded his Amberg officials to report on the progress of noble conversions, 'as you already know full well how much we value the holy cause of religion and the conversion of our subjects, especially that of the noble landowners'.[38] Whilst the struggle over patronage had exposed the Lutheran sympathies of a small section of the nobility, the conversion mandate finally revealed the full strength of Protestant opinion amongst them, as individuals or whole families wrestled with the agony of decision-making: some grudgingly submitting to instruction in the Catholic faith, others asking for more time to consider their position, and many, like Christoph Rummel, placing conscience over convenience and petitioning the Amberg government for permission to emigrate:

> Now God knows, in the bottom of my heart, how utterly pained and distressed I have been, and continue to be, that I would or could not dutifully follow or give total obedience to Your Electoral Highness in matters of faith, as I could in other, political, affairs, but this matter ... concerns not just my person, or my corporal and temporal duty, but equally my conscience and God's honour and Word. For this reason, therefore, I humbly ask Your Electoral Highness not to burden or pursue me with continual, terrifying worries in such a matter of conscience, against my conscience, faith and confession, but to permit me to remain in the practice of the Augsburg Confession, in which I was taught, instructed and raised by my dear parents from childhood and with which I grew up, and to allow me to leave the land.[39]

---

[38] 'Da euch doch mehr dann wolbewust, wie hoch wir unnß daß hailsame Religionswerckh und unnserer underthanen zumahlen der Adelichen landtsessen *Conversion* angelegen sein lassen': STAA, ORuR 423 (27 November 1628).

[39] 'Wann nun dann Gott weiß es von grundt meines Herzenß, mir leidenlich unndt gantz bekhümmerlich gewesen, wie auch noch ist daß Euer Churf. Durchl. ... ich in den ... glaubenß sachen nit solte oder khönte underthenig volgen unndt volkhommenen gehorsam wie in anderen politischen sachen leisten, unndt aber dieße sach ... nit meine Persohn, oder aber den leiblichen unndt zeitlichen gehorsamb allein, sondern auch mir zugleich daß gewissen, gottes ehr, unndt wort belanget thuet. Derhalben unndt deme allen nach so gelanget an Euer Churf. Durchl. ... mein hoch fleißiges bitten, die wollen mich in solchem *Consciens* handel, wider mein gewisen, glauben unndt *Confession* mit besorglicher immerwehrender bekhümmernuß nit beschweren unndt betreiben, sondern mich bey der übung Augspurgischer *Confession*, darinnen ich von meinen lieben Eltern von Jugendt auf underricht, gelehrt uferzogen, unndt damit also erwachßen bin verbliben, unndt mir auß dem [land] zu ziehen ... bewilligen lassen': STAA, ORuR 342 (30 May 1629).

Other noble correspondence produced equally vivid articulations of faith, as well as such indirect expressions of Protestant sympathy as the motto 'Gott mit uns' at the close of a letter or the continued use of the old calendar alongside the new. The slogan and the ten-day calendrical divergence were hallmarks of confessional allegiance every bit as telling as the crosses scratched at the heads of letters by Catholic correspondents.

The *Religionspatent* did not end Maximilian's struggle with the nobility. The government's attention now switched to the practical problems of enforcing the conversion mandate, assessing the reliability of noble conversions, negotiating the sales and transfers of the estates of noble emigrés, keeping such emigrés to the dates set for the sales and ensuring that they paid the *Nachsteuer*, a ten-per-cent property tax, before their departure.[40] In some cases noble emigrants attempted to circumvent the decree by continuing to adminster their Upper-Palatinate estates from their other lands in neighbouring territories.[41] It was a strategy which depended on the landowners' ability to retain amenable estate managers. On the Löschwitz estate at Wolframshof, for example, the bailiff pleaded ignorance of the government order forbidding him to readmit his emigré lord: a letter had indeed arrived, but as he was unable to read, he had simply sent it on to von Löschwitz, who had not chosen to inform him of its contents. At this the exasperated Catholic magistrate was driven to wondering whether the appointment by emigré nobles of illiterate administrators was not in itself a deliberate strategy![42] Such tactics enabled the nobility not only to preserve their own religious conscience and to minimize the costs of exile but also to continue employing and protecting their Protestant correligionists in the Upper Palatinate.

In the aftermath of the *Religionspatent*, many noble families appear to have hedged their bets, some members emigrating, others converting in order to retain possession of their estates. In the district of Waldeck-

---

[40] Emigrants were required to declare under oath (the so-called *juramentum emigrantium*) the value of their property and any debts, 'under the threat of confiscation of their property and goods if they knowingly conceal the slightest wealth, prejudicing their payment of the *Nachsteuer*': STAA, ORuR 194.

[41] This even included neighbouring Catholic territories where confessional policies were pursued less implacably. In February 1629, for example, the Bavarian officials at Amberg complained to the Catholic ruler of Pfalz-Neuburg that non-Catholic emigrants were being allowed into his territory, 'so that the work of reformation, which began with great effort and success, is somewhat stuck and made into a laughing stock': STAA, ORuR 89.

[42] 'Sie [the emigrants] ... ihre unterthanen ... auch nicht schreiben und lesens verrichtet zu verwaltern und voigten uffsetzen thun, und also durch dieses Mittel dass *dominium* ihnen vorbehalten': STAA, ORuR 429.

Kemnath, for example, where some 41 noble landowners had resided, of those whose fates are known, seven converted and kept their estates, five remained Protestant, emigrated and lost their estates through sale or confiscation, and some 16 others remained Protestant and emigrated but managed to keep their estates within their families.[43]

In the case of nobles who chose to stay and accommodate themselves to the Bavarian regime, the government was further confronted by the problem of ensuring that the task of receiving the nobility into the Catholic fold was assigned to suitably qualified clergy. This was at a time when there was a shortage of candidates for all of the suddenly vacant benefices in the Upper Palatinate as a whole. Religious instruction was the preserve of the clergy, but Maximilian's government intervened in the selection of the nobility's instructors, in the possible fear that the average priest might be duped or overawed by his powerful catechumens. In September 1627, for example, the authorities urged that five parishes which had been previously served by Calvinist *Adelsprädicanten* should now be staffed by Jesuits, arguing that 'since the nobility are well versed in their religion, there is a need for thoroughly trained people, few of whom are to be found among the normal secular priests who are assigned to the task'.[44]

The subject of catechumenical instruction and the reference to a nobility 'well versed in religion' return us to a problem posed at the start, that of assessing the balance between 'religious' and 'secular' motivation in the patronage struggles of the 1620s. For Maximilian (and doubtless for his picked officials), it seems clear that the goal of recatholicization was a spiritual one: with souls at stake, heresy could and would not be tolerated. If Catholic exclusivity also happened to bring with it a more quiescent, ordered, and productive society, this was to be accepted as a fitting reward for the pious, Anti-Machiavellian prince.[45] At the same time, and despite Maximilian's emphasis on genuine conversions, the Counter Reformation's success on the ground depended less on missionary zeal than on practical solutions to local legal, political, social, and economic obstacles, especially in the cautious years of phased recatholicization before 1628, when the elector was not yet

---

[43] Ziegler, 'Rekatholisierung', p. 446, n. 34.

[44] STAA, ORuR 558.

[45] On the theme of Anti-Machiavellianism, with particular reference to Maximilian and his Jesuit confessors Adam Contzen and Johannes Vervaux, see R. Bireley, 'Antimachiavellianism, the Baroque, and Maximilian of Bavaria', *Archivum Historicum Societatis Iesu*, 53 (1984), 137–59, and *The Counter-Reformation Prince* (Chapel Hill, 1990).

legally able to employ the *cuius regio* principle of the Peace of Augsburg
to enforce confessional uniformity. The wider confessional campaign
was therefore reduced to such disparate issues as piecemeal calendrical
reform, parochial reorganization, or disputed patronage rights, and was
cloaked (in the government's own words) by 'political pretext'.

An equally strong religious motivation appears to have characterized sections of the Upper-Palatinate nobility, whose rearguard action
on the battleground of ecclesiastical patronage has been followed
here. There is no reason to doubt the authenticity of the convictions of
those, like von Pertolzhofen or Mendl, who fought and lost on the
patronage issue and then chose to emigrate rather than convert to
Catholicism. At the same time, whatever their personal approach to
matters of faith, they took issue with the new Bavarian administration
in the first instance not through doctrinal declarations, but on a
conservative platform of the defence of traditional custom, law, and
privilege. The battle over patronage was an example of the way in
which early modern religious conflicts and confessional identities were
articulated through a variety of discourses, political, legal, and social,
rather than simply theological.

The dispute also reveals a blend of continuity and change which is
not without its paradoxes. For example, when Protestant religious
conviction was expressly articulated, it often had a conservative, nostalgic air, as in Christoph Rummel's references to the faith of his
parents. The tone was typical of the many aristocratic confessions of
faith which were prompted by the *Religionspatent*. At the same time,
a parallel can be drawn between the conservatism espoused by the
nobility and the attitudes expressed by other sectors of Upper-Palatinate society. One piece of evidence comes from the spring of 1628,
when Maximilian ordered a series of examinations to be conducted in
the territory's leading towns: Amberg, Neumarkt, Waldmünchen,
Nabburg, and Neunburg vorm Wald. The aim of the exercise (which
bears a superficial resemblance to the *referenda* conducted in a number
of German cities in the early sixteenth century on the question of the
adoption of the Reformation) seems to have been to gauge the extent
of potential resistance to the planned conversion decree. Although
here individual citizens were explicit in their confessional choice, their
justifications are illuminating. In all five towns, the vast majority
declared a desire to be allowed to retain their Lutheran allegiance, but
overwhelmingly they did so by appealing to their 'baptismal bond'
and a desire to maintain the faith of their parents in which they had
been raised. Kaspar Maier, Amberg's mayor, for example, declared
that he 'confessed with lips and heart the true evangelical religion in
which he had been raised from his youth ... in his heart and con-

science he could confess no other'.[46] Truth and tradition here went hand in hand. Correspondingly, in the towns as much as among the nobility and their tenants in the countryside, it was Catholicism which was seen as the novelty, upsetting established patterns of Protestant socialization as well as local political custom and traditional aristocratic privilege. During some 70 years of Protestantism in the Upper Palatinate new institutions had been introduced and assimilated and older ones maintained and accommodated to the new confessional climate. The traditional system of lay patronage was used by noble families, as ever, to entrench their own influence on their districts, although now with the added ingredient of applying it to defend their own, possibly (as in the case of the von Pertolzhofens) heterodox, brand of Protestantism.

The Catholicism reintroduced from the 1620s also naturally had its conservative aspects, although the opportunities for innovation created by the lengthy Protestant interlude perhaps made the Upper Palatinate a special case in the context of German Catholicism as a whole.[47] Its accommodating approach to traditional local popular religious culture, for example, was epitomized in the enthusiastic revival by the Jesuits of pre-Reformation pilgrimage sites, including some where chapels had been razed by Calvinist visitors but which had still continued to attract unofficial pilgrimages from their neighbourhoods right through the Protestant period.[48] Predictably, the return of Catholicism brought the reintroduction of medieval ecclesiastical institutions. Although restoration of the region's ancient monastic houses would have to wait until 1669 (and indeed was never fully realized), the episcopal functions which had been taken over by the Palatine electors at the Reformation reappeared in the 1620s.[49] They included the adjudication of disputed patronage rights. It is ironical, perhaps, that Konrad Teufel, one of a group of recalcitrant Protestant nobility summoned to Amberg in the

---

[46] STAA, ORuR 556.

[47] As Marc Forster has recently observed in the case of the Rhenish diocese of Speyer, German Catholic territories could exhibit a remarkable degree of traditionalism, as cathedral chapters or monastic foundations fought to preserve their authority, autonomy, and local devotional usages against the new spirit of universalism and centralization emanating from Rome: *The Counter-Reformation in the Villages. Religion and Reform in the Bishopric of Speyer, 1560–1720* (Ithaca and London, 1992), and his 'The élite and popular foundations of German Catholicism in the Age of Confessionalism: the *Reichskirche*', *Central European History*, 26 (1993), 311–25.

[48] Johnson, 'Recatholicisation', pp. 217–48. For a recent account of the role of pilgrimages and the cult of miraculous images in the promotion of the Counter Reformation in Bavaria see P. M. Soergel, *Wondrous in his Saints: Counter-Reformation Propaganda in Bavaria* (Berkeley, Los Angeles, London, 1993).

[49] Lippert, *Gegenreformation*, pp. 171, 181.

summer of 1629, gave as the explanation for his non-compliance the need to defend his patronage of the parish of Schwarzenfeld against the attentions of a rival noble in a hearing before the vicar general at Regensburg.[50]

A new feature exposed in the course of the recatholicization, however, was the determination of Maximilian to use all available means to realize his goals, including the overturning of custom and precedent, if (as with the patronal rights of specific individuals or the collective rights of the regional diet) they appeared to stand in his way. Losers in the process were the region's convinced Protestants, who were forced to choose between conversion and emigration, and the nobility and towns who saw the loss of traditional privileges. The clear winner was of course the new elector. It is a further irony that, in the case of the Upper Palatinate, Protestantism was defeated not so much by a reassertion of ecclesiastical power, but by the assertion of a new-found secular strength, that of the territorial ruler, the very force which is generally credited with the institutionalization of Protestantism in the first place. As the Upper-Palatinate nobility discovered, aristocratic *Herrschaft* could be superseded by the princely *Landesherrschaft* of a determined, proto-absolutist ruler. Bavarian Catholicism was thereby able to succeed where Palatine Calvinism had failed. In this respect Maximilian was right: times had indeed changed.

---

[50] STAA, ORuR 402 (28 June 1629).

PART FOUR
Education

Continuity and competition: Luther's call for educational reform in the light of medieval precedents

Markus Wriedt

In my opinion, it is necessary – particularly in these dangerous times – to order chapters and monasteries to return to their original state at the time of the Apostles and a long time thereafter, when all of their members were free to stay as long as they liked. For what else were chapters and monasteries than Christian schools in which pupils were taught the Holy Scriptures and Christian discipline, where people were educated to govern and to preach.[1]

With this reference to the apostolistic age and the first centuries, Martin Luther made it clear that he saw the Reformation as a return to early Christian principles.[2] Given the towering position of the Scriptures, early church institutions appeared as models with special authority. They were seen as particularly close to Jesus Christ and his revelation of the will of God. At the same time, the passage reflects the influence of Germanic law, which placed ancient custom above change and innovation.[3]

I am grateful to Andrea Vogt, Ken Farnhill and the editor for their help in translating this essay.

[1] 'Es were meynis bedenckens en nottige ordnung beszondern zu vnsern ferlichen zeytten/das stifft vnnd kloster widderumb wurde(n) auff die weysze verordenet/wie sie waren ym anfang bey denn Aposteln vnnd ein lang zeit hernach/da sie alle frey waren/eine(m) yderman drynnen zubleyben szo lang es yhm gelustet. Dan was sein stifft vnd kloster anders geweszen/den Christliche schulenn/darynnen man leret/schrifft vnnd zucht nach Christlicher weysze/vnnd leut auff ertzog/zu regieren vnnd predigen': Martin Luther, 'An den christlichen Adel deutscher Nation von des christlichen Standes Besserung' in Hans-Ulrich Delius et al. (eds), *Martin Luther: Studienausgabe* (Berlin, 1982), ii. 134, lines 15–21; see also pp. 158, 4–7.

[2] Cf. Eike Wolgast, 'Reform, Reformation' in O. Brunner, W. Conze, and R. Koselleck (eds), *Geschichtliche Grundbegriffe* (Stuttgart, 1984), v. 313–60; Gerald Strauss, 'Ideas of *Reformatio* and *Renovatio* from the Middle Ages' in Th. A. Brady Jr, H. A. Oberman, and J. Tracy (eds), *Handbook of European History 1400–1600: Late Middle Ages, Renaissance, and Reformation* (2 vols, Leiden, 1995), ii. 1–31.

[3] See Johannes Heckel, *Lex Charitatis: Eine juristische Untersuchung über das Recht in der Theologie Martin Luthers* (Cologne, 1973); Klaus Schlaich, 'Martin Luther und das Recht' in Knut Schäferdieck (ed.), *Martin Luther im Spiegel heutiger Wissenschaft* (Bonn, 1985), pp. 77–97.

In the first part of this essay I will attempt to sketch if – and to what extent – Luther's idea of early Christian schools is justified. In a second part, we will take a closer look at his own educational programme and examine where exactly reformed ideas challenged the medieval system. The third and final section will expand the theme of continuity and competition, assessing the specific blend between traditional and innovating features in the Reformation as a whole.

(i)

Ever since the creation of an 'established' church in the fourth century, tensions between secular–pagan education and Christian teaching have dominated the history of Western schooling. The responsibility for education swung like a pendulum to and fro between ecclesiastical and secular authorities. Although early medieval schools derived from classical Roman institutions, they became increasingly 'Christianized'; not so much in terms of teaching methods, but certainly in subject matter.[4] The sixth century proved an important turning-point: in response to the missionary challenge posed by the pagan Germanic environment, the educational emphasis shifted towards the sacramental and liturgical life of the church. Conversion to Christianity, at the time, was not merely a change of religion, but a much more wide-ranging *conversio* of lifestyle, culture, and manners of speech. From this perspective it is clear that a fundamental re-orientation was needed to develop a Christian educational system. The church had to break with established late Roman practices.

'Palace' or 'court schools' (*scholae palatinae*) catered for the leading nobility, but their curriculum was limited to the acquisition of basic administrative skills, primarily spoken and written Latin. It was important, therefore, to supplement this level with more sophisticated clerical education. The task was tackled in Central Europe by the Irish–Scottish mission and a new ideal of the ministry emerged wherever British monks established their foundations.[5] Boniface continued this tradition

---

[4] For developments in the early church see Henri-Irénée Marrou, *Augustinus und das Ende der antiken Bildung* (2nd edn, Paderborn, 1995), for a general survey Franz A. Specht, *Geschichte des Unterrichtswesens in Deutschland von den ältesten Zeiten bis zur Mitte des dreizehnten Jahrhunderts* (Stuttgart, 1885), Pierre Riché, *Education et culture dans l'Occident barbare* (3rd edn, Paris, 1962), G. Dagron, P. Riché, and A. Vauchez (eds), *Histoire du christianisme des origines à nos jours IV: evêques, moines et empereurs (642–1054)* (Paris, 1993).

[5] Cf. Arnold Angenendt, *Monachi peregrini: Studien zu Pirmin und den monastischen Vorstellungen des frühen Mittelalters* (Munich, 1972), his *Das Frühmittelalter: Die*

and erected schools for clerical novices in his Benedictine monasteries. This type of education, of course, was intended exlusively for members of the order (and the occasional aristocratic patron). The emerging gap in the education of the secular clergy was filled by Chrodegang of Metz through the foundation of cathedral schools.

Both kinds of institutions had their legal and financial basis in the Germanic *Eigenkirchenwesen*.[6] Local lords did not only take physical possession of churches and monasteries in their territory, but also exercised extensive spiritual supervision. It was inevitable that princes and emperors gradually extended these powers to ecclesiastical schools, and clerical education, only recently emancipated from secular influence, soon returned under worldly control. Duke Tassilo of Bavaria, for instance, decreed at the synod of Neuching in 774 that each bishop should found a school at his see and hire a wise man to teach according to Roman tradition. Furthermore, the 'admonitio generalis' of Charlemagne (789) ordered that every monastery and every diocese should teach psalms, musical notes, chants, the 'computus' (calendar calculation), and grammar. In addition, every school had to be in possession of dogmatically sound Catholic books, and the emperor recommended a careful examination of candidates for the priesthood at annual meetings of the diocesan clergy.[7]

Even traces of compulsory popular education can be detected. With reference to Caesarius of Arles and the Synod of Baison (529), the emperor and bishops called for the establishment of parish schools: Theodulf of Orléans, for example, demanded that in his diocese:

> the clergy should hold a school in every village and hamlet; if the pious give their children into the hands of a priest, he is not allowed to reject them and to refuse to teach them ... If the priests fullfill their duties with devotion, they shall not receive any money or payment above a small gift from the parents.[8]

These schools were to teach reading, writing, and ecclesiastical liturgy, alongside the Creed and the Lord's Prayer (to be expounded in the vernacular).

---

abendländische Christenheit von 400 bis 900 (Stuttgart, 1990), pp. 208–10 and 268–90, and Helmut Flachendecker, *Schottenklöster: Irische Benediktinerkonvente im hochmittelalterlichen Deutschland* (Paderborn, 1992).

[6] Peter Landau, 'Eigenkirchenwesen' in *TRE* (Berlin, 1982), ix. 399–404.

[7] For text and context of the 'admonitio' see P. Brommer (ed.), *Capitula episcoporum*, Monumenta Germaniae Historiae, cap. 1 (Hannover, 1984) [hereafter MGH, cap. 1], no. 22; Pierre Riché, *Ecoles et enseignement dans le Haut Moyen Age* (Paris, 1979), pp. 70–71; Josef Fleckenstein, 'Admonitio generalis' in *Lexikon des Mittelalters* (Munich, 1980), i. 156; Angenendt, *Frühmittelalter*, pp. 305–20.

[8] Theodulf von Orléans, 1. capitulas, c. xx, in MGH, cap. 1, p. 116.

Charlemagne's system, developed under the influence of Alcuin, was equally open to secular concerns. Apart from other topics, the reading of profane texts was introduced, and the liberal arts were taught as a preparation for studies of Holy Scripture. Ludwig the Pious, however, advised by Benedict of Aniane, refocused his educational policy on the training of clergymen. The Imperial Diet of Aachen (817) closed monastic schools to outsiders. Henceforth, monasteries ceased to provide public education and limited their teaching to their own needs. At the same time, the boarding school system enhanced the unity of clerical upbringing and training, a principle resuscitated in the sixteenth century by reformers of all confessional persuasions. In short, the church claimed full and exclusive responsibility for education.[9] As a result of tensions provoked by the reform movements of Cluny and Hirsau, however, internal monastic schools were also disrupted.[10]

At the same time, the level of education among kings and princes declined, so much so that cultured rulers such as Frederic II or Alfons X were regarded as exceptional by their contemporaries. From the thirteenth century, a growing number of observers complained about the deplorable educational standards of political leaders and about the unprecedented increase in the power of peasants and other commoners who were eager to learn.[11]

In a fresh educational offensive from the twelfth century, imperial and papal legislators began to regulate the fastly expanding range of new methods of teaching and study,[12] and eventually helped to establish corporate bodies of masters and scholars in 'universitates magistorum et scholarium' under central control. On the secular side, the 'Authentica

---

[9] Laetitia Boehm, 'Das mittelalterliche Erziehungs- und Bildungswesen' in *Propyläen Geschichte der Literatur* (Frankfurt, Berlin, 1988), ii. 143–81; Riché, *Education et culture*, and his *Ecoles et enseignement*.

[10] For a discussion of contemporary tensions between 'monastics' and 'scholastics', and the implications of a higher entry age for novices, see R. Kottje and H. Maurer (eds), *Monastische Reformen im 9. und 10. Jahrhundert* (Sigmaringen, 1989), H. E. J. Cowdrey, *The Cluniacs and the Gregorian Reform* (Oxford, 1970), H. Richter (ed.), *Cluny* (Darmstadt, 1975), and H. Jakobs, *Die Hirsauer* (Cologne, 1961).

[11] See, for example, Walter Map, *De nugius curialum* (c. 1200), Werner Rolevinck, *De gemine rusticorum* (c. 1500), and E. Holzapfel, *Werner Rolevnick's Bauernspiegel* (Freiburg, 1959).

[12] Martin Grabmann, *Geschichte der Scholastischen Methode* (2 vols, Freiburg, 1909–11) (teaching methods); André Vauchez (ed.), *Histoire du christianisme des origines à nos jours*, tome v: Apologée de la papauté et expansion de la chrétienté (1054–1274) (Paris, 1993), pt 3, ch. 3 (André Vauchez) and pt 5, ch. 3 (André Vauchez and Agostino Pravicini Bagliani).

habita', issued by Frederic Barbarossa around the time of the imperial diet of Roncaglia (not later than 1158), is viewed as a Magna Charta of the evolving university system: it provided for the safety and protection of scholars whilst travelling to and staying at the place of study, it prohibited their arrest for crimes committed by fellow countrymen, and it guaranteed them a free choice of court.[13]

On the ecclesiastical side, a new wave of legislation, beginning with the Lateran Council of 1123, endeavoured to expand papal jurisdiction and to consolidate the church's hold over education. The main elements were: (a) a commitment to the education and training of priests, (b) financial safeguards for teachers (salaries, benefices) and students (new foundations, scholarships, dispensations from residence requirements), (c) privileges of jurisdiction (universities and their members to enjoy immunity from local courts), (d) teaching licences, (e) institutionalization of courses and curricula (limited to certain social groups), and (f) protection of scholarly communities from local authorities. This blueprint for a centrally (in fact, papally) controlled dissemination of knowledge, however, soon fell victim to the dynamics of European state development. National and princely prestige, as well as ambitions of the academic communities themselves, ensured that university expansion failed to adhere to papal planning. Eventually, all institutions were allowed to offer the full range of faculties (arts, medicine, law, theology) and to award their own doctorates.[14]

The growth of the educational system from the thirteenth century, evident above all in the spread of the ability to read and write Latin beyond the clerical estate, cannot be explained by purely socio-economic or purely religious reasons, but depended on a whole range of interconnected factors: the establishment of universities, the foundation of mendicant orders, the increasing number of towns as centres of educational institutions, the emergence of an ambitious 'middle class' engaged in commerce, trade, and arts, the growing need for administrative and especially legal expertise in the nascent territorial and city states, and the rising demand for educational and edifying literature among the laity, to name but a few.[15] All of these tendencies combined

---

[13] W. Stelzer, 'Zum Scholarenprivileg Friedrich Barbarossas ('Authentica Habita')', *Deutsches Archiv für Erforschung des Mittelalters*, 34 (1978), 123–65.

[14] R. L. Benson and G. Constable (eds), *Renaissance and Renewal in the Twelfth Century* (Cambridge Mass., 1982); P. Classen, *Studium und Gesellschaft im Mittelalter* (Stuttgart, 1983); C. H. Lawrence, 'The university in state and church' in J. I. Catto (ed.), *The History of the University of Oxford* (Oxford, 1984), i. 97–150; *Università e società nei secoli XII–XVI*, Atti del nono convegno internazionale di studio tenuto a Pistoia nei giorni 20–25 settembre 1979 (Pistoia, 1982).

[15] For a more thorough discussion see Boehm, 'Das mittelalterliche Erziehungs- und Bildungswesen', and Walter Rüegg (ed.), *Geschichte der Universität* (vol. i, Munich, 1993).

to destroy the basic assumption that 'clerici' were 'litterati' and 'laici' 'illiterati', albeit without revolutionizing the social order. From the fourteenth century, princes started to found universities in Central Europe, and – alongside the pope – the emperor became one of the main patrons of learning.[16] With ever greater frequency, universities approached them for improved charters and privileges.

Elementary schools, too, had been revived by papal reform legislation in the twelfth century. As a result of the increasing economic and cultural importance of towns, however, magistrates started to intervene in the running of Latin schools, and to promote the establishment of German institutions. This, of course, forms one of the main precedents for Martin Luther's initiatives. Let us thus take a closer look at one particularly striking example: the quarrel about school reforms in Hamburg, starting in the late thirteenth century and culminating in the Reformation of the city in 1524.[17]

Since the foundation, by papal bull, of the grammar school at the church of St Nicholas in 1281, the new municipal institution co-existed with the old cathedral school established by Ansgar. Problems arose about the position of the *scholasticus* who supervised the schools, appointed the teachers, and determined tuition fees. Almost constantly, the citizens criticized him for neglecting his duties and for using his position for personal gain. In 1289, the *scholasticus* obtained archiepiscopal support to turn the cathedral school into an exclusively clerical institution and to run St Nicholas's school as an elementary school with no access to higher education. The move heightened existing tensions, provoked several lawsuits, and eventually resulted in an agreement in 1337, but a subsequent visitation showed that its clauses were not adhered to. The archbishop thus admonished the *scholasticus* to fulfil his duties, ordered a payrise for the teachers in both schools, and outlawed corruption in the appointment of staff.

Hamburg's ever-increasing demand for educated men to run its adminstration and trade then led the citizens to found German schools without papal approval. A bull of 1402 specifically forbade this practice and demanded the closure of illegal institutions. When, in 1472, the *scholasticus* Hermann Duker accused a priest and two lay teachers of founding a German school, the conflict over educational control re-

---

[16] Georg Kaufmann, 'Die kaiserlichen Universitätsprivilegien', *Deutsche Zeitschrift für Geschichtswissenschaft*, 1 (1889), 118–65.
[17] Cf. for the following Rainer Postel, *Die Reformation in Hamburg 1517–28* (Gütersloh, 1986), pp. 157–81.

sumed. The citizens supported the priest, resorted to active resistance, and finally closed St Nicholas's school. In return, Duker secured the excommunication of the city. To obtain absolution and to meet its legal costs after five years of conflict, the town council was forced to part with a large sum of money in 1477. The school reopened and a new institution, which specialized in the teaching of writing skills (*Schreibschule*) was founded with clerical permission. This, however, turned out to be the council's last defeat in its quest to obtain control over schooling within the city.

The outcome caused permanent friction between the ecclesiastical school officials and the citizenry. Tuition fees and teaching standards emerged as the main bones of contention: the *scholasticus* was regularly accused of diverting funds into his own pockets, and in 1522, the citizens complained that the teachers were 'idiots' who failed to educate their children. The laity was forced to spend large amounts of money for private tuition in schools outside Hamburg, while any priests prepared to teach within the town faced the wrath of the *scholasticus*. For these reasons the parents of the pupils at St Nicholas's school refused to pay any more fees. After several meetings and disagreements, the magistrates finally forced the schoolmaster Hinrick Banskow to transfer control of St Nicholas to the citizens of Hamburg. The council was to determine and collect the fees, while the citizens were free to appoint properly qualified teachers and to decide about the best possible education for their children. As a result, St Nicholas became a state school and the church lost its towering position.

Even such a brief survey suffices to illustrate the irreversible trend towards secular control over education in Hamburg, and other case studies from the fifteenth and early sixteenth century confirm this impression.[18] An increasingly self-confident citizenry claimed responsibility over schooling. Although most conflicts focused on economic issues, they point to the laity's emancipation from ecclesiatical supervision. Martin Luther himself, coming from a family which acquired wealth one generation before the Reformation, could be cited as an example. His programme reflected the ongoing readjustment of boundaries between church and state and the increasing assertiveness of late medieval individuals.

---

[18] See, for instance, Rudolf Endres, 'Das Nürnberger Bildungswesen zur Zeit der Reformation', *Mitteilungen des Vereins für die Geschichte der Stadt Nürnberg*, 71 (1984), 109–28; Reinhard Jakob, *Schulen in Franken und in der Kuroberpfalz 1250–1520* (Wiesbaden, 1994); Klaus Leder, *Kirche und Jugend in Nürnberg und seinem Landgebiet 1400 bis 1800* (Neustadt, 1973); Anton P. Brück, *Kurmainzer Schulgeschichte: Texte – Berichte – Memoranden* (Wiesbaden, 1960).

(ii)

It could thus be argued that Luther's reference to the educational system of the old church is not completely unfounded. In some periods, at least, monasteries and other ecclesiastical foundations had indeed provided 'Christian schools'. Given his view of early practices, papal interference and scholastic developments must have appeared as a travesty of the original model and it was in part the clericalization of traditional structures which triggered Luther's call for reform. Yet he found no explicit biblical proof to support this particular line of attack: the *formal* and *institutional* aspects of the Wittenberg reforms thus had to be bolstered by legal and socio-economic arguments: the superiority of Germanic over Roman legal principles and the validity of lay complaints about clerical manipulation of medieval schooling. The Scriptures, however, could serve as the prime authority for the definition of the *content* and ultimate *aim* of the educational programme, yielding ammunition against scholastic and humanist practices, and helping to develop a specifically 'reformed' curriculum.

The first part of Luther's key text 'To the mayors and aldermen of all German cities' (1524) lists three theological arguments for a renewed and stronger commitment to youth education:[19] first, to fight Satan, who strives to destroy God's creation; second, to retain God's mercy, which the Germans received in succession to the Jews, the Greeks, and the Romans; third, to understand and obey the commandments and the order of creation. In spite of Luther's subsequent emphasis on the responsibilities of secular authorities, these scriptural references should not be ignored: educating the young is not merely a matter of common sense, but also a theological imperative. As teachers and spiritual advisors, theologians have a duty to identify magisterial neglect and to suggest improvements in educational provision. Luther then merges this joint ecclesiastical–secular responsibility with medieval reform concepts, while distancing himself from a purely secularized overhaul of the system. This duality characterizes the whole of the Wittenberg programme.

The text attacks three distinct contemporary approaches: scholasticism, spiritualist-utilitarian tendencies, and humanism. Scholasticism is the most frequent target and denounced for a whole variety of rea-

---

[19] 'An die Burgermeyster und Radherrn allerley stedte ynn Deutschen landen' in WA, xv. 27–53.

sons:[20] in particular its ineffective, artificially contrived, and often ridiculous teaching system, which Luther had experienced himself. Ecclesiastical schools are described as 'ass's places and devil's schools',[21] because they fail to meet divine requirements, and Jesus' condemnation from Matthew xviii:6f is directed against them. Scholastic institutions abuse the children in their care, oppose the teaching of languages, and contribute to the decline of classical education. Their tuition methods and text books are branded as useless for a proper understanding of the Bible.

The anti-educational stance of spiritualist and utilitarian groups attracts the most substantial criticism.[22] The former are chided for their arbitrary exegesis of the Scriptures. Luther is at pains to prove that an exclusively spiritual interpretation must result in error, heresy, and ultimately total anarchy. Even the church fathers, otherwise held in great esteem, are cited as examples of a clerical and misleading reading of the Bible.[23] The utilitarians' hostility towards educating the 'middling sort' is denounced as a simplistic misunderstanding of lay life and priorities. Luther emphasizes the necessity to address real-life needs and to promote the spread of advanced knowledge. Political rulers, too, are reminded of their duty to look after their subjects.

The text finally distances itself from humanist reformers, particularly with regard to the ultimate aims of education. The knowledge of classical languages and other skills should not merely promote the development of autonomous individuals, but help to integrate them in the divine order and the earthly hierarchy of parental and magisterial authority. Even so, Luther does not ignore the more practical aspects of schooling: he calls for the study of languages, the extension of the scholastic *trivium*, and for didactical improvements: playful instruction on the one hand, and learning by imitation (*imitatio*) on the other.

Luther's letter to the mayors and aldermen gradually acquired programmatic quality, but it was written on the spur of the moment; its immediate importance should not be overstated. The author himself

---

[20] The crucial theological argument, the reversal of the Gospel (by means of which the devil attempts to lure man away from God) is not explicitly mentioned, but Luther must have felt that he had expounded this sufficiently on previous occasions.

[21] WA, xv. 31, 25.

[22] Cf. Ernst Kähler, 'Karlstadts Protest gegen die theologische Wissenschaft', *450 Jahre Martin Luther Universität Halle-Wittenberg*, vol. i: Wittenberg 1502–1817 (Wittenberg, 1952), pp. 299–312, and the report of Sebastian Fröschl in Karl Kaulfuss-Diesch (ed.), *Das Buch der Reformation geschrieben von Mitlebenden* (Leipzig, 1917), p. 289–90.

[23] Markus Wriedt, 'Die Verwendung altkirchlicher Autoritäten in der Debatte um die Schulreform im 16. Jahrhundert' in L. Grane, A. Schindler, and M. Wriedt (eds), *Auctoritas Patrum: New Contributions to the Reception of the Church Fathers in the 15th and 16th Century* (Mainz, forthcoming).

was extremely disappointed about its impact.[24] Friedrich Falk, who attempted to prove the letter's effect on a number of school ordinances, arrived at the conclusion that 'the historical influence of the text ... cannot clearly be ascertained. It is mentioned in letters soon after its appearance, but school foundations or regulations only rarely refer to it explicitly. The only direct quotation appears in the Göttingen church ordinances of 1531'. In contrast, works by Bugenhagen and Melanchthon seem to have had a more immediate effect.[25]

More important than a textual reference, of course, is the personal influence of Luther and his Wittenberg colleagues. All of the main reformers were involved in school foundations and there are numerous written statements outlining their views. Disregarding the subtler differences between Luther, Bugenhagen, and Melanchthon, the following elements emerge as the shared core of their programmes: all three advance theological arguments to define the *aim* of their educational reforms, and all see their engagement as an inevitable consequence of the requirements of the reformed religion. The basic concern is to educate the young generation in 'omnibus civitatibus, oppidis et pagis',[26] even though the necessity of comprehensive popular education was gradually toned down because of financial constraints. There is a strong emphasis on the learning of languages, especially Latin, but less explicit guidance about the position of German schools; confronted with an ever more pressing demand for new ministers, Latin may have been a natural priority. Even so, many school ordinances refer to Luther's demand for an adequate education for girls.[27]

---

[24] Martin Luther, 'Dem auserwählten lieben Freunde Gottes, allen Christen zu Riga, Reval und Dorpat in Livland' in WA, xii. 147–50; cf. Otto Albrecht, 'Studien zu Luthers Schrift "An die Ratsherren aller Städte deutsches Landes, daß sie christliche Schulen aufrichten und halten sollen" (1524)', *Theologische Studien und Kritiken*, 1 (Gotha, 1897), 771.

[25] 'Luthers Schrift an die Ratsherren der deutschen Städte und ihre geschichtliche Wirkung auf die deutsche Schule', *Lutherjahrbuch*, 19 (1937), 80 (quote); cf. Karl Hartfelder, *Melanchthoniana paedagogica* (Leipzig, 1892), pp. 125ff, Georg Mertz, *Das Schulwesen der deutschen Reformation im 16. Jahrhundert* (Heidelberg, 1902), p. 471, and Reinhold Vormbaum (ed.), *Die evangelischen Schulordnungen des 16. Jahrhunderts* (vol. i, Gütersloh, 1860); for Johannes Bugenhagen see Ralf Kötter, *Johannes Bugenhagens Rechtfertigungslehre und der römische Katholizismus: Studien zum Sendbrief an die Hamburger* (Göttingen, 1994).

[26] Franz Lambert von Avignon, *Reformatio ecclesiarum Hassiae* (1526), cap. xxx, quoted in Vormbaum (ed.), *Evangelische Schulordnungen*, p. 4.

[27] WA, xv. 47, 7–8. For the reception of this proposal see, for example, the church ordinances of Stralsund (1525), Schwäbisch Hall (1526), Braunschweig (1528), and Ulm (1531) in Vormbaum (ed.), *Evangelische Schulordnungen*, and Lambert, *Reformatio*, cap. xxxi; see also Falk, 'Luthers Schrift', 94–6, and Luther's letter to Else of Kanitz: WA Br., iv. 236.

The letter to the 'mayors and aldermen' also addresses the needs of academic élites. Luther recommends specific measures to assist the 'prodigy of learning', and some schools seem to have heeded this advice.[28] The adoption of the humanist *studium trilingue*, in contrast, was initially largely ignored. The study of languages remained a preserve of the universities – and thus primarily of those students preparing for an ecclesiastical career. Melanchthon, in particular, opposed more general tuition in Greek, Hebrew, and also in German.[29] Luther came to endorse this view in his 'Sermon admonishing [Christians] to send their children to school', where he recommended linguistic studies only for scholars.[30] The reading of classical writers was meant to enable the latter to learn by means of imitation; only Melanchthon, with his strong humanist connections, seems to have put some emphasis on an understanding of the content.

Even though Luther failed to mention religious education in the letter, the 1528-visitations of Saxony and his own catechetical writings suggest that it formed an implicit part of the programme. Special Bible-lessons can thus be found in nearly all school ordinances, none of which distinguish, in the 'modern' way, between worldly 'state' education and ecclesiastical instruction. Quite to the contrary, almost all assume a close relationship between teaching priorities and church doctrine. Many ordinances prescribe short prayer services at the beginning and the end of each day, with sermons, liturgical training, and choral exercises as further integral parts of the curriculum.[31]

To sum up, it is clear that Luther's educational programme had many medieval precedents: reallocation of ecclesiastical resources, appeals to the responsibilities of secular authorities, rejection of a church monopoly over schooling. Genuinely 'new', however, is the undivided supremacy of the Bible in determining the content and aims of education. The principle of 'sola scriptura' had been upheld throughout the Middle Ages, but there were arguments about who could interpret its ambiguous parts and who had the authority to settle the resulting disputes. Wittenberg's reformers knew no such doubts: no one was qualified to tamper with the word of God, for 'sacra scriptura sui ipsius interpres'.[32]

---

[28] WA, xv. 47, 13–16.

[29] Martin Luther and Philipp Melanchthon, 'Unterricht der Visitatoren an die Pfarrherren im Kurfürstentum Sachsen' in Delius et al. (ed.), *Studienausgabe*, iii. 406–62.

[30] 'Eine Predigt, daß man Kinder zur Schulen halten solle' (1530): WA, xxx/2. 508–88.

[31] Falk, 'Luthers Schrift', 102.

[32] Walter Mostert, '*Scriptura sacra sui ipsius interpres*: Bemerkungen zum Verständnis der Heiligen Schrift durch Luther', *Lutherjahrbuch*, 46 (1979), 60–96; for a late medi-

In the later years of the Reformation, particularly in the wake of the dispute between the spiritualists and evangelists, a need for 'Protestant' interpretation re-emerged, but in the early phase – from which our texts derive – such turbulences remain below the surface. At first, therefore, the new principle must have appeared as a welcome alternative to the frequent, and seemingly arbitrary, doctrinal interferences deriving from Rome.

Combined with the emphasis on the 'priesthood of all believers', the approach demanded the active promotion of 'critical' public reasoning and thus an energetic educational offensive. For Luther and his fellow reformers, the primary task lay in the establishment of a system of schools and universities to make as many people as possible familiar with the Bible, in order to enable them to interpret its meaning and to restructure their lives. Everything else was of secondary importance.

Church history, to return to one of the crucial theological arguments in the letter to the 'mayors and aldermen', unfolded as a process of precipitating decline until the second coming of Christ. Improved education was seen as a tool in the apocalyptic battle between God and Satan: the study of the past would alert people to God's omniscience and help them to understand the Scriptures and the fate of the world. It thus obtained an important place in school and university education, even though profane – and especially classical – historians were to be studied in strict subordination to the overall authority of the Bible.[33]

(iii)

Given this specific mixture between traditional and innovative elements in the Wittenberg reforms, what exactly is the place of the early sixteenth century in the transformation of the medieval into the early modern world? Did Luther's theses start a new era, or was he merely a 'forerunner of the Reformation'?[34] Is there a case for a fresh periodization in European history; should the years between the fourteenth

---

eval precedent of this allegedly Protestant axiom see Friedrich Kropatscheck, *Das Schriftprinzip der lutherischen Kirche: Geschichtliche und dogmatische Untersuchungen* (Leipzig, 1904).

[33] For a more detailed discussion see my 'Luther's view of history and the formation of an evangelical identity' in Bruce Gordon (ed.), *Protestant History and Identity in Sixteenth-Century Europe*, St Andrews Studies in Reformation History (Aldershot and Brookfield/Vermont, 1996).

[34] Heiko A. Oberman, 'Martin Luther: Vorläufer der Reformation' in E. Jüngel, J. Wallmann, and W. Werbeck (eds), *Verificationen: Festschrift für Gerhard Ebeling zum 70. Geburtstag* (Tübingen, 1982), pp. 91–119.

and sixteenth century be seen as one long 'era of reforms'? My concluding remarks shall address some of these issues.

Recent historiographical tendencies, especially the emphasis on the functional similarities of early modern confessions and the blurring of traditional dividing lines between the later Middle Ages and the Reformation, have fundamental implications for our interpretation of almost all areas of public and private life in the period.[35] 'Modernization' is now associated with late medieval reform movements as well as with the Reformation; the view of a 'redeemer', sent to resurrect a derelict church through a complete break with tradition, has long been abandoned. In fact, it has been turned upside down: fourteenth and fifteenth-century monastic reforms, for instance, are said to have been 'destroyed by the Reformation', and developments in territories east of the Elbe interpreted as a 'reaction to a crisis in modernization'.[36] Even the doctrine of the 'priesthood of all believers' was based on medieval precedent,[37] and by 1500 at the latest, the traditional dualism clergy – laity no longer corresponded to social reality; in terms of learning and spirituality, the dividing lines had become increasingly blurred.

The idea of the Reformation as a violent interruption of an ongoing process of modernization, however, cannot fully convince. Many late medieval initiatives had lost their momentum or had been undermined by their opponents; often, it was only the Reformation which brought them to a conclusion. Catholic confessionalization, pursued by the church hierarchy after it had overcome the first shock of the Reformation, in turn resumed late medieval reforms alongside the promotion of new forms of spirituality and organizations such as the Jesuits. In this sense, the centuries between 1350 and 1650 should indeed be seen as a long and interrelated 'era of reforms'.[38]

While the Reformation undoubtedly revived the dynamics of modernization in some cases, it would be wrong to claim that it was *only* the Reformation which could successfully alter existing structures. Innovation *was* possible under the old religious regime, even in core areas

---

[35] Summarizing: Heinz Schilling, 'Luther, Loyola, Calvin und die europäische Neuzeit', *ARG*, 85 (1994), 5–31.

[36] Kaspar Elm, *Reformbemühungen und Observanzbestrebungen im spätmittelalterlichen Ordenswesen* (Berlin, 1989), p. 18; Volker Reinhardt, 'Der Primat der Innerlichkeit und die Probleme des Reiches: Zum deutschen Nationalgefühl der frühen Neuzeit' in Bernd Martin (ed.), *Deutschland und Europa* (Munich, 1992), p. 90.

[37] Hans-Martin Barth, *Einander Priester sein: Allgemeines Priestertum in ökumenischer Perspektive* (Göttingen, 1990); Bernhard Lohse, *Luthers Theologie in ihrer historischen Entwicklung und in ihrem systematischen Zusammenhang* (Göttingen, 1995), pp. 308–10.

[38] Schilling, 'Luther, Loyola, Calvin', 19–20.

such as the cult of saints. Sixteenth-century iconoclasm was not the only way to alter public perceptions of images, for sacred painting had undergone significant changes from the fourteenth and fifteenth century.[39] Similarly, the 'rational' colour, form, and light compositions of Guido Reni (1575–1642) and other Catholic painters appear just as 'modern' as the oratorio-baroque of their Protestant equivalents.[40]

Many more examples could be cited. Returning to the subject matter of this essay, Luther must be seen as both continuing and competing with medieval precedent. To acknowledge this particular blend neither reduces the importance nor the quality of his reform-ideas, some of which, to finish on an oecumenical note, have long since been adopted in Roman Catholic theology.

---

[39] Dieter Koepplin, 'Reformation der Glaubensbilder: Das Erlösungswerk Christi auf Bildern des Spätmittelalters und der Reformationszeit' in *Martin Luther und die Reformation in Deutschland*, Ausstellungskatalog des Germanischen Nationalmuseums Nürnberg (Frankfurt, 1983), pp. 333–78.

[40] Schilling, 'Luther, Loyola, Calvin', 26.

CHAPTER ELEVEN

The Reformation and the evolution of Geneva's schools

William G. Naphy

It is an historiographical commonplace that Protestantism, especially Calvinism, was an urban phenomenon which placed considerable value on education.[1] Presumably then, one would expect to see an emphasis upon schooling arising in a town as it embraced the new religious ideas. No better place could be chosen to test this hypothetical link than Geneva itself and this essay will attempt to assess Calvin's impact on the provision of education in the city.

The role of the Reformation, however, cannot be judged without a closer examination of the chronological and geographical setting. Geneva shared many economic, political, and cultural ties with France, and if one assumes a broader regional perspective, it is soon apparent that there was widespread urban interest in education well before the religious changes. In fact, the spread of municipal schooling was clearly the result of rising *bourgeois* expectations and power rather than Calvinist ideology.[2] Modern French historiography focuses on the growth of royal and Jesuit institutions in the late sixteenth century.[3] However, Map 11.1 shows the extent to which urban areas had already established schools prior to Calvin's return to Geneva in 1541.[4] A compilation of the information provided by Marie-Madeleine Compère and Dominique Julia reveals that no less than 72 towns had schools dating

---

[1] Despite the lively debate, I simply accept that connecting urbanism and Calvinism is the prevailing historiographical view. On Genevan Protestantism and education: C. Borgeaud, *Histoire de l'Université de Genève* (vol. i, Geneva, 1900), esp. chs 1 and 2.

[2] On the structure of Geneva's councils and citizenship see the author's *Calvin and the Consolidation of the Genevan Reformation* (Manchester, 1994), pp. 92–4. The Genevan term *bourgeois* can be used as a synonym of the Swiss German *Burger* or citizen. What little rural education there was was a much later feature of Genevan education (cf. Notes 91–2).

[3] See G. Mialaret and J. Vial, *Histoire mondiale de l'Education* (Paris, 1981), and R. Chartier et al., *L'Education en France du XVIᵉ au XVIIIᵉ siècle* (Paris, 1976).

[4] From this date it is possible to speak of a Calvinist Reformation: P. Imbart de la Tour, *Les Origines de la Réforme* (Melun, 1948), i. 529. The map is the product of a synthesis of locations given in the works of Huppert, Mialaret and Vial, and Compère and Julia (see notes 3, 5, and 7).

Map 11.1   Distribution of French schools and colleges by 1541

from the fifteenth and early sixteenth centuries.[5] Approximately 12 were organized enough to be considered *collèges*.[6] Moreover, George Huppert's recent study underlines the depth of urban commitment to providing high quality education.[7]

The extent of the phenomenon is striking. Information on other areas of France is limited, but there is clearly a substantial concentration of

---

[5] *Les collèges français, XVIe–XVIIIe siècles, France du Midi* (vol. i, Paris, 1984).

[6] Crudely, a *collège* resembled a university, but did not award any degrees; it also included lower schools, which differentiated it from an academy. *Ecoles* provided primary and, perhaps, secondary education. Quasi-*collèges* (Versonnay and Rive) developed in Geneva.

[7] *Public Schools in Renaissance France* (Chicago, 1984), and see note 2 above.

schools in the Rhône–Saône basin – areas closely connected to Geneva.[8] Given the geographical pattern apparent in the map, it is tempting to speculate about a potential link between the historic success of Calvinism in a 'crescent' through southern France (from La Rochelle via Montpellier to Grenoble) and the distribution of pre-Reformation schools.[9] These towns, as will be shown below, had a tradition of struggles which pitted merchant and artisan élites against the clerical establishment. Convinced by the advantages of secular supervision, the laity had begun to take control of various functions (schooling and, to some extent, poor relief) well before the Reformation. This urban culture may well have been inclined to entertain (and later accept) yet more radical proposals. Perhaps, then, the relationship between Calvinism and education was that Calvinism spoke for, and to, a milieu already predisposed to support and provide education.

And yet, it is not sufficient to show that urban schooling was an increasingly common phenomenon in and around Geneva. The type and quality of education must also be examined to see if developments in the city, both before and after Calvin's arrival, departed from the established pre-Reformation pattern. For this purpose, one must first look at the organization and emphases of the schools in some detail.

The *collège* founded at Sens in 1537 by a bequest from one Philip Hodoard, displays many of the features common to these municipal schools. The bequest provided for a purpose-built structure (still used in the 1970s), its legal incorporation (*collège*), an overseer (*proviseur*), a board of trustees (mostly civil but including some clergy), and a specific staff structure (a principal/master and three teachers).[10] The analysis of other schools adds to this picture. In most, tuition was free (or occasionally means-tested) to city residents, with substantial fees for outsiders who boarded with the principal and supplemented his salary.[11] Normally, the principal contracted personally with the city for the schooling and the recruiting and paying of the teachers.[12] He retained the non-resident fees and the city prohibited any potentially competitive

---

[8] See, for instance, De la Tour, *Réforme*, i. 517.

[9] On the distribution of Calvinism: M. Greengrass, *The French Reformation* (Oxford, 1987), pp. 43–4.

[10] Huppert, *Schools*, pp. 19–22.

[11] Aix-en-Provence, 1522: F. Belin, *Histoire de l'Université de Provence* (Paris, 1896), p. 288; Huppert, *Schools*, p. 23. At Lectoure (1519): 'los enffans de la bila son quitis de collecta', ibid., p. 12; Mialaret and Vial, *Histoire*, ii. 305, 307.

[12] Huppert, *Schools*, pp. 23–4.

teaching (for example, by private tutors).[13] Finally, most contracts spelled out a fairly mild disciplinary régime and a humanistic curriculum.[14]

While this picture of a 'normal' municipal educational establishment is interesting, it begs one important question. Why did cities seek to provide such elaborate and expensive institutions? Apparently, there were a number of interconnected concerns.[15] First and foremost, while diocesan and monastic foundations provided some access to education, urban merchants had different educational goals. Ecclesiastical schooling was primarily designed to equip men for the clergy. Moreover, these schools were beyond magisterial control and were part of an educational network which took the town's children to distant universities and academies. Also, the merchants saw commercial value in educating their future heirs and appreciated the wider benefits for social order and stability by occupying children in schools.[16] This latter issue was of special concern as it limited youthful disorder and eventually promised to produce that most desirable of products, *gens de bien*, good citizens.

There was also broad agreement on how these schools should be administered. The ideological framework was provided by humanist ideas on education. Pierre Saliat, in 1537, expressed the prevailing opionion when he argued that the only schools appropriate for the education of the *enfans de bourgeois* were public, magistrate-controlled institutions.[17] Saliat's work supplied the basic justification for this view, while Parisian schools emerged as more practical models. *La coutume parisienne* spread with amazing speed. Students were divided into six grades with teachers specializing for each level.[18] Young students were enrolled to begin their education under *l'abécédaire*, who taught rudimentary reading and writing.[19] This trend towards conformity went so far that the Fête de St Rémy (8 October) became the first day of the school calendar throughout much of France.[20]

---

[13] Vienne, *c.* 1550: C. Faure, *Recherches sur l'Histoire du collège de Vienne* (Paris, 1933), 355; Huppert, *Schools*, p. 24.

[14] Ibid., pp. 41, 69–71.

[15] Cf. H. Vuilleumier, *Histoire de l'Eglise réformée du Pays de Vaud* (Lausanne, 1927), p. 397, which notes Farel and Viret's commendation of the Bernese generosity towards schools.

[16] N. Weiss , 'Le collège de Nevers et M. Cordier', *Revue Pédagogique* (1891), 405; Chartier, *L'Education*, p. 48; De la Tour, *Réforme*, i. 526; Vuilleumier, *Vaud*, p. 353.

[17] *Declamation contenant la manière de bien instruire les enfans* (Paris, 1537), translated from Erasmus, *Declamatio de pueris instituendis* (1529), ed. J. C. Margolin (Geneva, 1966).

[18] Narbonne, 1530: L. Narbonne, *L'instruction publique à Narbonne* (Narbonne, 1891), pp. 27–8.

[19] Huppert, *Schools*, p. 42.

[20] Cf. the 1558 contract in Lyon: Huppert, *Schools*, p. 50 (and note 10).

In addition to depending upon Parisian models, educational institutions turned to the capital for teachers. Paris (although outside the Rhône–Saône basin) was the best source for teachers because of the size of its university population. Bordeaux presents an excellent example of this commitment to hiring quality teachers. In 1533, its magistrates instructed the master of their newly-founded *collège* to recruit an entire staff at Paris. Master Tartas (a former Parisian principal), relying on municipal largesse, returned with 18 teachers, most with master's degrees.[21] Undoubtedly, Tartas returned to a school adhering to the national norm. Classes would have begun at nine, followed by a lunch break at eleven, with more classes from one to five.[22] Discipline would have been strict, but not severe – many educators advocated an understanding, supportive approach. Often, the magistrates (themselves parents) forbade corporal punishment in the schools, arguing that they would apply it at home.[23]

Beyond these features, the magistrates also showed a definite prejudice against clerics. In 1537, the council of Alais decided against employing a monk claiming that no person could serve two masters and, therefore, the Dominican could not perform the office of principal 'convenablement'.[24] Troyes, as late as 1576, was convinced that 'in our experience, when such masters [priests] are provided with benefices, they retire and no longer fulfil their duties'.[25] This complaint also underlay the dismissal of Master Damas, priest, from the principalship of Vienne's schools. His teachers complained that he was living off his benefice – neglecting the school. The magistrates wanted to sack him but could not fault his teaching skills, so they removed him for supplying the school with inferior wine in violation of his contract.[26] Finally, many cities were concerned that unmarried men, and especially priests, had no personal ties to the locality and were, therefore, more likely to depart for more lucrative positions.[27] This factor and other benefits of married teachers – two workers for the price of one – were emphasized by leading theorists such as Claude Baduel.[28]

---

[21] E. Gaullier, *Histoire du collège du Guyenne* (Paris, 1874), pp. 32–3.

[22] Auch, 1565: Huppert, *Schools*, 53.

[23] Saliat's recommendation (*Declamation*, p. 37): 'Il y en aura qui nous chanteront icy les oracles des Hebreux. Qui espargne la verge, il hait son fils. Tel chastiment peut estre convenoit jadis aux Juifs. Il faut maintenat interpreter plus civilement les dits des Hebreux'. See note 30 below.

[24] A. Bardon, 'Les écoles à Alais', *Mémoires et compte rendus de la société scientifique et littéraire d'Alais*, 20 (1899), 30.

[25] T. Boutiot, *Histoire de l'instruction publique à Troyes* (Troyes, 1865), p. 36.

[26] Belin, *Provence*, p. 277.

[27] Aix-en-Provence, 1543: ibid., p. 277.

[28] *Traicté de la dignité du mariage* (Paris, 1548): Huppert, *Schools*, pp. 64–5.

Therefore, one sees throughout pre-Reformation France – areas with close trading links to Geneva – the development of a national, educational model. Municipal authorities wanted an effective and efficient school organization. They wrested control of education from the ecclesiastical and private teachers to create a free, public educational system under firm magisterial supervision. They adopted the newest ideas in education, built the necessary structures, competed to attract the highest quality teachers, and girded themselves to meet the necessary burdensome expenses.

It is thus hardly surprising to find that Geneva strove to organize its schools according to the same model. The greatest difficulty facing the city, however, was that there was no separation between secular and ecclesiastical authority: Geneva's temporal overlord was the city's bishop. And yet, proof of the *bourgeois* determination to provide an independent, public school is the magistrates' battle to wrest control of education away from the cathedral canons.[29] Given that developments mirrored the above pattern, they can be discussed briefly.

Geneva's educational interests had an extensive and impressive pedigree dating from the medieval period. Bishop Ardutius, at the Third Lateran Council (1179), reported that his diocese provided free education for clerics and poor scholars. In 1227, the city arrested a teacher for offering private tuition in contravention of Genevan decrees. Later, in 1290, a master, Guillaume de Conflans, prescribed the study of grammar, logic, and philosophy in the schools. There is no better indication of Geneva's support for education (if not its desire to fund it) than the Imperial Bull (1365) of Charles IV granting the city the right to establish a university; the institution, however, never materialized.

The year before the bull saw the first evidence of direct magisterial involvement in education. Bishop Alamand de St-Joire referred to the 'schools of the city and the diocese'. Definitive proof of civil interest can be found in 1389, when the *Conseil Général* decided to construct a *collège* beside the Franciscan monastery. The money came from a bequest by François de Versonnay. A *recteur*, Jean de la Ravoire, was hired to teach grammar, logic, and the liberal arts (rhetoric and poetry);

---

[29] This section is indebted to H. Naef, *Origines de la Réforme à Genève* (Geneva, 1968), i. 278–99, and the introduction in K. Maag, *Seminary or University?* (Aldershot, 1995). On the chapter: J. Mercier, *Le Chapitre de Saint-Pierre de Genève* (Geneva, 1890); Abbé Besson, *Mémoires pour l'histoire ecclésiastique* (Nancy, 1759); H. Naef, 'La conquête du vénérable Chapitre de Saint-Pierre de Genève par les Bourgeois', *Bulletin de la Société d'Histoire et d'Archéologie de Genève*, 7/1 (1938/9), 35–128. On Geneva's environs: J. F. Gonthier, *Histoire de l'instruction publique avant 1789* (Annecy, 1887).

students were divided into three groups by ability and age. The institution (a secular foundation) was established with full ecclesiastical consent. Regulations were approved by Henri Fabri (the bishop's vicar general), Amadée de Charansonay (Prior of St-Victor, Geneva's Cluniac monastery), Pierre Blanc (Franciscan *gardien*), other clerics, and numerous leading citizens. The Collège included a chapel (St Nicolas and St Catherine) and provided a daily *Ave Maria* and *Pater Noster* for the founder's soul. Despite clerical involvement and these religious obligations, all teachers were state-paid and tuition was free to residents.

Clearly, the secular authorities exercized extensive control over the Collège de Versonnay. The regulations prohibited corporal punishment, especially the rod (*verge*). On 30 October 1459, the magistrates asserted their right to dismiss a *recteur* for mistreating students and bringing the Collège into disrepute.[30] In 1486, the city intervened to separate male and female students to improve morality, and on 9 June 1503 the civic officials pre-emptively cancelled classes to prevent the spread of the plague. Prior to this, but almost a century after the introduction of free education, the magistrates were forced to impose charges – the contemporary decline in Geneva's economy undoubtedly being a factor.[31] In 1483, the city had already allowed the principal to collect fees from (foreign) boarding students to supplement his meagre state salary.

In 1494, the city decided to rebuild the school. In spite of chronic financial problems the building was completed and inaugurated in the same year by the newly-appointed master, Jean Guency. Guency's brief principalship ended with a disagreement between council and canons over the control of the Collège. In 1495, the master was effectively sacked by the chapter – they refused to pay the small portion of his salary allotted to them. Apparently, the city acquiesced, for they agreed to sever all ties with Guency and to pay him all monies they owed him.

---

[30] There were other examples of magisterial involvement in student discipline: in September 1554, five students were arrested for sodomy. After ministerial advice, the city decided the students were too young for adult punishment. The youngest received private parental beatings and the older three were thrashed. All were burned in effigy. AEG/RC (Registres du Conseil)/(vol.) 48, fos 169ʳ–169ᵛ (27 Sep. 1554); M. Roset, *Chroniques de Genève* (Geneva, 1894), pp. 363–4, and my *Calvin*, pp. 188–9. On the usual penalty: AEG/PC (Procès Criminels)/1ʳᵉ Sèr., 502 (7–16 March 1554), 518 (7–23 Jan. 1555); RC/48, f. 181ᵛ (23 Jan. 1555); CO, xv. col. 69–70 (advice to *Petit Conseil*, March 1554): Lambert le Blanc (son of a royal *comptrolleur des finances*), Mathieu Durand (printer's helper), and four others were executed.

[31] On late medieval Geneva: E. W. Monter, *Calvin's Geneva* (London, 1967), pp. 1–35. On Geneva's economy: J. F. Bergier, *Genève et l'économie européene de la Renaissance* (Geneva, 1963); A. Babel, *Histoire économique de Genève des origines au début du XVIᵉ siècle* (Geneva, 1963).

However, the dispute only highlighted the problems inherent in an institution administered by the secular authorities but ultimately controlled by the church through the chapter's head, the *chantre*. The issue was resolved on 8 April 1502, when the magistrates assumed complete control of Geneva's schools. Undoubtedly this did not end the debate between the council and the chapter, but it appears that at this juncture the control of education became entwined in the more serious dispute between Genevans who supported the city's Savoyard episcopal ruler and those who longed for the city's independence and affiliation with the Swiss Confederation.[32]

As Geneva entered into a prolonged period of social and political turmoil, exacerbated by religious disputes, it is not surprising to discover that the Collège became disturbed and disorganized. Clashes occurred in the 1510s among the teachers as well as between ecclesiastical and magisterial officials. Early in 1518, the *Petit Conseil* (or senate – Geneva's highest civil body) asserted its right to hire and fire teachers according to 'ancienne coutume'. Apparently, the magistrates failed to carry the argument as the principal in question, Esserton, was sacked by the *chantre*, De Maurienne. On 26 September 1518, the senate, with the support of the larger *Conseil des Cinquante*, reiterated its supremacy and appointed a successor, Louis Beljaquet, without consulting De Maurienne.[33]

Beljaquet remained principal for five difficult years until resigning, in 1523, to pursue a career in medicine. He was troubled by rival teachers rather than the church. In 1518, the *faubourg* of St Gervais (across the Rhône from Geneva proper) had asked to establish a separate school. Under pressure from the opposing demands of St Gervais's residents and Beljaquet, the city agreed in 1520 to permit primary education in the suburb – for its residents alone. The magistrates protected Beljaquet's diminished monopoly by taking action against private tutors in 1520 and 1523.

Geneva's last pre-Reformation regent, Jean Christin, replaced Beljaquet. As the political chaos grew, his position became untenable. A supporter of the independence party, Christin quit Geneva in 1528 when Savoy temporarily re-asserted its control. His tenure was also troubled by competition from private tutors; the government was unable to secure his monopoly. City-wide public education effectively collapsed after his departure until the revolution's end in 1535. The Collège re-opened (as the Collège de Rive) at a new location, the former

---

[32] See Naef, *Origines*, esp. pp. 278–99. Note 29 above.
[33] After 1535, the *Cinquante* became the *Soixante*, cf. note 2 above.

Franciscan monastery – secularized along with other ecclesiastical properties by the revolutionary (and Protestant) party.[34]

One informative vignette survives from Christin's principalship. A former pupil, the notary Guillaume Messiez, recalled that under Christin ('un homme l'ictéré et deyjà ancien') he had studied 'Dispaute, Virgile ad Eneidos, Ovide, Cicero, Fauste et plusiers aultres'. This curriculum tallies well with that used throughout France. There, a 'normal' school programme involved these authors as well as Cato, Donat, Terence, Valla, Lineacre, Clénard, Pellisson, Horace, Quintilian, Sallust, Livy, Persius, Juvenal, and Aristotle (if Greek were available) – perhaps the 'plusiers aultres' taught by Christin.[35]

Before leaving the Collège de Versonnay to examine the early years of its successor, one cautionary remark needs to be made. The foregoing discussion has accepted the most positive interpretation of Geneva's pre-Reformation school situation. In fact, what has been said is the sum total of the knowledge of the Versonnay establishment. There is little doubt that the skeleton of the educational structure, as well as the magistrates' spirit in establishing it, were certainly in keeping with the prevailing French model. However, good wishes and a thorough outline on paper would not, of themselves, have created a school system.[36]

Mindful of this caveat and the paucity of detail on Geneva's schools, it should be clear that in every important feature they were analogous to the schools found in urban areas in France. It is unnecessary to prove that any specific institution was in fact a *collège* or not to conclude that the interest in free, public education was primarily an urban, *bourgeois* phenomenon aimed at curbing youthful exuberance and providing a city with productive, educated citizens.[37] Geneva's magistrates shared these desires and, insofar as possible, replicated this pattern in their city – before the Reformation.[38] The religious change had no immediate, appreciable impact upon the provision of education as the struggle between magistracy and chapter had been resolved before the revolu-

---

[34] Similar use was made of the church's wealth by the Bernese in the Pays de Vaud: Vuilleumier, *Vaud*, pp. 396ff (especially for founding the Lausanne Academy in 1537). Most secularized properties and goods were officially allocated to poor relief; cf. the essays of Cahill, Dykema, Fehler, and Maag in this volume.

[35] Huppert, *Schools*, pp. 59–60; P. Bénétrix, *Les origines du collège d'Auch* (Paris, 1908), pp. 74–5.

[36] Naef is optimistic about the Collège de Versonnay; Maag dubious. So little survives that any conclusions are tentative.

[37] Geneva's rural possessions were scant. Hence, 'local' necessarily implies 'urban'. Cf. notes 91–2 below.

[38] Explicit in Jean Girard's *L'Ordre*, quoted in E. A. Betant, *Notice sur le Collège de Rive* (Geneva, 1866), pp. 29–30: 'selon la maniere des ecoles ... selon la coustume des meilleurs colleges'.

tion. Clearly, the magistrates had no difficulty reconciling their adherence to late medieval Catholicism with their desire to control education. Primarily, this was because the schooling they provided differed fundamentally from the seminary education of the diocesan and monastic establishments.

The one significant change wrought upon the schools by the Reformation had already occurred two months before Calvin's arrival, in July 1536: the magistrates had relocated the Collège to Rive.[39] The newly independent magistracy hired Antoine Saulnier (from Morans in the Dauphiné) as *recteur* and he took an oath to the city-state on 8 March 1537.[40] He faced problems from the outset. There was a brief clash between Saulnier and the 'maistre de lescripture'.[41] Moreover, it is somewhat unclear how many other teachers assisted him as wages were disbursed to unnamed 'maistres'.[42] What is certain is that by early 1537, Saulnier was assisted by the famous teacher and educational theorist, Mathurin Cordier – fresh from the *collèges* of Paris, Nevers, and Bordeaux.[43]

Fortunately, the regulations of this new Protestant institution survive. They were printed by Jean Gerard on 12 January 1538.[44] Lessons began in the morning (at five), stopped for lunch (at ten), and continued into the evening. Latin, Greek, and Hebrew were taught, also French – 'laquelle [langue] n'est pas du tout à mépriser'. Basic, elementary education was entrusted to Cordier.[45] Advanced students were schooled in classical Latin to acquire 'vrai latin et élégant'. Lessons in Greek and Hebrew used the Bible as a textbook. Boarding students received extra tuition including maths. The religious content was left to Saulnier, who directed prayers before and after lessons. After dinner, all students assembled in the former monastery's hall where a student recited 'par coeur à haute voix les commandments de Dieu en français avec l'oraison de notre Seigneur at les articles de la foi'. A Bible chapter was read and everyone was expected to read a sentence from the Scriptures 'en diverses langues, chacun selon sa capacité'. This programme prevailed until

---

[39] C. E. Delormeau, *Mathurin Cordier* (Neuchâtel, 1976), p. 44.

[40] AEG/RC/30, f. 188ᵛ (8 March 1537). Saulnier arrived after Calvin.

[41] AEG/RC/31, f. 91ᵛ (13 Nov. 1537).

[42] Ibid., f. 133ʳ (14 Dec. 1537). Cf. AEG/RC/32, f. 47ᵛ (15 March 1539): a single payment for 'maystre de leschole'.

[43] Delormeau, *Cordier*, pp. 24–8, 32–3, 39–40.

[44] 'L'Ordre et manière d'enseigner en la ville de Geneva au Collège': Betant, *Rive*, after p. 26.

[45] Saulnier taught advanced students.

Christmas 1538, when the adherence of the Collège faculty to Calvin and Farel (expelled in April after a dispute with the magistrates) resulted in the dismissal of two teachers.[46] By January 1539, tensions in the city resulted in the removal of Saulnier and three further teachers, including Cordier.[47]

During Calvin's exile (1538–41) the Collège experienced serious difficulty. The new regent, Agnet, a native of the Bernese controlled Vaud, was beset by two major problems.[48] First, the staff was insufficient for the task; his sole helper was Claude Chavison.[49] Moreover, the city was unable to guarantee a sufficient wage even with a tuition fee – 'jouxte lay coutume ung solz pour mois'.[50] By 1540, Agnet's health declined and he resigned from preaching at the rural parish of Vandœuvres which had supplemented his salary.[51] The situation remained chaotic until Calvin's return in 1541 and Castellio's assumption of the principalship.[52]

In addition to staff troubles, the Collège suffered from a second major problem during Calvin's absence. In 1539, the state had decreed that all small schools (perhaps including the St Gervais school) were to be amalgamated with the Collège de Rive – although the Rive location

---

[46] Delormeau, *Cordier*, pp. 45ff. Farel was Geneva's premier Protestant preacher and persuaded Calvin to stay in Geneva. After 1538, Farel ministered in Neuchâtel.

[47] A. Roget, 'Mathurin Cordier' in his *Etrennes Genevoises* (Geneva, 1877), pp. 99–117.

[48] AEG/RC/33, fos 372ᵛ (10 Dec. 1539), 399ʳ (23 Dec. 1539).

[49] Ibid., fos 95ʳ (25 April 1539), 125ᵛ (16 May 1539). The ministers requested a *recteur* to help Chavison (Agnet): ibid., fos 260ʳ (26 Aug. 1539), 277ᵛ (8 Sep. 1539).

[50] Ibid., f. 35ʳ (18 April 1539). Agnet's annual salary was increased from 250 florins to 300. AEG/RC/34, fos 244ʳ (22 May 1540), 506ʳ (2 Nov. 1540), 510ʳ (5 Nov. 1540). For purchasing power cf. Bergier, *Genève*, and Babel, *Histoire économique*. Calvin was paid 500 florins, the other city ministers 250 florins, along with houses, foodstuffs, and intermittent gratuities. The city acknowledged the salaries' insufficiency. See my 'The Renovation of the Ministry in Calvin's Geneva' in A. Pettegree (ed.), *The Reformation of the Parishes* (Manchester, 1993), pp. 113–32, and J.-F. Bergier, 'Salaires des pasteurs de Genève au XVIᵉ siècle', *Bibliothèque historique Vaudoise*, 43 (1970), 165–8. Even sending guards 'mayson par mayson' failed to produce the necessary money: AEG/RC/35, f. 30ʳ (24 Jan. 1541).

[51] Agnet resigned his preaching post and received 30 florins for six months' work at Vandœuvres: AEG/RC/34, f. 560ʳ (14 Dec. 1540); RC/35, fos 6ʳ (10 Jan. 1541), 76ᵛ (15 Feb. 1541).

[52] A proposed new regent, Martans, was to replace Agnet who would retire to a small preaching post in rural Satigny at a pension of 200 florins. AEG/RC/35, fos 35ʳ (14 Feb. 1541), 91ᵛ (28 Feb. 1541). This plan failed and Cordier suggested a friend, Claude Budin, from Bordeaux: Ibid., f. 131ᵛ (29 March 1541). Even without a regent, the city hired two teachers, Estienne Roph (or Roux) and Pierre Mossard: ibid., fos 203ᵛ (14 May 1541), 255ʳ (5 July 1541). Upon Calvin's return, he was able to supply a new regent in the form of his friend Castellio: ibid., f. 240ᵛ (20 June 1541).

had been abandoned for some reason.[53] In August 1541, after Calvin's return, the Collège moved back to the Rive building from its interim location in the *chantrerie* attached to the cathedral of St Pierre. The *chantrerie* was not deemed 'bonement comode'.[54] However, after repairs and the addition of a garden it seemed suitable as a home for the city's new chief minister, Calvin.[55] Understandably, a private house was not comparable to the larger building which had served the Franciscans. Obviously, during Calvin's exile, the Collège had declined so severely as to meet in a private residence.

Before examining the Collège during Calvin's ministry, one should give some attention to the changes in the relationship of the educational institution with the magistrates. The most profound alteration emerges from the Ecclesiastical Ordinances of 20 November 1541. The Collège was once again placed under clerical control. In particular, the choice of teachers was left to ministerial discretion: 'Que nul ne soit receu s'il n'est apprové par les ministres'. The magistrates desired to retain at least the ambiguous powers which they had held under episcopal rule. To the assertion of church authority was added the phrase: 'l'ayant premierement faict scavoir à la Seigneurie et allors de rechef qu'il soit presenté au Conseil' and 'touteffois l'examen doibvra faict present deux les seigneurs du petit Conseil'.[56] Under the bishop's regime the state recruited and nominated teachers; the church authorities had right of final refusal. Theoretically, the ordinances reversed this arrangement and gave the initiative to the city's predominately foreign Company of Pastors.[57]

It would be incorrect to assume that this alteration to the educational administration was complemented by changes in the content or methods of the Collège. Humanist lessons still focused on language studies with the Bible as the primary text (as before, although with greater emphasis on the original languages of the Scriptures). Education remained the monopoly of the principal and his teachers and girls were separated from boys to maintain morality.[58] Thus for students, Calvin's return – indeed the Reformation – would have had little impact on the actual courses. The religious interpretations changed but in all other

---

[53] AEG/RC/33, f. 95ʳ (25 April 1539).

[54] AEG/RC/35, f. 273ᵛ (1 Aug. 1541).

[55] Ibid., f. 309ᵛ (4 Sep. 1541).

[56] *Seigneurie* could mean senate; technically, it encompassed all magistrates.

[57] J. F. Bergier et al. (eds), *Registres de la Compagnie des Pasteurs de Genève* (Geneva, 1964), i. 6. On Calvin and teachers: J. T. McNeill et al. (eds), *Calvin: Institutes of the Christian Religion* (Philadelphia, 1960), ii. 1057 (and n. 5).

[58] Girls received rudimentary schooling at *petites écoles*. Theoretically, higher education was available. However, the issue never arose.

respects schooling in Geneva remained true to the *bourgeois*-inspired methods and goals of the previous decades.

Sadly, the return of ecclesiastical stability and a lessening of the troubles and dislocations associated with Geneva's revolutionary period did not usher in an age of educational success. The Collège continued to confront two chronic problems. First, the city was unable to assume the entire cost of the faculty, which made it extremely difficult to attract and retain high quality teachers. Second, the ministers were determined to secure their ideal regent, Cordier, even at the cost of undermining the acting principal.[59]

Initially, the Collège seemed to recover under Castellio. In addition to Pierre Mossard and Estienne Roph, the city hired Guillaume Franc to teach the new metrical psalms.[60] The city also provided room in the 'mayson de la chambrerie', to 'Jaques Meraulx maystre descripture'.[61] Apparently, though, Meraulx was providing private tuition. Unable to pay a large staff, the city decided to tolerate rival schooling at the primary level. In June 1544, another 'maystre descripture' (Bernard Auguste) was permitted to offer tuition and, in February 1545, a foreign couple were allowed to open a school for boys and girls.[62]

While the edifice of a unitary, lay-controlled, and state-funded educational structure crumbled, the public teachers lamented their poverty. Castellio said that his salary was insufficient.[63] The regent's problems, however, were exacerbated by the lack of support which he received from the ministers in other areas. As early as December 1541, Calvin had informed Farel that he was negotiating with Cordier to bring him to Geneva.[64] The prospect of Castellio's replacement was broached to the *Petit Conseil* on 17 December 1543, with Calvin's announcement that a new principal had been located in Montpellier.[65] This move, which apparently took Castellio by surprise, led to a rapid deterioration

---

[59] Calvin wanted Cordier back in Geneva: Delormeau, *Cordier*, pp. 49–56 and CO, xi. col. 356–7 (letter to Farel, Dec. 1541).

[60] For 40–50 florins: AEG/RC/37, f. 61ʳ (16 April 1543). The salary rose to 60 florins, then 80 florins: ibid., fos 68ʳ (23 April 1543), 70ᵛ (24 April 1543). See Betant, *Rive*, p. 20: the salary eventually reached 100 florins. Geneva also hired other Psalm teachers: Franc (1543–5), Guillaume Fabri (1545–7), Louis Bourgeois (1547–56), Pierre Dagues (1556–9).

[61] AEG/RC/38, f. 27ʳ (8 Jan. 1544).

[62] Ibid., f. 242ᵛ (9 June 1544); RC, 40, f. 28ᵛ (19 Feb. 1545).

[63] 'Son gage ne peult soder a luy et a deux bachelleurs': AEG/RC/38, fos 30ʳ–30ᵛ (13 Jan. 1544), 36ʳ (21 Jan. 1544).

[64] CO, xi. col. 356–7 (letter to Farel, Dec. 1541).

[65] AEG/RC/38, f. 10ᵛ (17 Dec. 1543).

in his relationship with the Company of Pastors, culminating in his departure in June 1544.[66]

Regrettably for the Collège, the Montpellier candidate failed to materialize. Moreover, the ministers informed the magistrates that although they had found another available, and acceptable, replacement, the principal's salary was insufficient to entice the man to Geneva. The city was less than pleased with the revelation as it had already agreed to an increase in the wage and fees. Eventually, an acceptable formula was agreed upon and the new *recteur*, Charles Damont, was hired on 11 July 1544.[67]

However, this failed to bring tranquillity to Geneva's troubled Collège. By September, the new principal was involved in a personal dispute with one of the teachers, Mossard. Worse was yet to come: in March 1545, Calvin announced that the ministers had located and tentatively hired a new *recteur*, the long-sought Cordier, who was working in Neuchâtel. He was available for an agreed price of 500 florins. After negotiations, the city agreed to pay his removal expenses and a salary of 450 florins. All was for nought since, in May, Neuchâtel's magistrates refused to permit Cordier to leave. Then, the ministers attempted to attract François Déothée from Berne. He accepted the charge, but once again the plans were frustrated, as the Bernese leaders refused to release him from his obligations. Eventually, in July 1546, the city replaced the beleaguered Damont with Erasmus Cornier.[68]

Throughout all these machinations Damont remained unsure of his position.[69] Bereft of ministerial support and languishing in the impoverished state to which principals had become accustomed, the *recteur* strove to maintain the educational programme.[70] The problems he faced mounted at an alarming pace. In March 1545, the *Petit Conseil* noted that the Rive building was in desperate need of repairs. The psalm teacher, Franc, resigned because he could not survive on his meagre

---

[66] Ibid., fos 248ᵛ (13 June 1544), 257ᵛ–258ʳ (19 June 1533). On Castellio, see my 'Calvin's Letters: Reflections on their usefulness in studying Genevan history', *ARG*, 86 (1995), 67–89.

[67] AEG/RC/38, fos 262ᵛ–263ʳ (24 June 1544), 278ʳ (7 July 1544; the magistrates accepted 400 florins), 286ʳ (11 July 1544).

[68] Ibid., fos 286ʳ (1 Sep. 1544); RC/40, fos 59ʳ (20 March 1545), 81ʳ (13 April 1545), 102ʳ (4 May 1545), 216ᵛ (17 Aug. 1545), 221ʳ (21 Aug. 1545), 233ʳ (8 Sep. 1545), 260ʳ (13 Oct. 1545); 41, f. 146ᵛ (16 July 1546). Apparently, the city agreed to 500 florins: AEG/RC/40, f. 361ʳ (29 Jan. 1546).

[69] He was advised to apply to Calvin for a pastorate: ibid., f. 84ʳ (16 April 1545).

[70] Rectorial salaries rose from 250 florins in May 1540 to 500 in January 1546. However, the teachers' wages remained constant at 84 florins, with the principal providing supplements. This proved untenable and the city gave Mossard 160 florins: ibid., f. 335ʳ (24 Dec. 1545).

salary. Finally, the city continued to undermine the public school by sanctioning two more private tutors, Benoyt Bard and Jaques Merauld.[71]

Cornier's arrival brought no respite for the Collège. His salary was raised to 500 florins, which was nominally equal to Calvin's, but, as with previous *recteurs*, he was expected to supplement the teachers' low wages from his own pocket. By August 1546, scarcely a month after his arrival, Cornier was accused by Mossard of decreasing the usual supplement paid by the principal.[72] Upon this increasingly chaotic and tumultuous situation the magistrates and ministers attempted to impose some degree of order. They tried to mollify the dispute between the *recteur* and the teachers by ordering that all previous rules and traditions be codified into one comprehensive regulation.[73] By this point, the financial and personal problems had become critical. Cornier threatened to resign claiming he could no longer work with Mossard. Eventually, Mossard was allowed a month's leave of absence 'for business reasons' in the hope that harmony might be restored in the interim.[74] While the tensions were lessened, a magisterial committee of 1549 was forced to conclude that the underlying financial complaint was accurate.[75] The investigation had taken testimony from Cornier and a new teacher, Simon de Rostier, who gave irrefutable support to the committee's conclusions.[76] However, in April, before any decision could be taken, Cornier became fatally ill and died on 12 May 1550.[77]

To be brief, the unsettled conditions in the Collège continued without respite for the next five years until Calvin's victory over his magisterial opponents in 1555. The Rive building remained 'ruinous' though some minor repairs were undertaken.[78] The new *recteur*, Louis Enoch, clashed with two teachers.[79] He accused Jean Colinet of having lapsed into

---

[71] Ibid., fos 61ᵛ (23 March 1545), 202ᵛ (3 Aug. 1545), 323ʳ (11 Dec. 1545); RC/43, f. 63ᵛ (12 April 1548).

[72] AEG/RC/41, f. 184ʳ (27 Aug. 1546). Mossard was to cease complaining or face dismissal: AEG/RC/43, f. 132ʳ (10 July 1548).

[73] AEG/RC/42, f. 359ʳ (5 Dec. 1547).

[74] AEG/RC/43, f. 15 ᵛ (10 Aug. 1548); RC/44, f. 195ʳ (26 Aug. 1549).

[75] The *Petit Conseil* had convened a committee upon a complaint by Calvin: ibid., fos 212ʳ (13 Sep. 1549), 218ᵛ (20 Sep. 1549), 233ʳ–234ᵛ (7 Oct. 1549).

[76] AEG/RC/44, f. 237ʳ (11 Oct 1549).

[77] The city provided 20 florins for medical expenses: ibid., f. 370ᵛ (25 April 1550); RC/45, fos 1ᵛ (12 May 150), 4ᵛ (16 May 1550).

[78] Ibid., fos 142ᵛ (8 Dec. 1550), 270ᵛ (11 May 1551); RC/46, fos 233ʳ–233ᵛ (5 July 1552).

[79] The city 'decreed' harmony: AEG/RC/45, fos 89ᵛ (15 Sep. 1550), 92ʳ (16 Sep. 1550). On Enoch see Roget, 'Louis Enoch', *Etrennes* (1878), 33–46. Enoch's works included: *Prima infantia linguæ græcæ et latinæ simul et gallicæ* (Paris, 1546), *Partitiones grammaticæ* (Geneva: Crespin, 1551). Betant, *Rive*, p. 19, also lists *De puerili græcorum literarum doctrina liber* (Geneva: Estienne, 1555).

Catholicism, a charge partially admitted by the accused who was dismissed and jailed.[80] Enoch also argued with Léger Grimonet.[81] This constant bickering and fighting was, no doubt, the result of the magistrates' habit of appointing teachers without reference to, or consideration of, the principal.[82] The regent and his wife were charged with physically assaulting Grimonet.[83] Some relief was given when Nicolas Colladon, a French refugee, offered himself as a teacher in September 1552, and when Pierre Thodelle was hired on Calvin's recommendation two months later.[84] Colladon was promoted to the ministry soon afterwards but immediately replaced by Jean Barbier of Picardy, who had been recruited by Enoch.[85] The much maligned malcontent, Mossard, finally left on 22 March 1554 and was replaced by Pierre Duc of Toisse (Dombe) the following day.[86]

Although Calvin's troubles with the magistrates worsened from 1550–55 and the underlying problems besetting the Collège remained, it does appear that the *recteur* was finally able to attract and retain a sufficient number of congenial, qualified teachers. The overall situation improved further after the routing of the Perrinists in the summer of 1555.[87] Another teacher, the native Genevan Du Perril, was hired.[88] In response to Enoch's complaint that he could not support yet another member of staff, the magistrates undertook to pay Du Perril themselves.[89] Finally, on 17 March 1556, in response to a report from Calvin, the *Petit Conseil* decided to constitute a committee charged with restoring Geneva's divided and neglected educational system. The committee was especially advised by Calvin to find some way to integrate the numerous private schools into the state system.[90]

At this point, Calvin and the ministers were able to turn their attention to greater educational concerns. Not only did they encourage a

---

[80] AEG/RC/46, fos 271ᵛ–272ᵛ (13–15 Sep. 1552), 279ʳ (30 Sep. 1552); RC/47, f. 183ʳ (21 Nov. 1553).

[81] AEG/RC/45, fos 251ʳ (14 April 1551), 254ʳ (16 April 1551).

[82] Betant, *Rive*, p. 18. The Ecclesiastical Ordinances allowed ministerial advice on these appointments; the principal was not consulted. Effective ministerial control was gained after Calvin's political triumph (1555).

[83] AEG/PC/2ᵉ Sèr., 936 (7 April 1551). Violence was not unknown in the Collège: Pierre Mossard, a teacher, was prosecuted for cruelty (Betant, *Rive*, p. 17).

[84] AEG/RC/46, fos 278ᵛ (29 Sep. 1552), 314ʳ (25 Nov. 1552).

[85] AEG/RC/47, fos 79ᵛ–80ʳ (22 May 1553).

[86] AEG/RC/48, fos 24ᵛ–25ʳ (22–23 March 1554).

[87] On these disputes see my 'Baptisms, church riots, and social unrest in Calvin's Geneva', *SCJ*, 26 (1995), 87–97.

[88] AEG/RC/50, f. 24ʳ (31 Oct. 1555).

[89] Ibid., f. 35ʳ (12 Nov. 1555).

[90] AEG/RC/51, fos 52ᵛ–53ʳ (17 March 1556).

widening of the availability of education into Geneva's rural possessions, but they agitated for the creation of an advanced academy to
crown Geneva's public system.[91] In 1557, the senate agreed to finance
schools in the villages of Pigney, Chancy, and Cartigny.[92] Finally, on 17
January 1558, the decision was taken to proceed with the establishment
of the academy using the proceeds of the financial windfall provided by
the sale of properties confiscated from the Perrinists, the faction opposed to the growing political and economic influence in Geneva of the
French refugees and the French ministers.[93] For the first time in 60
years, Geneva had a complete educational system designed to provide
some schooling at every level. In addition, the city was able to expand
its teaching services into its rural hinterland and to create an academy
designed to attract students throughout Europe.

Admittedly though, this expansion of schooling had been at the expense
of many of the original *bourgeois* educational ideals. The new, enlarged
system was thoroughly dominated by the clergy and their concerns. As
Karin Maag has shown in her discussion of the academy's later years,
the magistrates fought to defend the needs of an urban élite. For example, they consistently strove to augment the academy's seminary programme with courses in law and medicine.[94] Nevertheless, the public
system remained under clerical control and its pinnacle was focused,
not on the educational needs of the small city-state of Geneva, but on
the wider, grander clerical requirements of the growing Calvinist movement in France and beyond.[95]

The basic character of primary education, however, remained the
same. Prior to the Genevan Reformation and revolution, the city had an
established educational system *à la mode française*. Geneva took civic
pride in its Collège which strove to rival those of its trading partners
and neighbours in south-eastern France and the Suisse Romande. The

[91] Geneva, the city-state, was smaller than Geneva, the diocese. Apparently, no schools
had existed in the few villages which Geneva controlled. Diocesan schools had merely
prepared students for an ecclesiastical career.
[92] AEG/RC/52, f. 234^v (1 Feb. 1557); RC/53, f. 125^r (4 March 1557). Jean de Lonnay
of Berry was hired at Chancy for 50 florins and 24 *sols* per student.
[93] AEG/RC/54, fos 29^r (30 Dec. 1557), 48^r (17 Jan. 1558).
[94] In addition, the magistrates wanted riding and fencing masters to attract noblemen.
They (and Beza) recruited legal and medical professors, a move never supported by the
other ministers, who considered it a distraction from the academy's aim – providing
ministerial training: Maag, *Seminary*, pp. 59ff, 123.
[95] The academy was not aimed at the local population: in 1559–1620, 2 672 students
were enrolled, 216 (8.1 per cent) were Genevan. Cf. Zurich (whose records are patchier)
with 529 students, of which 209 (39.5 per cent) were local: ibid., pp. 159–60.

goal of this municipal institution was clear: it was to provide the variety and quality of education necessary to equip the *enfants* of Geneva for the future and to allow them justly to bear the title *gens de bien*. These ideas and goals still underpinned and directed the local elements of Genevan education.

Many aspects of the development of education in Geneva under the Protestant ministers were counterproductive. Their consistent attempts to entice Cordier to Geneva severely undermined the position of other *recteurs*.[96] Presumably, this lack of support made it easier for the *Petit Conseil* to turn a deaf ear to the pleas for higher wages and an effective end to private tuition. However, the chaos in the Collège from the 1510s until 1555 must also be blamed upon the severe stress and strains in Geneva's institutions and society occasioned by the manifold changes which accompanied the city's revolution and Reformation. The upheavals associated with this period of turmoil must bear the lion's share of the responsibility for the unsettled conditions which prevailed in the school system.

What effect then did the Reformation have upon local education in Geneva? The basic principles, methods and curriculum of the Collège pre-dated the Reformation and were derived, not from desires for religious change, but from the growing self-awareness and self-assertiveness of the urban *bourgeoisie*. This rising élite, in Geneva and elsewhere, was determined that any *collège* would focus on the specific needs of the local community. The Reformation did not alter these attitudes and, apart from the academy, these concerns and goals continued to direct the provision of education. Also, it is essential to remember that, although the ministers were given immense leeway in directing the affairs of the schools, financial control always remained within the hands of the civil authorities. And yet, there were long-term changes relating to the effective control of the Collège; this passed, for a time, into clerical hands.[97] Also, perhaps crucially, the understanding of the goals of higher education became dominated by the ministers' desire to build a comprehensive seminary with interests well beyond Geneva's boundaries. In these areas Calvin re-established clerical control. Thus the ideological goal of schooling changed from a narrow focus upon the educational needs of the Genevan *bourgeoisie* to the far-reaching demands of the Calvinist movement for well-trained ministers.

---

[96] Delormeau, *Cordier*, p. 61.

[97] Maag, *Seminary*, on the re-establishment of magisterial authority after Calvin's death (1564). In brief, by 1600 the greatest limitation on magisterial influence and goals (such as teaching law and medicine) was not ministerial stubbornness but municipal poverty.

CHAPTER TWELVE

Financing education:
the Zurich approach, 1550–1620

Karin Maag

As the Reformation entered its consolidation phase in the latter half of the sixteenth century, certain issues which had been neglected in the anticipation of a more or less automatic conversion of Europe to the new religion could no longer be ignored. Catholic powers were regaining the advantage in many regions and Reformation leaders had to find ways to establish Protestantism more firmly in the hearts and minds of their fellow-citizens. This essay sketches the range of options in the key area of higher education and takes a closer look at the strategy adopted in one of the centres of the European Reformation.

The provision of better schooling was complicated by the fact that there were conflicting ideas about the purpose of learning and study. The laity tended to insist on local primary education, as it satisfied the wishes of most parents to see their offspring acquire some basic skills.[1] Higher education was of lesser interest, since only a very small percentage of lay people had any access to, or need for, further study. Ministers and civic leaders agreed, however, that a basic level of literacy and knowledge of the Bible deserved to be promoted among the population at large. Clergymen, supported by schoolteachers in more prosperous areas, undertook the task of teaching basic reading and writing skills, with a particular emphasis on the catechism, prayers and creeds of the church.[2] Through these efforts, backed up by enforced church attendance and closer magisterial supervision, most people gradually acquired a basic knowledge of the Reformed faith, albeit often by rote learning.[3] However, such educational efforts in no way provided the in-depth

---

[1] For the importance of local education in Geneva see my *Seminary or University? The Genevan Academy and Reformed Higher Education 1560–1620*, St Andrews Studies in Reformation History (Aldershot, Brookfield/Vermont, 1996), pp. 11–13.

[2] Gerald Strauss, *Luther's House of Learning: Indoctrination of the Young in the German Reformation* (Baltimore, 1978), pp. 17–18, 21–2. Pamela Biel, *Doorkeepers at the House of Righteousness: Heinrich Bullinger and the Zurich Clergy 1535–1575* (Berne, 1991), pp. 188–9.

[3] William Naphy, *Calvin and the Consolidation of the Genevan Reformation* (Manchester, 1994), pp. 110–11.

training necessary for a new generation of reformers and ministers, nor for the lawyers and city physicians who needed more specialized knowledge to exercise their professions. These men could acquire a higher level of skills in the Latin schools which had emerged in many pre-Reformation cities,[4] but the limited facilities offered there could not compete with the higher education available at Catholic universities.

In order to remedy the lack of centres of higher education in Reformed areas, some cities and principalities simply turned former Catholic universities into the pinnacle of their educational system. Heidelberg and Basle, for example, founded in the fourteenth and fifteenth centuries, respectively, became leading Protestant centres of learning and attracted a great number of students from areas without a pre-Reformation university.[5] Other territories, intent on training their élite locally in spite of a lack of existing institutions, created academies which offered a similar level of education. The Academy of Herborn, founded in 1584 by the rulers of Nassau-Dillenburg, was one such centre of learning, as was that of Geneva, founded by Calvin in 1559.[6] As more recent institutions, they had advantages as well as disadvantages. On the one hand, they could be more flexible due to the absence of established traditions and statutes, but on the other, they could not award degrees (a privilege which required a papal or imperial charter) and insufficient endowment often led to financial problems. The Academy of Herborn, for instance, floundered in the period prior to the Thirty Years' War because of the princes' over-generous support of its students.[7] Furthermore, the academies faced greater difficulties in drawing in top-level professors, because of the universities' more powerful financial and intellectual incentives. The short space of time spent by Joseph-Juste Scaliger, the famous French philologist, at the Genevan Academy is a case in point. Having fled to Geneva during the St Bartholomew's Day Massacre, he taught in the academy for only two years (1572–4), before returning to France. The fact that he accepted a call to the newly created University of Leiden in 1593 testifies to the greater attraction of a university position. Leiden was prepared to pay him a higher salary than Geneva could have ever afforded, for the sole privilege of his presence, since one of the clauses of Scaliger's agreement with Leiden specified that he would not be required to do any teaching.[8]

---

[4] See William Naphy's contribution to this volume.

[5] On Heidelberg see Johann Friedrich Hautz, *Geschichte der Universität Heidelberg* (2 vols, Mannheim, 1864), vol. ii.

[6] On the Genevan Academy see Maag, *Seminary or University?*

[7] Gerhard Menk, *Die Hohe Schule Herborn in ihrer Frühzeit (1584–1660): Ein Beitrag zum Hochschulwesen des deutschen Kalvinismus* (Wiesbaden, 1981), pp. 153–5.

[8] Eugène and Emile Haag, *La France Protestante* (10 vols, Geneva, 1966), vii. 6–9.

The academies clearly faced major difficulties in their attempts to achieve the sort of educational standards offered by the universities. By and large, both ministers and secular rulers agreed that the best way forward lay in investing as much as possible to try and attract famous professors in order to reap the financial benefits of visiting students. A local centre of learning also offered young citizens an opportunity for training without the dangers of foreign travel, and it allowed the magistracy and ministers to keep an eye on them while they pursued their courses. Yet while there was agreement on the need to provide funds for local academies, conflict persisted between lay and clerical authorities over the relative importance of secular and theological studies. Some, like Calvin and his ministerial colleagues in Geneva, saw the Academy's role as that of a seminary, whereas the magistrates sought to increase its international reputation (and revenues) by fostering more lucrative subjects such as jurisprudence.[9]

One city developed another approach. In Zurich, the educational opportunities available prior to the Reformation had been provided primarily (but not exclusively) by the clergy. The Dominicans ran a *studium* in their monastery, teaching philosophy and sometimes theology, but the sources for its history are patchy. Talented students could be sent on to centres of higher study, such as Paris, Heidelberg, or Vienna.[10] In Heidelberg, for instance, 42 Zurich students matriculated between 1420 and 1520, and the cathedral canons were allowed absences of up to seven years for study purposes.[11] Both the Grossmünster and the Fraumünster, Zurich's principal churches, operated Latin schools from the thirteenth century, teaching primarily Latin grammar, dialectics, and church music.[12] German schools, which focused on basic reading and writing skills, provided additional educational opportunities on a private basis. In all of these instances, the civic authorities had virtually no role to play, as the oversight of monastic teaching lay in the hands of the church, while the German schools operated independently.[13] Both the two Latin and German schools continued after the Reformation. The major change for the latter lay in their increasing oversight by the Zurich magistrates, so that from 1549 onwards, delegates from the city's senate supervised the teaching

---

[9] Maag, *Seminary or University?* , pp. 23–6.

[10] Martina Wehrli-Johns, *Geschichte des Zürcher Predigerkonvents (1230–1524): Mendikanten zwischen Kirche, Adel und Stadt* (Zurich, 1980), pp. 186–90.

[11] Heinrich Ernst, *Geschichte des zürcherischen Schulwesens gegen das Ende des sechzehnten Jahrhunderts* (Winterthur, 1879), p. 18.

[12] Ibid., pp. 9–23.

[13] Ibid., pp. 23–4, 33–8.

in these schools.[14] As for the Latin institutions, their curriculum was adapted by Bullinger to match the new religious climate: the curricula of 1532 and 1559 placed a strong emphasis on religious education, prescribing daily prayers, the study of the catechism, mandatory church attendance of all pupils, and the learning of Greek as well as Latin. The pupils were subdivided into five classes by 1546, and in an effort to ensure good standards, the magistrates indicated that before being admitted to the Latin courses, boys should have spent a year in a German school, learning the basics of reading and writing.[15]

Thus the continuity between pre- and post-Reformation education in Zurich was strong. The major change lay in the increasing role of the magistracy, particularly as the civic authorities also obtained control over the teaching budget of all Latin schools. The ministers and teachers played a vital role in day-to-day educational affairs, but the ultimate decision-making power lay in the hands of the city councils.[16] Higher education underwent a greater transformation, although some elements of Zurich's later practice, such as the policy of sending certain students to matriculate in other centres of learning, were not without medieval precedents.[17]

The Reformed city pursued two inter-related paths towards the provision of higher education. It established its own academy, the *Lectorium*, in the 1530s, and by the 1550s, ministers and magistrates had evolved a scheme which provided the best possible ecclesiastical or professional training at minimal cost to the city. In brief, while the *Lectorium* formed the linchpin of education in Zurich, the authorities simultaneously evolved a system of scholarships and travel bursaries to enable young men to study in other famous universities and academies across Europe. They could thus be taught by the most renowned professors of their day, without the need to maintain an expensive teaching staff in the local academy. This strategy is unique and, fortunately, well documented in the city's archives. The records show how education, even at a distance, had a significant local impact, as it brought together students, their parents, ministers, and magistrates in a complex organiza-

---

[14] Hans-Ulrich Bächtold, *Heinrich Bullinger vor dem Rat: Zur Gestaltung und Verwaltung des Zürcher Staatswesens in den Jahren 1531 bis 1575* (Berne, 1982), p. 212.

[15] Ernst, *Geschichte*, pp. 87–100.

[16] Bächtold, *Heinrich Bullinger vor dem Rat*, p. 189.

[17] On Catholic higher education in pre-Reformation Zurich see Hans Nabholz, 'Zürichs höhere Schulen von der Reformation bis zur Gründung der Universität 1525–1833' in E. Gagliardi, H. Nabholz and J. Strohl (eds), *Die Universität Zürich 1833–1933 und ihre Vorläufer* (Zurich, 1938), pp. 4, 10.

tion to provide members of the city's élite with the necessary skills for their respective careers.

The *Lectorium* evolved from the *Prophezei*, the scriptural exegesis sessions of the 1520s.[18] On top of daily philological analysis of the Old and New Testaments, Zurich began to offer courses in Greek, Latin, and, from 1541, in natural sciences, led by the famous Conrad Gesner.[19] The creation of the travel scholarships should not be seen as a result of the poor quality of domestic education, for it has been argued that Zurich was the best centre for Reformed theological study and training for the ministry, at least before the flowering of Geneva's academy in the last thirty years of the sixteenth century.[20] The *Lectorium* managed to attract professors like Conrad Pellican and Peter Martyr Vermigli, but its long-term prospects as a top-level centre of higher education were affected by restrictive municipal legislation, in particular by an act passed (against Bullinger's will) in 1562 which required professors to be citizens of Zurich.[21] Consequently, the *Lectorium* failed to attract large numbers of students from beyond its regional sphere of influence.[22] At the same time, such rules made the prospect of travel to other centres of learning even more attractive for the city's own students, since it became the only opportunity to hear distinguished foreign professors.

The funding for both *Lectorium* and scholarships derived chiefly from the resources of former Grossmünster canons. A total of 24 benefices had been attached to the church, providing each of the incumbents with money, wood, hay, wheat, wine, and financial assistance to pay for servants and the maintenance of their houses.[23] The chief obstacle to the reallocation of these funds was the fact that the benefices did not actually become available until the canons resigned, or failing that, until they died.[24] The longevity of the clergymen allowed only a very gradual accumulation of financial resources to invest in Zurich's educational system. Eventually, when all the benefices had passed into the hands of Zwingli's successors, they were divided into 18 parts, three of which went to the three chief ministers of the city, one to the overseer of the benefices, eight to the professors, teachers, and regents of the schools, and six to the students' scholarship fund. This last portion, however,

[18] Jacques Figi, *Die innere Reorganisation des Grossmünsterstiftes in Zürich von 1519 bis 1531* (Affoltern am Albis, 1951), p. 84.

[19] Fritz Büsser, 'Reformierte Erziehung in Theorie und Praxis' in his (ed.), *Wurzeln der Reformation in Zürich* (Leiden, 1985), p. 212.

[20] Figi, *Die innere Reorganisation*, pp. 92–3.

[21] Nabholz, 'Zürichs höhere Schulen', p. 28.

[22] StAZ, E II 479, *Album in Tigurina schola studentium*.

[23] Ernst, *Geschichte*, pp. 124–5.

[24] Nabholz, 'Zürichs höhere Schulen', p. 5.

was also used to cover repairs to school buildings, book purchases, and the administration of the former benefices.[25] Furthermore, the most immediate priority for any available funds was to pay for the salaries of Zurich's own professors, with student bursaries given a lower priority until more benefices had been vacated.[26] Mirroring practices elsewhere, Zurich's authorities sought to establish their own centre of higher education first. Given these circumstances, bursaries had to be small in the early years. Gradually, though, they rose from a modest 3 florins a year plus clothing (in 1527) to 14 florins and an allowance of grain (in 1529). By the 1550s, the *Studentenamt*, or student scholarship fund, offered bursaries of 10, 15, 20, and 25 florins to those who studied in the Latin schools of Zurich and the *Lectorium*, while, at the top of the scale, travel scholarships amounted to 40 florins a year.[27]

The need for student grants was pressing, for Zurich needed a substantial number of men to run its church, as there were approximately 140 clergymen and schoolteachers at work in the city and its extensive rural territory.[28] Eventually, replacements would be needed for all of these posts and the provision of financial support could help to recruit candidates and to bind them to the ruling élite. Furthermore, scholarships were required to assist those young men who were interested in the ministry, but too poor to afford the costs of study, and those from families who considered the ministry an unsuitable career for their offspring, because of the expensive training and the small size of ministerial salaries.[29]

The *Lectorium*, the Latin schools leading up to it, and the scholarship programme organised by Zurich were all overseen by the *Schulherr*, the minister responsible for educational matters. It was to him that students sent abroad wrote to report on their studies. The *Schulherr*, appointed on a yearly basis from 1560, kept a record of all matters dealt with during his tenure. The *Acta Scholastica* provide details of the various meetings and of those in attendance, normally the chief ministers and professors. The *Schulherr* and his colleagues were in day-to-day control

---

[25] Ernst, *Geschichte*, p. 125.

[26] Figi, *Die innere Reorganisation*, p. 87.

[27] Bächtold, *Heinrich Bullinger vor dem Rat*, p. 215.

[28] Heinz-Peter Stucki, 'Bullinger, der Zürcher Rat und die Auseinandersetzung um das Alumnat 1538–1542' in Ulrich Gäbler and Erland Herkenrath (eds), *Heinrich Bullinger: Gesammelte Aufsätze zum 400. Todestag* (2 vols, Zurich, 1975), i. 294. In contrast, Geneva only had a small number of rural parishes, and thus less need to train ministers for its own area, though it focused instead on sending significant numbers of ministers to France: Robert Kingdon, *Geneva and the Coming of the Wars of Religion in France 1555–1563* (Geneva, 1956).

[29] Bächtold, *Heinrich Bullinger vor dem Rat*, pp. 216–17.

of educational matters, but answerable to the council as the city's sovereign institution, which also controlled and disbursed the funds.[30] In most areas, including education, clergy and magistrates worked together, as in March 1529, when three *Ratsherren* met with Zwingli and Anton Walder to decide on the operation of the city's sponsorship scheme. They approved the following procedure: first, the schoolteachers were to identify the most talented students. Second, the boy's parents or guardians had to be asked whether they were willing to have their child trained for the ministry. Then the boy himself was to indicate whether he was interested in the career. If everyone agreed, the prospective scholarship candidate entered a one-year trial period, which allowed the city authorities, both clerical and lay, and the young student the chance to change their minds. The regulations explicitly permitted the latter to withdraw from the scheme without penalty, if he decided that he did not want to pursue a clerical career after all. The trial period also allowed the authorities to see him at work, and to dismiss him from the programme if he proved to be unruly or academically weak, without any further financial consequences.[31]

After his probationary year, the student was bound to obey the educational authorities in all matters. He had to promise to enter the service of the church and city at the end of his studies and was required to accept any teaching or ministerial post selected for him by the educational council, which included representatives from the clergy and magistracy. Finally, the regulations acknowledged that older students were normally allowed to travel abroad to complete their training. At the same time, scholars were warned that those who acted wilfully, without the permission of the educational council, would not only lose their prospective post, but also be liable to repayment of all the money they had ever received as part of the scheme.[32]

The regulations of 1529, applied retrospectively to the first scholars of 1527, gave the educational council and the magistrates total control over the programme. Essentially, once the one-year trial period was over, the student had little chance to change his mind without serious financial consequences. While a large proportion of the funds helped young men to study in the city's Latin schools and *Lectorium*, the travel scholarships were a significant feature of Zurich's educational policy, which created and reinforced international links with other European centres of learning. In what follows, a more detailed analysis of the

---

[30] Pamela Biel, 'Heinrich Bullinger and the office of minister' (Ph.D. Columbia University, 1988), pp. 167–74.

[31] Figi, *Die innere Reorganisation*, p. 88.

[32] Ibid., p. 89.

initiative shall help to determine what exactly the Zurich authorities had in mind for their most promising students.

The *Catalogi Scholae Tigurinae*, a list of scholars sponsored by the city, contains the names of 112 men who were allowed to travel to foreign educational institutions between 1569 and 1591, an average of slightly over five every year.[33] This list is not complete, as other names appear in the *Acta Scholastica*, kept by successive *Schulherren* since 1560.[34] Indeed, by 1573, the magistrates were concerned about their large number and poor behaviour, for the city fathers pointed out that the scholarship fund was overwhelmed by those who were running up debts, returning to Zurich, getting married, and unable to reimburse the city for its expenses. Therefore the magistrates ordered that all students should be trained in Zurich, apart from those with private means or other sponsors.[35] Clearly, the debts incurred by its students worried the city, because it had to advance the money until the ministers were established in salaried posts and able to repay their dues. Yet the magistrates' proposal to train everyone in Zurich had little effect: 12 students were sent out from the city in 1574 and no less than 16 students in 1580.[36]

Of the 112 names recorded in the *Catalogi Scholae Tigurinae*, 55, or nearly half, were only sponsored for one year, 24 for two years, 14 received funding for three years, and 19 for four years or more. The record for the highest number of scholarship renewals was held jointly by Adrian Frisius, sponsored for nine years between 1573 and 1581, and by Marcus Bäumler, supported for an equal number between 1583 and 1589, and 1591–2.[37] These men were clearly an exception, for over two thirds of the students were sponsored for two years at the most. There was very little likelihood for scholars to obtain degrees in this short period, given that in Heidelberg, for instance, the minimum number of years required for a Master of Arts was three. Degrees were clearly not the main objective of the Zurich scheme, even though the *Lectorium* as an academy could not award any either.

The regulations of 1529 indicated that the authorities looked for boys who had shown early academic promise as candidates for city bursaries. It is more difficult to tell what the requirements were for

---

[33] StAZ, E II 497, *Catalogi Scholae Tigurinae ab anno 1566*. The first scholarship records in the *catalogi*, however, date from 1569.

[34] Ernst, *Geschichte*, p. 109.

[35] Ibid.

[36] Ibid.; *Catalogi Scholae Tigurinae*, vol. vi, fos 7–8, vol. xiii, fos 9, 11.

[37] Ibid., vol. v, fos 4–5 – vol. xiv, f. 4; vol. xvi, f. 17 – vol. xxiv, f. 11.

those to be sent abroad. It seems that those who had reached a certain level of performance in the *Lectorium* were usually selected for a visit to a foreign institution, as a final stage of training before returning to Zurich and sitting examinations prior to becoming ministers or school-teachers. In 1560, the educational council updated the rules governing the scholarship programme in a document entitled 'Procedures to be followed in taking on boys for scholarships from the Grossmünster fund, and in dealing with them'. The ninth section of this document is particularly relevant, as it lays out the authorities' intentions regarding the travel bursaries:

> He who studies hard, behaves himself well and is making progress, so that one can trust that he will not wander away from the right path, can be sent to travel in foreign lands ... He should stay there until he is ordered to go elsewhere, and he is not allowed to choose for himself where he would like to go. Even in other lands, he should obey the regulations of this school, as if he were still here. And when he returns home from his travels, he should bring with him reports, letters, and seals from the schools and his professors and tutors, detailing his conduct, and he should not return without such testimonies. And when he returns, he must present himself before the education council, showing them his reports, giving them an account of his studies and of the schools he attended, and then obediently let himself be examined and placed as and when he receives orders to do so.[38]

Once again, those who wished to take advantage of the opportunity of foreign study at Zurich's expense were left in no doubt about their responsibilities. The obligation to provide reports from foreign universities indicates that the period of travel was not simply an opportunity to experience other cultures or to broaden one's horizons, but a means to acquire measurable skills. Indeed, in 1579, the magistrates stated this explicitly when they ordered that 'those who return from their travels should be asked to present an extemporaneous argument, to see how

---

[38] 'Weliche wol studiert, sich wol gehalten und dahin kommen sind, das man inen getruwen darff daß sy nit lichtlich mal abpasun werdin, die solligen sol man an die frömbde gon wandlen schicken ...'Daselbs söllend si bliben bis man sy anderswohin bescheidet, und sy gar nit gwal haben zu ziehen war sy wellend. Sy söllend auch an der frömbde grad sich diser schul und zuferordnungen halten, als ob sy daheimen werind. Und so sy ab der frömbde heim komend, söllend sie von den schulen und der selbigen gelerer und iren praeceptoribus kuntschaffe und brief und sigel bringen wie sy sich gehalten habind, und söllend an die selbigen nit heim komen. Und so sy dann heim komen, so man sy für die verordneten zu der leer fürstellen, also sollend sie ire kuntschaffen zeigen, rechnung von ire studia und schulen gäben, sich dannerhin examinieren und ordnen auch ghorsamlich bruchen lassen won und wie man inen bedarff': StAZ, E I 13, no. 21: 'Ordnung wie man die knaben an die Stipendia an der Stifft zu Dem Großmünster annemen un mit Inen umgan sölle' (1560).

their style has improved'.[39] Thus, students who received travel bursaries from Zurich had to prove that they had spent their time profitably by providing evidence of their performance from the institutions in which they had matriculated, and through examinations upon their return. For those who were away for longer periods of time, Zurich evolved a scheme of continuous assessment, which took the form of progress reports to be sent home at regular intervals. In these letters, the students detailed the courses they were following, the professors who were teaching them, and generally updated Zurich on their state of affairs. Through this correspondence, the educational council obtained valuable information about the various centres of learning, which allowed it to make informed judgements as to who should be sent to which particular academy or university. The careful distribution and re-distribution of students from the base at Zurich is the most impressive feature of the travel scholarship programme. For example, on 17 August 1563, the educational council decided:

> that Felix Trüb should go from Basle to Heidelberg, but that Hans Rudolf Bigel and Esaias Wegger should stay in Basle. Joachim Herter, Amandus Fisher, and Zacharias Schörli should stay in Heidelberg until further notice. Christopher Rutter, Rodolph Koller, and Johannes Huser should also stay in Marburg for the moment. Hans Jakob and Hans Wilhelm des Branwalden, to stay in Basle. However, Wilhelm Stucki should go to Tübingen. Johannes Steiner and Jakob Suter, presently in Berne, should move to Lausanne.[40]

Such decisions took place approximately every two to three months, as students in turn set out from Zurich, changed from one centre of learning to another, and eventually were summoned to return to the city.

At times the educational council took decisions which were based more on Zurich's own needs than on those of the students. For instance, on 15 July 1566, the *Schulherr* noted that:

> because of a lack of ministerial candidates awaiting posts, and because several such posts are vacant and unoccupied, we must urgently write to the following students in foreign places, and call them home: Abraham Hartmann, Heinrich Steiner, and Marcus Wydler from Geneva, Rodolph Haldenstein, Jakob Keretz, Georg Ottli and Jakob Pfründer from Marburg, and Jakob Kneul from Heidelberg.[41]

The students were soon employed. On 19 October, three months after his return, Jakob Kneul was assigned the post of regent of the senior

---

[39] Ernst, *Geschichte*, p. 107.
[40] StAZ, E II 458, f. 50ʳ (17 August 1563).
[41] Ibid., f. 80ᵛ (15 July 1566).

class in the upper Latin school, replacing Hans Heinrich Wirt, who had
been presented to a rural parish.[42] At times, therefore, the opportunities
offered by foreign study were overridden by Zurich's need to fill the
clerical and educational vacancies in its territory.

In spite of the risk of being recalled at a moment's notice, there was
no shortage of interest for the 40 florins bursary. The successful candidates included not only the most able students of the *Lectorium*, but also
some who had petitioned for a scholarship either personally or through
their parents. In 1580, for instance, Ludwig Lavater, one of the foremost city ministers of Zurich, asked the *Burgermeisters*, Zurich's chief
magistrates, to provide a scholarship for his son Heinrich who was
studying medicine at Heidelberg. Apart from providing funds for future
ministers, the city also supported medical studies, because of the need
for trained city physicians. In 1555, for instance, Kaspar Wolf and
Georg Keller were sent to Montpellier and Padua, respectively, to study
medicine.[43] Lavater pointed out that his son had attended the local
schools and those at Lausanne, Geneva, and Marburg for five years at
his father's expense before going to Heidelberg, and added that it was
not right for him to spend all his money on one son and to ignore the
needs of his other children. He also noted that the present city doctors
were all getting on in years, though not without adding 'God give them
a long life'. Finally, in an effort to convince the magistrates that he was
not trying to obtain money from them under false pretences, he recommended that they should ask his son to return to Zurich to be examined
and asked about the actual cost of his studies.[44] There is no record as to
whether Ludwig Lavater's petition succeeded.

In any case, the letter raises two interesting points. First, Lavater's
appeal to the magistrates was based as much on the city's need for
trained doctors as on his son's acute need of funds for his studies, and
second, he stressed that the training had already largely been paid for,
so that Zurich would not have to invest heavily nor wait long to reap
the benefits of Heinrich's training. Another student who sought a travel
bursary was Erasmus Kauffmann from Winterthur in Zurich's territory.
He wrote to the *Schulherr*, who dealt with the matter on 16 April 1567.
Kauffmann was also at Heidelberg and applied for the highest possible
level of funding, so that he would not be forced into the service of
another territory to support himself. The educational council, however,
did not want to proceed without a report on his academic progress and
decided to contact Thomas Erastus, who was a professor of medicine at

---

[42] Ibid., f. 84ʳ (19 October 1566).

[43] Ernst, *Geschichte*, pp. 96–7.

[44] StAZ, E I 13: Ludwig Lavater to the *Burgermeisters* (1580, n.o.d.).

Heidelberg at the time, and his colleagues to supply the necessary information.[45] On 19 August 1567, having obtained a positive report, the *Schulherr* noted that Kauffmann would receive the 40 florin scholarship.[46]

Zurich's students were sent to universities and academies all across Europe, including Catholic centres of learning such as Vienna, Paris, and the Italian universities. On the same day, the *Schulherr* reported that Johannes Wilhelm Stucki, who had been in Paris, was asking for permission to go to Italy. This was granted, but only for a year, after which time he was to return to Zurich. Furthermore, Johann Jakob Frisius was allowed to go from Strasbourg to Paris to pursue his studies there.[47] At that time at least, it was still possible for young men from Reformed areas to matriculate in Catholic universities, although these cases were few and far between. Indeed, the location to which the highest number of scholars were sent between 1569 and 1591 was Reformed Basle, where 31 Zurich students matriculated, followed by Heidelberg (23), and Marburg and Wittenberg (16 each). The academies were less popular: Geneva attracted seven sponsored students from Zurich, Lausanne six, and Strasbourg five.[48] The significantly greater share of universities might be interpreted as an attempt to obtain formal degrees, especially as two of Zurich's students are known to have graduated. Johann Jakob Koller, sponsored at Marburg and Geneva between 1578 and 1582, received his MA from the former institution in 1579, and Johann Jacob Ulrich, supported in 1588 and 1589 at Heidelberg, received a Marburg MA in 1590.[49] Yet overall, given the relatively short stays outlined above, it is more likely that the universities dominated because of their ability to recruit and retain the most distinguished professors.

Another objective of Zurich's travel bursaries was to enable students to benefit from the best Reformed centres of learning. The prime example of the importance of confessional allegiance is Heidelberg, where the number of Zurich students dropped significantly during the reign of the Lutheran Ludwig VI (1576–83). A mere 11 matriculated in those eight years, compared to 23, both sponsored and self-funding, between

---

[45] StAZ, E II 458, f. 91ʳ⁻ᵛ (16 April 1567).

[46] Ibid., f. 92ᵛ (19 August 1567).

[47] Ibid.

[48] *Catalogi Scholae Tigurinae* and *Album in Tigurina schola studentium, passim*. It has to be kept in mind, however, that several students' places of study are unknown. The total number of scholars matriculating in any one location could thus be higher.

[49] Sven and Suzanne Stelling-Michaud, *Le Livre du recteur de l'Académie de Genève (1559–1878)* (6 vols, Geneva, 1959–1980), iv. 213; *Historisch-Biographisches Lexikon der Schweiz* (7 vols, Neuchâtel, 1921–1934), vii. 118.

1568 and 1575, and an equal number between 1584 and 1591, after the return to a Reformed confession under the Palatine regent Johann Casimir.[50]

When students were recalled after their leave abroad, Zurich endeavoured to obtain an accurate account of their experiences and to reintegrate them into the city's academic world. On 14 May 1563, for instance, the *Schulherr* reported on the return of Wilhelm Weber and Wolfgang Ribenmann from Heidelberg and of Johannes Oswald Fäsi and Conrad Waser from Berne:

> After they told us where and with whom they had stayed, what lectures they attended, what reports and testimonies they were bringing back with them, and how many debts they still had to repay in foreign places, we ordered them sternly: 1. to attend the preaching services assiduously; 2. to attend diligently the theological lectures in the New and Old Testaments, as well as other lectures; 3. to respect all school ordinances regarding clothing appropriate to citizens [...]; 4. to repay their debts honestly; 5. to prepare for a general examination in languages, philosophy, and theology.[51]

The injunction to respect sumptuary ordinances reflects the authorities' fear of imported fashions and their insistence that returning students should be no different, in appearance at least, from those who had stayed behind. The fact that the scholars were ordered to attend lectures in the *Lectorium* even after their stay in other academies and universities shows that the travel bursaries were not intended as the conclusion of their formal education. Indeed, if anything, the Zurich authorities appear to have been very cautious in their endorsement of the learning acquired elsewhere. Overall, domestic training and examination retained a high priority.

The award of a travel bursary did not necessarily imply that the student's abilities were any higher than those of his peers who remained in Zurich. On 29 June 1563, for instance, a month and a half after his return from Geneva and Berne, Conrad Waser was examined by the educational council as to his preaching ability, 'and as his sermon was not well prepared, he was made to wait another six months because of

---

[50] Gustav Toepke, *Die Matrikel der Universität Heidelberg von 1386 bis 1662* (4 vols, Heidelberg, 1884–1904), ii. 30–164.

[51] 'Und nach dem sy verhört wo, by wem sy gsin, was sy ghört für Lectiones, was sy für kuntschaff und fürgeschriff habind, auch was sy an der frömbde und sons schuldig bliben, had man inen mit ernst bevholen. 1. Die predigen flissig zu besuchen. 2. Die Lectiones theologicas Novi et Veteris test. vorab demnach auch andere flissig zuhören. 3. allen ordnungen der schul mit heimischer geburlicher bekleidung und dem wandel zugeläben. 4. Ire schulden trüvolich zubezalen. 5. und sich angends uff ein gmein examen in linguis, artibus un theologica rüsen': StAZ, E II 458, f. 37ᵛ (14 May 1563).

the preaching'.[52] It is equally difficult to tell what effect the period of study spent elsewhere had on the student's future career. A longer and more detailed study is needed to compare the fortunes of those who obtained travel scholarships with those whose entire education took place in Zurich's Latin schools and *Lectorium*.

By providing travel bursaries for some of their most promising young men, Zurich's magistrates and ministers sought to achieve several objectives simultaneously. First, and building on a medieval precedent, they aimed to provide their students with an opportunity to encounter the academic world outside the city. Second, they sought to administer the funds gained from former ecclesiastical benefices in the most effective way, without allocating all of them to a single centre of training. The authorities were thus in a position to support education at various levels, catering for the religious as well as secular needs of the population. Third, Zurich's leaders wanted to ensure an adequate supply of physicians, schoolteachers, and ministers, who would be grateful to the city for its support during their years of study. The travel bursaries met all of these requirements and – like the *Lectorium* – they allowed the authorities to retain full control of the educational system without forcing them to compete with the better equipped universities. That the Zurich approach to higher education, and its scholarship system in particular, survived well into the seventeenth century is at least in part a measure of its success.

---

[52] Ibid., f. 46ʳ (29 June 1563).

PART FIVE
Poor relief

CHAPTER THIRTEEN

The burden of benevolence: poor relief and parish finance in early modern Emden

Timothy Fehler

People are contributing too much money to the poor: this was the judgement of Emden's church bookkeeper sometime around 1590. As a result, he argued, the church suffered a decline in its own income. A search of earlier sixteenth-century accounts had revealed that the last significant bequest to the church dated from 1541. Commenting on this fact, he noted in the margin of the book: 'Would that it were, that in our time we also gave to the gospel. In that time one gave to churches and cloisters; now one gives to poor institutions which were not around then'.[1]

While such a complaint against generous almsgiving might be surprising, it demonstrates that contemporaries perceived dramatic changes in social welfare. The quote intimates an awareness of institutional changes as well as of shifts in popular attitudes towards charitable giving. In order to assess the accuracy of the bookkeeper's perceptions, this essay will provide a long-term survey of poor relief for the case-study of Emden. It will examine continuity and change over the course of the sixteenth century and attempt to identify the catalysts for new developments at the time of the Reformation.

Many historians identify the sixteenth century as a turning point in the history of poor relief. Some even term the century 'the beginning of modern social welfare'.[2] In traditional historiography, the Protestant Reformation has often been seen as an important stimulus for changes in this area of study. Catholic social welfare, it has been argued, encouraged mere

---

[1] ArchGK, no. 364: *Liber Expensarum* (1572–95).

[2] Elsie Anne McKee, *John Calvin on the Diaconate and Liturgical Almsgiving* (Geneva, 1984), p. 93. Robert Jütte has argued that sixteenth-century poor relief involved 'a radical departure from the beaten paths of medieval charity': *Poverty and Deviance in Early Modern Europe* (Cambridge, 1994), p. 2.

'charity' in the form of indiscriminate individual alms-giving,[3] and it allowed the church full control over any charitable endowments.[4] Furthermore, many Protestant polemicists, including Luther, criticized the medieval system because of its links to Catholic religious doctrine, implying that 'good works' were motivated primarily by the donors' desire to improve their chances of salvation.[5] On the other hand, Protestantism, so the argument goes, developed a much more rational form of state intervention in social welfare, resulting in a far-reaching 'social policy'.[6] Lutheran theology in particular was identified as the prime cause of the poor relief changes of the sixteenth century.[7]

Such views can be traced back to the Reformation period itself. Contemporary Catholics in Lyon and Ypres saw their own town's social welfare reforms as being tainted with heresy. In 1527, for instance, the Catholic humanist Juan Luis Vives was disturbed that the Bishop of Tournai had ruled his poor relief treatise *De subventione pauperum* to be 'heretical and Lutheran'. Five years later, the Inquisitor of Lyon attacked a sermon by the French cleric and humanist Jean de Vauzelles, who had called for sweeping new welfare measures (which were eventually adopted). The Inquisitor said that the sermon was filled with errors and was 'pernicious to Catholic piety'. He argued further that Lyon had more to fear from a host of heretics than it did from an excess of poor vagrants.[8]

The traditional view of the Reformation impact on poor relief, however, has been revised by a number of recent studies. Poverty, vagrancy, and begging were persistent problems for both Protestant and Catholic cities throughout the sixteenth century. Case studies of individual towns or regions have shown that many of the hallmark social reforms were,

---

[3] See, for example, Ernst Troeltsch, *The Social Teaching of the Christian Churches*, trans. by Olive Wyon (2 vols, New York, 1931), i. 134. According to Troeltsch, the medieval church's 'reaction [to social suffering] did not take the shape of social reform, or of organic change: it was simply and solely the work of charity'.

[4] Ibid., pp. 133–8.

[5] Brian Tierney, *Medieval Poor Law: A Sketch of Canonical Theory and its Application in England* (Berkeley, 1959), pp. 46–8.

[6] Troeltsch, *Social Teaching*, ii. 557.

[7] This view was argued most comprehensively in two articles by Otto Winkelmann, 'Die Armenordnungen von Nürnberg (1522), Kitzingen (1523), Regensburg (1523) und Ypern (1525)', *ARG*, 10 (1912–3), 242–72, and 'Über die ältesten Armenordnungen der Reformationszeit (1522–1525)', *Historische Vierteljahrschrift*, 17 (1914/5), 187–228, 361–440.

[8] Natalie Zemon Davis, 'Poor relief, humanism, and heresy' in her *Society and Culture in Early Modern France* (Stanford, 1975), pp. 17, 52–5. Some Catholic regions were even hesitant to pass laws prohibiting begging on the grounds that such laws were 'Lutheran': Jeannine Olson, *Calvin and Social Welfare: Deacons and the Bourse française* (London, 1989), pp. 22–3.

in fact, adopted – to varying degrees – by most urban governments irrespective of their confession.[9] This essay attempts to continue the search for a more balanced understanding of Reformation change by means of a diachronic analysis of one of the most prominent Protestant cities.[10] It cannot aim to provide an in-depth theological or quantitative local study, but – in line with a general theme of this volume – it tries to evaluate the actual socio-economic impact of religious change on the everyday life of a local community.[11] For this purpose, the state and development of the poor relief system shall be examined at three crucial stages: in the late Middle Ages (i), during the first Reformation years (ii), and in the Confessional Age of the late sixteenth century (iii).

(i)

In medieval East-Frisian law codes, poor relief was primarily a matter of kinship obligation. Nevertheless, and in spite of the scarcity of the sources, it is also possible to detect a degree of organized poor relief from the few surviving contracts and testaments of the time. Mendicant Franciscans living in their monastery on Emden's outskirts provided some assistance, but organized charity in Emden at the end of the fifteenth century was primarily the responsibility of lay confraternities and hospitals (known as *Gasthäuser* in East Frisia and along the northern coast of the Netherlands). By that time, there is evidence for five lay confraternities (Our Lady's, St Clement's, St Ann's, St Jurgen's, and St Anthony's), with at least one *Gasthaus* in operation by 1500, and others emerging soon after.[12] Lay piety was as notable in Emden as in many other cities, a fact which is illustrated by the surviving testaments

---

[9] See, for example, Brian Pullan, *Rich and Poor in Renaissance Venice: The Social Institutions of a Catholic State* (Cambridge, Mass., 1971), Davis, 'Poor relief', Linda Martz, *Poverty and Welfare in Hapsburg Spain: The Example of Toledo* (Cambridge, 1983), and Lee Palmer Wandel, *Always Among Us: Images of the Poor in Zwingli's Zurich* (Cambridge, 1991).

[10] Emden has recently received increased attention by historians: Andrew Pettegree, *Emden and the Dutch Revolt* (Oxford, 1992), Heinz Schilling, *Civic Calvinism in Northwestern Germany and the Netherlands: Sixteenth to Nineteenth Centuries* (Kirksville/ MO, 1991), and *KRP*.

[11] For a detailed quantitative analysis of Emden's transition from its medieval poor relief system see my 'Social welfare in early modern Emden: the evolution of poor relief in the age of the Reformation and Confessionalization' (Ph.D. University of Wisconsin-Madison, 1995).

[12] Fehler, 'Social welfare', pp. 84–158; Johannes Stracke, 'Geistliche Laienbrüderschaften im ausgehenden Mittelalter', *EJb*, 51/52 (1971/72), 35–53.

which include frequent bequests to confraternites to ensure the salvation of the donors' souls.[13]

Housing for the poor in pre-Reformation Emden was provided primarily by the *Gasthäuser*, one of which – at least – was administered by a confraternity, the St Anthony's Brotherhood. Another institution, St Gertrude's *Gasthaus*, functioned as a private foundation with its own endowment, chapel, and priest, independent from the parish church. Around the turn of the sixteenth century, there was probably an increase in the number of poor people served by Emden's 'hospital' facilities. This could help to explain the fact that in 1505, St Gertrude's was moved from its central location near the parish church in the increasingly crowded 'old city' to the outskirts of the town, where it could expand more easily.[14] Another common method of supporting the poor was for an individual or married couple to establish a *Gotteskammer* which provided single-room accommodation for the poor. By the time of the Reformation, such foundations existed throughout the town; several were administered by the *Gasthäuser* and the confraternities, while others relied on private provision made in testamentary bequests.[15]

The scrutiny of surviving law codes provides some valuable insights into contemporary attitudes toward the poor. Most notably, medieval East Frisian law already distinguished between the 'shameless and greedy poor' and the rest of the poor[16] – those 'who cannot feed themselves from their own goods and who shame themselves to beg for bread, as well as anyone who can earn nothing and must seek alms without fraud in the streets and by the houses'.[17] By the early sixteenth century, the latter enjoyed the same degree of legal protection as clergymen and members of religious orders, just as *Gasthäuser* and houses for the poor apppeared in the same category as churches and monasteries.[18] Pre-Reformation Emden was clearly aware of the difference between 'worthy' and 'unworthy' poor.

---

[13] An example of the typical language used in these documents is the 1522 will of Tyge and Dedden Harren who left half of their goods 'to St Ann's Brotherhood for the salvation of both their souls': *EKP*, 1/193 and ArchGK no. 48. Almost all surviving pre-1500 testaments in East Frisia are contained in Ernst Friedlaender (ed.), *Ostfriesisches Urkundenbuch* (2 vols, Emden, 1878–81); the sixteenth-century notorial records (including testaments) are in *EKP*.

[14] ArchGK no. 81.

[15] Fehler, 'Social welfare', pp. 76–80, 148–55.

[16] W. J. Buma and W. Ebel (eds), *Das Emsiger Recht* (Göttingen, 1967), p. 235, no. 5[b].

[17] M. von Wicht (ed.), *Das Ostfriesische Land-Recht* (Aurich, 1746), lib. I, cap. 22, pp. 40–41.

[18] Ibid., cap. 21–22, pp. 39–42.

(ii)

The first evidence for Protestant preaching in East Frisia dates from the early 1520s. This essay cannot be the place to describe the progress of religious change in detail; suffice it to say that Emden did not experience a Lutheran Reformation like much of the rest of northern Germany. This was due in large part to East Frisia's traditionally strong intellectual connections with the Netherlands. Moreover, for the better part of a decade, the churches of East Frisia received virtually no regulation from the Count, Edzard I. Thus, by the time of Edzard's death in 1528, East Frisia contained a mixture of Catholics, Lutherans, Zwinglians, and Anabaptists. Edzard's 23-year-old son Enno then made the first attempts to bring order and unity to the confusing East Frisian religious scene by instituting Lutheran church ordinances.[19]

From an ecclesiastical perspective, Count Enno's attempts to introduce strict Lutheran guidelines for his territory in 1529 and 1535 failed miserably, due primarily to the theological resistance from the pastors of the larger towns such as Emden.[20] These early regulations are, however, especially important for the objectives of this essay because they contain the first poor relief instructions by the territorial authorities. Having redefined the liturgical framework for the East Frisian church, the documents proceeded to elaborate 'On the Beggars'. While the theological reforms failed, there is evidence from Emden to suggest that some of the poor relief recommendations were, in fact, implemented.

The relevant 1529 instructions opened with a rejection of the practice of maintaining foreign beggars in the territory. Furthermore, each parish was to elect two 'upright' men, who 'should concern themselves with the suitability of the ways through which the registered beggars might be maintained in their dwellings and not in front of the city gates or on the streets'.[21] Count Enno did not prescribe any one set of guidelines to be followed throughout the territory but charged the two elected overseers in each parish with the responsibility of thinking

---

[19] The sixteenth-century East Frisian church ordinances are discussed in Emil Sehling (ed.), *Die evangelischen Kirchenordnungen des XVI. Jahrhunderts,* Siebenter Band, II. Hälfte, 1. Halbband (Tübingen, 1963). After confirming his 1529 Church Ordinances which prescribed a Eucharistic liturgy on the model of Luther's 'German mass' (1526), Count Enno banned the Catholic mass and ordered the expulsion of Anabaptists from East Frisia in January 1530. These actions were not effective, and in 1531 Luther himself, although a supporter of Count Enno's attempts to establish religious uniformity in the territory, complained that East Frisia was dominated by the 'faithlessness of the sacramentarians' and that everyone there was 'allowed to teach whatever he wants': WA Br., vi. 16.

[20] Menno Smid, *Ostfriesische Kirchengeschichte* (Pewsum, 1974), pp. 142–3.

[21] Sehling (ed.), *Kirchenordnungen,* pp. 366–7.

creatively about appropriate ways to care for their own beggars and poor.

The practice of electing parish overseers was soon implemented in Emden, for we find reference to Emden's 'administrators of the poor' in records as early as 1532.[22] More careful investigation, however, implies that no entirely 'new' position was actually created. By comparing the earliest surviving names of the 'administrators of the poor' with the records of the parish churchwardens, we find that virtually all of the identified 'new' poor relief officers simultaneously held the traditional medieval office of churchwarden. This data suggests that the Emden church simply added a new function to an existing position when carrying out the 1529 Church Ordinances.[23]

Beyond this organizational modification, however, Enno's ordinances did little to alter the manner in which poor relief was provided in Emden. The suggested fundraising method was a continuation of a traditional Frisian practice, the *huusdelinge*, which had been devised for the support of priests and parochial worship. According to the medieval church regulations of the region, during the *huusdelinge* 'the people, [both] poor and rich' provided donations to their priests at regular intervals 'according to their means'.[24] Under Enno's 1529 instructions, however, the two 'newly' created poor officials were to collect the *huusdelinge* together with the pastor. The latter kept half for himself, but the other half now went to the overseers.[25] Yet, given the large number of beggars in Emden, the system of *huusdelingen* was insufficient to finance the parishes' poor relief needs. The ordinances offered no specific remedy to offset financial shortcomings but depended on the charity of the congregation to make ends meet: 'We are without doubt', exhorted the count, 'that our people, out of Christian love, will indeed know their duty and, each according to his ability, will not deny their help to the poor'.[26]

Given the models which Enno could have copied to reform social welfare, it is striking that his regulations did not attempt to modify East Frisia's traditional methods more dramatically. During the preparation of the church ordinances, the count had consulted with Johannes Bugenhagen, along with other Lutheran theologians. Enno had even

[22] *EKP* 2/179ᵛ.

[23] Fehler, 'Social welfare', pp. 213–19.

[24] From section 5 of the late-medieval Emsgauer Sendrecht: C. Borchling, *Die niederdeutschen Rechtsquellen Ostfrieslands* (Aurich, 1908), i. 134–5.

[25] Sehling (ed.), *Kirchenordnungen*, pp. 366–7. A fine of 10 Gulden was decreed against anyone who refused to participate in the *huusdelinge*.

[26] Ibid., p. 367.

received copies of Bugenhagen's recent ordinances for the German cities of Braunschweig (1528) and Hamburg (1529).[27] And yet, although the ecclesiology and liturgy of the East Frisian documents followed Bugenhagen's model very closely, they failed to include the same sort of detail and theological reasoning when dealing with the poor relief sections. Both Braunschweig and Hamburg established a 'common chest' for the care of their poor and provided thorough descriptions specifying which poor should be supported, why they deserved assistance, and how the chest should be administered. Enno, in contrast, relied on continuity in fundraising and the creativity of existing officers. Bugenhagen's ordinances, especially those for Hamburg, also endeavoured to regulate the local hospitals and confraternities, while their East Frisian counterparts noticeably omitted any mention of *Gasthäuser* or religious gilds. Thus, whatever his theological leanings, Protestant prototypes seem not to have influenced Count Enno's poor relief strategies for his territory. The common chest system of social welfare, normally considered a 'Lutheran' hallmark, was not implemented in Emden or East Frisia after the Reformation.[28] Instead, a solution was found which relied on the foundation of medieval parish finance, regardless of potential 'Catholic' associations.

From very early in his reign, Count Enno embarked on the dissolution of the East Frisian monasteries, with the profits diverted into his own coffers. However, the Franciscan house in the Faldern suburbs of Emden (the so-called 'Observanten toe Embden') was granted an exemption in the 1529 ordinances and allowed to lead a 'private' existence, perhaps due to its useful poor relief services. The friars went on to live on this site until the late 1550s.

Emden's confraternities continued to function throughout the first three Reformation decades. The citizens still remembered them in their wills, but from the 1520s for markedly different reasons. Whereas the pre-Reformation language reflected the importance of the charitable deed for

---

[27] The Braunschweig Church Ordinance of 1528 in Sehling (ed.), *Kirchenordnungen*, Sechster Band, I. Hälfte (Tübingen, 1955), pp. 348–455 (sections dealing with poor relief: pp. 445–55); the Hamburg Church Ordinance of 1529 in ibid., Fünfter Band (Leipzig, 1913), pp. 488–540 (dealing with poor relief: pp. 531–40). [Note that all other citations to Sehling, *Kirchenordnungen*, refer to his volume 7/II/1 on East Frisia, as in note 19 above.]

[28] Indeed, Jütte's blanket assertion is incorrect: 'All the Protestant systems of poor relief had certain points in common: all were based upon the idea of a "common chest"', which contained the funds from, among other sources, the monastic properties: *Poverty and Deviance*, pp. 105–6. Unlike Philip of Hesse (cf. the essay by Richard Cahill in this volume), Count Enno does not seem to have used the confiscated church property for educational, charitable, or religious purposes.

the salvation of the donor's soul, references to the poor relief activities of the confraternities become much more prominent in the wills and contracts of the post-Reformation period.[29] It is evident, therefore, that in response to the new theological climate, the confraternities shifted their emphasis from traditional religious activites to the care of the poor. This, no doubt, allowed them to survive the first Reformation challenge.[30]

Unfortunately, no *Gasthaus* or confraternity account books survive from the early period which would allow us to measure the financial impact of the initial Reformation decades.[31] Yet, increasing evidence for the brotherhoods' contractual obligations in the field of poor relief suggests that they played an important role, especially as Emden parish finances became tighter following Count Enno's confiscation of ecclesiastical property. There was no attempt to compensate the parishes with some form of common chest, and overseers could only appeal to 'Christian love' to finance their efforts. The traditional *huusdelinge* was also stretched farther than customary: while it had previously been used to supplement pastor and church, it was now expected to cover poor relief expenses as well.

Judging from a speech of an 80-year-old widow in 1593, the financial strains caused by the first Reformation changes were particularly hard and not easily forgotten. In that year (more than 60 years after the Reformation), Tobe Buttels still angrily recounted how Count Enno – 'at the time when the changes in the papacy and Gospel occurred' – had taken from Emden's parish church nearly all ecclesiastical revenues. Suffering severe financial hardship, the congregation made numerous appeals to the count to regain control over some of its goods, and although these requests were eventually heeded, 'in the meantime the preachers of the Gospel suffered great poverty' and were 'fed for long years and supported by the citizens who were fond of the Gospel'.[32] Moreover, whenever the pastors or overseers of the poor lacked popular support among their congregation, the financial situation became even

---

[29] This shift is especially noticable in the first four volumes of *EKP*.

[30] There was of course no dramatic change in the leadership and membership of the religious gilds. Three of the four administrators of St Anthony's serving in 1516, for instance, still held their positions in 1527, and one of them continued until at least 1535: Fehler, 'Social welfare', p. 130. Thus, while the traditional spiritual activities of the confraternities began to fade from the records, it is likely that many of these continued in practice for some time. Indeed, there is evidence that traditional notions of charity as a good work leading to salvation did not pass away completely with the Reformation: see, for example, Reiner van Klewert's testament from 1541, *EKP* 2/569.

[31] The sole remaining pre-Reformation confraternal account book (Our Lady's) ends in 1521: J. Stracke (ed.), 'Unser Lever vrouwen register', *EJb*, 51/52 (1971/72), 53–64.

[32] ArchGK no. 364, p. 4 (14 October 1593).

more desperate. People would go so far as to withhold even their mandatory *huusdelinge* contribution.[33]

Religious turmoil in the city of Emden, to summarize the effect of the first two to three Reformation decades, seems to have affected the people's financial generosity, but existing institutions and methods of poor relief remained largely unchanged. During the first half of the sixteenth century, Emden's welfare system was characterized by continuity rather than innovation.

(iii)

On the eve of the Reformation, the German harbour of Emden had been a politically, socially, and economically underdeveloped, even backward, town compared with other cities in the Holy Roman Empire. It was quite a small settlement with little or no political autonomy, no real social stratification, and few communal civic institutions. By 1560, however, Emden emerged as an important intellectual and political centre for the Reformed churches in northwestern Europe. Its position as 'Geneva of the North' and the rise of 'civic Calvinism' within its boundaries during the second half of the sixteenth century had considerable political, economical, and social consequences for the Netherlands and northwestern Germany.[34]

By 1595, a combination of swift changes had deeply altered public life in the town. Primarily 'between 1540 and 1580, Emden, the provincial town without proper urban constitution, social diversity, and transregional economic significance, developed into a metropolis with [a broad social differentiation and with] intellectual, economic, and political connections reaching over the continent and the seas'.[35] At about the same time, Emden's social welfare system underwent rapid and large-scale reorganization.

The confraternities were gradually replaced by other relief institutions, but not all declined in equal measure. By the late 1540s, St

---

[33] Without adequate parochial accounts, it is impossible to determine the actual extent of this problem. Count Enno complains in some detail about it in his 1535 Church Ordinances. He argued that many people had lost respect for spiritual leaders because of the proliferation of 'foolish and unlearned preachers' who had been teaching in the territory since the early 1520s (especially the 'rotten Anabaptists and similar wicked people'). 'Unfortunately, this is the only thing that the farmers have learned out of all the sermons which have occurred in the last 12 years [since the Reformation]: to give no one anything'. They had heard so many different teachings that they no longer took anyone seriously. Sehling (ed.), *Kirchenordnungen*, p. 386.

[34] See, for instance, references in note 10 above.

[35] Schilling, *Civic Calvinism*, p. 21.

Clement's had become the primary organization, and by the 1550s it had absorbed the assets of the other confraternities and modified its charter. Originally founded as a religous gild of shippers and merchants to provide spiritual assistance to its members, St Clement's evolved into a poor relief brotherhood, chartered to assist the families of its members and those who lost their goods or relatives at sea. The Catholic spiritual functions of the confraternity had finally disappeared. The fact that it was the shipper's gild which was allowed to survive reflects the central role that the harbour and the seafaring professions played in Emden's social and economic development. In the reorganization of social welfare, the town wisely maintained the institution which had traditionally provided assistance to its most important trades. Another of the conventional methods of poor relief – the provision of *Gotteskammern* – continued throughout the early modern period. Many of the early establishments were preserved, and an analysis of testaments from the later sixteenth century yields the occasional new foundation.[36]

Emden's recently created 'administrators of the poor' evolved into a new, more extensive institution in the middle of the century. Although the exact date is uncertain, the major points of transformation can still be detected. Shortly after the Polish reformer Jan Laski's appointment as superintendent in 1543, he endeavoured to unify the East Frisian churches and implement greater ecclesiastical discipline. While most of his ambitions remained unfulfilled during his short stint in office, Laski's most enduring institutional contribution was the creation of the Emden church consistory in 1544.[37] Composed of the most respectable lay members of the congregation alongside the pastors, the consistory was intended as a tool to oversee and deliberate matters of congregational church discipline. The consistory's earliest lay members appear to have been churchwardens,[38] who were now also in charge of poor relief activities. It soon became evident, however, that they could not cope with this additional burden, and their duties were thus entrusted to two new lay offices: 'elder' for church discipline and 'deacon' for poor

---

[36] Fehler, 'Social welfare', pp. 219–36 (development of confraternities); for *Gotteskammern* see, for example, *EKP* 10/244, 10/713–14, 12/992–993, 15/121, 15/272, and *KRP*, p. 746.

[37] Laski, whose ideas were more 'Reformed' than Lutheran, was forced to leave Emden following the Interim of 1548. He went to London, where he became superintendent of the foreign congregration which settled there under Edward VI. Working with this exile community, he was much more successful in implementing his ideal conceptions of congregational church discipline. For Laski's work in East Frisia see Smid, *Kirchengeschichte* (Pewsum, 1974), pp. 158–72, and for a complete bibliography on Laski , see his 'Jan Laski' in *TRE*, xx. 448–51.

[38] Smid raises this possibility in *Kirchengeschichte*, p. 166.

relief.[39] Whether the reorganization occurred during Laski's tenure cannot be determined, but by the time of the earliest surviving consistory minutes (July 1557), it is clear that there were approximately 20 local deacons of the church (so-called *Haussitzenden* deacons), each of whom was responsible for a specific part of the town.[40] Thus, as Emden's church underwent a development toward a more Reformed ecclesiology, its central organ of social welfare became the diaconate. This would remain the pillar of the system for several centuries, providing assistance not only for members of the church, but for most of the town's population.[41]

By the 1550s, large-scale institutional reform became inevitable for a city that was undergoing dramatic socio-economic changes. The 1554 arrival in Emden of Laski's London foreign congregation, following its expulsion by Queen Mary, and the subsequent flood of refugees from the Dutch Revolt were pivotal events in Emden's religious, political, social, and economic history.[42] Emden's population exploded (from around 3 000 at the start of the century to as much as 20 000 or 25 000 at its peak), housing and food shortages occurred, shipping boomed as many of the wealthier Dutch emigrants brought their trading contacts with them, but at the same time increasing numbers of less prosperous labourers arrived. The poor of Emden were no longer simply the local *Haussitzenden*, and the structures of social welfare which had gradually evolved throughout the first half of the century were suddenly tested and found wanting.

Hastened by the demographic and economic crisis, the trend towards centralization of traditional relief institutions spread to Emden's *Gasthäuser*. By the end of the 1530s, only St Gertrude's appears in the records. It seems that the assets and responsibilities of the earlier hospitals had become centralized into St Gertrude's which had moved to

---

[39] Cf. Calvin's view of the offices of the church in his Ecclesiastical Ordinances (1541) for Geneva: *Calvin: Theological Treatises*, vol. xxii, trans. by J. K. S. Reid (Philadelphia, 1954), pp. 58–72.

[40] It is at this time that the first account books of the deacons appear. With the increasing organization of the church came increased interest in rationalized recordkeeping. ArchGK nos 1117 and 1118 cover the period from 1561–78.

[41] Unlike the additional diaconates to be discussed later (foreign and *Becken*), the *Haussitzenden* deacons did not utilize the consistory to maintain proper church discipline among poor relief recipients. Although they were concerned that those on their regular rolls maintain a certain level of order, the *Haussitzenden* deacons were willing – at least on a short-term basis – to provide relief to most people who came to them in need.

[42] For the most recent and detailed discussion of the refugees' impact on Emden see Pettegree's *Emden and the Dutch Revolt*; cf. also Heinz Schilling, *Niederländische Exulanten im 16. Jahrhundert* (Gütersloh, 1972).

the outskirts of town in 1505. However, population growth over the course of the century meant that it effectively found itself once again in a city-centre location. Furthermore, during the ever-increasing refugee influx of the 1550s, existent facilities could simply not provide sufficient housing for the poor.

The ruling countess and the city authorities began to negotiate with the remaining Emden Franciscans to acquire their house for poor relief purposes. Although confessional differences were important in the desire to get rid of the friars (Jan Laski had been arguing for their expulsion since the early 1540s), it is the issue of poor relief which dominates the surviving records of the negotiations. According to the complaints of countess and town, the old *Gasthaus* complex was insufficient to provide relief for the 'common use and emergency needs of this city'. The countess wrote to the friars, asking them to 'depart from here with honor and good will', because 'our town Emden multiplies daily and takes in to itself both rich and poor out of foreign lands'.[43] These discussions led to an agreement which eliminated the last official Catholic presence in the town, as the remaining friars acquiesced and left upon receipt of a small stipend.[44] The town authorities planned to convert the friary's buildings into a new parish church, a school, a hospital, and an orphanage. There is evidence that by 1557 poor people were being supported by the city and housed on the site, which was much larger than the old *Gasthaus* complex. St Gertrude's began to sell its buildings and to move its operations to the old friary. In 1561, the so-called 'new *Gasthaus*' was in full swing and a renovation project began, funded by the hospital itself, the city, and by private subscriptions. While there had been earlier attempts to expel the friars on religious grounds (reinforced, no doubt, by the arrival of many Dutch Protestant refugees), it required a social and economic crisis to force the countess to get rid of the last Catholic institution.[45]

The 1550s, however, witnessed not only reorganization of existing facilities, but also the establishment of genuinely new institutions. Perhaps the most direct effect of the refugees on Emden's social welfare system was the creation of a special diaconate of the foreign poor around 1554. This enabled the wealthier Dutch refugees to finance and administer assistance for their poorer compatriots. Especially during the first two decades of its existence, the office was vital in establishing Emden's place as *moeder kerk*, or mother church, for the struggling

---

[43] The letter was composed in 1556; Staatsarchiv Aurich, Rep. 135, 12, pp. 3–4.

[44] For a fuller account of this transition see Fehler, 'Social welfare', pp. 291–311.

[45] The fate of the house was also affected by the fact that the few remaining elderly friars were becoming less effective in providing for the poor of Emden.

Reformed congregations in the Netherlands at the time of the Dutch Revolt.[46] During much of this period, the expenditure of the foreign deacons was far greater than that of their local *Haussitzenden* equivalents. Through the mid-1570s, for instance, the latter spent around 500–1 000 Gulden *per annum*, while the foreign deacons' disbursements shot up to over 3 500 Gulden a year at the height of the refugee influx after 1570. In 1571, they had 132 people on their 'regular' relief rolls and provided alms for an additional 600 'extraordinary' requests. 'Regular' recipients tended to receive anywhere between 20 to 60 Gulden a year, in accordance with the deacons' assessment of each individual case.[47] The effective care of thousands of immigrants allowed Emden to prosper as a city of refuge. By absorbing much of the financial pressures, the foreign deacons made it politically and socially acceptable to take in so many Dutch refugees, and the city profited greatly from the additional shipping and trading activities they generated.

Another innovation of the 1550s was the creation of the 'grain reserve'. Following two years of bad harvests and stimulated by demographic pressures, grain prices began to explode in 1557. In response to this crisis, a number of Emden citizens initiated the grain reserve as a way to maintain a stockpile of the commodity to be provided at low prices in times of need.[48] Although it was more than simply an emergency, stop-gap measure, the reserve has remained on the sidelines of most discussions of Emden's poor relief, due partly to the comparative lack of surviving documentation and partly because it was a private initiative, controlled neither by the church nor the city. And yet, it is an

---

[46] In many ways, the 'deacons of the foreign poor' functioned very similarly to the *bourse française* which provided for the French refugees in Calvin's Geneva: Olson, *Calvin and Social Welfare*. For a similar institution in England see Andrew Spicer's essay in this volume.

[47] The account books of both diaconates are housed in the ArchGK. For the *Haussitzenden* deacons in the mid-1570s see ibid. no. 1118. In 1571, the foreign deacons paid Pluenke Kammaecker, an old, sick woman, 20.6 Gulden for the year; Jannes Horst, an old man with a wife and two children, was given 41.6 Gulden, and Albert Timmerman's widow with her five children received 57.7 Gulden: ArchGK, *Fremdlingen Diakone*, 2nd account book, pp. 162–4. In comparison, the yearly salary of a day labourer in Emden would have been somewhere between 30–60 Gulden in 1577 and perhaps around 45–70 Gulden in 1593; in the 1570s, the salaries of Emden's three ministers were each between 200–300 Gulden (by 1593 all the ministers received over 500 Gulden per year): Fehler, 'Social welfare', pp. xv–xvi, 524–32, 562. The expenditures of the *Haussitzenden* deacons do increase dramatically at the end of the 1570s (perhaps due to the return of most of the wealthy Dutch merchants to the Netherlands after 1575 and a subsequent decline in the finances of the foreign deacons), jumping rapidly to 3 000 Gulden and steadily increasing each year so that after 1587 they were consistently providing over 10 000 Gulden to the local poor: ArchGK no. 3001. See Figure 13.1 and Table 13.1.

[48] Fehler, 'Social welfare', pp. 311–7.

important institution, for it represented a growing communal awareness in much the same way as the emerging ecclesiastical structures indicated a growing confessional identity in Emden.

While social and economic forces were the prime catalysts for most of the developments discussed above, the formation of one final institution reveals deep religious motives as well. It is at this stage that the local *Haussitzenden* diaconate of Emden underwent a transformation which – as far as comparisons with other towns in northwestern Germany are possible – was unique to Emden. Spurred on by a number of social and economic factors, including, for example, the price increases of 1556–7, the deacons encountered mounting problems providing for the poor of the city, which forced them to review the use of their resources.[49] As the debate developed, some participants began to operate with the theological category of the 'household of faith'. This ideal conception, which Laski shared with Martin Bucer, distinguished between a pure church made up only of those who participated in communion ('the household') and the wider community of the baptized.[50]

The Emden consistory decided in 1557 to establish a third diaconate in order to ensure that the poor 'members of the household of faith' were adequately cared for. A *Becken*, or dish, was ordered to be set up during communion services to collect donations for this purpose. The deacons of the *Haussitzenden* poor would continue to care for the 'common' poor of the city and church, but the consistory decided to elect three additional deacons to administer the fund for the 'household of faith'.[51] In this way, the poor of the congregation would not be left to beg, but according 'to the command of God's word and the nature of love' would be fully supported by the congregation.[52] Thus, the creation of the diaconate of the *Becken* was based on the twin pillars of Reformed theology and the belief that the people of God should not have to beg.

The consistory court minutes reveal that church discipline and poor relief became closely connected. Supervision of the poor now involved

---

[49] *KRP*, i. 1–2.

[50] Laski's church ordinances for his London congregation (1550) had instructed the deacons to distribute the alms conscientiously and wisely to the poor, 'especially to the members of the household of faith': *Forma ac Ratio tota ecclesiastici Ministerii* (1550), ed. A. Kuyper (Amsterdam, 1866), ii. 78; for Bucer's use of the term see, for example, *Mehrung götlicher gnaden und geists...* (1547), f. 91ᵛ, printed in Werner Bellardi, *Die Geschichte der 'Christlichen Gemeinschaft' in Straßburg (1546/1550): Der Versuch einer 'Zweiten Reformation'* (Leipzig, 1934), p. 130.

[51] *KPR*, pp. 12–13 (22 November 1557). For an analysis of the complete chronology and discussions which led to the creation of the *Becken* diaconate see Fehler, 'Social welfare', pp. 261–78.

[52] Sehling (ed.), *Kirchenordnungen*, p. 461.

not just control of moral behaviour, but also control of religious faith.[53] In the attempts to promote and stabilize Reformed beliefs and practices, poor relief – especially that administered by the *Becken* deacons – became an important tool with which the church could monitor its members and remove its dissidents. The new diaconate kept a close eye on the lowest social strata of the city, ensuring that the pious poor be cared for and that the congregation's reputation be preserved.

Although Emden's diverse set of poor relief institutions was, on the whole, effective, not everything always ran smoothly during the two decades when the deacons of the 'household of faith' existed. Stiff opposition came from the officers of the *haussitzenden* poor, who did not approve of this theological distinction between the needy and de-layed the introduction of the new *Becken* diaconate.[54] Additionally, once the new institution began to function officially, it found itself entangled in virtually perpetual disputes with the *haussitzenden* dea-cons, especially about the distribution of charitable bequests or ques-tions regarding their jurisdiction in specific social welfare cases.[55]

Moreover, data from the surviving documents suggests that the *Becken* deacons never gained widespread acceptance among the town's popula-tion. Between 1558 and 1578, dozens of surviving wills left bequests to the support of the *Gasthaus* and the *Haussitzenden* poor, while only a handful bequeathed money to the *Becken*[56] – despite the fact that the *Becken* deacons had been chartered to provide for the 'proper and most pious poor'.[57] This seems to suggest that most Emden testators favoured the town's traditional poor relief systems rather than the new concept of the 'pure' congregation. Given the *Becken's* lack of established endowments, which the older relief institutions possessed, the *Becken* diaconate ran into severe financial dificulties. These practical concerns, along with a general rejection of the religious notion of a 'household of faith', combined to motivate the dissolution of the *Becken* diaconate and its merger with the *Haussitzenden* deacons in 1578.[58]

---

[53] See, for instance, the case of Jacob and Prone de Boer who had accepted alms from the local Anabaptists and would no longer be allowed relief from the Reformed deacons until they renounced these connections: *KRP*, p. 159 (22 February 1563).

[54] *KRP*, pp. 34–5.

[55] Sehling (ed.), *Kirchenordnungen*, pp. 461–2.

[56] See Fehler, 'Social welfare', p. 387, n. 143.

[57] Sehling (ed.), *Kirchenordnungen*, p. 461.

[58] ArchGK no. 3001, fos 23–7; Sehling (ed.), *Kirchenordnungen*, pp. 461–2.

(iv)

The Emden bookkeeper was right. Superficially, the social welfare system at the end of the sixteenth century bore little resemblance to that at around 1500. The gradual evolution of poor relief institutions in the first half of the century (and the continuity of pre-Reformation practices even under the Lutheran Enno) was followed by a massive overhaul of the system in the 1550s. Developed in close connection with the church leadership, the changes were, nevertheless, undertaken primarily in response to dramatic population increases and dire economic and social circumstances.

The changes of the sixteenth century caused increasing financial responsibilities for the people of Emden. Count Enno's confiscation of church properties created the first major burden: more than ever before the parishioners were called upon to subsidize the church and the poor. After the middle of the century, the magnitude of the system demanded yet greater resources from the citizenry: there were simply more poor to provide for and, thus, more institutions to support. Donors met the increased financial burden with surprisingly little protest. In fact, the few surviving complaints were aimed not at the cost of maintaining the poor but at the use of poor relief funds to support the preachers.[59] The amounts involved were substantial, and welfare costs grew at a steadier and faster rate than either the church or city budgets throughout the last quarter of the century (see Figure 13.1 and Table 13.1).

Yet, in surprisingly few years during the second half of the century did the *Haussitzenden* deacons, for example, fail to take in enough revenues from voluntary donations and bequests to cover their expenses.[60] And, when one institution did run into problems, special collections around the town or loans from another institution generally met its needs.[61] Only the 'foreign deacons' seem to have had to impose

---

[59] See note 33 above for those who did not approve of half of their *huusdelinge* going to the pastor any longer. Similar complaints arose in the 1560s and 1570s over the maintenance of refugee ministers from the funds of both the foreign and *Becken* deacons. The latter complained that their function was not to use their scarce resources to support foreign pastors; and many in the refugee community complained that poor relief funds should not be used to maintain unemployed ministers who were unwilling to work while in exile: see, for instance, *KRP*, pp. 173, 191, 193, 420, and Fehler, 'Social welfare', pp. 350-2.

[60] Individual deacons were also expected to cover deficits from their personal finances at least on a short-term basis until they could be reimbursed from other income. The *Haussitzenden* deacons operated with end-of-year surpluses in their accounts with few exceptions until 1609, from which time they constantly gave out more than they took in (until 1648, when the account book ends): ArchGK no. 3001.

[61] This is, of course, with the notable exception of the *Beckon* deacons who had no

a compulsory rate on the wealthier refugees – they called it a 'voluntary assessment' – and they were forced to increase its frequency and to rely on assistance from international sources over the period of the Dutch Revolt.[62]

Year	City	*Hauss*. deacons	Church
1575	15 114	414	1916
1576	16 049		1768
1577	17 065	3049	2313
1578	12 339	4496	2278
1579	23 019	4215	1839
1580	12 171	6256	2242
1581		7761	2545
1582		7943	3433
1583		8009	3263
1584	25 482	8928	3167
1585	20 009	8735	2806
1586		9938	3835
1587		10 759	3620
1588	19 954	9666	2475
1589	38 189	11 493	3106
1590	33 525	10 639	3619
1591	21 070	10 305	2917
1592	21 107	9716	2655
1593	21 659	9932	2962
1594	31 557	10 423	3093
1595	23 835	12 473	2935

Table and Figure 13.1

Yearly expenditure (in round Gulden) of the city, the *Haussitzenden* deacons, and the church of Emden, 1575–95. The city budget is characterized by extreme variations (note the peak in 1589–90, caused by extraordinary building projects), church spending remains more or less stable, while the deacons disburse nearly three times as much in 1595 compared to 1578[63]

revenues from traditional property holdings, no compulsary rate, and far from enough voluntary contributions: Fehler, 'Social welfare', ch. 5.

[62] Ibid., pp. 352–71.

[63] Sources: *Haussitzenden* deacons: ArchGK no. 3001; Emden church: ArchGK no. 364; city: Stadtarchiv Emden, Alte Kamerei, 2/18, 2/20, 2/23, 2/24, 2/25: city account books.

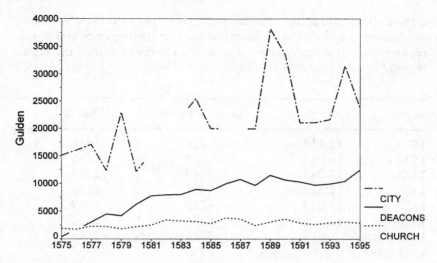

Figure 13.1

Emden's achievement in early modern poor relief was remarkable,
both in terms of institutional variety and in the speed and effectiveness
of response. Rather than being inherently Protestant, the pattern of
reform responded to specific socio-economic needs, maintained as much
continuity with the traditional institutions as possible, and combined
the current religious (the Reformed diaconate) with civic (the citizen
'committee of the grain reserve') priorities. Even the fascinating example of the 'deacons of the household of faith', whose creation was
driven almost entirely by a Bucerian theological concept, is an exception which proves the rule. Struggling with insufficient financial endowment and a lack of voluntary support, it remained but a temporary
phenomenon. Many of the citizens viewed it not as a new institution
created of economic necessity but as a theological invention, and despite their commitment to the Reformation and church discipline, most
were more interested in supporting institutions which cared for a larger
segment of the civic community.

CHAPTER FOURTEEN

Poor relief and the exile communities

Andrew Spicer

By the later Middle Ages a number of different institutions had developed in the southern Netherlands which served to aid the vulnerable members of society. Hospitals helped the poor and the sick and in some cities they accommodated invalids and the elderly. There were houses in most larger towns which provided temporary shelter for travellers and pilgrims. Monastic foundations helped the afflicted and some additional assistance derived from brotherhoods or confraternities.[1] The poor were also helped through the *tables des pauvres* which had been established during the fourteenth and fifteenth centuries in northern France and Flanders to distribute relief within individual parishes.[2] Similar developments occurred in England, with churchwardens and religious gilds becoming more actively involved in the provision of assistance in the late fifteenth and early sixteenth centuries.[3]

In spite of the wide range of institutions, the system was not comprehensive. At Ghent, for example, despite a rise in the number of foundations operating by 1500, there was no overall increase in poor relief.[4] The medieval approach failed for a number of reasons: help was often restricted to church festivals or particular saints' days. The assistance provided could vary from place to place and be limited to those living within a particular parish. Furthermore, funds were depleted through administrative expenses, the cost of holding services, and in the case of one brotherhood, the *O.L. Vrouwe Broederschap* at 's-Hertogenbosch, money was spent on lavish meals for the members.[5]

---

[1] W. P. Blockmans and W. Prevenier, 'Poverty in Flanders and Brabant from the fourteenth to the mid-sixteenth century: sources and problems', *Acta Historiae Neerlandicae*, 10 (1978), 40–45.

[2] N. Z. Davis, 'Poor relief, humanism, and heresy', in her *Society and Culture in Early Modern France* (Cambridge, 1987), pp. 37–8.

[3] M. K. McIntosh, 'Local responses to the poor in late medieval and Tudor England', *Continuity and Change*, 3 (1988), 220.

[4] Blockmans and Prevenier, 'Poverty in Flanders and Brabant', 54.

[5] Ibid., 42, 49; R. S. Duplessis, *Lille and the Dutch Revolt: Urban Stability in an Era of Revolution 1500–1582* (Cambridge, 1991), pp. 138–9.

Charitable giving was in part motivated by the benefit that accrued to the donor's soul and in some cases linked with masses for the dead.[6] Well into the sixteenth century, the citizens of Lille continued to found obits which provided relief for the poor who attended their anniversaries.[7] Some assistance, however, was more calculating and less spiritual in its intent. At Ghent the city authorities annually provided funds for organizations which dispensed relief as well as directing fines in their direction. It was hoped that this would predispose the poor towards the administration.[8] Magistrates, after all, were well aware that poverty and starvation could result in food riots such as those seen at Lyons in 1529.[9]

During the fifteenth and early sixteenth century attempts were made in various cities to repress begging and to develop a more rational and effective system of relief for the deserving poor.[10] The most controversial reforms were undertaken at Ypres where a 'common chest' was established in 1525. The mendicant orders denounced this as heretical, but the fundamental principles were upheld by the Sorbonne in 1531.[11] 'The Order for the Poor of Lille' (1527) reorganized the city's many charitable institutions, establishing a common fund supervised by a committee of *ministres généraux des pauvres* appointed by the municipal authorities.[12] These measures served to undermine the role of the church in the provision of relief and brought it more firmly under secular control. Similar developments in charitable relief can be observed in other towns within the southern Netherlands such as Bruges or Mons, and in France at Lyons, Nîmes, Paris, and Toulouse, for example.[13]

---

[6] Blockmans and Prevenier, 'Poverty in Flanders and Brabant', 39–40, 53.

[7] Duplessis, *Lille and the Dutch Revolt*, p. 138.

[8] Blockmans and Prevenier, 'Poverty in Flanders and Brabant', 40–41.

[9] Davis, 'Poor relief, humanism, and heresy', pp. 27–8.

[10] B. Pullan, 'Catholics and the poor in early modern Europe', *TRHS*, 5th Series 26 (1976), 17–18.

[11] F. R. Salter (ed.), *Some Early Tracts on Poor Relief* (London, 1926), pp. 32–4.

[12] Duplessis, *Lille and the Dutch Revolt*, pp. 140–43.

[13] P. Bonenfant, 'Les origines et le caractère de la réforme de la bienfaisance publique aux Pays-Bas sous le règne de Charles-Quint', *Revue Belge de Philologie et d'Histoire*, 6 (1927), 207–14, 225–30; J. Decavele, *De dageraad van de Reformatie in vlaanderen (1520–1565)* (Brussels, 1975), pp. 117–26; R. A. Mentzer, 'Organisational endeavour and charitable impulse in sixteenth-century France: the care of Protestant Nîmes', *French History*, 5 (1991), 5–6; Davis, 'Poor relief, humanism, and heresy', pp. 38–40; B. B. Davis, 'Poverty and poor relief in sixteenth-century Toulouse', *Historical Reflections*, 17 (1991), 286–7, 291–6; B. B. Diefendorf, *Beneath the Cross: Catholics and Huguenots in Sixteenth-Century Paris* (Oxford, 1991), p. 20.

However, the emergence of the Reformed church provoked a resacralization of the system. There was an attempt to recover the responsibility from the secular authorities and to return it to the now reformed (and Protestant) Church.[14] In Geneva, the city hospital had been reorganized before Calvin's arrival with *procurators*, who ran the institution, and *hospitalers*, who cared for the sick. Calvin attempted, through his Ecclesiastical Ordinances of 1541, to integrate this municipal system into the structure of the Reformed church by giving the officials of the city hospital the title of deacon. But since the hospital saw itself as reliant upon the municipal authorities rather than the Reformed church, the officials continued to use their former titles. While this attempt failed, the *bourse française*, which was established to succour the refugee population of Geneva, came increasingly to perform the role associated with the diaconate.[15]

The Reformed communities generally devised their own systems of poor relief. At Nîmes there had also been a gradual attempt to rationalize and remodel the city's welfare institutions during the late fifteenth and early sixteenth centuries. However, when the Reformed came into the ascendancy within the city, they preferred to develop their own more distinct systems of relief rather than to rely on the municipal institutions. Their reasons were twofold: first, as the Reformed Church's legal position was uncertain, their grasp on municipal office was tenuous and vulnerable. Second, the provision of poor relief through their church ensured that these resources reached the faithful rather than Catholics.[16]

While in such cases the Reformed *chose* to direct poor relief through their ecclesiastical channels, in the churches 'under the cross' this was a necessity. As the latter established themselves in the Netherlands they began to provide relief for the faithful, just like the similarly oppressed Anabaptists.[17] Collections for the Reformed poor were sometimes organized during the *presches* held during the summer of 1566.[18] At 's-Hertogenbosch a Catholic contemporary commented: 'They [the Cal-

---

[14] R. W. Henderson, 'Sixteenth-century community benevolence: an attempt to resacralise the secular', *Church History*, 38 (1969), 421–8.

[15] J. E. Olson, *Church and Social Welfare: Deacons and the Bourse française* (London, 1989), pp. 30–32, 251.

[16] Pullan, 'Catholics and the poor', 20; Mentzer, 'Organisational endeavour', 4–7. See also Davis, 'Poor relief, humanism, and heresy', p. 58.

[17] A. L. E. Verheyden, *Anabaptism in Flanders 1530–1650: A Century of Struggle* (Scottdale Pa., 1961), p. 31; A. C. Duke, *Reformation and Revolt in the Low Countries* (London, 1990), p. 117.

[18] P. M. Crew, *Calvinist Preaching and Iconoclasm in the Netherlands, 1544–69* (Cambridge, 1978), p. 105; Duke, *Reformation and Revolt*, pp. 138–9.

vinists] set up a common purse and distributors of alms and they contributed sometimes thirty guilders or more, some indeed gave the rings from their fingers'.[19] Money was also, on occasion, distributed to the poor who came to these meetings, and as a result more and more beggars and vagabonds attended. The Reformed were certainly criticized for effectively buying the support of the poor through their more effective systems of relief.[20] However, some municipal charities were similarly prepared to restrict assistance to those who regularly attended their parish church and were good Catholics.[21] The established systems of poor relief were thus challenged during the *presches*, and during the iconoclastic fury at Erquinghem-sur-la-Lys, near Armentières, claims were made that the churches' goods were being redistributed for the benefit of the poor.[22]

Poor relief and welfare provision was not the sole financial concern of the Reformed churches. Calvinist communities were cut off from some of the traditional sources of income such as tithes, and congregations also had to pay for the maintenance of their ministers as well as on occasion for their education and training. In fact the French Synod decreed that one fifth of all money collected for the poor should be used for the education of the ministry.[23] Besides these regular demands, there were also exceptional calls upon the community's resources. For example, at Armentières in the Southern Netherlands during the summer of 1566, the deacons collected money for the poor but in addition there were house-to-house collections for the construction of a Protestant temple as well as for what became known as the Three Million Guilders Request.[24] This collection was ostensibly an attempt to purchase religious freedom from Philip II, but became a source of funds for raising

---

[19] H. van Alfen (ed.), *Kroniek eener kloosterzuster van het voormalig Bossche klooster 'Marienburg' over de troebelen te 's-Hertogenbosch in de jaren 1566–76* ('s-Hertogenbosch, 1931), pp. 1–2.

[20] A. Pettegree, *Emden and the Dutch Revolt: Exile and the Development of Reformed Protestantism* (Oxford, 1992), pp. 133–4, 232; G. Moreau, *Histoire du Protestantisme à Tournai jusqu'à la veille de la Révolution des Pays-Bas* (Paris, 1962), p. 138.

[21] G. W. Clark, 'An urban study during the Revolt of the Netherlands: Valenciennes, 1540–1570' (Ph.D. Columbia University, 1972), pp. 84–5; Pullan, 'Catholics and the poor', 20.

[22] C. Rahlenbeck, 'Les chanteries de Valenciennes: épisode de l'histoire du seizième siècle', *Bulletin de la Commission de l'Histoire des Eglises Wallonnes*, 1st Series 3 (1888), 176; J. M. Regnault and P. Vermander, 'Armentières au temps des troubles religieux du XVIe siècle, 1545–1574', (M.A. Université de Lille III, 1972), p. 164.

[23] J. Quick (ed.), *Synodicon in Gallia Reformata* (2 vols, London, 1692), i. 137, 210.

[24] P. Beuzart, 'La Réforme dans les environs de Lille, spécialement à Armentières en 1566 d'après un document inédit', *Bulletin de la Société de l'Histoire du Protestantisme Français*, 78 (1929), 52, 53, 54–5.

forces for the Reformed cause during the First Revolt of the Netherlands.[25]

The suppression of the Reformed churches on the Continent during the 1560s, particularly in the wake of the *Wonderjaar* of 1566, resulted in a steady stream of exiles to England and the Empire. Reformed churches had been established in London during the reign of Edward VI and were refounded at Elizabeth's accession. The influx of refugees led to the creation of new communities at Sandwich (1561), Norwich (1565), Southampton (1567), Maidstone (1567), and Canterbury (1575). The emigrants from the French Wars of Religion, particularly after the Massacre of St Bartholomew's Day, swelled the existing congregations and resulted in the development of new ones such as Rye.

During the fifteenth century immigrants from the Low Countries had established several fraternities in London, which attracted not only the poorer immigrants but also the more wealthy.[26] Inevitably, social welfare became an even more pressing concern for their sixteenth-century successors, because in addition to the more usual objects of relief, the new exile communities also had to help those who arrived as refugees. Many people fled from the Netherlands leaving behind property, businesses, and goods subsequently confiscated by the *Conseil des Troubles* and depended on the Reformed communities for relief. In Geneva the *bourse française* had been established to deal with the refugee problem.[27] Yet not all of those who fled from the Netherlands should be characterized as penniless refugees; some were able to escape with considerable resources or had entrusted their property to relatives who remained on the Continent.[28] Furthermore, like their co-religionists who belonged to the churches 'under the cross', the exiles were excluded from existing local provision. The Reformed churches were therefore forced to develop their own distinct system in order to cope with these exceptional demands as well as with the more conventional needs of their members. While this has been examined for a number of case studies, there is as yet no comparative analysis of the system practised by the foreign congregations. This essay will focus on the relief provided by the French-speaking exile churches.

---

[25] On the Three Million Guilders Request see Pettegree, *Emden and the Dutch Revolt*, pp. 143–4.

[26] S. L. Thrupp, 'Aliens in and around London in the fifteenth century' in A. E. J. Hollaender and W. Kellaway, *Studies in London History* (London, 1969), pp. 263–4.

[27] Olson, *Church and Social Welfare*, pp. 37–49.

[28] A. Spicer, 'The French-speaking Reformed community and their Church in Southampton, 1567– *c.* 1620' (Ph.D. University of Southampton, 1994), pp. 41, 82–3.

The provision for the poor and in particular the role and responsibilities of the deacons were carefully defined in the Discipline of the French church in London, which was drawn up by Nicholas des Gallars in 1561. This derived in part from Jan Laski's *Forma ac ratio*, which emphasized the sacred nature of the deacons' responsibility for the poor by confirming them in office with the laying-on of hands. The Discipline also closely followed Calvin's Ecclesiastical Ordinances as was evident in the definition of the deacons' role.[29] The text distinguished between 'les vns estoient deputez à receuoir, dispenser & conseruer les biens des pauures ... les autres pour auoir soin des malades & les penser'. Not only does this definition repeat almost verbatim the draft Ecclesiastical Ordinances, des Gallars' Discipline also refers directly to the situation in Geneva with its city hospital. Such a distinction was of little validity in London so, in view of the comparatively small size of the London church, these two roles were combined.[30]

Des Gallars' Discipline provided detailed guidelines about the administration of the common chest and the provision of relief. The deacons were to meet weekly to report on the needs of the poor and others who sought money from the church, even though they were later given permission to provide help in emergencies without waiting for the consent of this meeting. The officers were expected to reach a unanimous decision about the provision of relief, but the opinion of the appropriate elder or the consistory could be sought if necessary. These discussions were to remain confidential 'pour euiter les murmures complaintes, & querelles'.[31] Money dispensed by the deacons was to be carefully recorded. The 1588 Discipline required them to monitor their disbursements and to visit the families within their district, with an elder, every month. The deacons were to question the poor as to their needs each week and to visit the recipients of relief every three months to assess whether their assistance should be increased or decreased.[32]

The deacons were also required to maintain detailed accounts about the money received by the church from each donor and to submit them to the consistory every month. Originally, all the church resources were held together, but soon two distinct funds developed, one for the relief

---

[29] A. Pettegree, *Foreign Protestant Communities in Sixteenth-Century London* (Oxford, 1986), pp. 121, 202. For the role of Jan Laski see also Timothy Fehler's essay in this volume.

[30] N. des Gallars, *Forme de police ecclésiastique instituée à Londres en l'Eglise des François* (London, 1561), f. 16; Olson, *Church and Social Welfare*, p. 251.

[31] Des Gallars, *Forme de Police*, fos 16ᵛ–18.

[32] 'Discipline of the French churches in England, 1588' in W. J. C. Moens, *The Walloons and their Church at Norwich, their History and Register, 1565–1832*, PHS i (1887–88), p. 293.

of the poor and the other for the maintenance of the ministry, and this arrangement was confirmed in the 1588 Discipline. The latter also placed the deacons more formally under the authority of the ministers who were to preside over their meetings, although when this was not possible one of the officers could preside.[33]

All French-speaking exile churches established in Elizabethan England were expected to conform with des Gallars' 1561 Discipline, but there was some divergence in local practice.[34] At its most simple level, the provincial churches differed in the number of deacons that they employed, each adapting the Discipline according to their needs. While des Gallars' Discipline recommended the election of eight deacons for the London church, the sizeable Canterbury community initially possessed six deacons, while at Southampton there may have been only two or three.[35]

In spite of these detailed regulations, relatively few sources have survived. There are deacons' accounts for the small Walloon community at Sandwich, for the period 1568 to 1572, and another set for the London church from November 1572 to December 1573. Further financial papers have survived from the Canterbury church, in particular the accounts for the support of ministers for the period 1594 to 1604. The deacons' records for Canterbury only survive from the early seventeenth century.[36] These financial documents can be supplemented by a number of other important sources such as consistory records and testamentary evidence.

According to the various Disciplines money was to be collected by the deacons at the end of sermons and other services, and they were to record each donation carefully.[37] While in London, during the early

---

[33] Des Gallars, *Forme de Police*, fos 16ᵛ–18; 'Discipline of the French churches', p. 293.

[34] It is important to note that historians have used different Disciplines when discussing the role of the deacons in the exile churches: W. J. C. Moens used the 1588 Discipline, but F. W. Cross that of 1641 (see notes 32 and 35). For variations in the different versions see Spicer, 'The French-speaking Reformed community', pp. 185–6.

[35] Des Gallars, *Forme de police*, f. 16; Spicer, 'The French-speaking Reformed community', p. 207; F. W. Cross, *History of the Walloon and Huguenot Church at Canterbury*, PHS xv (1898), p. 49.

[36] HLL, MSS/J27 Sandwich French Church: Poor Relief Accounts, 1568–72; French Church, Soho Square, London, DL/MS194: Deacons' Account Book, 1572–3; CDRO, French Church Records U47/B: Elders Accounts, 1594–1604, U47/C: Deacons Accounts, 1631–41. There is a descriptive account of the Sandwich records: W. J. C. Moens, 'The relief of the poor members of the French Churches in England', *HS*, 5 (1894–6), 321–42.

[37] Des Gallars, *Forme de Police*, fos 16ᵛ–17.

1570s, such collections could yield up to £25 each month, only relatively small amounts were raised by the Sandwich congregation and in some weeks nothing at all was received. These sums were supplemented by regular house-to-house collections amongst members of the community. The London church was able to suspend these briefly, but the influx which resulted from the St Bartholomew's Day Massacre led to their resumption.[38] These collections were in addition to the house-to-house collections made by the churches for the maintenance of ministers and the education of future pastors.[39] At times of exceptional need, there were attempts to raise further sums by similar means or, as occurred in London, by appealing to the wealthier members of the community.[40] By the early seventeenth century Canterbury held an annual collection before the onset of winter in order to cover the extra payments which were made during this period.[41] However, not all communities relied upon the same strategy. The church at Norwich was criticized by the Colloquy in 1604 for failing to hold regular collections for the maintenance of the ministry and the relief of the poor.[42]

The exile communities were closely associated with the development of the 'new draperies' in England and this industry provided another and important source of income for the churches. Some of the revenue of the Norwich congregations came from a third of the fine which was imposed on those who sold cloth outside the cloth halls, in contravention of local regulations.[43] Money also seems to have been raised from either the sale or the regulation of cloth produced at Sandwich. A section of the deacons' accounts is headed 'S'ensuisant les receptes des baies quy penny a la baie done au pouvre de l'eglise de Sandewye franchoise'. The accounts also refer to receipts from the 'bailli de la draperie' as well as fines concerning the production of cloth.[44] The Dutch church in London, during a period of financial crisis, managed to

---

[38] Pettegree, *Foreign Protestant Communities*, pp. 211–12; Moens, 'The relief of the poor members', 326.

[39] A. Spicer, '"A Faythful Pastor in the Churches": ministers in the French and Walloon communities in England, 1560–1620' in A. Pettegree (ed.), *The Reformation of the Parishes: The Ministry and the Reformation in Town and Country* (Manchester, 1993), pp. 200, 206.

[40] Pettegree, *Foreign Protestant Communities*, pp. 210, 213.

[41] Cross, *History of the Walloon and Huguenot Church at Canterbury*, p. 92.

[42] A. C. Chamier (ed.), *Les actes des Colloques des églises françaises et des Synodes des églises étrangères refugiées en Angleterre 1581–1654*, PHS ii (1890), p. 47.

[43] 'Norwich Booke of Orders for the Straunders [sic]' in Moens, *The Walloons and their Church at Norwich*, p. 260.

[44] HLL, MSS/J27, pp. 2, 34, 64, 93, 103, 125, 153; M. F. Backhouse, 'The Flemish and Walloon communities at Sandwich during the reign of Elizabeth I (1561–1603)' (Ph.D. University of Southampton, 1992), pp. 103–4.

persuade the Corporation of London to institute a levy of $^1/2$d. per cloth, on bays which were bought by foreign merchants from Blackwell Hall.[45] There is no evidence that the Southampton community benefited in this way from the production of the 'new draperies', although the industry was not as closely regulated as in Norwich and Sandwich.

The Sandwich deacons' accounts reveal other potential sources of income, such as fines for non-attendance at meetings of the consistory.[46] Money was raised from the rent of houses which were leased on behalf of the poor, and the officers may also have borrowed money from the members of their congregation. This was certainly the case in London where loans were procured in order to overcome serious financial crises. In Southampton an elder, Anthoine Jurion, was owed 18s. by the French church when he died in 1578.[47]

One of the most important sources of revenue, albeit irregular, came from gifts and bequests. The 1561 Discipline required that there should be a poor box placed in the church for such occasional donations made when the deacons were not present.[48] Attention has been drawn by Patrick Collinson to the generous gifts made to the poor of the French church in London by men such as William Whittingham, Sir Francis Hastings, Thomas Cartwright, Nicholas Fuller, and various Marian exiles. The financial support of the Bishop of London, Edmund Grindal, was crucial to the church during the crisis which followed the St Bartholomew's Day Massacre. Although the situation in London was unusual, with prominent Protestants, courtiers, and exiled Huguenot leaders attending the church's services, some of the provincial churches did also occasionally benefit from exceptional acts of charity.[49] A number of bequests were made from the estate of Robert Nowell: £10, for example, was left to the poor strangers in Southampton and £5 to the poor of the French and Dutch churches in Norwich. The latter also benefited from the queen's visit to the city in 1578 during which £30 was given to the exile churches, £11 to the Walloon church, and £19 to

---

[45] Pettegree, *Foreign Protestant Communities*, p. 209.

[46] Backhouse, 'The Flemish and Walloon Communities at Sandwich', p. 104. At Norwich those who failed to attend meetings of the Politic Men or fell asleep during the same were also fined: R. Esser, 'Social concern and Calvinistic duty: the Norwich strangers' community' in *Het Beloofde Land: Acht opstellen over werken, geleven en vluchten tijdens de XVIe en XVIIe eeuw* (Dikkebus-Ieper, 1992), p. 178.

[47] HRO, Wills 1578/B/53; Backhouse, 'The Flemish and Walloon Communities at Sandwich', p. 104.

[48] Gallars, *Forme de Police*, f. 17^v.

[49] P. Collinson, 'The Elizabethan Puritans and the foreign Reformed churches in London' in his *Godly People: Essays on English Protestantism and Puritanism* (London, 1983), pp. 262–3, 269–70; Pettegree, *Foreign Protestant Communities*, pp. 212, 271–2.

the Dutch.[50] The queen does not seem to have been equally generous when she visited either Southampton or Sandwich. Generally, however, most provincial communities could not expect such generous patronage as the London churches. At Southampton relatively few prominent figures attended the services – the queen's surgeon, Dr John James, and the Dean of Guernsey, Dr John After, are probably the only notable examples – and generous donations were thus rather less likely.[51]

Although the exile churches were frequently the object of appeals for assistance, for example from the church at Wesel, from Geneva, or in particular from the Netherlands, they were also the recipients of relief.[52] In 1568 the Bishop of Lincoln, Nicholas Bullingham, organized a collection throughout his diocese for those who had fled from religious persecution in France and Flanders.[53] The French churches appealed to the Kirk of Scotland in 1576, 'bewailing their sorrowfull estate and condition, and desiring the almes collected be the bretheren to be sent to them'; a further collection was made for them in 1587, and a proportion of this money found its way to Canterbury.[54] Some exile churches also found themselves in a position to help each other. The Southampton congregation seems to have been relatively prosperous in its early years and was able to contribute £2 (in December 1568) and a further gift of £1 10s. (in November 1569) for the relief of the poor at Sandwich. In 1577 the church wrote to Canterbury enquiring after the state of the poor at that church because they were considering sending them a donation. Unfortunately we do not know the outcome of this enquiry.[55]

---

[50] Moens, *The Walloons and their Church at Norwich*, p. 44; A. B. Grosart (ed.), *The Spending of the Money of Robert Nowell of Reade Hall, Lancashire ... 1568–80* (Manchester, 1877), pp. 102–5.

[51] H. M. Godfray (ed.), *Registre des Baptesmes, Mariages et Jeusnes de leglise wallonne de Southampton et des Isles de Jersey, Guernsey Serq, Origny &c.*, PHS iv (1890), pp. 8, 13; Spicer, 'The French-speaking Reformed community and their Church', p. 60.

[52] *Livre synodal contenant les articles résolues dans les Synodes des églises Wallonnes des Pays-Bas* (2 vols, The Hague, 1896), i. 69; A. M. Oakley (ed.), *Actes du consistoire de l'église de Threadneedle Street, Londres*, vol. ii: 1571–7, PHS xlviii, (1969), pp. 36, 57; J. H. Hessels (ed.), *Ecclesiae Londino-Batavae archivuum, epistulae et tractus* (3 vols, Cambridge, 1889–97), ii. 412–19; J.-F. Bergier et al. (eds.), *Registres de la Compagnie des Pasteurs de Genève* (Geneva, 1964 –), iv. 214, v. 259, vi. 155–7.

[53] PRO, SP 12/46/37.

[54] CDRO, French Church Records U47/A1: Actes du Consistoire, p. 49; *Acts and Proceedings of the General Assemblies of the Kirk of Scotland from the year MDLX* (Edinburgh, 1839), pp. 356, 379–80; D. Hay Fleming (ed.), *Register of the Minister Elders and Deacons of the Christian Congregation of St Andrews ... 1559–1600* (Edinburgh, 1890), p. 610.

[55] HLL, MSS/J27, pp. 8, 49; CDRO, U47/A1 p. 81.

Legacies provided an important source of revenue: 60 per cent of the 250 wills drawn up by members of the London community between 1550 and 1580 included some sort of bequest to the poor.[56] This was also an important source in the provincial context, where a similar pattern emerges. There are occasional references in the deacons' accounts at Sandwich to money which was left to the poor or to pieces of cloth sold on their behalf.[57] At Canterbury, 54 of the 92 wills which survive for the period 1586 to 1628 include bequests made to the poor.[58] Approximately 20 wills were drawn up by members of the Southampton community between 1567 and c. 1620, while they were still living in the town; in view of the small size of the congregation this is a not inconsiderable number. Thirteen of these wills included bequests to the poor.[59] Other beneficiaries included the ministers and the church as a whole. In addition bequests were made by people who had left Southampton. For example, Chrestienne de Preseau wrote fondly about her time in the town and made a gift both for the relief of the poor as well as the maintenance of the ministry in the town. A prominent merchant, Richard Etuer, who had migrated to London in the early 1580s remembered not only the Southampton corporation but also the French church when he died in 1603. He also made donations to the French churches in Cambridge [sic] and at Norwich as well as the Reformed churches in Paris, Rouen, and Dieppe.[60] Etuer was not a refugee but of Channel Island stock; other Islanders such as Thomas de Lecq, who died in the town while on business, also left money to the church.[61] In contrast there were only a handful of legacies made by natives of Southampton.[62]

In London the bequests for poor relief generally ranged from 5s. to £5, but smaller sums were also given as token gestures.[63] The Southampton bequests also generally fall within the this range – the smallest amount bequeathed was 3s. and the largest £20, given by Michael

---

[56] Pettegree, *Foreign Protestant Communities*, pp. 198, 201.

[57] HLL, MSS/J27, pp. 73, 137.

[58] B. Magen, *Die Wallonengemeinde in Canterbury von ihrer Gründung bis zum Jahre 1635* (Frankfurt, 1973), p. 232.

[59] Spicer, 'The French-speaking Reformed community', pp. 218, 220.

[60] Guildhall Library, London, Commissary Court of London, 1593 Reg. 18, f. 60: Christiana de Preseau; PRO, PCC Prob. 11/102.

[61] HRO, Wills 1578/B/31.

[62] They were: Robert Bulbecke (PRO, PCC Prob. 11/72), Nicholas Caplin (HRO, Wills 1611/A/19), Peter Caplin (ibid., 1609/A/15), John Cornish (ibid., 1611/A/28, PRO, PCC Prob. 11/118), Susanne Cotten (HRO, Wills 1618/A/18), Hugh Dervall (PRO, PCC Prob. 11/72), William Linche (ibid., 11/129).

[63] Pettegree, *Foreign Protestant Communities*, p. 201.

Heroult in 1576 'to the poore strangers afflicted for the worde of gode nowe remayninge in England'.[64]

The disbursements made by the deacons were wide-ranging; according to the Disciplines the deacons were responsible for the care of the poor and the sick. The churches also had a special responsibility to care for the widows and children of deceased ministers.[65] A distinction was made in the deacons' accounts between the ordinary payments to the poor, which were made on a weekly basis, and more exceptional payments. Money was given in London for the purchase of a blanket (2s.) or a mattress (7s.), for example. The deacons were also keen to help the poor to help themselves; accordingly they provided one person with 2s. 6d. to purchase the tools of his trade. Their Sandwich colleagues regularly bought cloth which could be made into shirts for the poor and their children, as well as buying shoes for them. Money was provided for the purchase of firewood and, in November 1569, the deacons supplied faggots of wood. They also administered a store of mattresses for the use of the poor.[66]

The Sandwich deacons became involved in producing bread for the community's poor. In February 1569 the deacons bought twelve bushels of wheat which was ground and baked to produce 80 loaves of good bread, worth 3d. each, and 59 loaves of 'putare' bread, worth 2d. each to be dispensed weekly with a lower rate of poor relief. This policy was repeated several times, but ultimately stopped due to the opposition of the Sandwich authorities concerned to protect the interests of the local bakers.[67]

The maintenance of the sick and the poor was among the deacons' principal expenses. In some cases regular weekly payments were made to the elderly and the disabled. Occasional disbursements were also made to the doctor for visiting the sick or to the apothecary. At London the deacons were responsible for a poor house for the elderly and disabled, while at Sandwich they built a wooden isolation hut for those suffering from the plague and employed Michiel Ortint and his wife as

---

[64] HRO, Wills 1583/Ad/10; PRO, PCC Prob. 11/58.

[65] Chamier (ed.), *Actes des Colloques*, p. 13.

[66] French Church, Soho Square, DL/MS194, fos 23, 29, 59ᵛ; HLL, MSS/J27, pp. 50ᵇⁱˢ, 62, 90, 94, 105, 126, 174; Pettegree, *Foreign Protestant Communities*, p. 204; Moens, 'The relief of the poor members', 334–5.

[67] HLL, MSS/J27, pp. 17, 22, 25, 27, 31, 34, 35, 37, 38, summarized in Moens, 'The relief of the poor members', 329–31; M. F. Backhouse, 'The strangers at work in Sandwich: native envy of an industrious minority, 1561–1603', *Immigrants and Minorities*, 10 (1991), 81–2.

nurses.[68] At Southampton the sick seem to have been lodged with members of the refugee congregation. A soldier from Wambrechies near Lille who fled to Southampton was lodged with a member of the community, one Jan le Merre. At the time of his death in 1570, it was noted that he had been ill for a long time and at great expense to the poor funds. One Jacob Dixt, a native of Antwerp, was taken from a ship coming from Spain and 'aiant este mis au despens des poures sur quelques logis, ou il fut pense par lespace de 8 ou 9 semaines, finablement vint a trespasser le 17e Jour de feuerier 1573'.[69]

The care of orphans was another responsibility of the church. From the Sandwich deacons' accounts it is clear that money was provided for the nursing, food, and clothes of such children. Members of the congregation looked after them in return for financial assistance from the deacons. The care and welfare of orphans seems to have varied between the different communities. At Sandwich the Flemish church agreed regulations for the purpose in 1566 – this was before the Walloon congregation left the town and may have also applied to them. These regulations stated that guardians were to be appointed, who had to appear before the consistory each year in order to give account of their maintenance expenses as well as to report on the child's godliness and understanding of the catechism. In communities such as Norwich and possibly Canterbury, the responsibility for overseeing orphans fell to the Politic Men, who were responsible for the exile community's civil affairs.[70]

A similar institution does not seem to have existed in Southampton. A testament drawn up in 1583 bequeathed 10s. to the consistory for the care of the testator's son. More specific arrangements were made by Magdalen Mesnier for the provision for her six children. She left all her possessions to the deacons John Hersant and Vincent Nerin, who were to care for her offspring until they came of age; the remaining estate was then to be divided amongst the surviving children. Mesnier wrote her will in 1589 and the deacons were not finally discharged of their duties until 1613.[71]

The deacons were concerned that the church should not be unduly burdened by the care of orphans. The Canterbury community wrote to London in 1577, possibly influenced by the terms of the Pacification of Ghent, suggesting that those orphans who had property in the Nether-

---

[68] Pettegree, *Foreign Protestant Communities*, pp. 203, 297; HLL, MSS/J27, pp. 1, 43, 138–39, 140–41, summarized in Moens, 'The relief of the poor members', 336–7.
[69] Godfray (ed.), *Registre*, pp. 100–101.
[70] Esser, 'Social concern and Calvinistic duty', pp. 177–8; Backhouse, 'The Flemish and Walloon Communities at Sandwich', pp. 136–40.
[71] HRO, Wills 1583/B/13, 1589/B/39, 1613/A/81.

lands should be sent back to the Continent; the London church did not consider this to be a good idea.[72] When Perronne Bino remarried in May 1572 the elders of the Southampton congregation ensured that provision was made for her children from her late husband's estate.[73] The problem of apparently disinherited orphans was addressed by the Colloquy in 1601. The meeting concluded that where an orphan had been left and was a burden on the church, the person(s) who had inherited the estate should be admonished to support these children and be reminded of their Christian duty.[74]

Another regular payment made by the deacons was the money given to *passant*. Refugees passing through Sandwich were given financial support to stay at local hostelries or to pay for lodgings. As well as food and lodging, they were provided with money either to return to the Continent or to move on to another exile community. A Pierre Locart from Tournai was given 7s. to stay with his family at the Black Eagle in Sandwich and then a further 5s. to travel on to London. The deacons also occasionally covered expenses incurred *en route*: 3s. was recorded for lodgings at the Black Horse of Lille.[75] Such payments were a serious drain upon the church's finances, particularly for communities such as Canterbury and Norwich. There were therefore attempts to ensure that those passing between the various communities were genuinely poor rather than merely vagabonds surviving on handouts from the exile churches.[76]

This problem had been identified by the churches 'under the cross' at a much earlier stage. The French congregations had repeatedly dealt with the issue and stated at the National Synod of Paris in 1565:

> that abuses committed by divers Vagrants may be prevented, who wander up and down with Attestations from Ministers whereof they serve themselves at all times and places, shamelessly begging from the Churches and thereby robbing God's true poor of their necessary relief. This assembly adviseth Ministers for time to come, rarely to give such Attestations, and when they do, to none but those who upon their particular knowledge are assured to be Persons of true Godliness, and of an upright Conscience, and groaning under pressing Necessities, specifying in their Attestations the Name, Quality and Abode of those to whom they give them and what Relief has been administered to them, mentioning also the Day and Place from whence they parted, whether they go, and upon what occasion. And such as bear them shall bring them forthand get

---

[72] Cross, *History of the Walloon and Huguenot Church at Canterbury*, p. 94.
[73] Godfray (ed.), *Registre*, pp. 83, 84.
[74] Chamier (ed.), *Actes des Colloques*, p. 41.
[75] HLL, MSS/J27, pp. 85, 95; Moens, 'The relief of the poor members', 335.
[76] Chamier (ed.), *Actes des Colloques*, pp. 10, 32.

them renewed in every Church through which they pass by the Ministers, who shall always specifie what hath been given them, and the Day when, until such time as they be come unto their Journey's end. And before May next all churches shall be advertised of this present Canon, that so all former Certificates given in any other form than this abovementioned, may be accounted null and void, and torn in pieces.[77]

These concerns were reiterated by subsequent French synods and also by those of the Walloons in the Netherlands. At the Synod of Emden in 1571 there was an attempt 'to reduce the heavy burdens of the churches, which daily increase from the fickleness of those who move so quickly from place to place and who, on the pretext that they are needy faithful, appropriate alms which are intended for co-religionists in distress'. The synod went on to set down detailed guidelines, which reflected the French regulations concerning the movement of the faithful between communities.[78]

Although the stranger churches in England were prevented from sending representatives to the Synod of Emden, the articles were circulated among them so that they could not have been unaware of these restrictions on the movement between congregations.[79] The issue also appeared on the agenda of several meetings of the Colloquy of the French churches when the articles of the Synod of Emden were reiterated. For example, in 1586 the Colloquy stated that those who travelled between the communities without reason should not be provided with a testimony and would not be given assistance, and at the following meeting in 1588 it was ordered that the amount of money provided by the deacons should be stated on the testimony. By 1595 the need to discriminate between *passant*, who were entitled to support, and common vagrants had become especially pressing. As a result the Colloquy required that claimants be asked about their means for making a living, their destination, and their reasons for going there. The *passant* were only to be given sufficient money to travel to the next congregation. The subject surfaced again in 1606, when it was stated that the attestations should refer to the good faith and conduct of those who passed between the churches, demonstrating, in fact, that they were co-religionists. The Norwich church was later censured by the Colloquy for not conforming to these measures.[80]

---

[77] Quick (ed.), *Synodicon in Gallia Reformata*, i. 60, 73, 76, 117, 137, 192, 349.

[78] F. L. Rutger (ed.), *Acta van de Nederlandsche synoden der 16de eeuw* (Utrecht, 1889), pp. 81–4.

[79] Oakley (ed.), *Actes du consistoire de l'église de Threadneedle Street*, p. 56; Pettegree, *Foreign Protestant Communities*, pp. 256, 269.

[80] Chamier (ed.), *Actes des Colloques*, pp. 10, 13–14, 32, 49, 56, 58.

These concerns about the payments made to *passant* reflect in part the increasing difficulties that the exile churches faced in meeting their obligations. At times of crisis, such as in the wake of the St Bartholomew's Day Massacre, the exile churches found it difficult to raise sufficient money for the relief of the poor. Furthermore by the early seventeenth century the exile congregations were in decline. The more settled conditions in France and the Low Countries reduced the influx of refugees to a trickle; many indeed had returned to the Continent while those who remained were becoming increasingly integrated into their host community.[81]

In the light of these financial difficulties, it became increasingly important to ensure that members of the congregation contributed according to their means. This was certainly not a new problem for the deacons. As early as 1561 it was suggested that their accounts should not be publicly presented because if people saw that there was too much money, they might not contribute as generously.[82] In the wake of the Massacre of St Bartholomew's Day, the deacons of the French church in London decided to visit those who did not contribute adequately to the relief of the poor.[83] This problem inevitably became more acute as the communities began to experience financial difficulties. In 1586 the Colloquy addressed the problem of those who failed to contribute to the maintenance of the ministry and other church expenses. Offenders were to be made aware of their ingratitude, if this failed they could be called before the consistory, and in case of further resistance the church should seek the assistance of the magistrates.[84] The Canterbury congregation protested to the Colloquy in 1601 concerning a certain Jean Lore who was suspected of having the means to support the poor but refused to do so. The Colloquy supported the censures imposed by the Canterbury consistory and at the following meeting urged the church to seek the assistance of the magistrates.[85]

Another problem came to the fore at the meeting of the Colloquy in 1601. Pierre Truye and Nicholas de Corte from Norwich were pre-

---

[81] On the integration of the community in Southampton see A. Spicer, 'A process of gradual assimilation: The exile community in Southampton, 1567–1635' in R. Vigne and G. Gibbs (eds.), *The Strangers' Progress: Integration and Disintegration of the Huguenot and Walloon Refugee Community, 1567–1889. Essays in memory of Irene Scouloudi, HS*, 26 (1995), 186–98. For evidence of financial difficulties see Spicer, '"A Faythful pastor in the Churches"', p. 204, and Chamier (ed.), *Actes des Colloques*, pp. 5, 7, 20.

[82] E. Johnston (ed.), *Actes du consistoire de l'église française de Threadneedle Street, Londres*, vol.i: 1560–5, PHS xxxviii (1937), pp. xxi, 31.

[83] Pettegree, *Foreign Protestant Communities*, p. 213; Oakley (ed.), *Actes du consistoire de l'église de Threadneedle Street*, pp. ix, 65–6, 130.

[84] Chamier (ed.), *Actes des Colloques*, p. 10.

[85] Ibid., pp. 40, 43.

sented for refusing 'de fournir a l'entretien des pauvres et autres charges de l'Eglise, sous pretexte d'être surchargez'.[86] By the early seventeenth century members of the refugee congregations had steadily become subject to a number of local dues from which they had previously been exempt.[87] According to the Book of Orders issued by the corporation in 1571, members of the Norwich congregation were obliged to contribute 'for the discharge of all manner of dewties growenge to the preste and clarke of the same parishes', and in 1606 legal opinion was given that this also included payments to the parochial poor relief system.[88] The exiles at Canterbury had been included in local tax levies, but from the early seventeenth century they were also obliged to contribute to the support of the town's poor.[89]

It was therefore understandable that as the refugees became integrated into their host community they became less willing to consider the needs of the exile churches. Truye and de Corte were censured for their failure to contribute, and duly suspended from the Lord's Supper, but as a result they left the Walloon congregation to join the parish church. With the approval of the Colloquy, the assistance of the Bishop of Norwich was sought and he was called upon to reprimand the offenders.[90] A similar situation developed at Canterbury, where the church found itself in chaos in 1606: some of its members had departed to the parish churches in order to avoid their contributions and the censures imposed by the consistory were ignored.[91]

The system of poor relief which operated in the exile churches should be seen in context. Intercession-related support and monastic almsgiving, which had marked the medieval period, were of course no longer available and alternative strategies had to be developed. Given the worsen-

---

[86] Ibid., p. 42.

[87] At Southampton some wealthier members of the congregation occasionally contributed to the town's poor relief system, but they did not benefit from these funds, even at times of crisis such as during the 1583–4 plague epidemic when special collections were held by the town authorities: SRO, SC5/3/1, fos 189–90, SC5/17/1, SC13/2/10, SC10/1/3–4, SC10/1/6–9.

[88] 'Norwich Booke of Orders', pp. 255–6; Moens, The Walloons and their Church at Norwich, p. 61.

[89] A. M. Oakley, 'The Canterbury Walloon congregation from Elizabeth I to Laud' in I. Scouloudi (ed.), Huguenots in Britain and their French Background, 1550–1800 (Basingstoke, 1987), p. 68.

[90] Chamier (ed.), Actes des Colloques, pp. 42, 44, 45, 49; Moens, The Walloons and their Church at Norwich, pp. 55, 60–62; C. M. Vane, 'The Walloons community in Norwich: the first hundred years', HS, 24 (1984), 135.

[91] Chamier (ed.), Actes des Colloques, p. 49.

ing socio-economic circumstances after 1520, this need was all the more pressing. The English state was forced into action too: during the sixteenth century parliamentary legislation attempted to prevent vagrancy, unemployment, and to ensure the adequate distribution of poor relief. These efforts culminated in 1598 in the Vagrancy and Poor Relief Statutes, which firmly established the principles of punishment for vagrancy, a compulsory poor rate, and the provision of employment for the able-bodied. The process was often preceded by local initiatives and in some areas by the partial implementation of earlier legislation. At Southampton begging was regulated and a compulsory poor rate introduced after an act of 1552, while reforms implemented at Norwich may have influenced the statutes of the 1570s.[92]

Against the background of an evolving welfare system in their host country, the exile churches provided their own well-organized programme for poor relief. For in their case, it was not only a matter of coping with the general social problems of the time, but also with specific 'religious' crises such as the St Bartholomew's Day Massacre. As in other Reformed churches poor relief was to an extent 'resacralized' and the resulting system must have been impressive. At Norwich, where the exile community was established in 1565, there are some tantalizing similarities between the city's welfare scheme of 1570 and the practice of the exile church. The city appointed 'deacons in everi ward ... to haue the oversight of the poor of theire warde'. They were also responsible for reporting the various instances of poverty and 'all moni or other thinges [was] gyven to be done by the deacons'.[93] While towns were prepared to exploit the exile communities by requiring them to contribute to the municipal systems of relief, they clearly recognized the advantages of the congregations' efforts which reduced the burden on the native population. In 1586 one of the benefits of the exile churches in Norwich was seen to be the £40 *per annum* which was paid in poor relief by the Walloon congregation, with a similar amount being distributed by the Flemish church.[94] As late as 1634, when the position of the exile churches was attacked by Archbishop Laud, their important welfare function was cited in their defence. The Canterbury corporation pointed out that the Walloons spent £153 *per annum* on poor relief. If the privileges of the churches were removed, the city feared that the

---

[92] SRO, SC10/1/1: 1552 Poor Relief Book; P. Slack, *Poverty and Policy in Tudor and Stuart England* (London, 1988), pp. 119, 122–8, 149–50; for the socio-economic circumstances see ibid., p. 6.

[93] R. H. Tawney and E. Power (eds), *Tudor Economic Documents* (3 vols, London, 1924), ii. 322–3.

[94] Moens, *The Walloons and their Church at Norwich*, p. 45.

burden would fall disproportionately on the city parishes, and the poorer parishes in particular.[95]

The exiles may have felt themselves unfairly burdened by the cumulative financial demands made upon them for the relief of the poor. As members of a Reformed exile community they were also subject to the church's strict discipline and the consistory was prepared to criticize those whom they considered ungrateful of their assistance.[96] However, the support for the poor offered by the strangers' church seems to have been more generous than parish relief in the early seventeenth century. In Canterbury, payments of about 2s. per week or more were made by the exiles compared with 6d. from parish sources.[97] In this case, as for most of the Elizabethan period, the exile congregations offered a more coherent system of welfare than that evolving within their host communities.

---

[95] A. Oakley, 'Archbishop Laud and the Walloons in Canterbury' in W. M. Jacob and N. Yates (eds), *Crown and Mitre: Religion and Society in Northern Europe since the Reformation* (Woodbridge, 1993), p. 40.

[96] Hatfield House, Salisbury MSS, CP64/37; BL, Landsdowne MS 161, f. 127.

[97] Oakley, 'Archbishop Laud and the Walloons in Canterbury', p. 40.

Index

Due to pressures of space, the following conventions have been adopted: individual dioceses and members of the ecclesiastical hierarchy appear under 'popes' or '(arch-)bishops', orders of monks and friars under 'regular orders', mayors and aldermen under 'town officials', and (parish) churches under the respective place-names. Evaluations of the three main themes of the volume (see p. 12) can be found under 'continuity/change', 'religious/secular factors', and 'winners/losers'. A page-number succeeded by 'n' denotes a reference to a footnote, but only authors mentioned in the main text are listed here. The editor is grateful to the contributors and Michelle Webster for their help in preparing the index.